The American Republic

Charles M. Redenius
The Pennsylvania State University

David M. Billeaux
Oklahoma State University

Martin W. Slann
Clemson University

The American Republic

Politics, Institutions, and Policies

West Publishing Company

St. Paul   New York   Los Angeles   San Francisco

Production credits

Copyediting Elaine Linden
Index Virginia Hobbs
Design David J. Farr, IMAGESMYTH, INC.
Artwork Alice Thiede, CARTOGRAPHICS
Cover Sandra Kapitan
Cover image The Granger Collection

COPYRIGHT © 1987 By WEST PUBLISHING COMPANY
50 W. Kellogg Boulevard
P.O. Box 64526
St. Paul, MN 55164–1003

Printed in the United States of America

Library of Congress Cataloging-in-Publication Data

Redenius, Charles, 1941–
The American Republic.

Bibliography: p.
Includes index.
1. United States—Politics and government.
I. Billeaux, David M. II. Slann, Martin W.
III. Title.
JK274.R32 1987   320.973   86–24695
ISBN 0–314–28509–1

Photo credits

i Robert A. Walsh; **1** Burt Glinn, Magnum; **3** The Granger Collection; **4** National Archives; **6** Library of Congress; **7** Suzanne Vlamis, Wide World Photos; **11** Paul Conklin, Monkmeyer Press; **13** Bill Fitz-Patrick, the White House; **19** The Bettmann Archive; **20** Guy Gillette, Photo Researchers; **22** Paul Conklin, Monkmeyer Press; **24** Hugh Rogers, Monkmeyer Press; **27** Library of Congress; **29** Elliott Erwitt, Magnum; **33** Bettmann Newsphotos; **35** Historical Pictures Service, Inc.; **36** American Philosophical Society; **37** The Bettmann Archive; **38** American Philosophical Society; **39** Library of Congress; **41** (*left*) The Bettmann Archive; **41** (*right*) The Granger Collection; **43** (*top left*) Library of Congress; **43** (*top right*) The Bettmann Archive; **43** (*lower left*) The Bettmann Archive; **43** (*lower right*) Library of Congress; **47** The Bettmann Archive; **49** New York Historical Society; **50** Library of Congress; **51** Library of Congress; **53** The Bettmann Archive; **54** (*left*) Library of Congress; **54** (*left center*) Dictionary of American Portraits; **54** (*right center*) Dictionary of American Portraits; **54** (*right*) Library of Congress; **55** (*left*) Library of Congress; **55** (*left center*) Independence National Historical Park Collection; **55** (*right center*) Library of Congress; **55** (*right*) Dictionary of American Portraits; **57** Library of Congress; **64** Library of Congress; **67** Wide World Photos; **68** Historical Pictures Service, Inc.; **71** Roger Mallock, Magnum; **72** (*top*) Historical Pictures Service, Inc.; **72** (*bottom*) Bahnsen, Monkmeyer Press; **74** Library of Congress; **75** Lanks, Monkmeyer Press; **76** Library of Congress; **87** Paul Conklin, Monkmeyer Press; **88** Strix, Monkmeyer Press; **89** (*left*) Suzanne Vlamis, Wide World Photos; **91** Mimi Forsyth, Monkmeyer Press; **92** Historical Pictures Service, Inc.; **103** Brown Brothers; **108** Jan Lukas, Photo Researchers, Inc.; **113** Gilles Peress, Magnum; **117** Wide World Photos; **120** The Granger Collection; **122** Wide World Photos; **127** Elliott Erwitt, Magnum; **131** The Bettmann Archive; **132** Barry Thumma, Wide World Photos; **139** Wide World Photos; **141** (*top*) Paul Conklin, Monkmeyer Press; **141** (*bottom*) Paul Conklin, Monkmeyer Press; **144** Wide World Photos; **145** Ralph Ginzburg, Wide World Photos; **146** Teresa Zubala, Picture Group; **149** Mimi Forsyth, Monkmeyer Press; **157** Jan Lukas, Photo Researchers; **163** Paul Conklin, Monkmeyer Press; **167** Courtesy of office of Congressman Tom Ridge; **169** AP/Wide World Photos; **172** Duricka, Wide World Photos; **173** Paul Conklin, Monkmeyer Press; **177** Courtesy of office of Congressman William Frenzel; **178** Paul Conklin, Monkmeyer Press; **181** David M. Grossman, Photo Researchers; **182** Pete Souza, the White House; **184** Paul Conklin, Monkmeyer Press; **185** J. Scott Applewhite, Wide World Photos; **193** The Bettmann Archive; **195** Library of Congress; **196** Library of Congress; **197** Library of Congress; **200** Liza Berg, Gamma-Liaison; **201** Library of Congress; **204** Terry Arthur, the White House; **205** AP/Wide World Photos; **207** Copyright 1985, by Newsweek, Inc. All Rights Reserved. Reprinted by Permission.

Credits continued following index

Contents

Preface

On September 17, 1987, the United States celebrates the bicentennial of the Constitution. On July 4, 1986, Americans, and much of the rest of the world, observed the 100th birthday of the Statue of Liberty. The national celebrations surrounding these historic events have convinced us that the time is ripe for a text in which the standard topics of American politics are animated by a historical and values-oriented approach to the study of American government. We are further convinced that only through a careful examination of historical developments and American ideals can we gain a well-rounded appreciation of why our political system produces the types and kinds of public policies it does. This approach forms the background to the entire work and we believe that our text is most fully intelligible when this historical and values-oriented approach to the policy process is kept in mind.

Our sense that we were on the right track was confirmed by how well our reviewers responded to our text and how quickly they drew us back to that approach when we strayed from it. To them we owe a deep debt of gratitude that cannot be fully captured by our acknowledgment of their assistance. We can only say that our text has benefited immensely from their suggestions and from their concern for the text's integrity. They have given of themselves and we trust they feel the same pride in this text as we do. Since two of these individuals, Danny Adkison of Oklahoma State University and Charles Dunn of Clemson University, are also our colleagues, we know from first-hand experience the value of collegiality. No less valuable, however, were the contributions of:

Lon Felker of East Carolina University,
Walter Jones of Memphis State University,
Henry Kenski of the University of Arizona,
Margaret Kenski of Pima Community College,
Ed Sidlow of Northwestern University, and
Martha Zebrowski of the City College of New York.

No author of a scholarly paper, let alone a textbook, can produce a final product without the dedication of a secretarial staff, library assistants, and reference librarians. We wish to recognize and to applaud Gladys Brown, Wendy Eidenmuller, and Vaunita Struble for their patient, understanding, and always-helpful contributions to our efforts. Patricia Gainer and Steve Sandbakken of the Penn State-Behrend College Library provided assistance on occasions too numerous and too painful to recall.

The birth pangs of our text were also considerably eased by our editor and production team at West Publishing. Clark Baxter's keen interest in our text kept us plugging away. Peggy Adams was always cheerful and kept the production schedule on track. Caroline Smith provided some gentle nudges that improved our thinking about how best to market our text in a highly-competitive arena.

Finally, with the completion of this textbook, each of us has learned once again that a wife is truly one's better-half. To our wives, Marilyn Betit Redenius, Ana Martinez Billeaux, and Ruth Isaac Slann, we dedicate this textbook with the affection that triumphed over the trials of authorship.

The American Republic

The role of government and its relationship to the individual has been changed so radically that today government is involved in almost every aspect of our lives. Political, economic, and racial forces have developed which we have not yet learned to understand or control. If we are ever to master these forces, make certain that government will belong to the people, not the people to the government, and provide for the future better than the past, we must somehow learn from the experience of the past.
Bernard Baruch

Chapter 1

Analyzing a Changing America: Values, Institutions, and the Policy Process

Chapter Outline

Introduction
Political, Economic, and Demographic Change: 1780s–1980s
Changes in the Pattern of Interests: 1780s–1980s
Ideals Derived from the Declaration of Independence and the Constitution
Values or Ideals Derived from the American Historical Experience
Contemporary Political Problems
Conclusion

Introduction

Since the Declaration of Independence in 1776 and the adoption of the Constitution in 1789, our political institutions and the values Americans hold have undergone significant changes. Revolutionary advances in the technology of communication and transportation, the dramatic growth of governmental programs, the advent of formidable challenges to America's economic and military supremacy, and the rise of ideologies hostile to the American way of life have all combined to produce a society that would barely be recognizable to Americans of only a few generations ago. These changes, we argue in this text, have had a direct impact on the policies of the national government.

At one time or another throughout our history, the national government has been held responsible for all that has happened, good or bad (recognizing that it is sometimes difficult to tell good from bad). Today, the role of government, and particularly that of the national government, has become the focus of intense debate. We are unsure what its role in economic matters, social problems, or international affairs should be. We can agree only that government is, and will surely remain, a presence in all our lives.

The complexity and confusion of public policies confounds most average citizens. The surgeon general warns us that the use of tobacco is dangerous to our health, while we continue to subsidize tobacco farmers and to encourage the export of tobacco products. We are told that a good citizen pays taxes and refrains from cheating in filing a tax return, but at the same time, special interests compete to secure tax advantages. Anomalies such as these strongly suggest a lack of coherence in governmental policies.

Throughout this text, we discuss how the American federal system works and why, sometimes, it doesn't. In either case, the values Americans hold, organized interests, and the institutions of government all contribute to uncertain and unpredictable policy outcomes, despite the best of intentions. Americans have come to expect that government will (somehow) reconcile competing policy interests. The nation's wheat farmers in the middle 1980s were filing for bankruptcy in record numbers and many of them blamed government policy. For the wheat farmer, it was the worst of times. But for

Policymakers (and political scientists) must often make choices among competing points of view.

American consumers, it was the best of times be cause they were able to purchase their groceries at relatively low prices, also a result of public policy.

All this would seem to suggest a simple truism: It is impossible for public policy makers to satisfy all parties to a conflict. One party will benefit and the other will bear a cost. If policy makers provide a subsidy for wheat farmers, they can do so only by increasing the economic burden for some other group. In the ongoing struggle to change the allocation of costs and benefits, policy makers must mediate the conflict between competing groups while striving for fairness and equity. Under such conditions, the policy process will at best produce imperfect results.

Yet that should not be an occasion for despair. Politics, like any other human enterprise, will record some notable successes and some unexpected failures. We have had plenty of both during the two centuries of American independence! However, the United States is one of the oldest, if not the oldest, **democracy** in the world. Our success must be more than a fortunate set of historical accidents. And, despite the warning that it is better not to know how either sausages or laws are made, we are convinced that good government requires a body of citizens who are aware of, and concerned about, how public policies affect their lives.

In this text, we examine how the values Americans hold have shaped our democracy; how those values gave rise to two of the most remarkable political documents the world has ever seen, the Declaration of Independence and the Constitution; and how those values have interacted with our political institutions to produce a distinctive policy-making process, in both its strengths and its weaknesses.

Because the United States is basically a free society, the faults of the policy process are readily apparent. Cartoonists, political commentators, opposing interests, religious leaders, civil rights activists, conservationists, and a host of others are quick to point out the government's shortcomings. But many of these shortcomings, for example, welfare dependency and an expensive, burgeoning bureau-cracy to administer welfare programs, are often unintended and unforeseen consequences of dealing with complex social issues. The question is whether we can solve them.

The Founding Fathers recognized that an imperfect species could hardly produce a perfect government. They sought to create a form of government that although resting on republican foundations would be flexible enough to accommodate the changes that the future was sure to bring. This bedrock of political principle underpins American democracy, and is one of the chief reasons why the form of government adopted in 1789 endures today. By recognizing that change was inevitable, the Founding Fathers ensured the success of our political institutions.

Welcome to the Land of Freedom—an ocean steamer passing the Statue of Liberty: scene on the steerage deck

One dimension of the nation's change is illustrated by this 1882 photo of Washington, D.C.

The Founders were also aware that any given policy is the result of complex interactions involving strongly held values, organized political interests, and governmental institutions. Given this context, they knew there was no guarantee that the policy process would always produce the most desirable results. All these factors add to rather than detract from the strength and durability of our government. Had flexibility, openness, and willingness to experiment been lacking, the immense changes of the last two hundred years would have overwhelmed the American government. We stress the great extent of change because perhaps more than any other factor, it is the velocity of social change that distinguishes the last two centuries from the previous two centuries. The next section describes some of the changes that have had a marked impact on our form of government.

Political, Economic, and Demographic Change: 1780s–1980s

In the 1780s, the United States consisted of thirteen former colonies on the Atlantic coast, occupying a land area of 889,000 square miles, whose western boundary was the Mississippi River. By the 1980s, the United States included fifty states, the District of Columbia, the commonwealth of Puerto Rico, and several territories, occupying a total of 3.6 million square miles. The first census in 1790 counted less than four million inhabitants, approximately one-fourth of whom were nonwhite. Only 10 percent of the nation's population lived in an urban area. Philadelphia was the largest city with a population of about forty thousand.

By the middle 1980s, Americans numbered 240 million, approximately 12 percent of whom were nonwhite. Natural increase provided the greatest growth, but the forty million immigrants who came throughout the nineteenth century and into the twentieth made a major contribution. Seventy percent of the population now lives in an urban area. The New York metropolitan area with more than fourteen million people is the nation's largest, but the fastest growing areas, such as Atlanta, Houston, and Los Angeles, are in the Sunbelt.

Using a variety of sources, economists have determined that the gross national product (GNP), the total of all goods and services produced in a year, for the 1780s was roughly $3 billion. By 1987, GNP had grown to $4.5 trillion (twice as much as the next largest GNP, the Soviet Union's). During the

TWO CENTURIES OF POPULATION GROWTH

A brief comparison with other major industrialized nations illustrates how dramatic the population growth of the United States has been over the last two centuries.

Population
(in millions) *

Country	1780s	1980s	Percentage of Increase *
France	20	54	225
Russia (Soviet Union)	40	275	700
United Kingdom	7	55	800
United States	4	240	6,000

* All figures are approximate.

first half-century, the national government expended $1.09 billion, and until 1900 had spent a total of only $16.5 billion. By the middle 1980s, expenditures had grown to $1 trillion per fiscal year, with a deficit that surpassed $200 billion. In the 1780s and 1790s, the national debt was actually reduced. By the 1980s, interest on the national debt stood at more than $140 billion per year, an amount exceeded only by spending on Social Security and national defense.

In the 1780s, negative government was the prevailing philosophy: "That government which governs least governs best." For many, the only two appropriate functions of government were to guarantee domestic tranquility and to protect the country against foreign invasion. Although these may sound like the conditions for laissez-faire **capitalism,** with its focus on a free market economy, such an economic system had little appeal for the leaders of the new nation. Neither Alexander Hamilton nor Thomas Jefferson, who were the leading economic thinkers in the United States, could be accurately described as a laissez-faire capitalist.

Hamilton espoused an economic philosophy that was more mercantilist than capitalist. As the first secretary of the treasury, Hamilton urged the Congress to adopt economic policies whereby the federal government would direct the nation's economic development. Although Jefferson viewed Hamiltonian policies as essentially government grants of economic privilege to the affluent and he supported efforts to end such practices,[1] he was not opposed to government actions that would benefit all Americans: Witness his purchase of the Louisiana Territory in 1803, which doubled the size of the United States. The Scottish economist Adam Smith, in contrast, the leading exponent of laissez-faire capitalism, had proposed an end to all government regulation of the economy as a precondition for healthy economic growth.

Since the 1930s, the prevailing theory of government, despite some resistance from the political right, is that of positive government, or the welfare state. This theory maintains that the national government has the primary responsibility for addressing the nation's social and economic problems. The size of the federal deficit in recent years, however, has caused this theory of government to come under attack. In 1985, Congress passed the so-called Gramm-Rudman budget bill, mandating across-

FRANKLIN D. ROOSEVELT (1882–1945) AND THE RISE OF WELFARE CAPITALISM

A new era in American politics began during the presidency of Franklin D. Roosevelt. Before his tenure of office, the national government's economic and social role was minimal. All that was changed by the Great Depression.

Herbert Hoover's inability or unwillingness to use the powers of the national government to combat the Depression led to Roosevelt's smashing victory in 1932. On taking office, he rallied the American people by declaring that "the only thing we have to fear is fear itself." Roosevelt insisted the American people were not the helpless victims of a system they had themselves created, and he promised action.

The New Deal called for both government intervention in the economy and the creation of government programs to alleviate the suffering caused by the Depression. In a whirlwind "Hundred Days," Congress enacted the necessary legislation that created a broad array of agencies to deal with the nation's problems. Among the most important were the AAA (Agricultural Adjustment Agency), the CCC (Civilian Conservation Corps), the NRA (National Recovery Administration),

and the TVA (Tennessee Valley Authority).

Although many of these agencies have either ceased to exist or are no longer important, virtually all of the national government's social programs trace their origins back to the 1930s. Today, these programs account for approximately 40 percent of the federal budget. The largest single expenditure is for Social Security, which by itself accounts for almost 30 percent of federal spending.

Roosevelt shattered the two-term precedent established by George Washington by being elected to the presidency four

times (1932–1944). He also led the Democratic party to a position of dominance that it held until the 1980s. Although crippled by polio, Roosevelt must be ranked along with Theodore Roosevelt and Woodrow Wilson as among the most vigorous presidents of the century. His leadership, however, was not without its critics. Probably no other president since Abraham Lincoln has been so bitterly hated by his opponents, just as none has been so deeply loved by his admirers.

Whatever may be the final verdict on Roosevelt's presidency, he must be credited with one achievement: He restored the faith of the American people in their capacity to shape their destiny, in their form of government, and in their future. By the time Roosevelt died in April 1945, less than three months into his fourth term, the New Deal had waged a largely successful war on the Depression, and the United States had waged a successful two-ocean war against Germany and Japan. Perhaps more than any other American, Franklin Roosevelt played a pivotal role in the vast changes that swept over this nation in the twentieth century.

the-board cuts in government expenditures to reduce the federal deficit. Despite this cost-cutting effort, budget projections for the next several years show an increase in federal expenditures.

Given this level of governmental spending, the United States can best be described as having a mixed economy rather than a **laissez-faire economy.** Yet the appropriate governmental role in eco-

nomic matters is still open to vigorous debate. Most Americans agree that the national government has a responsibility to assure a minimum level of economic well-being for every individual. A conservative president like Ronald Reagan recognizes this consensus. However, what concerns President Reagan and the conservatives is the growth of the social programs that originated in the New Deal of the 1930s. Such programs now make up nearly half of the federal budget. Government expenditures for Social Security and Medicare in the middle 1980s, for example, stood at more than $270 billion, or approximately 28 percent of the federal budget. A half-century ago, Social Security did not even exist.

The problems associated with an industrial society not only have impacted on governmental policies but have also affected how Americans earn their living. Choice of occupation, location of the workplace, skills and education required, compensation, and length of the workday have all undergone far-reaching changes. With the emergence of computer technology, it seems likely that even more profound changes are just over the horizon. Table 1.1 indicates how industrialization has affected workers at selected points in our history.

The table reveals a massive shift from the primary, mainly agricultural, sector to the tertiary, or services, sector brought about in part by governmental policies that enhanced farm productivity. The table, however, does not reveal the dramatic rate of growth in the number of women workers in the past two hundred years. Women employed outside the home in the 1780s were rare. By the early 1980s, women accounted for approximately 43 percent of the labor force. For the first time in the nation's history, more married women work outside the home than are housewives. Finally, this table indicates only implicitly the role of technological developments, such as computers, in economic growth. Such developments, of course, play a deci-

There are not only a lot of us, but as this photo of Fifth Avenue in New York shows, most of us are employed in the tertiary sector.

sive role in determining the composition of the labor force.

Despite all the changes of the last two centuries, American society has maintained certain constants of interests and values. The following sections identify and evaluate what we view as some of the most significant changes and some of the most important, enduring characteristics of American politics.

Changes in the Pattern of Interests: 1780s–1980s

In the 1780s, Americans were faced with problems arising from four major sets of interests:

(1) the commercial classes, located principally in the north,
(2) southern plantation owners,
(3) large and small states, and
(4) East and West.

Overall, these interests were a compound of economic, political, and geographic factors. The commercial classes worried whether the new government would be able to protect their interests as creditors against debtors, most of whom were small farmers. Southern plantation owners were anxious that slavery and the slave trade not be interfered with. The large and the small states were

Table 1.1
Labor Force Participation Rates: Percentages for Selected Years

	1790	1860	1900	1950	1960	1980
Primary Sector (agriculture, fishing, forestry)	(80)	59	38	12	7	2
Secondary Sector (industry, construction, mining)	(10)	20	38	33	36	32
Tertiary Sector (services: professional, administrative, transport, commerce, education)	(10)	20	24	55	57	66

Source: World Bank, *World Development Report, 1981* (New York: Oxford University Press, 1982), Table 19.

determined to protect their independence and **sovereignty** in the new Union. Smaller eastern states such as Connecticut, Rhode Island, and Delaware were understandably fearful of newer and bigger states that would inevitably be carved out of the old Northwest Territory and the other territories that stretched to the Mississippi River.

Interest competition in the 1980s, by contrast, involves a bewildering variety of claims on the government.[2] Major influences on the policy-making process today include the business community, organized labor, and farm interests. Civil rights, ethnic, religious, and linguistic groups also play important roles. Nor can the influence of women and gay liberation groups be ignored. An important milestone in women's participation in the political process was the precedent established at the 1984 Democratic National Convention where a woman, Geraldine Ferraro, was named to the party's ticket. Environmentalists and conservationists, weaker in influence than in the 1970s, remain a force to be reckoned with.

Urban areas, of which there were very few in the 1780s, are today led by energetic mayors who often bypass the state governments to seek assistance from the national government. Over the last two decades, interests groups focusing on specific issues like school prayer and abortion have captured the attention of policy makers. Better-informed consumers, although not well organized nor particularly well led, have also gained recognition.

Perhaps the single biggest change, is the emergence of the nation as a whole as an "interest group" on the international stage, especially the ideological rivalry between the United States and the Soviet Union. Many Americans are convinced that the Soviets represent a threat to freedom, to economic prosperity, and to world peace.[3] As a consequence of this rivalry, both nations feel compelled to expend large sums of money on national defense and to form military alliances with their ideological counterparts.

Despite the complexity of interest competition in the 1980s, we can assess the power or influence of competing groups in three ways: First, the recognition and success (or failure) of an interest can be measured by institutional influence. If an interest is "represented" by a cabinet position, a congressional committee, or a justice on the Supreme Court, that group's interests are likely to be adequately protected by governmental policy. On the other hand, the absence of such institutional representation probably means that a group's interests are not being adequately protected by public policy. Given these criteria, it can be argued that organized labor is more likely to be adequately protected than consumers.

Second, changes in the composition of government spending may reflect a group's changing influence. Although farmers have a cabinet position and congressional committees servicing their interests, their share of the federal budget dollar (and their contribution to the federal deficit) has declined over the last decade. This would seem to indicate that farmers as a group are less influential than they used to be. By contrast, governmental programs for the elderly experienced rapid budgetary growth during the same period.[4] This has been largely a consequence of numbers. By 1984, approximately 25.2 million Americans were sixty-five or over, 22.1 percent of the population. As their number increases, older Americans will see their electoral influence further enhanced nationally and in congressional districts located in such states as Arizona and Florida.

Third, efforts by a group to enhance its status can indicate, in a rough way, the influence of that group. The struggle over the Equal Rights Amend-

AMERICAN WOMEN IN THE 1980s

By 1983, a process that had long been under way reached a milestone. For the first time in American history, more women worked outside the home than in it. Women are entering the labor force in record numbers and in most blue- and white-collar professions. Such a dramatic social change has far-reaching implications. How, for example, will the daily absence of women from the home affect child rearing? What will be the social consequences of job competition between men and women (and between women and women)? Will the size of the family continue to shrink? The effects of this social transformation are still uncertain.

THE "GRAYING" OF AMERICA

Like most industrialized societies, the United States is experiencing significant demographic change. Persons sixty-five and over are the fastest growing population group. As Americans live longer, the United States is becoming an ''older'' country. This has important implications for the economy, employment, leisure, and, of course, the Social Security system. By the end of this century, the over sixty-fivers will constitute the largest voting bloc by age. They may not vote as a bloc, but their numbers will give them the ear of politicians of both major parties. Early in the twenty-first century, however, this group may be competing with the next fastest growing age group, those over eighty-five!

ment is a case in point. That that amendment failed of adoption by only three states is one indicator of the newly won influence of women. President Reagan as a candidate in 1980 announced he would name a woman as his first appointment to the Supreme Court. He has also included women in his cabinet. In 1984, Walter Mondale became the first major party presidential candidate to have a woman as his running mate. As women's organizations mature, both political parties will become increasingly sensitive to women's electoral strength. Despite the absence of large numbers of women in the highest echelons of government, their power is growing.

Clearly, interest competition in the 1980s is significantly different than it was in the 1780s. In the next two sections, we explore the values that have shaped that competition then and now.

Ideals Derived From the Declaration of Independence and the Constitution

Three sets of values are derived from the Declaration and the Constitution.

1. **Natural Rights.** The value or ideal of natural rights influences how Americans think about

politics. Thomas Jefferson in the Declaration of Independence drew upon the natural rights philosophy for the theoretical underpinning of that document, coupling the ideal of equality with the rights of life, liberty, and the pursuit of happiness, whereas the framers of the Constitution restored the right of property to its original place in John Locke's philosophy. Unfortunately, these rights have never been fully reconciled. Equality, liberty, and property often conflict with one another. Some have even suggested that these rights are fundamentally irreconcilable. Yet the nation's history shows that Americans have insisted on the protection of property rights, have been willing to fight and die for their freedom, and have sought to expand the reach of the ideal of equality.[5]

2. **Popular sovereignty.** Both in the Declaration and in the Constitution, the Founding Fathers maintained that Americans have a right to choose, not only their rulers, but also their form of government. The suffrage amendments—Fifteenth, Seventeenth, Nineteenth, Twenty-third, Twenty-fourth, and Twenty-sixth—have expanded the meaning of popular sovereignty. Although recent decades have seen a decrease in voter participation, the people's right to govern themselves still retains its vigor. One measure of this vigor is the increased amount of time and money that seekers of public office devote to electoral politics. Political parties and interest groups are important institutions through which the ideal of popular sovereignty is put into political practice.

3. **Limited government.** Both the Declaration and the Constitution clearly state that limits exist to the exercise of political power. Indeed, the Declaration insists that the people have a right of revolution if the government usurps their rights. The Constitution, as a more conservative document, does not go quite so far, but it does include three sets of provisions that explicitly limit the exercise of power—the **Bill of Rights,** the Civil War amendments, especially the Fourteenth, and Article I, Sections 9 and 10. Over the course of American history, the Supreme Court, the most authoritative interpreter of these provisions, has for the most part protected the rights of the people against governmental intrusion. Economic conservatives have also found the value of limited government a powerful

weapon supporting their arguments against government intervention in the economy.

Values or Ideals Derived from the American Historical Experience

Economic **individualism** is undoubtedly the single most important value growing out of the American experience. Although some authors equate economic individualism with capitalism, there are significant differences between the two. In its eighteenth-century origins, economic individualism did not display the social unconcern, the cutthroat competition, or the amassing of great fortunes of the laissez-faire capitalism of late nineteenth century America.

The foremost economic individualist of the nation's early years was Benjamin Franklin. His pithy sayings, such as "A penny saved is a penny earned," are still part of the American value system. Yet Franklin's individualism was benign. He subordinated economic values to political values, and he sought to ensure that the social costs of his individualism did not unduly harm other people. Furthermore, Franklin devoted most of his adult life to public service. In all these characteristics, Franklin stands in vivid contrast to the business leaders of the late nineteenth century.

Andrew Carnegie, J. Pierpont Morgan, and John D. Rockefeller, heirs of the industrial revolution, insisted that political values be subordinated to economic values. In support of this position, they employed both the traditional ideal of limited government and the prevailing economic **ideology,** which held government intervention in the economy to be unnatural and harmful. Nor were most of the economic giants much concerned with the social costs of industrialization. William Henry Vanderbilt, when admonished that his actions were contrary to the public interest, exclaimed "The public be damned!" Virtually none of them sought public office. Not until the second or third generations did the heirs of such business leaders as DuPont, Heinz, Kennedy, and Rockefeller enter public life.

Somewhat surprisingly, the rise of laissez-faire attitudes in the business and financial worlds was actually accompanied by the decline of Adam Smith's free enterprise model. Smith's model called for competition in industry, an absence of monopoly, mobility of labor, free flow of capital investments to where profit opportunities were greatest, and freedom from government intervention in the economy. By the late nineteenth century, most of these conditions had vanished.

The twentieth century has seen an even greater departure from Smith's model.[6] Almost 40 percent of economic activity in the United States today occurs under largely noncompetitive conditions. Although monopolies are rare, the American economy is dominated by oligopolists, a few giant corporations that control a given market. Restrictive professional practices and unionization limit mobility of labor. A number of restrictions from the public and the private sectors hedge the flow of capital investments. Government intervention in the economy is all-pervasive.

Yet corporations are far from helpless in the face of government intervention. They can transform their economic power into political influence in a number of ways. Businesses form political action committees (PACs) to contribute money to the campaigns of potential supporters in Congress. Corporate advertising and marketing techniques are used for political ends. Business interests lobby public officials. Legal action to protect corporate interests has a rich history. Corporate officers who become public officials can influence not only the making of public policy but also its implementation. Through all these efforts, corporations attempt to secure policies favorable to business interests.

Advocates of governmental restrictions on corporate power like Philip Green, Fred Harris, and John Kenneth Galbraith are concerned not only with corporations' excessive political influence but also with the consequences of economic individualism particularly the existing widespread inequalities of wealth and income.[7] They point to the fact that the top 20 percent of the population owns more than 75 percent of all personal wealth, whereas the bottom 20 percent owns .02 percent. The picture is hardly better when we look at the distribution of income. In 1984, the top 40 percent earned more than 67 percent of all income, whereas the bottom 40 percent earned less than 16 percent, about the

LOSING THE WAR ON POVERTY?

The poverty rate today remains higher than it was in the 1970s and early 1980s. Though the median income for the nation as a whole continues to grow, the increases for the affluent have been much greater than for the poor. Between 1980 and 1984, the median income for the poorest 40 percent of the population actually declined more than $500, from $12,966 to $12,489. During the same period, the median income of the top 40 percent increased almost $1,800 from $43,531 to $45,300. Apparently, the saying "The rich get richer and the poor get poorer" still holds true. Moreover, poverty is not equally distributed among racial groups in America. In 1984, the poverty rate stood at nearly 34 percent for blacks, nearly 28 percent for Hispanics, but just 11.5 percent for whites. Perhaps most disturbing of all, the poverty rate for children, especially minority children, is extremely high and continuing to rise. More than half of all black children under the age of six, for instance, were living in poverty in 1984.

slaveholders, whereas the latter made the attempts of blacks to escape their oppression hardly less perilous.

The Civil War freed the slaves, and three constitutional amendments—the Thirteenth, Fourteenth, and Fifteenth—were adopted to protect the rights of the newly freed blacks. But the new legal rights were rarely secured by the courts, and race prejudice was not eradicated. Indeed, black leaders such as W.E.B. DuBois, Marcus Garvey, and Malcolm X claimed that such prejudice was part of the very fabric of American political life. The fact that Congress passed no civil rights legislation from 1875 until 1957 supports their claims.

Yet it was not only blacks and Indians who suffered from discrimination. Virtually every immigrant group faced the animosity of earlier immigrants. The nineteenth-century Know-Nothing party, a semisecret organization hostile to all foreigners, especially immigrant Catholics, was perhaps the most virulent institutional expression of American nativism. In the southwest, Mexican Americans were subjected to the same forms of ra-

same as the top 5 percent.[8] Even more discouraging to reformers is the fact that this pattern has remained virtually unchanged since World War II. It has also meant that despite government efforts to reduce poverty, somewhat more than 14.4 percent, nearly 35 million people in 1984, still fell below the **poverty line** as officially defined by the federal government. Yet it should be pointed out that other democracies such as France and Italy have greater inequalities of wealth and income than does the United States.

A second set of values derived from the American experience is racial and ethnic prejudice. Race discrimination is an inextricable fact of American history. The English colonists quickly adopted the practice of excluding the Indians from lands they desired. As early as 1619, blacks were imported as slaves to labor on the tobacco and cotton plantations. Although the three-fifths compromise embedded in the Constitution and federal fugitive slave laws represented political compromises, the former affected the political representation of white

The daughter of a sharecropper in central Louisiana

cial discrimination by "Anglos" that had plagued blacks and Indians.

Income statistics for the last several decades reveal that the nation's racial and ethnic minorities tend to cluster near the bottom of the scale. Unemployment rates for these groups are much higher than for whites and they are far more likely to live in segregated neighborhoods or in substandard housing. Viewed from their perspective, the United States still has a long way to go before the ideal of racial and ethnic equality becomes an effective reality.

Since the 1950s, the nation has been moving incrementally toward that goal. Supreme Court decisions, congressional legislation, and executive action are important indicators of the nation's commitment to ending racial and ethnic discrimination as official policy.[9] Yet the bitterness surrounding school desegregation, busing, open housing, and affirmative action all reveal that the struggle for racial justice is far from over.

In an effort to secure their rights, various ethnic and racial groups have organized themselves to pursue their goals through pressure politics, electoral politics, and legal action. Jesse Jackson's pursuit of the Democratic nomination for the presidency in 1984 is the most dramatic example of these efforts. A related goal of civil rights activists is to increase citizen awareness that the United States is a great nation precisely because of its racial, ethnic, religious, cultural, and linguistic diversity.

A final set of values derived from the American experience has as its focus anti**communism,** or more accurately, anti-Soviet communism. Ironically, throughout most of the nineteenth century, the United States and pre-Soviet Russia were not unfriendly powers. When, for example, Russia sold Alaska to the United States in 1867, it was in part because of Russian fears that its greatest rival, Britain, would eventually annex Alaska to Canada and then be in a position to harass the Russian empire from the east. The isolationist United States could be relied on to abstain from international adventurism.

All this changed abruptly in 1917 when the Communists seized power in Russia and established the Soviet Union. At that time, the United States, like most western democracies, responded with shock and horror that a small Communist party, preaching revolution and the abolition of private property, now controlled a major country. Both communist ideology and Soviet nationalist aspirations have challenged the United States, confirming Alexis de Tocqueville's prediction in the 1830s that the twentieth century would be witness to a struggle between the two nations that would "sway the destinies of half the globe." [10]

Several factors lend further support to the idea that American sentiment is largely directed against Soviet communism. First, no other communist country is seen as threatening to American interests as the Soviet Union. Indeed, the American government has directly and indirectly given aid to communist countries that are viewed as anti-Soviet. Second, America's military forces and alliances are focused on the Soviet Union. The nation's principal military alliance, the North Atlantic Treaty Organization (NATO) is widely recognized as an anti-Soviet alliance. Third, the expansion of communism into the third world is almost always perceived by American policy makers as Soviet inspired. This is particularly true of American perceptions of the troubles in Central America. Fourth, American officials oppose participation by communists in the governments of Western European democracies on the grounds that they are in fact under Soviet control. Finally, America's relationship with China, the world's largest communist country, is conditioned in many ways by the fact of Chinese hostility towards the Soviets. American policy makers, in fact, become uneasy whenever any steps toward the relaxation of tension between the two communist giants appear likely.

Anticommunist sentiment is reinforced by the value of economic individualism. Communist **collectivism** threatens not only this strongly held value but also freedom itself. For the economic individualist, political and economic freedom go hand in hand. Perhaps the foremost spokesperson for this view is Milton Friedman, who in *Free to Choose* goes even farther and insists that economic freedom and political freedom are inextricably linked.

Communism, particularly in its Soviet form, is seen by many Americans as antithetical to the most important part of their nation's heritage. Thus, it comes as a shock that the containment of communism is a foreign policy that did not emerge until after the close of World War II.[11] Prior to that war,

RONALD REAGAN AND THE REPUBLICAN RESURGENCE

The Republican party under the leadership of Ronald Reagan is enjoying its greatest success in more than a quarter of a century. Indeed, some Republicans are harboring visions of a realignment of the two major parties that will restore the Republican party to the dominance they held from 1860 until 1932. Some observers question, however, whether it is the president or the party that has captured the people's imagination.

The personal characteristics of Ronald Reagan clearly account for some aspects of the Republican resurgence. Reagan's communication skills, his engaging manner, his ability to reduce complex issues to simple decisions, his willingness to project this nation's power, his populism, his attacks on government spending for social programs, his persistence in pushing for tax reform, and his almost uncanny ability to know when to exercise his power have thrilled his supporters and disheartened the Democrats.

Reagan's achievements are all the more remarkable given his age, his background, and his marital history. The president has succeeded in bridging the generation gap more successfully than any president since John Kennedy. His career as an actor in largely "B"-grade movies hardly seemed the training for executive office at the state level, let alone the presidency. And his divorce would have spelled doom for many a lesser politician.

But easily the most remarkable has been Reagan's ideological shift from New Deal Democrat to conservative Republican. No other politician has made such a dramatic shift and succeeded. In doing so, Reagan now holds many of the values that large numbers of Americans feel strongly about. This, perhaps more than any other factor, accounts for the president's popularity.

If, in 1988, the Republican party continues its resurgence (which was somewhat checked when they lost control of the Senate in 1986), it may well be the case that both Ronald Reagan and the party are espousing the values and the policies that most voters favor. If the resurgence stalls, then the electoral success of the Republican party will have to be attributed to, arguably, its most charismatic leader since the party's founding.

the United States did not have a large standing army or navy. The growth of the defense budget, of a munitions industry, of armaments trade, of military assistance, of multi-lateral military alliances, are all post World War II phenomena.

Contemporary Political Problems

In the preceding sections of this chapter, we have contrasted conditions that existed at the founding of the nation with those of the present. This section examines some of the problems that policy makers will have to grapple with over the next several decades. Although these problems may seem disparate, they are in fact closely related.

Domestically, policy makers must deal with the uneven functioning of the economy. Since the national government plays such an important role in shaping the economy, the impact of public policies on business conditions is critical to the nation's economic health. The strategies policy makers can employ are limited by the problem of federal deficits and the constraints of Gramm-Rudman. At the same time, both liberals and conservatives agree that vigorous economic growth is necessary if the nation is to reduce the gap between the haves and the have-nots. Statistics show that women and minorities suffer the most when the economy grows slowly.

The nation must also deal with a variety of troubling environmental questions. How strict should clean air and clean water standards be? What should be done about acid rain? Who should regulate the disposal of toxic wastes? What relationship should exist between environmental policies and energy policies concerning the use of coal, the nation's most abundant energy resource? How will the western states grapple with the demographic trends that already are placing severe demands on water resources and on a fragile environment? What kinds of policies are necessary to conserve the nation's topsoil and also to prevent the most productive farmlands from being taken over by urban developers? What is the proper balance between economic growth and environmental protection? How can the nation develop environmental standards to guide technological innovation? These are the kinds of questions this generation and the next must come to grips with.[12]

It is in the international arena, however, that America faces perhaps its greatest challenges. Although the ideological conflict between the United States and the Soviet Union remains paramount, that position is being increasingly challenged by the problems of economic development in the poorer nations of the world.[13] From one perspective, the East versus West ideological conflict that now claims primacy is being superseded by the North-South economic split.

Unfortunately, these two dimensions often overlap. Central America is a case in point; that regional conflict has important elements of both ideology and economics. Critics of American policy in that region insist that the United States must turn away from a blind anticommunism and recognize the legitimate aspirations of all the groups contending for power. These critics also see America's policy toward Africa and Asia as inadequate in addressing the needs of the **developing nations** on those two continents.

In defense of American policy makers, we can say that long-range plans for development assis-

tance are often frustrated by the short-term fact of communist subversion. The Marshall Plan, an American-financed effort to rebuild the war-torn economies of Europe and Japan after World War II, succeeded because the enemy had been vanquished. Policy makers today must balance the efforts to combat ongoing insurgency against the more uncertain benefits of future economic development. It may be true that we could most effectively check the spread of Soviet communism by a program of economic assistance to the developing nations. But policy makers cannot ignore the political threats that would undermine any such program.

United States foreign policy must also deal with the problems of apartheid in South Africa; with trade barriers and import restrictions; with the debt problems of developing countries; and with religious and national conflicts in the Middle East, Northern Ireland, and the Islamic nations. This nation must also assist in the building of more effective international organizations that will reduce the possibility of armed conflict, slow the arms race, reduce the risk of nuclear war, and aid in the search for peaceful solutions to international disputes. Given the power and wealth of the United States, we cannot escape the responsibility of a world leadership role.

Conclusion

This text examines the values, institutions, and policies of the American national government. In studying that government we are studying a wide-ranging set of processes whereby the American people attempt to cope with (but do not necessarily resolve) problems that affect significant numbers of people. The institutions of the national government are actually only one part of a complex whole that has many nongovernmental participants. In a pluralist society such as the United States, nongovernmental groups play important roles in making public policy and in allocating resources.

Political societies must also respond to societal changes. In this chapter, we have explored some of the profound changes that have occurred since the 1780s. The United States has evolved from an agrarian nation of less than 4 million people to an industrial giant of more than 240 million people.

Nineteenth-century America practiced negative government. As late as 1900, 90 percent of all federal employees worked for the post office: there was virtually no federal bureaucracy. By contrast, the twentieth century has witnessed the growth of positive government and a mixed economy. The budget of the federal government now accounts for more than 20 percent of GNP, and federal employment stands at nearly three million.

During the last two centuries, the pattern of interests has undergone some dramatic shifts. These shifts are reflected in the institutions of government—in the makeup of the president's cabinet, the committees of Congress, and the personnel on the Supreme Court. As new groups gain influence, changes in the pattern of government spending appear, as well as sustained pressures for policy changes.

Despite these massive changes, American ideals have proven strong enough to carry the nation through revolution, civil war, and economic depression. The values reflected in the Declaration of Independence and the Constitution—natural rights, popular sovereignty, and limited government—are widely regarded as the cornerstones of American democracy. Many critics, however, suggest that the values derived from the nation's historical heritage—economic individualism, racial and ethnic prejudice, and anticommunism—must be harmonized with democratic ideals if the United States is to become a more just society.

As the nation looks to the future, certain persisting problems—the health of the economy and the environment and the complexities of foreign affairs—will need to be addressed in new and innovative ways that require, first of all, vigorous leadership and widespread political participation. The task of policy makers is to forge new policies that fit American ideals to the needs of contemporary society.

 ## Glossary

Bill of Rights The first ten amendments to the Constitution containing provisions that limit governmental authority to infringe on certain fundamental political and personal rights. In important respects, bills of rights represent the implementation of the political principle of limited government.

Capitalism In the 18th and 19th century capitalism displaced mercantilism as the dominant economic philosophy. As a system of political economy, capitalism calls for private ownership of the means of production and a supply-demand market economy to distribute goods and services, and insists on the primacy of the profit motive, or economic self-interest.

Collectivism A system in which the state is perceived as the sole legitimate institution for directing both economic and political matters. Some, but not all, collectivist societies are socialist in nature.

Communism A political, economic, and social theory based principally on the writings of Karl Marx and Friedrich Engels. According to Marx, communism is a higher stage of development than socialism. When communism is achieved, the state will "wither away"

because all the economic contradictions plaguing society will have been eliminated.

Democracy A form of government in which the people rule directly. Today, the term *democracy* is often used interchangeably with *republic* (see Chapter 2). Three key principles underly democratic theory: popular sovereignty, limited government, and majority rule and minority rights.

Developing nations A term used to describe nations that have not industrialized. Most of these countries are located in the Southern Hemisphere, suffer from overpopulation, and have high levels of poverty.

Ideology A set of values that influences what people believe to be the proper form of government and the appropriate type of economic system. In the twentieth century, the dominant "isms" or ideologies include capitalism, communism, socialism, and democracy.

Individualism The doctrine that the interests of the individual are superior to the interests of the state and that the state exists to serve the interests of the individual rather than the reverse.

Laissez-faire economy "Hands off," meaning that government should not intervene in the economy except under carefully limited conditions. The market is viewed as the most efficient allocator of scarce resources and government intervention as almost always producing a less efficient, thus more costly, allocation.

Limited government (or **Constitutionalism**) The political principle that governmental power is limited by natural law and natural rights and that governments cannot justly invade these rights.

Natural rights A corollary of natural law that assumes all humans are endowed with certain rights that may not be abridged or invaded by political authorities. Jefferson called these rights unalienable.

Popular sovereignty The right of the people to create, alter, or abolish their form of government.

Poverty line The level, as defined by the national government, below which the income of a family of four is insufficient to meet the basic needs of food, clothing, and shelter. In the middle 1980s, this figure was $10,000.

Sovereignty The supreme power, independence, and freedom from external control of a state. Federal systems lodge sovereignty in the central government, whereas states retain their sovereignty in confederacies.

Three-fifths compromise An agreement reached at the Constitutional Convention by northern and southern interests, in which slaves were to be counted at the ratio of three persons for every five slaves for purposes of both representation and taxation.

 ## Suggestions for Further Reading

Allen, Frederick Lewis. *The Big Change: America Transforms Itself, 1900–1950.* New York: Harper, 1952. Although somewhat dated, this is still an entertaining and insightful account of the emergence of modern America.

Commager, Henry Steele. *The American Mind.* New Haven, Conn.: Yale University Press, 1950. A classic American intellectual history that focuses on the changes in American society from 1890 to 1950.

Hartz, Louis. *The Liberal Tradition in America.* New York: Harcourt, Brace and World, 1955. One of the standard accounts of the roots and manifestations of American political culture from a liberal's perspective.

Hofstadter, Richard. *The American Political Tradition.* New York: Knopf, 1948. Must reading for those interested in the political ideas that have shaped the American experience from the Founding Fathers to the New Deal.

Lowenthal, David. *The Past Is a Foreign Country.* New York: Cambridge University Press, 1986. A persuasive account of how the nation's history has shaped our understanding of contemporary America.

Murray, Charles. *Losing Ground: American Social Policy, 1950–1980.* New York: Basic Books, 1984. By the author's own admission, this is a contentious interpretation of governmental efforts to aid the disadvantaged.

Rodgers, Harrell R. *The Cost of Human Neglect.* Armonk, N.Y.: M.E. Sharpe, 1982. Presents an interesting and powerful argument that concern for the disadvantaged is justified for practical as well as moral reasons.

Rosenbaum, Walter A. *Energy, Politics, and Public Policy.* Washington D.C.: Congressional Quarterly Press, 1981. Excellent introduction to the political and policy problems in supplying energy to a modern industrial economy.

Slater, Philip. *The Pursuit of Loneliness.* Boston: Beacon Press, 1976. A critical and questioning look at some problematic features of American political culture.

Thurow, Lester C. *The Zero-Sum Society.* New York: Penguin Books, 1980. Examines the ways our political culture, policy process, and economic system may be combining to hamper effective economic policy making.

Tuchman, Barbara. *The March of Folly: From Troy to Vietnam.* New York: Random House, 1983. A noted historian examines how (and why) entire societies, but especially their governments, make incredibly stupid and often disastrous mistakes.

Udall, Stewart L. *The Quiet Crisis.* New York: Holt, 1963. Eloquent plea by a former secretary of the interior for a land policy that conserves and protects the natural environment.

Yergin, Daniel. *Shattered Peace: The Origins of the Cold War and the National Security State.* Boston: Houghton Mifflin, 1978. Analyzes the theory and practice of containment (of the Soviet Union) as a foreign policy.

*Man's capacity for justice makes democracy possible, but man's inclination to injustice
makes democracy necessary.*
Reinhold Niebuhr
Democracy is the worst system devised by the wit of man, except for all the others.
Winston Churchill

Chapter 2

The Nature of
American Democracy:
Principle and Practice

Chapter Outline

Introduction
The Democratic Triad: Principles and Practices of American Democracy
Common Misunderstandings Concerning the Nature of Democracy
Conclusion

Introduction

Democracy is a Greek word that means rule by the people. Most of us have heard that many times. But what is "rule by the people"? Does it mean "the people rule themselves" or "self-rule"? And what is that in practice? Does it mean everyone can "do their own thing"? What does "people" mean? Does it mean all the people? All at once? What do we mean by "rule"? Making decisions? About what? Voting? For what—or whom? Quite frequently, other familiar phrases are offered to help clarify the nature of democracy: statements like "government by the consent of the governed," **"majority rule"**, and **"minority rights."**

As the foregoing suggests, democracy defies easy definition. Unlike communism, it is not an ideology. No single, universally accepted democratic philosophy or doctrine exists. Modern democra-

cies reflect the contributions of various political philosophers such as John Locke, Jean Jacques Rousseau, John Stuart Mill, and for the American democratic variant, Thomas Jefferson and James Madison.[1]

Given such difficulties, can we adequately explore the meaning of democracy in a short chapter? No, but we can emphasize the basic values and major procedural elements that represent the mainstream of modern democratic thinking. Let's begin with some important observations about democracy. First, democracy is basically about political participation. It is probably fair to say that participation is the central core or essence of democracy.

What is the value of individual involvement in the making of political decisions and the assumption of responsibility for governing ourselves? Traditional or "classical" democratic theory rests on the notion that such participation in decisions that

Saving the Hudson. Participation is the essence of democracy.

affect our life helps to develop our character and our self-reliance. It contributes vitally to the full realization of our capacities and is necessary for the maintenance of self-respect and individual dignity. In short, the essence of democracy is political participation, and the value of participation is the fostering of individual human dignity.

But how can such participation be organized and carried out? Direct individual participation through holding public office or making policy is impossible. Even in ancient Greece, where the idea of democracy originated, most Athenians did not participate in political life. Citizenship was sharply limited, excluding women, slaves, minors, and those without property. Such restrictions had the advantage of allowing free, adult, male, property holders to assemble and to vote on virtually all important issues.

Even if those restrictions existed in twentieth-century United States, the size of the nation would present insuperable obstacles to direct democracy. A voting assembly like that of Athens would include 170 million Americans of voting age. If each were seated in an area of just one square yard, the enfranchised group would occupy fifty-five square miles—approximately the size of the District of Columbia. Debate would be equally difficult. Even if each person were given just fifteen seconds to speak, it would take longer than an average lifetime—eighty-one years—for everyone to be heard—and only on one issue!

To overcome the problems of direct democracy, the United States, as well as other nations, have adopted the notion of "representative" government. In Abraham Lincoln's words, the role *of the people* is to participate in selecting leaders who are given the power *by the people* to make political decisions *for the people.* This vision of democracy sees a close relationship between a politically active, aware, and well-informed citizenry and wise public policies.

Lincoln's vision also sees a close link between democratic principles and democratic practices. Throughout our nation's history, there has been a continual search for ways to bring practice closer to principle, a perennial testing of practice against principle, and a constant inquiry into why practice has fallen so far short of principle. And although our democratic principles are much older than our Constitution, they have developed in ways unique to the American culture.[2] In the next section, we examine three democratic principles and explore the various ways these principles have been translated into practice.

The Democratic Triad: Principles and Practices of American Democracy

Popular Sovereignty

This theory or principle can be defined as the right of the people to create, alter, or abolish their form of government. Although this may sound quite familiar and commonplace to us, in the eighteenth century political authority was exercised almost exclusively by monarchs or the privileged classes. The idea of popular sovereignty, embodied in the Declaration of Independence and the Constitution, represented a dramatic shift in political thinking. In the Declaration, Jefferson asserted that governments derive their just powers from the consent of the governed. The Preamble to the Constitution proclaims that it is the people who are forming a more perfect union.

In the United States, as well as in most democracies, the principle of popular sovereignty is put into practice by universal suffrage, competitive political parties, and periodic elections. From our perspective, a country that lacks these features is nondemocratic. Communist regimes and right-wing dictatorships can be contrasted with western democracies because they typically do not allow competitive political party systems to exist, nor do they hold regular elections.

Although limited in the early years of this nation's history, the suffrage (the right to vote) has been gradually extended to include all citizens over the age of eighteen. Competitive political parties were well established by the presidential election of 1800. Periodic elections have taken place since the adoption of the Constitution. Indeed, elections were even held during the Civil War and World Wars I and II. No other nation can claim as long a history of uninterrupted elections. On the other hand, contemporary problems such as the denial of the vote to ethnic or racial groups, the lack of effective two-party competition in certain parts of the country, and the decline in voter participation remind us that

ALTERNATIVE VIEWS OF DEMOCRACY

Democracy is a cause that is never won, but I believe it will never be lost.

Charles A. Beard

Democracy substitutes selection by the incompetent many for appointment by the corrupt few.

George Bernard Shaw

All the ills of democracy can be cured by more democracy.

Alfred E. Smith

The doctrine that the cure for the evils of democracy is more democracy is like saying that the cure for crime is more crime.

H.L. Mencken

a gap still exists between the theory and the practice of popular sovereignty.

Limited Government or Constitutionalism

This principle holds that certain rights (they may be called natural rights or human rights) are retained by the people and may not be intruded on by government. As we noted in Chapter 1, limited government rests on the philosophy of **natural law** and natural rights. Governments are granted only those powers necessary to protect the natural rights of the people. Such grants of power to the government are best accomplished through a social contract, that is, through an instrument whereby the people create their government.

In effect, the people create a government to protect rights that are essentially prepolitical in nature. The implication is that people are human beings before they are citizens or subjects of political authority. Thomas Jefferson, in the Declaration, specified equality, life, liberty, and the pursuit of happiness as being among the natural rights. Today, some human rights advocates such as Michael Harrington argue that these rights include a right to a job and a right to health care.[3] Despite uncertainty

about the precise nature of rights, little if any disagreement exists that governmental power ought to be limited.

American democracy puts the theory of limited government into practice in several ways. The Constitution defines and limits the powers of government. Article I, Sections 9 and 10, contain explicit prohibitions that constrain both the national and state governments. The Constitution divides power between the national government and the state governments. Congress, the president, and the federal courts are granted certain powers, but other constitutional provisions enable each branch to "check" the power of the other branches. The first ten amendments to the Constitution, known as the Bill of Rights, constitute an impressive list of limits on governmental powers. The Civil War amendments, the Thirteenth, Fourteenth, and Fifteenth (but especially the Fourteenth), restrain the state governments in virtually the same ways as the Bill of Rights does the national government.

These citizens are free to gather together and express opinions because government has "limited" powers to regulate such activity. Such limits to government power are essential to meaningful participation and thus democracy.

COMMUNIST DEMOCRACY?

Though Americans consider communist countries like the Soviet Union and China to be undemocratic, many of them make vigorous claim to be democracies. Some use the term *Democratic Republic* in their official name, and all of them describe their regimes as "people's democracies." This illustrates the virtual universal acceptance of, and homage to, democracy in the modern world. It also demonstrates that the term means different things to different people. The communists define a genuine democratic government as one that governs "for" the people, identifying and serving their "true interests." Participation of and by the people is not important, and adherence to the elements of the "democratic triad" is unnecessary. Since almost all governments claim to be governing for their people, clearly this definition would apply to virtually any country. When the term *democracy* is applied to nations as different in principle and practice as the United States and the Soviet Union, we are reminded of Humpty Dumpty's comment in Lewis Carroll's *Through The Looking Glass* that "When I make a word do that much work, I pay it extra."

All these constitutional provisions limit governmental power. When government exercises power, the federal courts can be called on to determine whether due process (a fair and nonarbitrary way of acting) has been followed.[4] Unfortunately, these provisions have not always proven effective, but they have given Americans a goal to strive for.

Political Equality/Majority Rule and Minority Rights

Political equality: Many Americans are deeply ambivalent about the meaning and reach of equality.[5] An insistence on equality is often seen as conflicting with the value of individualism. Racial prejudice has undermined the ideal of racial equality. Large numbers of men and women do not embrace the notion of sexual equality. At least part of the failure to adopt the Equal Rights Amendment can be traced to these sentiments. Persistent, wide gaps in income and wealth among different groups

documents that equality has traditionally lacked an economic content.

Yet the ideal of equality has a strong appeal to Americans. The principle that all human beings have the same worth and identical natural rights is deeply rooted in the American tradition. Jefferson voiced this conviction in the Declaration when he said: "We hold these truths to be self-evident, that all men are created equal." As American democracy has evolved, Jefferson's words have assumed a more universal meaning. We are now more reluctant to argue that the idea of equality contains implicit racial, sexual, or economic limits. From the perspective of this nation's minorities, women, and the poor, however, the acceptance of a wider meaning for equality has been frustratingly slow.

Americans have perhaps been readiest to accept the notions of equal opportunity and equality before the law. Equal opportunity means that society should not create nor tolerate artificial barriers to individual achievement. But Americans are far less sympathetic to the notion of equality of result— that everyone should be guaranteed equal outcomes. We can agree that everyone should have a fair start, but we believe our freedom would be impaired if there were no winners and no losers.

Equality before the law implies that all are bound by the law. In other words, no individual or group is above the law. Government officials as well as private individuals are subject to legal sanctions. Part of the furor over Gerald Ford's granting of a pardon to Richard Nixon can be traced to the feeling that Ford's action placed Nixon above the law. For many Americans, the saying "A government of laws and not of men" captures the notion of equality before the law.

As a principle of democracy, equality has yet another meaning. Equality signifies equality of rights concerning political participation; government should place as few restrictions on political activity as possible. Individuals in a democratic society have a right to express themselves, disagree with government policy, seek to change existing law, run for public office, and have no fear of government reprisal if they undertake any or all of these actions. It is here that the contrast between democratic and nondemocratic regimes is perhaps most vivid.

Traditionally, as we noted, equality in the United States has not been accepted in the economic

Equality in America has traditionally not had an economic content.

some people more heavily than others. Because the Constitution contains only minimal barriers to seeking public office, nearly everyone can throw their hat in the ring. The First Amendment protects virtually all forms of peaceful, political activity. Finally, the Fifth and Fourteenth Amendments' due process clauses ensure that the exercise of governmental power is equitable and that the law is fairly and equally applied.

Majority Rule and Minority Rights: The principle of majority rule and minority rights is closely related to the principle of political equality. In a society of political equals, the theory of majority rule holds that the majority should prevail. Yet even a majority has no right to infringe on the natural, "prepolitical", rights of the minority. Jefferson gave this position its classic statement in his first inaugral address when he declared that "the will of the majority is in all cases to prevail, that will, to be rightful, must be reasonable; that the minority possess their equal rights, which equal laws must protect, and to violate which would be oppression." [6] Majority rule does not empower the majority, no matter how large, to impair wrongfully the natural rights of the minority.

At bottom, this philosophy of democratic government rests on moral considerations. Governments possess the power to invade the rights of the people, but they are not morally justified in doing so. Indeed, a hallmark of democracy is the recognition of a close nexus between the concepts of natural rights and limited government. But, as is the case with all ideals, governmental practice sometimes violates political principle. The internment of Japanese Americans during World War II is a notable instance of government officials invading the rights of a minority.

In the United States, the practice of majority rule has contributed to the development and persistence of two major political parties that have to forge a majority at the polls to govern. During every electoral campaign, Democrats and Republicans, as well as the minor parties, try to attract such a majority. Given the success of the two major parties, minor parties tend to become quickly discouraged and either disband or, in the hope of gaining at least a share of power, join some other party with a more realistic chance of attracting majority support.

sphere. Americans have permitted and indeed encouraged economic inequality. The value of economic individualism—expressed in the drive for economic success—has often clashed with the value of equality. As a consequence, the United States is a democratic society in which both equality and individualism exist in uneasy balance. In such a society there are bound to be glaring examples where equality is subordinated to the drive for wealth.

Thus the several meanings of equality have yet to be fully accepted or implemented. Yet equality has found expression in a number of constitutional provisions. In Article I, the Constitution bars the granting of titles of nobility, which are the foundation of a class society. The First Amendment forbids an established church, ensuring an equality among religions. The Fourteenth Amendment's equal protection clause has been interpreted by the Supreme Court to prohibit racial discrimination and malapportionment, that is, weighting the votes of

SURE, "FREEDOM OF RELIGION" IS ALL FINE AN' GOOD, BUT....

...TH' GOVERNMENT SIMPLY MUST BRING THESE WEIRDO CULTS UNDER CONTROL....

...NOBODY WANTS TO RESTRICT NORMAL RELIGIONS....

....WE JUST WANT TO WEED OUT TH' DEVIANTS....

BEN SARGENT
©1979 The Austin American-Statesman

The party that gains a majority controls the government and make policy.

The principle of minority rights finds expression in the formation and activity of interest groups. In one sense, interest groups are organizations that seek to protect the rights of minorities (the members of the group) against majority intrusion. For example, the American Medical Association lobbies against national health insurance, labor unions against right-to-work laws, and ethnic groups against racial discrimination. Their success has encouraged a proliferating number of minorities to emulate their organization and strategies, thereby broadening the ways interest groups translate the principle of minority rights into political practice.

The First Amendment is also a powerful weapon that transforms principle into practice. A number of First Amendment provisions protect the rights of minorities. The free exercise of religion clause has been interpreted by the Supreme Court to permit Amish communities to establish their own schools free from state regulation. The Supreme Court has also used the language of this amendment to bar legislation that infringed the rights of free expression of political minorities, to shield the right of association from state intrusion, to forbid prior gov-

ernmental censorship of political tracts, and to ensure separation of church and state.

Common Misunderstandings Concerning the Nature of Democracy

In the previous section we examined the democratic principles of popular sovereignty, limited government, and political equality. We also explored how those principles were implemented in American political life. This section analyzes two common misunderstandings many Americans share about the nature of democracy. As a nation, we are perhaps no more ethnocentric (feeling that we are superior) than any other nation. Quite naturally, we tend to identify democracy with our form of government. American institutions and practices are touted as examples that other nations should strive to emulate. Yet if we classify the world's democracies by institutional patterns, we find ourselves in the minority. Most democracies follow the British system of parliamentary government, which is characterized by an executive drawn from and serving at the pleasure of the legislature. Only France and Mexico have adopted the American system of presidential government, which features an executive separately elected and serving a fixed term.[7]

Americans also tend to see a close relationship between the economic system and the political system. Communism and fascism are regarded as incompatible with democracy because these ideologies refuse to accept one or more of the principles of democratic practice: competitive political parties, periodic elections, and enforceable limits on governmental power. We also see such regimes as hostile to property rights. From the American perspective, capitalism and democracy are inextricably linked. Yet once again, a careful look at some of the world's leading democracies reveals considerable variations in the relationship between the political system and the economic system. An examination of both institutional patterns and economic systems will help to clarify their relationship with democracy.

Institutional Patterns and Democracy

We can see from Table 2.1 that no relationship necessarily exists between the institutions of gov-

Table 2.1
Institutional Patterns in Major Nations

	USA	Britain	China	India	Japan	USSR	W. Germany
Written Constitution	Y *	N *	Y	Y	Y	Y	Y
Separation of Powers	Y	N	N	N	N	N	N
Checks and Balances	Y	N	N	N	N	N	N
Federalism	Y	N	Y	Y	N	Y	Y
Judicial Review	Y	N	N	N	N	Y	N

* Y=yes, N=no.

ernment and the presence of democracy in any given country. Put another way, democracy cannot be identified with any particular institutional pattern. Democratic principles—popular sovereignty, limited government, and political equality—can be put into practice in different countries in different ways. A nation's political heritage, its political culture, and its level of political and economic development all play important roles in determining the relationship, if any, between institutional patterns and democratic government.

Table 2.1 also shows that nondemocratic regimes may share some of the same outward institutional patterns as democratic nations. The most distinctive institutional features of American democracy cannot be found in Great Britain, a nation widely accepted as one of the world's leading democracies, whereas the Soviet Union and the People's Republic of China, the two foremost communist powers, have two or more institutional features in common with the United States. As we noted, what most clearly sets nondemocratic systems apart from democracies is their nonadherence to the democratic triad in either theory or practice. Nondemocratic societies do not accept the theory of popular sovereignty and none of them tolerate competitive political parties. Nor are political leaders in these countries chosen through periodic, competitive elections. Finally, nondemocratic systems subscribe neither to the theory nor to the practice of limited government. Although nondemocratic regimes may have written constitutions, such documents normally lack provisions that ef-

fectively limit governmental power. Violations of human rights by governmental authorities are not uncommon when political power is perceived as absolute. Such regimes typically have neither an independent judiciary that can ensure due process in legal proceedings nor judicially enforceable equal protection provisions in their legal codes. Also, nondemocratic systems are often characterized by a privileged class or party that effectively denies both political equality and majority rule.

Economic Systems and Democracy

Since the industrial revolution began around 1750, the relationship between political systems and economic systems has grown exceedingly complex, so that it is difficult to specify precisely at what point representative institutions mark a political system as democratic. Much the same uncertainty plagues the designation of economic systems. The transition from **feudalism** through **mercantilism** to capitalism is more an exercise in historical scholarship than a series of historical events. All we can safely say is that both political and economic systems have evolved over long periods of time and both have undergone fundamental changes.[8]

In the course of this nation's history, the United States has passed through several stages of economic development. During the early years, the government acted on mercantilist principles; that is, it played an important role in directing economic affairs. Alexander Hamilton as President Washington's secretary of the treasury was perhaps the new nation's most ardent mercantilist. His *Report on Manufactures* and his role in creating the First Bank of the United States are classic mercantile actions.

By the time of Andrew Jackson's administration, 1829–1837, government policy had undergone significant change. Indeed, Jackson's veto of the bill to recharter the Second Bank of the United States has often been cited as opening the door to laissez-faire capitalism. The dominance of the Republican party after the Civil War ensured that government economic policy would reflect an even more antiinterventionist attitude.

At the turn of the century, J. Pierpont Morgan's role in creating the United States Steel Corporation highlighted the rise of corporate capitalism. Whereas individual entrepreneurs dominated late nine-

ANDREW JACKSON (1767–1845) AND THE RISE OF AMERICAN DEMOCRACY

Although the Preamble to the Constitution reads, "We, the People," not until Andrew Jackson was elected to the presidency in 1828 did that phrase become truly meaningful. Jackson rose to the presidency in part because of the expansion of the suffrage to include virtually all white males over twenty-one. More important, he was widely perceived as the embodiment of the common man who had made good.

Indeed, it seems as though Jackson's whole life was a shining illustration of how the American dream can become a reality. Born in poverty in the South, he had worked hard to become one of the landed gentry in the West. He had served as an enlisted man in the Revolutionary War and earned fame as the hero of New Orleans in the War of 1812. He had lost large sums of money to eastern banks, and as president, Jackson would destroy the archetype of such banks—the Second Bank of the United States. Throughout his life, he retained an almost unbounded faith in the capabilities of ordinary Americans. Jackson himself, with little formal schooling, had been a teacher, lawyer, judge, congressman, senator, and president. If he could do it, he firmly believed, men of like

intelligence and ambition could do the same.

As president, Jackson vigorously applied his democratic philosophy. His inauguration was attended by large numbers of people from the western regions who, to see their hero, stood on the velvet-covered chairs in the White House in their muddy boots. Jackson proclaimed that since he was the only federal official elected by all the people, it was he who was the "voice of the people." To ensure that the people served in the national government, he called for a "healthy" rotation in office. His opponents (and many later scholars) marked this as the introduction of the

spoils system. During his two terms as president, Jackson opposed all efforts to secure government grants for the privileged. It was on this ground that he vetoed the bill to recharter the Second Bank of the United States.

His pithy, perhaps apochryal, sayings also enhanced his popularity. "I have no respect," Jackson reportedly said, "for a man who can spell a word only one way." When John Marshall handed down a decision Jackson did not like, he fumed: "This decision is too preposterous. John Marshall has made his decision, now let *him* enforce it." And in his famous veto message, Jackson declared: "There are no necessary evils in government. Its evils exist only in its abuses."

Jackson towered over his age, yet so thoroughly captured its spirit that ever since it has been known as the era of Jacksonian democracy. Not only was he a great military hero, a great public figure, a great party catalyst, he was also, and most important, a great *popular* leader. Few other presidents have contributed so much, and with so much passion, to the principles and practices that make up American democracy.

teenth-century capitalism, corporate capitalism is characterized by giant corporations which are operated by managers who typically own only a very small percentage of the stock issued by the corporation. This development was, ironically, accompanied by a more positive role for the government in the nation's economy. Theodore Roosevelt, the first

progressive president, challenged the preponderant influence of the giant corporations and insisted that economic power must be subordinated to political authority.

The worldwide economic collapse that touched off the Great Depression of the 1930s marked a new phase in economic development. Franklin

ARE ALL NONDEMOCRACIES ALIKE?

Are all nondemocracies alike? Of course not! Nondemocratic governments are found in by far the majority of the world's nations, in countries that differ greatly in political culture, traditions, and political and economic development. It should not be surprising that their regimes reflect these differences. One important way in which they diverge is along the authoritarian–totalitarian dimension. These two broad types of regimes, although similar in their rejection of the principles of the democratic triad, differ in their basic goals and practices. Authoritarian governments are mainly interested in controlling and limiting the political activity of their citizens. They are largely concerned with retaining power, and often deal very harshly with vocal political opponents. But they will not seek to interfere greatly with the religious, economic, and cultural activities of an individual's life. They don't really care what the citizen's opinions, beliefs, and preferences are, as long as that person does not attempt to organize a political opposition around them. The military regimes in Chile, Paraguay, and Uruguay are good examples of authoritarian regimes.

Totalitarian governments are more ambitious. Guided by a system of beliefs encompassing all realms of human activity, they attempt to control all aspects of life to achieve compliance with an ideology. Such regimes are interested not only in the obedience of their citizens but also in their active acceptance of the ideology. These governments do not tolerate competing belief systems, such as religion, and require even artistic expression and tastes to conform to the ideology. Marxism-Leninism and fascism are the most famous, or infamous, ideologies underpinning totalitarian regimes, associated with the Soviet Communist and German Nazi regimes, respectively. But any universal ideology can be used as the basis for totalitarian rule, including religions. The "Islamic Republic" established by the revolution in Iran under the leadership of the Ayatollah Khomeini is a modern example. No government has been wholly successful in totalitarian control, but the effort creates a different political atmosphere than that of the authoritarian regime.

Roosevelt's New Deal policies initiated the evolution of welfare capitalism, which calls for an enlarged government responsibility for the healthy functioning of the economy and for government programs for the economically disadvantaged. Despite some minor deviations since Roosevelt's presidency, welfare capitalism remains the basis for government economic policy.

Great Britain went through roughly the same stages of economic development as did the United States. Following World War II, however, Great Britain and the Scandinavian countries elected socialist parties to govern their respective nations. Since then, virtually every Western European democracy has voted a socialist party into power. The election of Francois Mitterrand, the socialist president of France, indicates this trend is still very much alive.

Few scholars, however, would argue that the election of socialist parties necessarily means an end to democracy.[9] In most instances, the coming to power of a socialist party strongly implies disaffection with the malfunctioning of capitalist economies, not with representative political institutions. And until the mid-1970s, nations with extensive welfare systems such as Denmark and Sweden did enjoy high rates of economic growth. This seemed to suggest that socialist parties could manage economic matters more effectively than their conservative, capitalist counterparts.[10] Even Italy and West Germany, have passed from corporate capitalism through welfare capitalism to the election of socialist parties. In West Germany, as in Great Britain, political power has alternated between socialist parties and more conservative parties that favor welfare capitalism. Japan, a democracy since 1947, has favored conservative governments. However, the Japanese socialist party represents the most serious opposition in a multiparty system.

No modern nation with a developed economy has retreated to the stage of corporate capitalism. Once welfare capitalism is in place, the issue is not whether to have government intervention in the economy but rather how extensive that intervention should be. In the United States, the Reagan administration has sought to limit certain social programs, but it has not undertaken their wholesale elimination. A broad consensus still exists on the need for such programs.

The trend of economic modernization, regardless of the economic attitudes of government officials, has been toward greater political direction of the economy. Two prime examples are West Germany and Japan where the government plays a decisive role in economic matters.[11] Although our values of limited government and economic individualism make such an extensive role for the American government unlikely, no complex, industrial, interdependent, urbanized society is immune from this phenomenon. Although we may regret this development, the tendency in America, as in other mature industrial societies, is toward a more positive role for the government in economic concerns.

What implications does a pervasive role for government in the economy have for our form of democracy? This is an important and controversial question. As we mentioned earlier, Americans have traditionally associated democracy with capitalism and defined limited government as including strict limits on government economic activity. Government involvement in the economy, scholars such as Milton Friedman continue to claim, necessarily results in the loss of freedoms and rights vital for meaningful democracy. Others scholars such as Michael Harrington point to the history of Western Europe since World War II and argue that no logical incompatibility exists between democracy and **socialism.** The experience of these countries, at least to date, seems to suggest that socialist parties can adopt an extensive role in the economy, and still adhere to the principles of the democratic triad.

Several factors make it unlikely that a strong socialist party will develop in the United States in the foreseeable future, however. First is a tradition of economic individualism reaching back at least to Benjamin Franklin, a tradition reinforced by a wariness of the national government's authority that originated with the colonists' experiences with the British crown.

Second, the American working class has never been as alienated nor had as strong a sense of class consciousness as has been the case in other Western nations. Even during the colonial era, American society never experienced the sharp class distinctions between the hereditary nobility or ruling class and the common people that was feudalism's legacy to European societies. Status in the United States has tended to be based on wealth rather than bloodlines, which has encouraged aspirations of upward mobility. The attainment of status has depended on individual effort, not on collective political effort. Class consciousness in America was also hindered by ethnic and racial cleavages among the working class. Intense competition for jobs, property, and other scarce resources in the struggle for upward mobility, has tended to aggravate these cleavages rather than enhance a working-class consciousness.

A third factor accounting for the absence of a strong socialist party is the relative rapidity with which the right to vote was extended to all adults. This opportunity to participate in politics, realized fifty to seventy-five years earlier in the United States than in much of Europe, helped to counter the alienation generated by the industrialization of the late nineteenth century. It also provided an outlet for political activity across a broad range of issues that often reached beyond a common working-class identity.

Finally, socialist parties are unattractive to most Americans because of the uneven effectiveness of their economic programs. Their perceived associa-

Norman Thomas, six time candidate for president on the Socialist ticket between 1928 and 1948. A powerful voice for democratic socialism and opponent of Russian Communism and totalitarianism.

tion with communism and the denial of human rights reinforces this sentiment. The American nation, which recovered from the depression of the 1930s and considers itself one of the world's freest countries, is not very likely to risk existing institutions to gamble on socialism.

Although the Constitution does not mandate any particular economic system, these factors exert a powerful influence on the economic policies of our government. In the United States, capitalism and democracy are apparently inextricably linked.

Conclusion

Democracy is both a political process and a political result. As a process, it is most concerned with ideals to work for, rather than with the design of a system to protect the status quo. Written constitutions, institutional patterns, economic systems, and patterns of interests may be helpful in defining a given stage of democracy, but none is essential to a definition of democracy.

Nor is democracy simply a set of political principles divorced from everyday life. Rather, it is a form of government that continually seeks to bring political practices closer to democratic ideals. Although any nation is bound to fall short of attaining such ideals, they must remain an animating force in society for democracy to retain its vitality.

American democracy should not be confused with such institutional features as separation of powers, welfare capitalism, or the influence of business and labor. Instead, an analysis of our form of government should focus on the ways this nation has sought to translate the democratic principles of popular sovereignty, limited government, and political equality/majority rule and minority rights into practice. The health of the two major political parties, the level of political participation, the vigor with which civil rights and liberties are protected and expanded, governmental adherence to due process, and the openness of our society to dissent are important measures of how effectively democratic principles are being implemented.

It is more difficult to assess nondemocratic regimes because they are typically closed societies that resist efforts at analysis and evaluation. Nonetheless, when any regime departs from the democratic triad, when one party dominates the government, when the limits to governmental power are poorly defined, and when force and violence are perceived as acceptable instruments of political power, such a society is clearly nondemocratic. This is true regardless of the relationship between the political system and the economic system.

When analysis focuses on political practice rather than political rhetoric, the sharpest differences between American democracy and nondemocratic regimes become apparent. Yet as this nation's minorities, women, and poor are aware, government officials and the American public are often satisfied with rhetoric alone. They do not feel the urgency of closing the gap between ideal and practice. Until this seeming complacency is overcome, officials and ordinary citizens will not recognize just how keenly aware the disadvantaged, both here and abroad, are of America's shortcomings.

 **Glossary**

Feudalism A system of political economy dominant in Europe from the ninth to about the fifteenth century, based on the relationship between lord and vassal and characterized by land being held on condition of homage and service.

Majority Rule The political principle that assumes the majority has a lawful right to prevail in elections and to make public policy.

Mercantilism The system of political economy prevailing in Europe after the decline of feudalism. Under mercantilist doctrines, governments sought to direct economic development through (1) the accumulation of precious metals, (2) establishing colonies and a merchant marine for colonial trade, and (3) developing industry and mining to produce a favorable balance of trade.

Minority rights The political principle, based partly on natural rights, that assumes the existence of certain rights so crucial to human freedom that the majority cannot justly infringe on or deny them to a minority. Freedom of speech and of worship are examples.

Natural law   A political concept that assumes there exists a "higher law" emanating from God or Nature that is immutable, moral, rational, and objective and that should govern all human relationships.

Republic   A representative form of government where the people choose their rulers in competitive elections.

Socialism   A system of political economy that developed in the nineteenth century as a reaction to the excesses of capitalism. Under socialism, the means of production are publicly owned and goods and services are distributed according to the dictates of a central plan drawn up by the state.

 ## Suggestions for Further Reading

Cohen, Carl. *Democracy.* New York: The Free Press, 1971. An unusually lucid and very thorough discussion of democracy. A good book with which to begin serious study of the concept.

Dahl, Robert. *Dilemmas of Pluralist Democracy.* New Haven: Yale University Press, 1982. Examines in a thoughtful fashion the major theoretical problems that plague modern western democracies.

Domhoff, G. William. *The Powers That Be.* New York: Vintage Books, 1979. A highly readable example of the substantial literature that criticizes American government for being "elitist" rather than democratic.

Gilder, George. *Wealth and Poverty.* New York: Basic Books, 1981. Modern restatement of the view that government programs are an inefficient way to create wealth or combat poverty. Exerts a great influence on conservative policy makers.

Lowi, Theodore. *The End of Liberalism.* New York: W.W. Norton, 1979. Lowi presents a powerful argument that too little autonomous governmental authority and too much power widely distributed to private organized interests perverts democracy rather than improves it.

Macpherson, C.B. *The Real World of Democracy.* New York: Oxford University Press, 1966. Brief and highly readable discussion of how democracy manifests itself in communist, underdeveloped, and Western contexts.

Pennock, J. Roland. *Democratic Political Theory.* Princeton, N.J.: Princeton University Press, 1979. Good overview of the major variants of democratic theory and the central issues surrounding the concept.

Redenius, Charles. *The American Ideal of Equality: From Jefferson's Declaration to the Burger Court.* Port Washington, N.Y.: Kennikat Press, 1981. Chronicles America's struggle to come to terms with the value of equality.

de Toqueville, Alexis. *Democracy in America.* New York: New American Library, 1956. A classic description of American political culture. Written from the perspective of a European in the early nineteenth century, it serves to remind us how different and novel the values, principles, and practices characterizing American democracy were.

I still have a dream. It is a dream deeply rooted in the American dream. I have a dream that one day this nation will rise up and live out the true meaning of its creed. We hold these truths to be self-evident that all men are created equal. ... And if America is to be a great nation, this must become true.
Martin Luther King, Jr.

Chapter 3

The Declaration of Independence

Chapter Outline

Introduction
The Declaration as a Guide to the American Revolution
The Declaration as a Statement of American Political Thought
Two Phases of the American Revolution
Why the American Revolution Succeeded
Conclusion

Introduction

The Declaration of Independence, a revolutionary document, gave birth to the United States as a sovereign nation in 1776. For more than two centuries, it has been the basic statement of this nation's ideals. Abraham Lincoln recognized this when he called the Declaration "the sheet anchor of the American republic." And at Gettysburg, he referred to the Declaration rather than the Constitution when he spoke of the founding of the new nation. The United States, he said, had been "conceived in liberty, and dedicated to the proposition that all men are created equal."

Lincoln's words, however, do not capture for us the revolutionary nature of this document. At the time of the War of Independence, the vast majority of people in the Western world lived under some form of monarchial regime rather than in a republic, were routinely taxed without their consent, and were economically exploited by the state. The Declaration was a revolutionary challenge to those con-

THE LONG–TERM CONSEQUENCES OF THE FRENCH AND INDIAN WAR (1754–1763)

Britain and the American colonies fought a war against France and her Indian allies for control of Canada and the Mississippi Valley. Britain's victory ended French rule in Canada and effectively brought to a close France's role as a major power on the North American continent. After the war, Britain sought to pay at least part of its huge war debt by imposing new internal taxes on the American colonies. These taxes, and the colonists' resistance to them (the Boston Tea Party, for example), mark the beginning of the American Revolution.

ditions. Although it established no legal rights or duties, the Declaration wielded (and continues to wield) its greatest influence as a statement of democratic ideals.

Yet we must not overlook the fact that the Declaration was also brilliant propaganda. Its leading purpose was to provide a philosophical and legal justification for the American Revolution. Such a justification would call attention to the differences with Great Britain that had driven the American colonies into revolt.

By the 1760s and the 1770s, three differences had become glaringly apparent, that caused the colonists to question ever more seriously the relationship between the British government and the colonies. First, the long-standing relationship of crown and Parliament to the colonial governments had been upset by the imposition of new internal taxes, partly due to expenses the British crown incurred in the French and Indian War. Such drastic interference in domestic colonial affairs was a marked departure from the autonomy and the self-government permitted the colonies for most of their history. This interference also had an important economic dimension. Mercantilism, the dominant economic theory, assumed the mother country had a right to exploit her colonies for the profit and the welfare of the empire. British efforts to implement mercantilist doctrine had the effect of uniting New Englanders and Virginians in opposition to the mother country's advantageous trade laws.

Lost Moments in American History

'In calling for the declassification of this sensitive document, Mr. Jefferson forgets that it touches on the decision-making process leading to a major war.'

Reprinted from The Commercial Appeal

Second, the colonists differed with King George III and his ministers in Parliament over their rights as British subjects, claiming that taxation without representation violated these rights. Both the king and Parliament summarily rejected petitions by the colonists for a redress of their grievances.

Finally, the British government and the American colonists were at odds over the limits of governmental power. The colonists claimed allegiance to the crown but denied Parliament's authority to legislate for the colonies. Parliament retaliated with a series of acts designed to assert legislative jurisdiction over the colonies. The Declaration of Independence was the colonists' ultimate response.

As a justification of the American Revolution and a concise statement of American political thought and ideals, the Declaration merits close examination. Such an examination highlights both the premises of the Declaration and the reasons for that document's continuing significance.

The Boston Tea Party

The Declaration as a Guide to The American Revolution

"When in the Course of human events, it becomes necessary for one people to dissolve the political bands which have connected them with another, and to assume among the Powers of the earth, the separate and equal station to which the Laws of Nature and of Nature's God entitle them, a decent respect to the opinions of mankind requires that they should declare the causes which impel them to the separation."

In this opening paragraph, Thomas Jefferson, the Declaration's principal author, makes three critical points. First, he asserts that the colonists no longer consider themselves to be a part of the same people as those residing in the British Isles. Americans are now "one people" separate and distinct from the British nation. This represented a profound departure from earlier revolutionary documents. Indeed, as late as 1774, Jefferson had written a pamphlet entitled "A Summary of the Rights of British America." Even at that date, the colonists thought of themselves as British subjects. Two years later, in 1776, the Second Continental Congress rejected this position.

The sentiment that the United States was something different, even something special, was also growing. A twentieth-century political sociologist has argued that Americans saw themselves as founding the "first new nation."[1] Here was a country that was comparatively removed from the politics and problems of late eighteenth-century Europe. Americans were not Europeans, and at some indistinguishable point in their history, they ceased to be English. From our perspective, we can mark the Declaration of Independence as the first authentic statement of distinctively American political thought. Not coincidentally, it came at the beginning of the nation's history as a separate political community.

At the same time, though, the Declaration was consistent with a stream of political thought that had actually originated in Britain more than a century earlier. This stream included such diverse movements and individuals as the Levellers and Diggers, the Scottish "commonsense" philosophers, James Harrington (1611–1677), Richard Hooker (1554–1600), John Locke (1632–1704), and religious dissenters like the Puritans.

JOHN LOCKE (1632–1704)

Many of the ideas, and even some of the language, used to justify the American Revolution are to be found in the writings of John Locke, the leading English political philosopher of the seventeenth century. Such Lockean phrases as "life, liberty, and property," the "consent of the governed," and "the majority have a right to act and conclude the rest," have become hallmarks of democratic theory. Besides being a landmark of Western political thinking, Locke's *Two Treatises of Civil Government* includes a clas-

sic defense of the right of revolution. Yet Locke was by no means a revolutionary. For most of his adult life, he was a member of the British establishment, and his one foray into colonial politics was to draft a feudal constitution for the Carolinas. This constitution was never successfully implemented. At his death in 1704, Locke was recognized as one of England's foremost philosophers. As later events would reveal, his influence on American political thinking was perhaps greater than that of any other single person.

Ironically, political thinkers justified the American Revolution of 1776 for the same reasons that their earlier counterparts had justified the **English revolutions** of the 1640s and 1680s. Higher and more noble laws had to be upheld in the face of an oppressive regime that was in fact governance by usurpers. By using English political thought to underpin their revolt, Americans were furnishing the British with a bitter reminder of the unforeseen consequences of revolutionary doctrines.

Second, Jefferson employed natural law, as well as Nature's God, to justify the American Revolution. His reasoning was deceptively simple, but at the same time contained devastating consequences. As Britain, the mother country, did not abide by the commands of natural law, the colonists possessed a **right of revolution**. In making this argument, Jefferson launched a powerful attack on the notion of the divine right of kings. For the author of the Declaration, neither God nor natural law invested ultimate political power in the hands of a king or his government. Rather such power rested in the body of the people. The effect of Jefferson's logic was to transfer the source of political legitimacy from the ruler to the ruled. The Declaration embodied the concept of popular sovereignty, that is, the

right of the people to create, alter, or abolish their form of government.

The third critical point was Jefferson's appeal to both a domestic and an international audience. By citing the grievances against the British crown, Jefferson sought to show that the struggle with Great Britain was not a hasty, ill-conceived revolt on the part of the colonists but the result of long-term abuses. He repeated nearly every serious charge that was lodged against the king from the beginning of the revolutionary period in 1763 to 1776. For domestic purposes, this list was a powerful reminder of the British attempt to reduce the colonies to utter subjection to the crown. Internationally, the list was intended to reveal the seriousness of the independence movement and to induce France and Spain to become America's allies. Both domestically and internationally, the Declaration had the desired propaganda effect of building support for the American Revolution.

Whereas the Declaration's first paragraph gave reason for the revolution, the second contains the heart of American political thought. Here Jefferson was able to articulate the core of what Americans had come to believe as a result of their hard-earned colonial experience of more than 165 years. Jeffer-

King George III

dition. By doing so, Jefferson is able to ground these truths in a tradition reaching back to the Greeks. If the historical roots are insufficient to command assent, Jefferson asserts these truths are "self-evident." For Jefferson, this means that certain truths are so fundamental, so basic, and so obvious that they need not be proven. Like the axioms in Euclidean geometry, such as "The shortest distance between two points is a straight line," we simply assume such statements to be true.

"... that all men are created equal, that they are endowed by their Creator with certain **unalienable Rights,** that among these are Life, Liberty, and the pursuit of Happiness."

Because he was a slaveholder, Jefferson cannot be considered a completely committed **egalitarian.** Yet in the Declaration, the ideal of **equality** becomes a force to be reckoned with.[3] Jefferson goes beyond asserting that the Americans and the English are equals to encompass the equality of all people. His statement is a direct attack on the very foundations of a class society. In the natural order, people are not divided into classes; nobles and commoners are human-created distinctions. Ultimately, Jefferson's ideal of equality can be seen as an attack on all forms of inequality whether racial, sexual, or economic. So powerful was the American conception of equality that by the time of Andrew Jackson's presidency (1829–1837), the French observer Alexis de Tocqueville cited equality as the fundamental characteristic that distinguished the American republic from European nations.[4]

Equality during the Jacksonian era meant equality of political rights. Voting and running for public office had been extended to include most white men who owned property. Equality also meant equal before the law; the law recognized no privileged classes. That all white men should have the same opportunity to advance their lot in life was also widely accepted. Against these positive dimensions of equality must be set its darker side. Equality was largely empty of meaning for black slaves, Indians, and women.[5] Nor did equality encompass economic equality, especially equality of result. Even today most Americans are uneasy with the notion of economic equality and many of them would deny that a person has a right to a job or a right to health care.

Despite the importance of equality in Jefferson's Declaration, the Revolution was not fought because

son himself viewed the Declaration as "an expression of the American mind."[2] By examining that paragraph, we can gain a clearer understanding of American political thought and the political ideas and values that underpin it.

The Declaration as a Statement of American Political Thought

"We hold these truths to be self-evident, ..."

This phrase includes ironically, both the strengths and the weaknesses of Jefferson's argument. The word *hold* can only mean "believes" or "assumes." Jefferson is not saying that Americans can prove these truths, but rather that Americans believe in them so strongly they are prepared to fight and die for them. The truths that concern him are not facts; they are something far loftier and far less certain of attainment—moral values and ideals.

In the first paragraph, Jefferson used the natural law tradition to justify the American Revolution. In the second, he deduces natural rights from that tra-

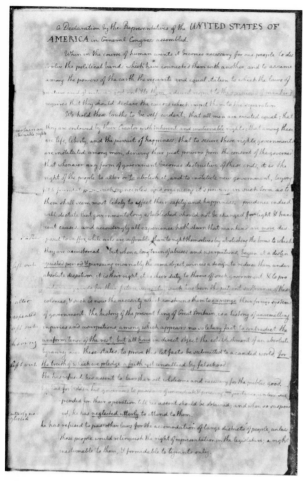

A manuscript copy of the Declaration of Independence in Thomas Jefferson's handwriting

the British had failed to enforce equality, whether economic, political, or social. Rather, the government in London had, through ignorance and insensitivity, angered the colonists by continually violating the individual rights and liberties they had long claimed as Englishmen. For most members of the Second Continental Congress, Jefferson's ideal of equality had more complicated and more radical implications than they were prepared even to consider, let alone accept.

The Revolution of 1776 did not have grandiose goals. In this respect, it differed from the French Revolution of 1789 and more closely resembled the English revolutions of the 1640s and 1680s. What Americans sought was a redress of what they perceived as legitimate grievances. They gave little thought to leveling society and recreating it from the ground up. Unlike the French thirteen years later, the Americans did not attempt to achieve both equality and liberty. They focused their energies on securing freedom.

"... that they are endowed by their Creator with certain unalienable Rights, ..."

Jefferson's Declaration speaks of unalienable rights—rights that are so basic and essential to human freedom that individuals cannot give them away nor sell them, nor can government or society justly deprive individuals of such rights. In essence, the government can intrude on these natural rights under only very carefully limited conditions.

Although Jefferson does not cite them, historical foundations existed for the American conception of rights that reinforced these moral considerations. These foundations were rooted deep in English history and in colonial history as well. Many of the colonists, particularly in New England, had fled from Britain because of religious persecution. For such dissenters as the Puritans and the Pilgrims, their hard-fought right to worship as they pleased was threatened by the English government with its established church. The American colonists also had more than 150 years of experience with the English common law, that is, law based on court decisions and custom rather than legislation.

American political leaders also recognized the importance of the thirteenth century Magna Carta that limited the authority of the crown.[7] As British subjects, the colonists embraced the seventeenth-century protections that the British Parliament had enacted—the Habeas Corpus Act and the Bill of Rights. Thus Jefferson's language had the support of both the logic of the natural law tradition and the weight of English history.

Yet the concept of unalienable rights can conflict with the notion of majority rule. For example, a majority, no matter how large, cannot justly deny individuals freedom of speech, establish a state religion, or deprive a person accused of crime due process of law. In all these instances, the concept of unalienable rights places limits on the power of the majority to make decisions. Thus in a democracy, an inherent tension exists between majority rule and unalienable rights or, put another way, between majority rule and minority rights.

" ... that among these are Life, Liberty, and the pursuit of Happiness."

THOMAS JEFFERSON (1743–1826) AND AMERICAN POLITICAL THOUGHT

Thomas Jefferson is one of the most compelling figures in American history and American political thought. As a Virginian and a southerner, he embodied many of the beliefs and attitudes that remain a vital part of the American creed. In the Declaration of Independence, he stated in enduring form the heart of American political thinking. Jefferson insisted that a decentralized form of government was most consistent with a republican philosophy. Throughout his long life, he bitterly opposed those who would have preferred a monarchy.

The ideal citizens of a republic were not aristocrats but yeoman farmers working their own land. The fundamental purpose of all government was to foster the conditions whereby each individual could pursue happiness. Government was never to be viewed as an instrument of class rule. A strict, rather than broad, construction of constitutional powers would ensure that governments would not infringe on the inalienable rights of citizens.

Jefferson's opposition to the Federalist party led to the founding of the Democratic-Republican party, which dominated American politics through the Jacksonian era. Elected to two terms as president (1801–1809), he ranks as one of America's greatest presidents.

The most significant achievement of Jefferson's later years was his founding of the University of Virginia, which incorporated almost completely his educational philosophy. On July 4, 1826, the fiftieth anniversary of the Declaration of Independence, Jefferson died at Monticello, his Virginia mountaintop home.

Jefferson's phrase substitutes "pursuit of happiness" for John Locke's "life, liberty, and property." There were several reasons for this. First, Jefferson's understanding of the ends of government was more subtle than Locke's. Ideally, government should seek to create the conditions for the realization of each individual's potential. Jefferson's pursuit of happiness envisions a broader and more humane role for government than Locke's narrower concern with the protection of property.

Second, Jefferson was convinced that property was not a natural right, but rather a right acquired on entering into society. Finally, property in the colonies had, as a practical matter, always been viewed as an alienable right. Property could be bought and sold, was acquired and transferred through legal proceedings, and was simply another item of commerce.

This choice of language, however, does not mean that economic matters were not an important contributing factor in the American Revolution. Besides the imposition of new internal taxes, colonial trade was closely regulated by the British government. As opposition to British rule increased, that regulation became even more oppressive in the eyes of colonial merchants and shipowners. The navigation acts, which added new burdens, were termed "the Intolerable Acts" by the colonists.

All this was aggravated by the British government's adherence to mercantilist doctrine.[8] Based partly on a nation's right to exploit its colonies for the welfare of the empire, this doctrine not surprisingly, worked against free trade, made debtors of many in the New World, and in general exacerbated the uneasy sense of economic dependency experienced by the American colonists.

"That to secure these rights, Governments are instituted among Men deriving their just powers from the consent of the governed."

The rights Jefferson seeks to secure are natural

Drawing by Dana Fradon. © 1972 The New Yorker Magazine, Inc.

"Founding Fathers! How come no Founding Mothers?"

rights, which, as we earlier noted, are prepolitical in nature. In this context, prepolitical has three different levels of meaning. First, natural rights are prepolitical because they presuppose that humans are moral creatures and not simply political subjects. In other words, we believe that although laws may bind us, we should not be forced to do what our conscience forbids. A person opposed to the use of force, for example, should not be compelled to serve in the armed forces.

Next, natural rights are prepolitical because they are natural as opposed to artificial. They are derived from natural law or are conferred by God and thus are not merely human-created rights. Finally, natural rights are prepolitical because such rights imply a **social contract** and a limited government. In the United States, the Constitution functions as this nation's social contract and the Bill of Rights places limits on the power of government.

In all this, Jefferson was drawing on John Locke. Although he died nearly three-quarters of a century before the American Revolution, Locke had set out the arguments that Jefferson employed so effectively. A happy people, Locke reasoned, would not rebel. They had no interest or purpose in doing so. Only when arbitrary and corrupt government abuses the authority placed in it by the people will they rise up. In the *Two Treatises,* published in 1689, Locke held that

great mistakes in the ruling part, wrong or inconvenient laws, and all the slips of human frailty will be borne by the people without mutiny or murmur. But if a long train of abuses, prevarications, and artifices, all tending the same way, make the design visible to the people, and they cannot but feel what they lie under, and see whither they are going, 'tis not to be wondered that they should then rouse themselves, and endeavor to put the rule into such hands which may secure to them the ends for which government was first erected....[9]

None of the American colonists expected the British government to be perfect. They did, however, expect it to be sensitive to their aspirations—or at least to try to be. The Americans had given the London government plenty of opportunity. Since the middle 1760s, they had tolerated one outrageous and unjustified act after another. Even in a time of dismally slow communications, they felt a full decade of politically loutish behavior was more than they should be expected to endure.[10]

In the eyes of the colonists, the British government had refused to recognize that its power was limited or that Parliament derived its "just" powers from the consent of the governed. By imposing internal taxes and burdensome trade regulations, the British government was wielding unjust powers that invaded the rights of the people. By insisting on the consent of the governed, Jefferson sought to ensure that a government would exercise only those powers granted to it by the people.

"That whenever any Form of Government becomes destructive of these ends, it is the Right of the People to alter or to abolish it, and to institute new Government, laying its foundation on such principles and organizing its powers in such form, as to them shall seem most likely to effect their Safety and Happiness."

Jefferson clearly envisions a right of revolution resting with the people if their rights are trampled on. This right is implicit in the notion of popular sovereignty. When governments act irresponsibly, they must expect the people to reassert their sovereign right to alter the existing form of government. Not to reassert this right would be to submit to tyranny. As the Declaration makes evident, the American people had too long an experience with self-government to submit peacefully to British incursions on their rights.

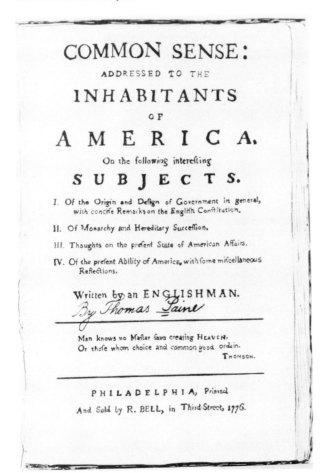

Thomas Paine

On this note, Jefferson brings the part of the Declaration that summarizes American political thought to a close. He then turns to a recitation of the circumstances that precipitated the Revolution. This list of grievances comprises nearly half the Declaration and covers the events of the 1760s and the 1770s that led to the break in 1776. There are more than twenty grievances that Jefferson considered important enough to mention and that the Second Continental Congress accepted when they adopted Jefferson's Declaration. The cumulative effect of these charges shows Jefferson's mastery of existing rhetorical techniques. The Declaration's power and effectiveness resides not only in its enunciation of American political thought but also in its persuasiveness in stating the American case for independence.

After the list of grievances against the crown, Jefferson continues with a paragraph that chastises the British Parliament and the English people for their insensitivity to the American colonists' aspirations. This paragraph reveals the completeness of the break between the colonies and the mother country. The Americans had hoped for reconciliation, but the intransigence of the king, the acquiescence of the Parliament in the crown's usurpations, and the disregard for the petitions of the American colonists left the Americans with no choice but to declare their separation and independence.

Jefferson concludes the Declaration by reiterating the appeal to popular sovereignty, by declaring the colonies independent, by insisting that the new states are absolved from any allegiance to the British crown, and by asserting that the newly independent United States has all the powers and rights of other sovereign nations. The Declaration's closing sentence is a ringing call to the American people to support the nation's bid for independence: "And for the support of this Declaration, with a firm reliance on the Protection of Divine Providence, we mutually pledge to each other our Lives, our Fortunes, and our sacred Honor."

For the American colonists, revolution was a last resort. Only after everything else had been tried, including an appeal to common sense, did the colonists reach the decision to resist a wayward government with force. The British should have known better; John Locke had warned of the consequences of misgovernment nearly a century before the Declaration.[11] Jefferson was convinced that Americans by rebelling were simply acting out an honorable tradition, part of which holds that the people and not public officials decide when the government is behaving itself. Jefferson's Declaration remains the most eloquent and succinct expression of this sentiment.

The Declaration of Independence marks a pivotal point in the American Revolution. By looking at the revolutionary events that both preceded and followed the Declaration's adoption, we can gain a clearer understanding of why the American Revolution succeeded so brilliantly and why the French and Russian revolutions produced such mixed results.

Two Phases of the American Revolution

It is helpful to think of the American Revolution as having two phases.[12] The first phase consisted of destroying the existing political relationship with Great Britain. The second consisted of creating a new set of political institutions to govern the newly independent states. As might be expected, there was a good deal of overlap between the two phases. Somewhat more surprising is the length of the revolutionary period; it lasted for nearly a quarter century. Table 3.1 lists some of the more important events and their respective dates.

As the table reveals, the American Revolution was crowded with many critical events.[13] If the revolutionary generation had failed to meet these crises successfully, the independence movement would have been doomed. Equally important, if the revolutionary generation had been less able, the effort to establish a new and stable form of government might have ended less happily.

Table 3.1
The Two Phases of the American Revolution

Destruction of the Old Order: 1765–1783
  Stamp Act Congress, 1765
  Committees of Correspondence, 1772–1773
  First Continental Congress, 1774
  War of Independence, 1775–1781
  Second Continental Congress, 1775–1781
  France enters the war as an ally, 1778
  Spain enters the war as an ally, 1779
  Peace treaty signed, 1783

Creation of a New Order, 1776–1789
  Declaration of Independence, 1776
  Articles of Confederation proposed, 1777
  Articles of Confederation adopted, 1781
  Government under the Articles of Confederation, 1781–1789
  Annapolis Convention, 1786
  Constitutional Convention, 1787
  Government under the Constitution, 1789–

Here the American Revolution stands in vivid contrast to the French and Russian revolutions. The French Revolution engendered numerous excesses and eventually fell victim to Napoleon's dictatorship. In Russia, about 150 years later, the revolution also fell short of its professed goals. Following the overthrow of the tsar, Russia was plunged into a civil war that pitted various groups competing for power against one another. Although the Communist party was able to establish a stable government, the Marxian vision of a classless society where the state has withered away is still a distant prospect in the Soviet Union. In the next section, we examine three primary reasons why the American Revolution succeeded so notably.

Why The American Revolution Succeeded

Although the end results of the American Revolution were frequently in doubt and were achieved only with considerable difficulty, virtually every aspect of the Revolution was, on balance, marked by success. One system of government was displaced by another through armed conflict. Rivalries between states were temporarily put aside. Even in the midst of uncertain and trying circumstances, the revolutionary leaders were able to create a new and stable form of government. Its foundation, the U.S. Constitution, is at two hundred years the oldest written constitution in the world.

The reasons for the success of the American Revolution are many and complex, but three factors seem to stand out. First, many of the revolutionary leaders of phase 1, the destruction of the existing order, were not, for a variety of reasons, leaders in the second phase.[14] Several important radicals of the earlier period were not even in the country at the time of the Constitutional Convention: John Adams was in England as American ambassador, Thomas Jefferson was in France to succeed Benjamin Franklin as ambassador, and Thomas Paine was there to aid in the French Revolution.[15] Other radicals refused to be considered for election as convention delegates, whereas some, such as Sam Adams, failed to be elected. Still others simply chose to stay away.

We need to keep in mind, though, that even the radicals who had fomented the Revolution in its earliest days were not *that* radical. After all, Adams

Famous signers of the Declaration of Independence not involved in the Constitutional Convention

Patrick Henry

Samuel Adams

John Hancock

John Adams

WHY DID ORDINARY AMERICANS FIGHT IN THE WAR OF INDEPENDENCE?

In 1842, a young historian had a conversation with Captain Levi Preston of Danver, Massachusetts, who had fought at Concord and Lexington sixty-seven years earlier. His reasons for joining the patriot cause have a pungency of expression often found in New England speech.

"Captain Preston, why did you go to the Concord Fight, the 19th of April 1775? . . . My histories tell me that you men of the Revolution took up arms against 'intolerable oppressions.' "

"What were they? Oppressions? I didn't feel them."

"What, were you not oppressed by the Stamp Act?"

"I never saw one of those stamps. . . . I am certain I never paid a penny for one of them."

"Well, what about the tea tax?"

"Tea tax, I never drank a drop of the stuff; the boys threw it all overboard."

"Then, I suppose you had been reading Harrington, or Sidney and Locke, about the eternal principles of liberty?"

"Never heard of 'em. We read only the Bible, the Catechism, Watts's Psalms and Hymns, and the Almanack."

"Well, then, what was the matter? and what did you mean in going to the fight?"

"Young man, what we meant in going for those red-coats, was this: we always had governed ourselves and we always meant to. They didn't mean we should."

Source: Mellen Chamberlain, *John Adams, Statesman of the American Revolution: With Other Essays and Addresses, Historical and Literary* (Boston: Houghton, Mifflin, 1898), pp. 248–249.

and Jefferson became the new country's second and third presidents. Moreover, the United States in the 1780s and 1790s was so sparsely populated, so extensive in its territorial domain, and so mindful of the English tradition of civil liberties [16] that any group of radicals (or reactionaries) who attempted to establish an authoritarian regime would be faced with a hopeless task. Communication and transportation were still primitive. Anyone dissatisfied with the existing government could simply move to the frontier where there wasn't any. Politically and geographically, the environment combined to produce a setting in which democratic government could emerge and flourish.

The second reason for the success of the American Revolution was the willingness of the competing interests—North and South, large states and small states, creditors and debtors—to compromise their differences. Of especial significance is the fact that these competitors had to bargain and compromise numerous times over the nearly twenty-five years of the revolutionary effort, an ability that proved extremely useful at the Constitutional Convention.[17]

Of the three reasons for the Revolution's success, the third was the most remarkable. The government under the Articles of Confederation accepted the work of the Constitutional Convention and submitted the Constitution to state conventions for ratification. This is all the more striking because the convention delegates had clearly exceeded their authority. The convention was called merely to revise the Articles of Confederation. As we shall see in the next chapter, the Founding Fathers very early in the convention debates abandoned the idea of revising the Articles and instead wrote an entirely new constitution. Only when that new constitution was adopted and the new government formed did the second phase of the Revolution come to a close.

Conclusion

In analyzing the Declaration of Independence, indeed analyzing any document, behavior and tradition are as significant as the words used. Documents, including the Declaration and the Constitution, are often silent on the most troublesome issues. The list of grievances in the Declaration, for example, does not directly address the larger problem of economic exploitation that is an inherent part of any colonial system. Nor do the words *slave* or *slavery* appear anywhere in the Constitution. Textual analysis has to go beyond the words and phrases used if we hope to achieve an accurate appraisal of any document. We have sought to scrutinize the Declaration of Independence with these cautions in mind.

As a succinct statement of American ideals, the Declaration of Independence has no peer. It enunciates a revolution in the principles and ideals that underpin government. The people, rather than being the subjects of political power, are now proclaimed to be its sole legitimate originator. Moreover, the natural rights of individuals cannot be justly denied. Governmental power is limited and not absolute. These principles—popular sovereignty, natural rights, and limited government—constitute our understanding of democratic government.

The Declaration also justifies the American Revolution. Drawing on natural law and citing numerous grievances against the crown, Jefferson produced a rhetorical masterpiece. The Declaration's philosophy, however, raises it above mere propaganda. This philosophy is what gives the Declaration its greatness, its timelessness, and its universal appeal.

Yet the Declaration was only one event in a series of events that comprised the American Revolution. The first phase of events saw the destruction of British rule in the colonies and the second phase witnessed the creation of a new system of government. From a number of perspectives, the success of the American Revolution stands in vivid contrast to the more mixed results of the French and Russian revolutions.

Of all the factors contributing to the success of the Revolution, three stand out: First, was a marked change in leadership from the first phase of the revolution to the second. Next, the competing interests were willing over a long period of time to reconcile their differences through compromise. Third, the government under the Articles of Confederation allowed itself to be superseded by the Constitution. In the next chapter, we examine how this came about.

 ## Glossary

The English revolutions   The political upheavals from the 1640s to the 1680s wherein the English people sought to limit the autocratic power of the crown.

Equality   An ideal that holds all people are of the same worth and have identical rights. In the United States, the ideal of equality has often come into conflict with the notion of property rights.

Egalitarian   A person or group committed to the ideal of equality.

Right of revolution   An eighteenth-century concept that the people have a right to rebel against arbitrary and tyrannical government.

Social contract   In political philosophy, the idea that legitimate governments are created by the people. Written constitutions are often viewed as social contracts between the people and their government.

Unalienable rights   Jefferson's term for natural rights. Unalienable rights cannot justly be given away, taken away, or usurped by government.

 ## Suggestions for Further Reading

Bailyn, Bernard. *The Origins of American Politics.* New York: Random House, 1970. An incisive study of the prerevolutionary and revolutionary eras that makes certain contemporary features of American politics more understandable.

Catton, Bruce, and William B. Catton. *The Bold and Magnificent Dream.* New York: Doubleday, 1978. This work captures the mythic quality of the founding days of the American republic.

Foner, Phillip S. *We, the Other People.* Urbana: University of Illinois Press, 1976. Chronicles the use of the Declaration of Independence by various disadvantaged groups in their efforts to achieve their political goals.

Hofstadter, Richard. *The American Political Tradition: And the Men Who Made It.* New York: Knopf, 1948. Landmark study that analyzes the thought of ten key political leaders, among others, from the Founders to Franklin D. Roosevelt.

Mason, Alpheus T., and Richard H. Leach. *In Quest of Freedom.* 2d ed. Englewood Cliffs, N.J.: Prentice-Hall, 1976. One of the first-rate surveys of American political thought that makes extensive use of original materials.

Parkes, Henry Bamford. *The American Experience: An Interpretation of the History and Civilization of the American People.* New York: Vintage, 1959. As its title indicates, this work interprets, in a highly readable and persuasive fashion, the significance of American history and civilization.

Peterson, Merrill D., ed. *The Portable Thomas Jefferson.* New York: Viking, 1975. An excellent and extensive collection of the writings of this Renaissance man.

Skidmore, Max J. *American Political Thought.* New York: St. Martin's, 1978. Brief chronological survey, with a good bibliography, of most of the major figures in American political thinking.

Smith, Page. *A New Age Now Begins: A People's History of the American Revolution.* New York: McGraw-Hill, 1976. The first volumes in a narrative history of this nation that evoke a sense of what this era meant to the common man and woman.

White, Morton. *The Philosophy of the American Revolution.* New York: Oxford University Press, 1978. Includes a careful discussion of the revolutionary nature of the Declaration of Independence.

The Constitution of the United States was made not merely for the generation that then existed, but for posterity—unlimited, undefined, endless, perpetual posterity.
Henry Clay

Chapter 4

The Constitution: Creating a Republican Form of Government

Chapter Outline

Introduction
From the Articles of Confederation to the Constitution
The Articles of Confederation Contrasted with The Constitution
The Constitutional Convention: Membership, Consensus, Conflict
The United States Constitution: Provision and Practice
The Meaning of a "Living" Constitution
Conclusion

Introduction

In this chapter, we examine the nation building of the crucial decade of the 1780s. Once again, we see that the values held by the American people influenced the form of government that was eventually adopted. We also explore how changing conditions, values, and circumstances affected the interpretation of the Constitution and the practices and policies of the national government.

After the Revolutionary War, the problem of what kind of nation had been forged by the independence movement became more urgent. The thirteen former colonies had led a largely separate life, in some cases for as much as a century and a half. Virginia, for instance, had been founded in 1607 and Massachusetts in 1620. Not until 1765, when the colonies convened the Stamp Act Congress to protest a tax imposed by the British Parliament, had they taken the first hesitant steps toward independence and union.

The War of Independence compelled the colonies to unify, but the **Articles of Confederation,** proposed in 1777 and adopted in 1781, did not require the thirteen original states to relinquish their sovereignty to the newly created central government. Many Americans began to question whether the thirteen separate political entities loosely bound together by the Articles was indeed a nation.[1]

From the Articles of Confederation to the Constitution

Even before the close of the war, the Articles' defects became obvious, particularly to those interested in an energetic national government. The states failed to meet the central government's requisitions for money and refused to recognize its authority in trade matters. Rhode Island, for example, blocked Congress's attempt to levy an excise tax on imports. Certain states, such as New Jersey and New York, created trade barriers hampering interstate commerce. In other instances, the states hindered the war effort by their frequent failure to cooperate with one another. Consequently, in 1785, only four years after adoption, calls were heard for revisions of the Articles of Confederation.

The proposed revisions focused on issues that would define and clarify the nature of the Union.

What should be the proper relationship between the state legislatures and the central government? Which should be sovereign? Should the Union of the states be a confederation with the state governments dominant or a federation with the national government supreme? Only after these fundamental questions were answered could proposals to enhance the scope of the national government's power to tax and to regulate commerce be considered.

Even a cursory examination of the two major plans at the Constitutional Convention reveals the centrality of these issues. Proponents of the Virginia Plan fostering a strong national government were bitterly opposed by the advocates of the New Jersey Plan, which favored a limited central government. So divisive was this conflict, the work of the convention nearly collapsed before the Connecticut Compromise resolved the impasse. Table 4.1 briefly describes the features of each plan and the compromise.

Table 4.1
Paths to Compromise About the Nature of the Union

Virginia Plan

A set of nationalistic proposals, submitted by Governor Edmund Randolph of Virgina to the Constitutional Convention of 1787, that called for replacing the Articles of Confederation and creating a national government with ample powers. The plan provided for a two-house national legislature based on state population or wealth, a national executive, and a federal judiciary. Congress would be granted the power to disallow state laws as well as a broad power over matters affecting the entire nation.

New Jersey Plan

A counterproposal submitted by William Paterson of New Jersey to the Constitutional Convention. Paterson's proposals, in addition to expressing the views of small states and states' rights advocates, sought only to revise the Articles of Confederation. The New Jersey Plan retained the essential features of the government under the Articles, mainly a single-house Congress where each state, regardless of size, had only one vote. Although the power of Congress would be enhanced, the plan carefully limited the reach of the national government.

Connecticut Compromise

An agreement, often called the "Great Compromise," reached at the Constitutional Convention that resolved the struggle between large states and small states over representation in Congress. Under its terms, seats in the House of Representatives would be apportioned according to population, and each state legislature would elect two individuals to serve in the Senate. By satisfying the demands of the small states for equal representation in the Senate, the large states were able to persuade the small states to accept many features of a strong national government.

Despite the importance of the question of how the Union should be structured, another set of conflicts actually precipitated the Constitutional Convention. Disagreements between moneylenders and borrowers had been increasing throughout the revolutionary period. In several states, both North and South, these conflicts had resulted in violence, in the capture of the state legislature by debtor interests, and in the forcible closing of state courts. **Shays's Rebellion,** which broke out in Massachusetts in 1786, was the incident that brought matters to a head. Daniel Shays, a Revolutionary War officer, led a group of disgruntled farmers in a protest against imprisonment for debt, the foreclosure of mortgages, and other laws that favored creditors.

Although the "rebellion" was quickly crushed, propertied interests throughout the states were alarmed as never before. Laws passed by **agrarian**-dominated state legislatures that prevented mortgage foreclosures were one thing, but armed insurrection was another. Creditor-debtor conflict made many Americans uneasily aware of the stark differences between the commercial classes and agrarians. As creditors, the commercial classes saw their prop-

THE CONSTITUTION AS AN UPPER–CLASS DOCUMENT

Did the Constitution create a government to protect and serve the interests of the propertied? Some historians have made this argument. Charles Beard, in *An Economic Interpretation of the Constitution of the United States*, insisted that in drafting the Constitution the framers were primarily concerned with securing their property interests. To "prove" his case, Beard analyzed the backgrounds and property-holdings of the convention delegates and the speeches they made in the convention debates. His analysis led him to the conclusion that a link existed between the economic interests of the delegates and the views they espoused.

Although Beard's thesis has been challenged by other historians, his interpretation still has many advocates. Indeed, among revisionists and certain leftist historians, Beard did not go far enough. They contend that not only the Constitution's framing but also the nation's entire history is best explained by examining closely the economic motives and actions of the governing classes.

Daniel Shays led farmers in a violent protest of the circumstances which were pushing small farmers off their lands and into debtors prisons in the 1780s.

erty interests threatened when contracts such as mortgages were jeopardized. As debtors, the agrarians felt their property interests, the lands they farmed, were threatened when mortgages could be so easily foreclosed.

Both these issues, the nature of the Union and creditor-debtor conflicts, demonstrated to the convention members that the government under the Articles of Confederation lacked the balance essential to good government. To correct this deficiency, the delegates had to solve two related problems. First, ways had to be found to compel the central government to control itself while remaining in balance with the state governments. A federal structure of government; separation of legislative, executive, and judicial power; **checks and balances;** and the **supremacy of law** required by Article VI were all designed to establish the proper balance between the central government and the state legislatures. Even these proved insufficient, and a Bill of Rights and **judicial review** were added later to improve the balance.

JAMES MADISON (1751–1836):
THE FATHER OF THE CONSTITUTION

Although only thirty-six at the time of the Constitutional Convention of 1787, James Madison, in the opinion of most scholars, made the most substantial contribution and had the greatest impact on the document that shaped the Union. He was the principal architect of the Virginia Plan and was instrumental in making it the agenda of the convention. Learned in political theory and conversant with the great works, Madison was the foremost political theoretician of his day. At the outset of the convention, he took it on himself to keep careful notes of the deliberations. Most of what we know today about the debates comes from those notes. During the struggle for ratification, Madison joined with Alexander Hamilton and John Jay in authoring *The Federalist Papers*. After ratification, he played the dominant role in the adoption of the Bill of Rights.

Madison and Jefferson were lifelong friends. Together they forged the political party, the Democratic-Republicans, that was to wrest power from the Federalist party. As Jefferson's secretary of state, Madison was heir apparent to the presidency and the only blot on a brilliant career came while he was president. His inept leadership during the War of 1812 caused him to lose much of his popularity. After the close of his presidency in 1817, Madison retired to Montpelier, his Virginia home, where he prepared his notes on the Constitutional Convention for publication and also worked with Thomas Jefferson to establish the University of Virginia. At his death in 1836, Madison was one of the last survivors of the delegates to the Constitutional Convention.

Second, ways had to be found to control the "excesses" of the people. James Madison, recognized as the father of the Constitution for his contributions to that document, argued in **Federalist No. 51** that "ambition must be made to counteract ambition. ... It may be a reflection on human nature that such devices should be necessary to control the abuses of government. But what is government itself but the greatest of all reflections on human nature? If men were angels, no government would be necessary. ... In framing a government which is to be administered by men over men, the great difficulty lies in this: you must first enable the government to control the governed; and in the next place oblige it to control itself." [2]

Whereas Thomas Jefferson in the Declaration of Independence was optimistic about human nature, the convention delegates saw only the darker side. As a consequence, the Founding Fathers provided for a number of checks on the will of the people.

The only office of the national government for which the people voted directly was the House of Representatives, and even this exercise of the vote was limited by the suffrage requirements of the state legislatures. In some states, this meant property qualifications and in other states religious qualifications. Such restrictions effectively denied the vote to as much as 70 percent of the adult population. In the first national election in 1788, for example, only about 100,000 electors voted out of a total population of nearly 4 million.

The convention delegates also limited the power of the state legislatures to pass certain kinds of legislation. For example, Article I, Section 10, bars states from impairing the obligations of contracts. This provision was specifically designed to limit the power of state legislatures that might be captured by agrarian majorities. Other constitutional language that protected the property interests of the commercial and creditor classes included clauses in Article I,

Section 8, that dealt with congressional power to enact bankruptcy laws, to coin money, and to establish uniform standards for weights and measures.

The framers' intent was to establish a republic, that is, a representative form of government, and not a democracy where the people govern directly. A direct democracy was out of the question for two reasons. First, the United States was already too large for direct participation in government. Second, and more important, the convention members saw democracy as an inherently unstable and unbalanced form of government that could easily, and would ultimately, deteriorate into mob rule.

The Articles of Confederation Contrasted With the Constitution

Under the Articles of Confederation, state sovereignty was preserved largely intact; the central government was, in actuality, not a government at all.

Indeed, the confederation could be described most accurately as a league of friendship among sovereign states. By contrast, the Preamble to the Constitution assigns sovereignty to the people. It is the people, and not the state governments, who were establishing "a more perfect union." Table 4.2 contrasts the two documents.

The Congress created by the Articles was a one-house body with expressly delegated powers. Members represented the states and not the people. No matter how large the state legislative delegation, each delegation had only one vote. All legislation required the concurrence of nine states. Congress had neither independent power to tax nor power over interstate and foreign commerce. Both the Congress and the state governments could coin money and make bank notes legal tender. Even the delicate question of which entity, the central government or the states, could act authoritatively in foreign affairs had not been definitively resolved.

ALEXANDER HAMILTON (1754–1804): ARDENT NATIONALIST

Alexander Hamilton was a leading figure in the Revolutionary years and in the adoption of the Constitution. He authored 51 of the *Federalist* papers which advocated the ratification of the Constitution. Even today, these papers are considered the most brilliant exposition of the principles underpinning the Constitution. As a New Yorker and a Northerner, he embodied in many ways the political beliefs and attitudes that came to be synonymous with Northern interests. Hamilton championed the commercial classes throughout his life. As Washington's Secretary of Treasury, he drafted a report on manufacturing that called for a strong, centralized government directing and fostering economic develop-

ment. By insisting on the doctrine of implied powers, and a broad, as opposed to a narrow, construction of constitutional powers, Hamilton sought to justify an energetic

government. He also used these arguments to justify the creation of a national bank. From his perspective, the principal end of government involved the protection of property, particularly property in the form of contracts. Government was an instrument of class rule that shielded the property-owning classes from popular "excesses". A strong, national government and the protection of property rights became the leading principles of the Federalist Party that Hamilton helped found. In the presidential election of 1800 he rallied support for Jefferson, thus thwarting Aaron Burr's presidential ambitions. Four years later Burr ended his and Hamilton's political career by killing Hamilton in a duel.

Table 4.2
Articles of Confederation Versus the Constitution

Articles of Confederation	Constitution
State sovereignty	Popular sovereignty
One-house Congress with expressly delegated powers	Two-house Congress with broad interpretation, via necessary and proper clause, of enumerated powers
Congress represented states	Congress represents both states (Senate) and people (House of Representatives)
Vote of nine states required to enact laws	Simple majority of both houses required to enact laws
No power to tax	Congress granted taxing power
No power to regulate interstate and foreign commerce	Congress granted power to regulate interstate and foreign commerce
States and central government could coin money	Only federal government authorized to coin money
No separate executive branch	Executive branch with separate powers
State courts only	Federal and state courts
Unanimous consent of the states required for amendments	Proposal by two-thirds of both houses of Congress; ratification by three-fourths of either state legislatures or state conventions
State supremacy—central government could not directly affect individuals	National supremacy—both the federal and the state governments directly affect individuals
Adopted by state legislatures	Ratified by state conventions
No bill of rights	A bill of rights added in 1791

By contrast, the Constitution established a two-house Congress with broad powers made possible by the **necessary and proper clause** in Article I, Section 8. A national bicameral legislature was a stroke of political genius, allowing the states representation in the Senate and the people in the House of Representatives. Only a simple majority of both houses was required to pass legislation. Congress was also granted an independent power to tax and to regulate commerce. To overcome the confusion over the currency, only Congress could coin money. Finally, by excluding the state governments from the field of foreign affairs, the Founding Fathers made the national government the sole voice of the United States in that arena.

The colonies' experience with arbitrary executive power created such wariness that the sponsors of the Articles of Confederation made no provisions for a separate executive branch. Nor did the Articles establish a bureaucracy responsible to the executive. All administrative tasks were lodged in the committees of the Congress. These defects were so serious that by the time the convention delegates met, the creation of a separate executive branch was in little doubt.

The language of Article II of the Constitution produced an executive with such potential that presidents, particularly in the twentieth century, have been able to dominate virtually all facets of American politics. Part of the explanation for this lay in the almost universal assumption that George Washington, whose adherence to republican principles was unquestioned, would be the first president. As a result, the executive article was not burdened with restrictions that would have severely limited presidential authority. Without them, the presidency has evolved into the dominant branch of the national government.

The Articles also failed to create a national judiciary, that is, federal courts that could adjudicate disputes between states, hear cases involving individuals, or exercise jurisdiction over lawsuits where the contestants lived in different states. All legal controversies under the Articles were tried in state courts, which, on occasion, reached decisions that came into conflict with each other. Under the Articles, there was no national court that could reconcile these conflicting decisions.

These weaknesses—the lack of a separate executive branch and the absence of national courts—were exacerbated by another perceived defect of the Articles. Many political leaders, including Alexander Hamilton and James Madison, were convinced that to be truly effective, the central government must possess direct authority over the people. Under the Articles, the states were not required to surrender their sovereignty. As a consequence, the laws of the central government did not directly affect the citizenry. Article VI remedied this defect by providing for national supremacy; the article ensures that both federal and state laws bind individuals and that both levels of government can prosecute them for breaking the law.

Finally, since the government under the Articles did not possess direct authority over the people, virtually no one thought a national bill of rights was necessary. All the state constitutions adopted after the colonies declared independence in 1776 contained bills of rights. The drafters of those constitutions believed such bills adequately protected the rights of the people against intrusion by the government.

The national government created by the Constitution, however, inspired much anxiety. Those opposed to the Constitution argued forcibly that the lack of a bill of rights seriously endangered the liberties of the people. So telling was this argument that the Constitution's adoption might have been delayed had not George Washington and James Madison, two of the most important figures at the convention, agreed that the first Congress under the Constitution should propose a bill of rights that would be sent to the state legislatures for ratification.[3]

The Constitutional Convention: Membership, Consensus, Conflict

Membership

Some of the leading radicals of the independence movement were not present in Philadelphia in 1787. As we noted in Chapter 3, John Adams, Thomas Jefferson, and Thomas Paine were in Europe. Sam Adams failed to be elected a convention delegate. John Hancock, the boldest signer of the Declaration of Independence, was not a member of the Massachusetts delegation. Nor would Richard Henry Lee agree to serve in the Virginia delegation. But it was Patrick Henry who furnished the most pungent reason for not participating: He "smelt a rat in Philadelphia tending towards monarchy" and stayed in Virginia.[4]

Of the fifty-six signers of the Declaration of Independence in 1776, only eight were delegates at

George Washington presiding at the Constitutional Convention

the Constitutional Convention in 1787. Yet the convention still had many men of proven ability.[5] The members included arguably the two most distinguished Americans, George Washington and Benjamin Franklin and others only slightly less eminent—James Madison, Alexander Hamilton, Gouverneur Morris, Edmund Randolph, James Wilson, George Mason, Roger Sherman, John Rutledge, Oliver Ellsworth, Elbridge Gerry, Rufus King, and William Paterson. Of the thirty-nine delegates who were most active at the convention, these men made the most substantial contributions.

Consensus

The compromises agreed to at the Constitutional Convention were possible only because a substantial consensus prevailed among the convention members. No one doubted that the Union was passing through a very critical period. Virtually all the delegates recognized that the Union's collapse would almost certainly bring to an end the independence of some, if not all, of the states. For them, and for many others, forging a "more perfect" union was essential to survival.

It was a foregone conclusion that the government established must be a constitutional republic, that is, a government of limited powers representative of, and responsive to, the governed. Americans had fought a war to resist irresponsible and unrepresentative government. Convention members also agreed that no single faction, interest, party, branch, or level of government should dominate, so they embedded the doctrine of checks and balances in the structure of the Constitution.

Most of the delegates recognized that the failure to separate the legislative, executive, and judicial functions was one of the fundamental deficiencies of the articles. Although the details of the relationships among the three branches of government would need to be specified, no one questioned the wisdom of separating them. Finally, the central government's inability to affect individuals directly was another widely recognized defect of the articles. To be truly national in character, the central government must be able to exercise direct authority over the people. The grant of authority established in the Preamble to the Constitution and in Article VI was acceptable to the states and to the ratifying conventions because national officeholders who sought to usurp power could be removed in the next election.

Conflict

Easily the most serious disagreement at the convention involved the question of representation of large states and small states in the new form of government. North and South also argued about how slaves should be counted, if indeed they should be. Randolph's Virginia Plan favored the large states and called for a single-house Congress that would enhance their political power in the Union. The small states countered with Paterson's New Jersey Plan, which was actually a continuation of the representation mode of the Articles.

After a long and sometimes bitter struggle, the delegates agreed to the Connecticut Compromise. That compromise provided for a two-house Congress with the upper house, the Senate, protecting

Benjamin Franklin

Edmund Randolph

George Mason

Elbridge Gerry

the interests of the small states, and the lower house, the House of Representatives, reflecting the voting strength of the large states. North and South reconciled their differences over the enumeration of slaves by agreeing to count five slaves as three people for purposes of representation, desired by the South, and the same ratio for purposes of taxation, desired by the North.

Northern and southern interests also clashed over the regulation of commerce. In this instance, the agreement reached favored southern plantation owners. The Constitution prohibited taxes on exports, while requiring a two-thirds vote in the Senate to ratify treaties. Thus the income of southern planters from the export of cotton and tobacco was protected, and no trade agreements affecting exports could be reached without the concurrence of the southern states. Farmers as well as other exporters benefit even today from this provision designed with far different political purposes in mind.

No other nation had ever established a republican executive. As we noted earlier, the anxiety about a strong executive hovered over the Constitutional Convention. None of the delegates wished to repeat the colonial experience where royal governors were largely free of legislative and popular control. Length of the executive's term of office, the question of reeligibility, and the manner of election dominated the convention debates, but in the end, the Constitution left the contours of the presidency to be determined by future holders of the office. This decision by the framers enabled other strong presidents—Jefferson, Jackson, Lincoln, the two Roosevelts—to shape the presidency to meet the nation's needs.

The Treaty of 1783, which concluded the Revolutionary War, had fixed the Mississippi River as the western boundary of the United States. How the new territory was to be administered and under what conditions new states would be admitted were critical questions bearing on the nature of the Union. The small states on the Atlantic coast worried about the large states that might be carved out of the trans-Appalachian territory. This issue pitted the established East against a West that was virtually unrepresented at the convention.

Since the delegates could not reach an agreement, they granted Congress the power to make rules for governing the public domain and the power to admit new states. The issue of East versus West and the fears of the small states were dampened by the admission of Vermont as the fourteenth state. When Vermont, a small eastern state, entered the Union as an equal, it set a precedent for the admission of large western states as equals. Kentucky came in soon after Vermont and settled the issue for some time. Only after vast new tracts of land had been acquired by the Mexican War of 1846–1848 did the issue reawaken with a vengeance.

Finally, the convention members differed over how power should be divided between the national and the state governments. Political theory since Thomas Hobbes, a seventeenth-century English thinker, and perhaps as far back as Jean Bodin, a sixteenth-century French philosopher, had insisted that sovereignty could not be divided. The choice facing the framers seemed clear: Either the United States would be a confederacy or it would have a unitary government with all sovereignty reserved to

John Rutledge

Oliver Ellsworth

William Paterson

Roger Sherman

the central government. The Founding Fathers resolved the problem brilliantly by inventing **federalism,** a form of government that divided sovereignty between the national government and the state governments.

The Constitution's Preamble, Article VI, and the method of ratification by state conventions rather than by state legislatures indicate that the delegates intended the national government to be supreme. However, they did not destroy state sovereignty. Three-quarters of a century later, the Civil War would be fought to establish conclusively that the Constitution had created a federal government rather than a confederacy.

The United States Constitution: Provision and Practice

Although Table 4.3 outlines the functions of a written constitution, we must note that the Constitution as a paper document furnishes only a framework for government. Life must be breathed into its provisions, it must be interpreted, and over time its meaning must be modified. By looking at the Preamble, the seven articles, and the amendments we can explore how changing conditions and values have altered the meaning of the Constitution and how new circumstances affect the practices and policies of the national government.

The Preamble

The Preamble opens with the phrase "We, the People," revealing the framers' commitment to popular sovereignty. But the Founding Fathers were also careful to limit the people's right to participate in politics. Checks on the popular will—such as suffrage restrictions, limiting the number of elective federal offices, omitting provisions for the initiative, referendum, and recall, and prohibiting the impairment of the obligations of contracts—ensured that government would be able to control the people's extreme behavior. The Preamble also argues indirectly for a federal form of government as opposed to a confederacy. If the framers had meant that the states should be supreme, they would have crafted the appropriate language. The Preamble might have read, "The Sovereign States in order to

form a more perfect union" rather than "We, the People."

The First Three Articles

Together, the first three articles establish a government of separated powers where independent branches check one another's actions. The Founding Fathers believed that placing all governmental authority in one branch or one level of government would inevitably lead to tyranny. By balancing one power center against another, they hoped to ensure the longevity of a republican form of government.

Yet neither **separation of powers** nor checks and balances, doctrines that are fundamental ele-

Table 4.3
The Functions of a Written Constitution

A written constitution's principal function is to legitimize, that is, make legally binding, the relationship between the government and the people. To establish a democratic form of government requires the consent of the people. Written constitutions that provide for popular consent can furnish a basic framework for a democracy.

Other important functions of written constitutions include the following:

Enabling	The people grant, delegate, or assign power to the government. Key questions: Who has lawful authority to do what? How is power distributed among the executive, legislative, and judicial functions of government? Who determines the relationship between levels (national-state, national-local, state-local) of government?
Limiting	The constitution constrains the exercise of power by government officials to preserve certain rights of the people. Key questions: Who is constrained? Congress, president, courts, states? What rights are protected against arbitrary governmental intrusion by constitutional provisions, such as a bill of rights? What is the appropriate balance between individual rights and community needs?
Structuring	The constitution creates governmental institutions and establishes how public policy will be made. Key questions: Who ensures that each institution does not exceed its authority? What is each institution's role in making public policy? What extraconstitutional institutions (such as political parties and interest groups) influence the policy-making process?

GOUVERNEUR MORRIS (1752–1816)

Much of the credit for the felicitous wording of the Constitution belongs to Gouverneur Morris. As head of the committee that prepared the final draft, he played the leading role in arranging the articles in their present order and in polishing the clauses until they shone. Throughout the debates, Morris was prized for his open willingness to surrender his opinions when the debates convinced him to do so and for a readiness to make the best of measures in which he had been outvoted. Although occasionally abrasive, his wit often leavened the debates when they became overheated. Morris was also adept at using his wit to make the best of a bad situation. As a young man, he had lost a leg in a carriage accident. A friend who was commiserating on his loss noted that the amputation would have a good effect on his morals because it would reduce impulses toward dissipation. Morris rejoined: ''My good sir, you argue the matter so handsomely, and point out so clearly the advantages of being without legs, that I am almost tempted to part with the other.''

ments of American politics, are explicitly stated in the Constitution. Whereas the first three articles establish separate branches of government, they prescribe neither the meaning nor the scope of separation of powers. Much the same can be said for checks and balances—dividing power so that one type of authority offsets or counterbalances another—although examples, such as the presidential veto and senatorial consent to presidential appointments, occur throughout the first three articles.

Article I provides for the legislative branch of the national government. It is the longest article and contains the most impressive grant of powers, reflecting the Founding Fathers' desire that Congress be the dominant branch.[6] Even so, the chief executive has gradually absorbed some prerogatives originally thought to be exclusively legislative. But it was the rise of political parties that has had perhaps the greatest impact on the internal operations of Congress. Because Article I is silent on the issue, the two major parties determine how committees should be organized and what procedures should be employed in selecting congressional leaders. The majority party in either chamber has a majority on every committee and chooses the chair. Congressional leadership positions for each house are also chosen from members of the majority party. Sometimes, as in the Reagan years, the Democrats will control one house while the Republicans control the other.

Article II creates the executive branch of government. The framers, fearing a strong executive, did not give the president an impressive set of powers. Yet executive power has grown over time through custom and practice and, most significantly, through the strong personalities that have occupied the office.[7] During his presidency (1901–1909), for example, Theodore Roosevelt enlarged upon the nineteenth-century activist precedents of Andrew Jackson (1829–1837) and Abraham Lincoln (1861–1865).

Even where the Constitution appears explicitly to limit executive authority, presidents have increased the range of their power. The Constitution mandates senatorial ratification of all treaties. Yet through the use of so-called executive agreements, presidents can make international agreements that are treaties in all but name and do not require senatorial ratification.

Presidents have also assumed certain roles, such as manager of the economy, when Congress was unable or unwilling to act.[8] In other instances, Congress has aided and abetted the executive's quest for leadership (as a policy initiator, for example) by granting power to the president. When Congress gave the president the authority to formulate the federal budget, they effectively ensured executive dominance of the policy-making process. Constitutional grants of power have also been imbued with new meaning as a result of changed circumstances. When the United States emerged as a world power in the twentieth century, the president's power as commander in chief, the power to recognize foreign governments, and the power to formulate treaties took on heightened significance.

The use—and abuse—of presidential power is not without risks, however. In 1974, Richard Nixon claimed executive privilege in an effort to deny access to his taped conversations. Congressional committees and Special Prosecutor Leon Jaworski sought those tapes for their investigations into the alleged Watergate coverup. A unanimous Supreme Court held in *United States v. Nixon* that the president's claim of executive privilege could not be sustained and that he must obey Jaworski's subpoena. The Court's decision, loss of support in Congress, a hostile press, and adverse public opinion led to Nixon's resignation. Under more normal circumstances, however, it remains true that an astute chief executive has a more impressive set of powers than the language of Article II indicates.

Article III deals with the federal courts. Although it requires only the Supreme Court, Article III gives Congress the power to establish other federal courts. Congress has exercised this power in creating the courts of appeal and the federal district courts. Judicial review, the most significant power of the courts, is not explicitly provided for in the Constitution. Chief Justice John Marshall claimed this power for the courts in a unanimous decision in the famous case of *Marbury v. Madison* (1803).[9]

In his opinion, Marshall held that the Supreme Court had the power to nullify those laws of Congress that were contrary to the Constitution. To support his argument, the chief justice observed that Article VI unequivocally states that the Consti-

---

Marbury v. Madison 1 Cranch 137 (1803)

Opinion of the Court by Chief Justice John Marshall

The question whether an Act repugnant to the Constitution can become the law of the land, is a question deeply interesting to the United States; but, happily, not of an intricacy proportioned to its interest. It seems only necessary to recognize certain principles, supposed to have been long and well established, to decide it.

That the people have an original right to establish, for their future government, such principles as, in their opinion, shall most conduce to their own happiness, is the basis on which the whole American fabric has been erected. The exercise of this original right is a very great exertion; nor can it nor ought it to be frequently repeated. The principals, therefore, so established, are deemed fundamental. And as the authority from which they proceed is supreme, and can seldom act, they are designed to be permanent.

This original and supreme will organizes the government, and assigns to different departments their respective powers. It may either stop here, or establish certain limits not to be transcended by those departments.

The government of the United States is of the latter description. The powers of the legislature are defined and limited; and that those limits may not be mistaken, or forgotten, the constitution is written. To what purpose are powers limited, and to what purpose is that limitation committed to writing, if these limits may, at any time, be passed by those intended to be restrained? The distinction between a government with limited and unlimited powers is abolished, if those limits do not confine the persons on whom they are imposed, and if acts prohibited and acts allowed, are of equal obligation. It is a proposition too plain to be contested, that the constitution controls any legislative act repugnant to it; or, that the legislature may alter the constitution by an ordinary act.

Thus, the particular phraseology of the Constitution of the United States confirms and strengthens the principle, supposed to be essential to all written constitutions, that a law repugnant to the constitution is void; and that courts, as well as other departments, are bound by that instrument.

tution is the supreme law of the land. Laws passed by Congress that are contrary to the Constitution, he argued, must be invalid or the notion of supreme law is empty. He concluded his opinion by citing the provisions of Article III and *Federalist* No. 78, where Alexander Hamilon had insisted it was the peculiar function of the courts to interpret the laws. Marshall structured his opinion in such a way that neither President Jefferson nor the Congress was able to counter or to refute this assertion of the power of judicial review.

The power of judicial review has enabled the federal courts to play a significant policy-making role throughout this nation's history. In recent times, the Miranda warning (the police obligation to inform individuals accused of crime of their constitutional rights), busing of public school students to achieve racial integration, and a woman's right to have an abortion all highlight the Supreme Court's importance as a policy maker in extremely sensitive areas.

Articles IV Through VII

Article IV is called the federal article because it deals with interstate relations. The nature of federalism requires constitutional provisions that establish the ground rules for relations between and among the states. The full faith and credit clause, for example, ensures that the legal acts of one state are binding in all other states: A person married (or divorced) in one state is considered married (or divorced) in all the other states. Other provisions of this article deal with the privileges and immunities of citizens, the admission of new states to the Union, and the guarantee by the national government of a republican form of government in every state. In the past, these provisions were the subject of bitter conflicts, some of which reached the Supreme Court. Today, few disputes arise in this area.

Article V spells out how amendments are proposed and ratified. Although there are two modes for proposal, all twenty-six amendments were proposed by a two-thirds vote of both houses of Congress. The other method, proposal by a congressionally authorized national convention that has been applied for by two-thirds of the state legislatures, has never been used. Of the two modes for ratification—three-fourths of the state legislatures or three-fourths of state conventions—the lat-

IS THERE DANGER IN ANOTHER CONSTITUTIONAL CONVENTION?

Article V furnishes the mechanism by which the states can ask Congress to convene a constitutional convention. Could such a convention do what the Founding Fathers did? They wrote an entirely new constitution, which provided for a mode of ratification different from that found in the Articles of Confederation. Many people believe the talent assembled in Philadelphia in 1787 can never be matched and any convention today would be tampering with a supreme work of political genius. Jefferson spoke of these concerns in a letter to Samuel Kercheval in 1816: "Some men look at constitutions with sanctimonious reverence, and deem them like the ark of the covenant, too sacred to be touched. They ascribe to the men of the preceding age a wisdom more than human, and suppose what they did to be beyond amendment. ... We might as well require a man to wear still the coat which fitted him when a boy, as civilized society to remain ever under the regimen of their ... ancestors." Jefferson obviously did not believe that the Constitution was sacrosanct. And others have occasionally called for a new constitutional convention to remedy perceived evils. But although times may change, human nature tends to remain conservative. In the absence of political upheaval, few people would be willing to undergo the traumatic changes a new constitution would produce.

ter has been used only for the Twenty-first Amendment, which repealed Prohibition.

The procedures for proposal and ratification show further the framers' intention that Congress should be the dominant branch. Congress determines both how amendments will be proposed and how they will be ratified. Neither the president nor the Supreme Court has any direct or immediate role. If the Founding Fathers had intended the United States to be a confederacy, the convention delegates would have placed control of the amending process in the state legislatures. As it stands, Congress can bypass them altogether by calling for ratification by state conventions, as was the case with the Twenty-first Amendment. Finally, the amending procedure reveals yet another check on the power of the people; They have no direct involvement in the amending process.

Article VI, the national supremacy article, is another way the framers sought indirectly to locate sovereignty in the national government. When combined with the language of the Preamble, with Article V, and with the method of ratifying the Constitution, the framers' intent to establish national supremacy seems clear. But at the time of the Constitutional Convention, the sentiment among the American people in favor of state sovereignty was too strong to be challenged directly.

Yet the language of Article VI provided a legal ground on which to base an argument for national supremacy. In *McCulloch v. Maryland* (1819), Chief Justice Marshall declared that Maryland could not tax a bank created by the federal government. Marshall pursued the same goal of national supremacy in *Gibbons v. Ogden* (1824), where he held that the commerce power of Congress could not be interfered with by the states. These decisions alone, however, were insufficient to ensure national supremacy. A Civil War and three constitutional amendments, the Thirteenth, Fourteenth, and Fifteenth, were finally necessary to end the insistence on state sovereignty.

Today, the most important factor ensuring national supremacy is the Sixteenth Amendment, which provides for a tax on incomes. By the middle 1980s, federal revenues from personal and corporate income taxes stood at more than $450 billion.[10] This figure exceeds the revenue collected by all fifty states. Indeed, most states are dependent on the federal government for as much as 24 percent of their budgets. The augmented United States role in international affairs in the twentieth century has also contributed to national supremacy. This tendency is reinforced by the Constitution's prohibition against state involvement in foreign policy. Since World War II the United States has exercised a world leadership role that often dominates the nation's consciousness. Opposition to the expansion of communism, the increasing importance of international trade, and the instability in much of the Third World ensure that America will continue to be deeply involved in world politics.

Article VII specifies how the Constitution was to be ratified. The Founding Fathers might have opted for submitting the Constitution to the state legislatures as mandated by the Articles of Confed-

THE STRUGGLE FOR RATIFICATION OF THE CONSTITUTION

Immediately after the close of the Constitutional Convention, both those in favor of and those opposed to ratification swung into action. The supporters, quickly dubbed Federalists, included many who had been convention delegates. However, some delegates—the most prominent being Elbridge Gerry, George Mason, and Luther Martin—and others noted for their revolutionary activity—George Clinton, Patrick Henry, and Richard Henry Lee—joined the Anti-Federalists. They attacked the work of the framers on the grounds that it placed too much power in the hands of the national govenment, that it would destroy the state governments, and that it lacked a bill of rights. All these charges were answered brilliantly by Alexander Hamilton, John Jay, and James Madison in the *Federalist*. But not until the Federalists acceded to the demand for a bill of rights was ratification assured. The narrow margin for ratification in a number of the state conventions, particularly Virginia and New York, was due to the Federalists' promise. Moreover, four conventions specifically insisted that their ratification was contingent on the adoption of a bill of rights. Rhode Island remained intransigent and did not ratify until 1790. Even then it did so only because the other states vowed to treat Rhode Island as a foreign power.

eration. But the strong sentiment in favor of state sovereignty and Rhode Island's delayed ratification show the framers were aware that the Constitution might not attract the support of all thirteen state legislatures. In fact, several state legislatures viewed the Constitution as transferring far too much power to the central government.

On the other hand, the framers were leary of submitting the Constitution directly to the people, many of whom might regard it as too conservative a document and thus at variance with the ideals of the Revolution. Astutely, the Constitution's authors decided to require the assent of only nine state conventions. This had the additional benefit of indirectly arguing for national supremacy while avoiding the uncertainties of securing ratification from either recalcitrant state legislatures or an aroused people.

The Amendments

Most scholars believe that the promise to add a bill of rights contributed to the momentum for ratification. By quickly agreeing that the first Congress established under the Constitution would propose a bill of rights, the Federalists crippled the opposition. Shortly after his inauguration, George Washington urged Congress to keep its promise. James Madison, who had been elected speaker of the House, acted on Washington's advice. Congress proposed twelve amendments in 1789, ten of which were ratified in 1791. These amendments furnish an excellent example of what is meant by limited government.

The First Amendment is a bold assertion of certain fundamental political and individual rights: freedom of speech and press, freedom of religion, freedom of assembly and petition. Its opening words, "Congress shall make no law," clearly imply that government has no power to infringe on these rights. Despite this unequivocal language, both the national and state governments have sought to restrict the scope of the First Amendment.

The Supreme Court, for example, has fashioned at least four doctrines that affect freedom of speech and of the press. Justice Oliver Wendell Holmes enunciated the clear and present danger test, the earliest doctrine, in *Schenck v. United States* (1919), when he argued that the distribution of a pamphlet could be restrained if the words used and the circumstances prevailing were such that dangerous conditions existed and a public disturbance was imminent.

Five years later, Justice Edward T. Sanford forged a more restrictive doctrine in *Gitlow v. New York* (1925), which stated that speech need only reveal a "bad tendency" to be suppressed. The third doctrine, the preferred position rule, argues that if a conflict arose between First Amendment freedoms and other constitutional rights, the former should prevail. Balancing, the final doctrine, calls for the Court to weigh competing constitutional rights

" WHAT'S A NICE GIRL LIKE YOU DOING IN A PLACE LIKE THAT?"

Schenck v. United States
249 U.S. 47 (1919)

Opinion of the Court by
Justice Oliver Wendell Holmes

But the character of every act depends upon the circumstances in which it is done. The most stringent protection of free speech would not protect a man in falsely shouting fire in a theatre and causing a panic. It does not even protect a man from an injunction against uttering words that may have all the effect of force. The question in every case is whether the words used are used in such circumstances and are of such a nature as to create a clear and present danger that they will bring about the substantive evils that Congress has a right to prevent. It is a question of proximity and degree. When a nation is at war many things that might be said in time of peace are such a hindrance to its effort that their utterance will not be endured so long as men fight and that no Court could regard them as protected by any constitutional right.

---

without giving preference to any particular set of rights. This doctrine can be used both to sanction and to justify governmental intrusion on rights found in the First Amendment.[11]

Fourth Amendment provisions protecting individuals against unreasonable searches and seizures allow even greater latitude for interpretation. Such words as *unreasonable, probable,* and *particularly* readily lend themselves to the High Court's decisional process. Because these words are inherently ambiguous, both federal and state courts have sought to give them some substantive meaning. Courts must also strike a balance between protecting the privacy of individuals and protecting society from lawbreakers.

These efforts are especially significant because many provisions in the Bill of Rights are concerned with the rights of individuals accused of crimes. Besides the Fourth Amendment, the Fifth, Sixth, and Eighth Amendments include such important protections as due process of law, trial by jury, and a ban on cruel and unusual punishment. In each of these areas, the Supreme Court has handed down landmark decisions. Some of these decisions, made by an activist Court under Chief Justice Earl Warren in the 1960s, are the exclusionary rule forbidding admission of evidence seized illegally (*Mapp v.*

Ohio), the famous "Miranda warning" of a suspect's right to legal counsel during questioning by police (*Miranda v. Arizona*), and a poor person's right to a lawyer (*Gideon v. Wainwright*).

Next to the Bill of Rights, the Civil War amendments—the Thirteenth, Fourteenth, and Fifteenth—are among the most important. In seeking to ensure national supremacy, these amendments also represented an effort to transfer the protection of individual rights from the state governments to the national government.[12] The Supreme Court has used the Fourteenth Amendment's due process and equal protection clauses to make most of the provisions of the Bill of Rights binding on the states.

Of the remaining amendments, six (including the Fifteenth) have had the effect of democratizing the Constitution. The Fifteenth, Seventeenth, Nineteenth, Twenty-third, Twenty-fourth, and Twenty-sixth have expanded participation in electoral politics, removing virtually all the restrictions the Founding Fathers thought necessary to secure a balanced government. Only the **electoral college** remains as a significant limit on the suffrage, because in presidential elections the public is in fact voting for electors and not directly for the president. The political advantage it gives to states with both large and small populations helps to ensure that in the

absence of some powerful reform movement, the electoral college will persist.

The Meaning of a "Living" Constitution

In this chapter, we have explored how changing conditions, values, and practices have modified the Constitution's meaning. By examining the processes by which the Constitution has kept abreast of the times, we can better appreciate why it has endured. Congress, the president, and the Supreme Court have all played important parts in modifying the intent, if not the language, of the Founding Fathers. Even the states have altered the Constitution's meaning. As a result, we have a "living" Constitution, flexible enough to meet changing needs and circumstances.

Despite changing interpretations, the Constitution's underlying principles remain largely intact. The framers' strategy of laying down general rules rather than detailed definitions allowed these principles to gain acceptance and to evolve over time. As noted earlier, neither the doctrine of separation of powers nor that of checks and balances was spelled out in the Constitution. The Founders sensibly avoided the rigidity that plagues the constitutions of several of our states.

In some instances, the framers were dealing with principles that they could not, for both political and theoretical reasons, define precisely. This was certainly true for federalism, which they invented to placate the states while establishing a national government with broad powers. We know today that the national government's exercise of its taxing, spending, and commerce powers has contributed to national supremacy. The Supreme Court's interpretation of the Fourteenth Amendment has also enhanced the power of the national government. Yet the states remain vital elements in the federal system, having the principal responsibility for education, for highways, and for local government.

The Constitution comes closest to making explicit one of its underlying principles in Article VI. It states quite plainly that the Constitution shall be the supreme law of the land. This provision did not prevent the national government and the states from engaging in numerous disputes over which level of government was supreme. Yet by providing

THE BICENTENNIAL OF THE CONSTITUTION

Nineteen eighty-seven marks the two hundreth anniversary of the Constitution. Ironically, this historic event comes amidst calls for another constitutional convention. Since we have not had one in two hundred years, perhaps it is time we did. Or is it? Constitutions, especially written ones, seldom last for two centuries. Our Constitution's longevity can be traced in part to its flexibility. It shuns the rigidity of ideology in favor of broad political principles. It also persists because of what it doesn't say as well as what it does.

By sketching only the framework for a government and by using language that could be adapted to changing conditions, the Founding Fathers crafted a document that has kept up with the times. Such a strategy ensured that the underlying principles and the basic structure of government would be preserved while new policies could be forged to meet the needs of the nation.

Calls for changes to the Constitution are not new. Every generation has expressed its dissatisfaction with current problems by seeking to amend or to revise the Constitution. However, the vast majority of Americans are convinced of the Constitution's soundness. It is highly unlikely that they would seriously entertain any basic changes to the document that has served the nation so long and so well.

All these factors have contributed to making our Constitution the world's oldest written instrument of government.

for the supremacy of the Constitution, the framers made a subtle but ultimately successful argument for national supremacy.

Ambiguity about which branch or level of government should be the authoritative interpreter of the Constitution contributed to the emergence of the doctrine of judicial review. Although challenged many times in this nation's history, judicial review has been accepted as one of the cornerstones of American constitutional government. This doctrine also made the Supreme Court a coequal branch of government. The policy making of the Supreme Court, however, has not always been appreciated. During the 1930s, President Franklin Roosevelt

tional amendment which would overturn the Court's rulings on abortions.

The very nature of a written constitution, particularly in the context of American politics, implies a limited government. Together, the Bill of Rights, the Civil War amendments, and Article I, Sections 9 and 10, contain the most important restraints on governmental authority. Yet none of these provisions details the precise meaning or scope of limited government. This has been left to the courts to determine. Without effective limits on power, no government can be characterized as a democracy. This nation's courts, by enforcing such limits, make a vital contribution to American democracy.

challenged the Court's opposition to the New Deal. In the 1960s, Senator Everett Dirksen sought a national convention to deprive the Court of jurisdiction in reapportionment disputes. In the 1980s, a number of religious groups demanded a constitu-

Conclusion

By avoiding explicit statements of the Constitution's underlying principles, the Founders ensured

Women march for suffrage in Washington, D.C.

its flexibility and adaptability. These principles have not escaped modification, but none has been altered fundamentally. If the framers were alive today, they would recognize immediately the vitality of these principles at both the national and state levels of government. The Constitution's longevity would also confirm for them the wisdom of their methods.

However, we believe they would be surprised to learn how important political parties and interest groups have become. Neither parties nor groups were mentioned in the Constitution, yet no significant policy decisions are made without their input. Their activity and influence make them the most significant extraconstitutional institutions that participate in policy making.

The values of economic individualism and anticommunism have also shaped our understanding of the Constitution. Economic individualism goes back to colonial times. Anticommunism is a twentieth-century phenomenon. No important area of public policy escapes their influence. Although the Constitution mandates neither economic policies based on economic individualism nor an ideological outlook dominated by anticommunism, these values are deeply rooted in the American consciousness, and no analysis of American politics can ignore their significance.

The United States Constitution, the oldest and most successful written instrument of government, has proven equal to the challenges of a nation vastly different from what it was two hundred years ago. Geographical expansion, industrialization, immense population growth, urbanization, and the emergence of the United States as the leader of the Western world have all occurred without any significant alteration of the Constitution. Although the nation is faced with many difficult and intransigent problems—poverty, recurring recessions, urban decay, vestiges of racism and sexism, drug abuse, toxic wastes, acid rain—few people would argue that the Constitution exacerbates these problems or that a new and different constitution is needed to resolve them.

 ## Glossary

Agrarian A person or group who favors an equitable division of landed property. In the revolutionary era, conflicts between agrarians and the commercial classes, particularly over mortgages, contributed to the calling of the Constitutional Convention.

Articles of Confederation The first constitution of the United States. Proposed in 1777 but not adopted until 1781, the articles established a form of government in which the states retained much of their sovereignty.

Checks and balances Dividing power so that one type of authority offsets another. The president's veto is a classic example of an executive check on the legislature.

Electoral college A group of people called "electors," popularly chosen in each state, that officially elects the president and vice president. Each state has an elector for each senator and representative.

Federalism The division of power between different levels of government, one level being ultimately sovereign. Considered by many scholars to be the most brilliant invention of the Founding Fathers.

The Federalist A series of essays, eighty-five in all, that both argued for and explained the Constitution. Alexander Hamilton and James Madison authored the bulk of the essays, John Jay the remainder. Widely regarded as both a brilliant exposition of the principles underlying the Constitution and an important work of political theory in its own right.

Judicial review The power of the courts to determine whether an act is contrary to the Constitution. Chief Justice John Marshall claimed this power for the courts in *Marbury v. Madison* (1803).

Necessary and proper clause The provision in Article I, Section 8, also known as the elastic clause, which became the basis for a broad construction of the Constitution. By authorizing Congress to make all laws "necessary and proper" for carrying out its enumerated powers, the Founding Fathers ensured the adaptability of the Constitution and diminished the need for frequent constitutional amendment.

Separation of powers The distribution of governmental power among separate branches to prevent its concentration in a single institution.

Shays's Rebellion An uprising in Massachusetts in 1786–1787 that alarmed the creditor and commercial interests and contributed to the calling of the Constitutional Convention. The "rebels" were mostly indebted farmers, workers, and craftsmen, who organized to seize control of courthouses that had ordered the confiscation of their property.

Supremacy of law The political principle that asserts that the government as well as individuals are bound by law.

 ## Suggestions for Further Reading

Beard, Charles. *An Economic Interpretation of the Constitution.* New York: Macmillan, 1983. A book that challenges traditional thinking about the Constitution, arguing that the framers constructed a powerful government that could pay its debts so they could personally realize a profit on earlier investments.

Brown, Robert. *Charles Beard and the Constitution.* Princeton, N.J.: Princeton University Press, 1956. A leading counter to the arguments of Charles Beard concerning the motives of the framers of the Constitution. Brown's arguments suggest that Beard, at the very least, overstated his case.

Conant, Michael. *The Constitution and Capitalism.* St. Paul, Minn.: West, 1974. Detailed examination of the Constitution as a foundation for a capitalist economic system.

Farrand, Max. *The Framing of the Constitution of the United States.* New Haven, Conn.: Yale University Press, 1913. In a concise fashion, the editor of Madison's Constitutional Convention notes carefully examines the deliberations of that body.

The Federalist Papers. New York: New American Library, 1961. A standard edition that includes an introduction by Clinton Rossiter, a distinguished historian.

Jensen, Merrill. *The New Nation: A History of the United States During the Confederation, 1781–1789.* New York: Random House, 1967. One of the first works to examine the nation-building process that occurred during this crucial decade.

Kelly, Alfred H., and Winfred A. Harbison. *The American Constitution: Its Origins and Development.* 6th ed. New York: Norton, 1982. A standard work on constitutional history that merits careful reading.

McDonald, Forrest. *We the People: The Economic Origins of the Constitution.* Chicago: University of Chicago Press, 1958. Forcefully argues that Beard's thesis overemphasizes economic self-interest as a motivating factor of the convention delegates.

Padover, Saul K., and Jacob L. Landynski. *The Living United States Constitution.* 2d ed. New York: New American Library, 1983. Includes a brief recounting of the Constitution's framing, sketches of the framers, and excerpts from a number of important Supreme Court decisions.

Rossiter, Clinton. *1787: The Grand Convention.* New York: Macmillan, 1976. A very readable account of the events and personalities of the Constitutional Convention.

The government of the Union, like that of each State, must be able to address itself immediately to the hopes and fears of individuals; and to attract to its support those passions which have the strongest influence on the human heart. It must, in short, possess all the means, and have a right to resort to all the methods, of executing the powers with which it is intrusted, that are possessed and exercised by the governments of the particular States.
Alexander Hamilton,
The Federalist

Chapter 5

The Politics of Federalism

Chapter Outline

Introduction
Dividing Power Between Levels of Government
Nationalization of Power in the Federal System
Political Protection of the States in the Federal System
The Politics of Federalism: Intergovernmental Relations
Conclusion

Introduction

The federal structure established by our Constitution was an effort to create a balanced governmental system—a central government strong enough to be effective and state governments strong enough to insulate the citizens from absolute central control. In achieving some balance, the framers' federal invention would have to be judged a success, for the national and state governments continue to function as separate sovereign entities to this day. But the exact nature of the division of powers has often been a highly controversial issue in American politics. This question prompted much debate when the Constitution was ratified and resulted in the inclusion of the Tenth Amendment, which explicitly grants to the states the "reserved powers" only implied in the original document. Disagreement over the rights of the states in the **federal system** animated major controversies before the Civil War, when debate centered on concepts such as the following states' rights doctrines:

interposition—a doctrine holding that the states had the power to interpose themselves between the national government and their citizens when they felt that a national law being imposed on their citizens was unconstitutional

concurrent majority—an argument, put forth before the Civil War by John C. Calhoun, holding that all parts of the country must concur in the decisions of the national government. In the absence of such concurrence, each state has the right to accept or reject national decisions

nullification—a doctrine holding that states had the right to declare national law null and void and to secede from the national Union.

The disagreements culminated finally in outright warfare over the states' right of secession. As the national–state balance has shifted in favor of the national level in recent decades, the controversy over the proper division of power in the federal system has again become a central issue of political debate.

One reason to study federalism, then, is that it is a continuing issue in American politics that has a great impact on our political processes. Our electoral process is federated, with all members of Congress being elected from the states or subunits created by the states. Even the only truly national

John Calhoun, intellectual force behind such notions as "concurrent majority" "nullification" and "interposition"

offices, president and vice president, are selected through an electoral College system which, through custom, requires candidates to assemble coalitions of state-by-state-determined "units" of electoral votes to obtain the necessary majority. Our national parties are really federally organized, reflecting the electoral system within which they compete. Much national domestic policy involves or is actually administered by state and/or local governments.

Most strikingly, many of the issues that dominate the political agenda take on a decidedly geographical or territorial cast due to the federal nature of our politics. Political conflict and competition develops between the states or regions themselves because of differing political and economic interests. Witness the clash of the Sunbelt versus the Snowbelt over energy and economic development policy in the 1970s and early 1980s.

The central role of the state and local governments in the administration of national policy make such regional and state conflicts extremely important for national policy making. National politics and government are, to a large extent, **intergovernmental relations,** involving shared authority and power for joint action. In such a system, effective national policy often depends on a high level of cooperation between the state and national governments. But owing to differences in interests, consensus on one national policy by all the states is often quite difficult to attain. National politics is thus frequently dominated by the process of resolving such conflicts.

The notion of federalism and the values it reflects—local autonomy and responsibility, government "close to the people," decentralized public authority, and so on—remain strongly held by the American people. Ironically, this commitment to lo-

cal control and decentralized authority has not resulted in less government, but in the creation of many governments. Collectively, we are governed by about 19,000 municipalities, some 17,000 townships, 3,000 counties, and thousands upon thousands of single-purpose special districts, such as school districts, transit authorities, sewage disposal districts, and the like. All in all, we are governed by almost 80,000 overlapping governmental entities.[1] Most of us live under the jurisdiction of at least six such units, though in urban areas the number can be much higher. As a result, government in the United States is a complicated and sometimes chaotic process. To make sense of government in America, we have to try to make sense of federalism.

DOES FEDERALISM MEAN "DROP DEAD"?

Just how deeply the United States's commitment to federal principles runs was clearly illustrated by the reaction of many Americans and their political representatives to the financial crisis of New York City in 1975. Facing bankruptcy, the city of New York turned to the national government for aid in meeting its financial obligations. Arguing essentially that New York should learn to live within its resources, President Ford expressed the feelings of many non-New Yorkers in vowing to veto any legislation providing federal aid. This position prompted the *New York Daily News* to respond with one of the decade's most famous headlines: "FORD TO CITY: DROP DEAD." Later, after New York had taken many stringent measures to put its finances in order, Ford and Congress agreed to provide some federal aid. But even then, this legislation was strongly opposed by legislators from the more rural states of Kansas, Nebraska, North and South Dakota, and the South who argued it was unfair that their citizens should be required to help save New York City and that such help set a dangerous precedent for other cities that might want national help with their local problems. Some observers have found it curious that national aid to our own largest city can be more controversial than similar economic assistance to foreign nations around the world. This may be one of the odder effects of our belief in federalism.

Dividing Power Between Levels of Government

Essentially, federalism is a way of dividing political authority between the national government and the smaller, more local levels of government. It is not, of course, the only way to make such a division of authority. Political scientists identify two other general categories, the **confederative** and **unitary**, in addition to the federal system. To better understand what federalism is, let us examine how it differs from these other general ways of dividing power.

The federal system embodied in the Constitution was intended to strengthen the national government, and it differs from the confederative form in several ways to produce this end. First, in a federal form, the national government derives its authority from the people directly and governs them directly in such matters as taxation, regulation of interstate commerce, and raising an army. In the confederative arrangement, the national government is created by the states, has no powers not granted it by the states, has a relatively narrowly defined authority and set of functions, and can act only indirectly through the state governments when dealing with the people. Second, in the federal system, the laws of the national government are supreme when in conflict with state legislation. In a confederation, the national government cannot enforce its provisions on the member governments but must depend on them to enforce its authority.

Finally, a federation allows neither level of government to abolish the other or fundamentally change the makeup of the federal union. A confederation allows the state governments to dissolve the national government or alter the makeup of the Union by individual secession if it is perceived to serve a state's interests.

Unlike the federal system in which the central government is considered supreme, in a confederation the components clearly possess the ultimate authority or "sovereignty" and are dominant over the central units. The best examples of such an arrangement in the modern world occur in our international organizations like the United Nations and NATO, in which the component governments are nation-states like the United States, Great Britain, the Soviet Union, and so on. The international organization reflects the basic characteristics of a confederation: (1) It has only those powers granted to it by its member nations; (2) Its authority and functional mandate are narrowly defined; (3) It has no direct contact with or authority over the citizens of its member governments and thus has no source of money and materiel for its operations independent of the voluntary contributions of the member governments; (4) It cannot enforce its provisions on member governments, for they retain ultimate sovereignty; (5) The member governments are free to withdraw from the organization at their pleasure.

In contrast to the extreme decentralization of the confederation is the unitary system. As the name implies, in this type of arrangement all power is unified in the central government. Such subnational governmental units that exist are created by, receive their authority from, and can be eliminated at the discretion of the central government. The amount of authority delegated by the central government in a unitary system varies from those in which the lesser governments are no more than administrative agencies of the national government to those in which the subnational governments are given substantial power to tax and spend for locally chosen programs. Sometimes the granted authority is so large that the component governments appear to operate with the same autonomy enjoyed by those in a federal system. Despite the functional similarities in a case such as this, however, any unitary system remains legally very different from a federal system. Unlike the federal arrangement, in the unitary system the central government has the

power to unilaterally alter the authority and makeup of the component government or even decide to eliminate it altogether if it sees fit.

The unitary form is by far the most common arrangement for the division of power among modern nations. Perhaps the clearest example is France, where a long historical tradition of centralization is reflected in a unitary government with strong central authority. A somewhat looser unitary arrangement occurs right here in the United States. The relationship between the state governments and their lesser units are essentially unitary in nature. City, county, and village governments have proven useful, effective, and popular, and enjoy considerable autonomy within their domains. However, they are created, receive their authority from, and have their scope of functions defined by the state governments, and ultimately exist at the pleasure and for the convenience of this higher-level government. Though we often think of our federal system as having three levels or "tiers" (the national, state, and local), in fact only the national and the state governments have a truly federal relationship. The cities, counties, and villages are creatures of the states in a unitary system.

A truly federal relationship means, then, that each level of government is legally independent of the other. Federal systems can differ on the means they employ to divide power, however. For instance, in the case of the United States, the Constitution assigns certain specific powers to the national government and reserves all remaining powers to the states. The Canadian federal arrangement uses the reverse strategy, granting specific powers to the provinces and giving the remaining powers to the national government. Others have granted specific powers to both levels of government. But regardless of the means, there is always an effort to grant important powers to each level to maintain a rough balance between them.

In the American case, the Constitution sought to establish a balance by granting to the national Congress **enumerated powers** such as laying and collecting taxes, borrowing money, regulating interstate commerce, coining currency, raising an army and navy, establishing a post office, and declaring war. Importantly, the Constitution also granted Congress the power to "make all laws which shall be necessary and proper for carrying into execution the foregoing powers ..." This necessary and

In a unitary system, education is the responsibility of the national government. A long tradition of local control of public education is an important source of support for federalism in the United States.

proper clause gives to the national government **implied powers** and expands its authority far beyond the specifically listed enumerated powers.

In the original document, the Constitution also left the powers of the states to implication, for it makes no specific provision for them. Uneasiness over this lack of specificity led to the adoption of the Tenth Amendment, which states that "the powers not delegated to the United States by the Constitution, nor prohibited by it to the States, are reserved to the States respectively, or to the people." In practice, these **reserved powers** grant broad authority to the states to legislate for the "health, safety, and morals" of their people, often called simply the "police power." In effect, the state governments are free to legislate on any matter not expressly forbidden them by either the national constitution or their own state constitutions.

In extending the national government's enumerated powers with those powers implied by the necessary and proper clause and reserving general police powers for the states, the Constitution actually provides both levels of government in the federal system with rather broad grants of authority. Understandably, such broad grants of power overlap and conflict from time to time. Foreseeing such a possibility, the framers in Article VI of the Constitution also included the supremacy clause, stating that the Constitution and the laws of the United States "shall be the supreme Law of the Land . . . the Constitution or Laws of any State to the Contrary notwithstanding." The supremacy clause

clearly makes the national government superior in the federal system in cases where state and national law conflict.

But the supremacy clause does not make the national government all powerful. Owing to the broad grants of authority given to both the national and state governments, there is no neat division of functions between them. In practice, both levels of government are involved in many functions. The area of education is a good example. Principally a state responsibility, day-to-day educational policy is delegated by the states to local school districts. The autonomy of these districts varies, but all are dependent on the state for financial aid, state teacher certification, and regulation of areas as diverse as janitorial service and the quality of instruction. The national government is also involved in education through providing technical aid, subsidized milk and school lunches, and aid to geographical areas "impacted" by federal installations such as military bases, prisons, hospitals, and the like. Historically, the national government made grants of land for public education, on some of which have grown our great state universities.

Our federal system does not divide power between the levels of government into neat and sharply-distinguished functional layers. Instead, each level of government tends to be involved in most governmental functions. Some have argued that our federal system should be thought of not as a layer cake, with distinct and separate planes of governmental activity, but as a marble cake with complexly interrelated and inseparable swirls of governmental activity by different levels of government in all functional areas.[2]

The division of powers in the federal system as it functions today is frequently termed **cooperative federalism,** a fairly recent development replacing the **dual federalism** that emerged after the Civil War. Dual federalism, a doctrine that emerged from post-Civil War Supreme Court decisions held that the national government and states were equally sovereign in their own spheres of action and that these two spheres could and should be kept distinct. Since the Great Depression, the cooperative character of American federalism has become much more predominant. This substantial shift illustrates that the roles of the state and national governments have never been absolutely fixed. The system has been able to change and adapt to new circumstances and conditions, although the fundamental structure remains the same.

Nationalization of Power in the Federal System

The adaptation to new circumstances and conditions during the last fifty years has brought with it an expansion of governmental activity at all levels of the federal system. It has also brought increased national government involvement in functions that were once considered strictly state or local concerns. Cooperative federalism has thus seen a substantial shift of power to the national government. The discussion that follows examines both the reasons for the nationalization of power and the means by which it has taken place.

Why the National Government Has Grown More Powerful

The most basic reason for the increasing influence of the national government is the growth of the nation itself, from a weak, relatively poor, sparsely populated, agricultural society to a relatively wealthy, powerful, densely populated, industrial nation. The governmental needs of the nation have changed. Many of our problems have become national in scope, requiring national solutions. Air and

This air pollution released in Chicago may affect conditions in Michigan, Indiana, or Ohio. The lack of respect for state boundaries of such modern problems has contributed to the nationalization of power.

In response to the Great Depression, the government became directly involved in providing employment. Here, young men work in a Civilian Conservation Corps project.

water pollution, the provision of adequate energy supplies, inflation and unemployment, and organized crime are problems that do not respect state and local political boundaries. The causes of such problems in a particular state may in large part lie outside its boundaries and thus beyond the scope of its governmental jurisdiction and resources. Adequately coping with such problems often calls for the scope and resources of a national government.

The immediate catalyst for the expansion of the national government's influence has been national crises like war and economic depression. The full-fledged national mobilization required to fight World Wars I and II led to an expanded role for the national government and greater national acceptance of such a role even after the wars were over. Perhaps the single most important impetus for expanded national governmental power, however, was the Great Depression. Not private enterprise, charitable organizations, nor state and local governments were capable of coping with this national economic disaster. The national government had power over the currency, the banking system, interstate commerce, and a good tax base. Its success, however limited, in cushioning the effects of the Great Depression substantially weakened the popular bias against government regulation of the economy.

A final reason for the continued expansion of national governmental power is that growth itself tends to engender growth. Once a national government program is established, groups that benefit from the program organize and work for its maintenance and expansion. These groups include influential business and other private interests, as well as the state and local governments themselves. Since their interest in national government programs is motivated by the economic and political benefits to be derived by their constituents, the pressure for maintaining these programs tends to continue regardless of whether Republicans or Democrats are in charge and regardless of whether the nation is experiencing economic prosperity or recession.

How the National Government Has Grown More Powerful

These motives for the growth of national power do not explain how such growth has been possible. Do we not have a Constitution that determines the distribution of power between the levels? As we discussed earlier, the Constitution does grant specific, enumerated powers to the national government and reserves all other powers to the states. However, the language of the Constitution is so vague as to require Supreme Court interpretation of various clauses that have been crucial to the nationalization of power. For the most part, the Court's interpretations have tended to favor the interests of the national government and opened the way for the nationalization of the federal system.

The first significant interpretation was of the meaning and scope of the necessary and proper clause of the Constitution. The issue essentially was whether the term *necessary* meant "indispensable" or merely "convenient" or "appropriate." In the famous *McCulloch v. Maryland* case of 1819, the Supreme Court was asked to determine whether the national government had the power to establish a national bank. Although given no specific power to establish such a bank, Congress had done so as "necessary and proper" for carrying out its power to raise money by taxation or borrowing. Maryland argued that such a bank was not indispensable for exercising the power to raise monies. The United States, on behalf of McCulloch, the chief cashier of the Baltimore branch of the U.S. Bank, argued that Congress had those powers that were "appropriate" for carrying out its enumerated powers under the necessary and proper clause. The Court under Chief Justice John Marshall ruled for the latter interpretation. This broad definition of the meaning of the

necessary and proper clause widened the scope of Congress's implied powers and laid the foundation for the nationalization of power.

Two specifically enumerated powers have also been of special importance for the nationalization of power—the interstate commerce power and the power to tax and spend for the general welfare. Again, their importance was established by favorable interpretations by the Court. The first significant decision concerning interstate commerce power came in the case of *Gibbons v. Ogden* in 1824 and focused on the meaning of the term *commerce*. Did it refer just to the buying and selling of goods, or did it apply to all forms of intercourse between two states including, as in *Gibbons v. Ogden,* human passengers on steamboats? The Marshall Court again attached the broader interpretation to the term, widening the scope of the national government's reach under the commerce clause.

A second major milestone in the expansion of the national government's power over interstate commerce came much later and focused largely on the meaning of the term *interstate.* Until recently, interstate commerce was defined as only those activities that actually and directly involved the crossing of state boundaries. Thus the jurisdiction of the national government was limited largely to transportation and communication activities. It could not regulate manufacturing and mining, for example, nor the local sale or distribution of products. This interpretation led the Court to strike down as unconstitutional a national law designed to limit the practice of employing child labor in industry. In the 1940s, however, the Court changed the meaning of interstate commerce from economic activity that directly *involves* interstate commerce to any activity that economically *affects* interstate commerce. Given the highly interdependent character of the modern American economy, virtually any commercial activity might be argued to affect interstate commerce.

Two examples illustrate the scope and versatility of the interstate commerce power under this broad definition. In *Wickard v. Filburn* (1942), the Court found the interstate commerce power applied to a farmer's growing feed to fatten his own chickens, even though the grain never left the farm, because this practice economically affected the interstate market for the grain. As this case suggests, the Court would consider almost no economic activity beyond the scope of the interstate commerce power under this interpretation. This power also allows the national government to regulate activities of commercial enterprises that are not essentially economic in nature. For example, the equal treatment of minorities and elimination of segregation required under the Civil Rights Act of 1964 is enforced on private business through the interstate commerce power. In 1964, a small restaurant in Birmingham, Alabama, attempted to avoid compliance with the law by restricting its business exclusively to an intrastate market. In *Katzenbach v. McClung,* the Court ruled that the restaurant fell under the Civil Rights Act because its operation affected the market of those restaurants directly in interstate commerce.

The power to tax and spend, the second enumerated power that has played a vital role in the expansion of national power, was also subject to an important early interpretation by the Supreme Court. In *McCulloch v. Maryland* (1819), the question was whether the power to tax and spend was subsidiary to the other powers or whether it stood alone in addition to them. The question is extremely important, for if the power is subsidiary, the national government's taxing and spending power could be used only for activities over which it had specific authority. On the other hand, if the power was considered independent and in addition to the others, it could tax and spend for activities over which it otherwise had no control. The Court adopted the latter interpretation.

In a later case, the Court also decided not to interfere with the right of Congress to establish conditions under which its monies can be spent. These broad interpretations of Congress's power to tax and spend have provided the legal foundation for the federal **grants-in-aid** to the states. Though

Through its use of interstate commerce power, the national
government has eliminated practices such as this in America since 1964.

Our unparalleled system of super highways is a product of
national-state financial cooperation.

they vary somewhat in type and method of distribution, grants-in-aid are generally cash payments
to state and local governments for purposes specified by Congress. In essence, the national government pays the state or local government to do
something that it cannot do directly or in the absence of federal money the state or local government would not choose to do at all. In the latter
case, the grant-in-aid results in the national government effectively making policy at the state and
local level. For example, it is unlikely that the states
would ever have independently created the interstate network of four-lane highways on their own.
The benefit for each state would not match the cost
incurred. But with the passage of the National Defense Highway Act, Congress made available funds
for such a system and its maintenance that made
the project attractive to the states. The national

government in effect paid the states to do something it wanted but had no power to do, and the
states did something they would not otherwise
have done.

A problem for the states and localities is that
once such money has been accepted and investments in popular spending programs have been
made with federal money, it is hard to do without.
Like a person on drugs, the states want more money, and they go through serious political withdrawal symptoms if they are cut off. They become
dependent on it and relinquish some of their freedom of policy choice because of that dependence.
For example, if the national government decides to
conserve energy and save lives by having a nationwide fifty-five-mile-per-hour speed limit, the only
way it can do that is to induce the state legislatures
to pass such a speed limit in their states. The in-

JOHN JAY (1745–1829)

Despite an illustrious career during the American Revolution and the early years of the republic, John Jay remains the least known of the authors of *The Federalist*. Given the many contributions he made, this relative obscurity is somewhat surprising. Jay served in both the First and Second Continental Congress. Indeed, he was president of the Continental Congress from December 1778 to September 1779.

Jay's diplomatic skills earned him several prestigious appointments. He was minister to Spain, helped to frame the Treaty of Paris of 1783, which ended the war with Great Britain, and served as secretary of foreign affairs from 1784 until the government was reorganized under the Constitution. During the ratification debates, Alexander Hamilton, a fellow New Yorker, called on Jay to draft several of *The Federalist* papers where Jay's foreign policy expertise would be invaluable.

George Washington appointed Jay to be the first chief justice of the United States Supreme Court in 1790. In 1794, while still chief justice, Jay went to England and negotiated the Jay Treaty, which resolved several issues that had troubled relations between that nation and the United States. Jay found the work of the Supreme Court to be so unrewarding that he resigned in 1795 to become governor of New York.

With his keen mind, Jay understood the necessity for balance in the new republic. Federalism was at that time an untried mode of governing a nation. Until his death in 1829, Jay worked to ensure a healthy balance between the national and state governments and to lay down the principles that would help federalism to evolve as the nation grew.

---

ducement is legislation that would make any state without the desired speed limit ineligible for federal highway grants. The states, dependent on the money for maintenance of existing highways, have little choice but to pass the speed limit. To choose to forego the grant money would mean either deteriorating roadways or higher state taxes for the citizens. Either might mean political suicide for state legislators.

The Court has also determined that it will not inquire into the *motive* of a tax passed by the national government. This means taxation can be used not only as a means of raising revenue but as an indirect means of regulating activity as well. For example, if Congress wished to discourage the consumption of tobacco or liquor, it could greatly increase the excise tax on these products. In the 1980 presidential campaign, candidate John B. Anderson suggested a $.50 per gallon gasoline tax to conserve fuel. Tax credits

in the income tax code function in much the same way. Congress reduces the taxpayer's tax burden if he or she does what Congress wishes. The Energy Conservation Tax Credit, for example, encouraged homeowners to conserve fuel by allowing them to write off the cost of insulating their homes on their federal taxes.

Through taxation and spending, the national government possesses an indirect power to legislate for the public health, safety, and morals of the citizens. The Constitution formally reserves such "police" powers to the states. Through the use of grants, however, the national government can influence the states to use their powers to serve the purposes of the national government. The key to the expanded use of grants in the twentieth century was the passage of the Sixteenth Amendment establishing an income tax. This tremendous increase in taxing power gave the national government a substantial and permanent revenue advantage over the states and provided the resources needed to engage in extensive grants-in-aid. Through taxes and tax credits the national government can also exercise an indirect and limited police power directly on the citizen. The size and complexity of the tax code is evidence that it has been used.

The national government, through legal interpretations of the Supreme Court and constitutional amendment, is now involved in an almost unlimited range of activities. But despite the nationalization of power, the states remain important and their interests are not left unprotected in the federal system.

Political Protection of the States in the Federal System

Though the national Congress can legislate directly or indirectly in almost any area and thus possesses great power in the federal system, we should remember that Congress is made up entirely of representatives chosen from the states. States are equally represented as geographical units in the Senate, and the House of Representatives is made up of individuals from substate congressional districts. The constituencies of these senators and congressmen are entirely state and local district entities. Elections are organized and contested within the states and sub-

LATIN AMERICA MAY BE CLOSER THAN YOU THINK

Among the factors that make each state different is its unique ethnic make-up. In a sense the United States has been formed by successive waves of immigration from different parts of the world, each bringing a distinctive cultural flavor to the American mix. Perhaps none has had a more distinctly regional impact than the latest tide of immigration flowing predominantly from Latin America. The states of the Southwest and Florida each have significant, though different, Hispanic populations.

Hispanics make up about 19% of the residents of both California and Arizona and in New Mexico nearly one-third of the population speaks Spanish in the course of everyday conversation. Unlike other areas of the Southwest, however, few of New Mexico's Hispanics are recent immigrants from Mexico. Instead, they are mostly descendents of Spanish settlements dating from the colonial era. Hispanics have always been important in New Mexico's politics. For many years a "balanced ticket" in New Mexico meant one Spanish and one Anglo senator and the offices of governor and lieutenant governor split between the groups. For many years Albuquerque, New Mexico's largest city, has been represented in Congress by a member of the Hispanic community, Manuel Lujan.

In Texas Hispanics have only recently begun to exercise any independent political impact. Though making up at least 21% of the state's population (not counting illegals) they have tended to be somewhat

more segregated and less prosperous in Texas. The greatest concentration of Hispanics occurs in an area sometimes called "Mexamerica" extending from the Rio Grande north to San Antonio and west to El Paso. El Paso is poor and predominantly Mexican, while San Antonio is more prosperous and has elected an Hispanic, Henry Cisneros, as Mayor. His election in 1981 represented perhaps the most significant political breakthrough for Hispanics in Texas to date.

Florida's Hispanic population is smaller, about 10% of the population, and more geographically concentrated than in the Southwest. It is also predominantly Cuban rather than Mexican in origin. The Cuban exile community began to form in the Miami area after Castro's revolution in Cuba and has become large and economically successful. With size and economic success has come political influence. Both Miami's mayor and the manager of surrounding Dade County are from the Cuban community. The size and success of the Hispanic community has also allowed it to exist as a separate linguistic community with little need to assimilate. This has recently led to political tensions in Florida. Some English-speaking southern Floridians feel threatened enough to sponsor a movement to make English Florida's official language, and state legislators are considering amending the state Constitution to require that all government business be conducted in English.

ject to the concerns and issues peculiar to the state and its districts.

The political clout retained by the states in the federal system is given added impact by the decentralized organizational structure of the United State's two major parties. American political parties are fundamentally pragmatic rather than ideological; that is, they are basically interested in winning elections and gaining power, not in furthering any particular set of principles. To win elections, they have organized themselves in accordance with the electoral structure, which is decentralized along the lines of the federal structure. The major parties are thus also organizationally decentralized along the lines of the federal structure. The basic organizational unit is the state party organization, and its substructure reflects the politically significant local political substructure of the state. The national parties are little more than loose associations of state party organizations. As a result, actual candidate selection is a function of the state and local party organizations, and campaign funding, for the most part, is also derived from state and local sources. The electoral success of party candidates is thus dependent on a local constituency rather than national party leadership. When the national interest, or the interests of the national party in Congress, collide with the interests of the representative's local constituency, then, political self-interest dictates that the legislator vote with the local interests in most cases.

Members of Congress also promote and defend the interests of their states and localities as members of the legislative body that controls the appropriation and allocation of national government monies. Congressional leaders will seek to secure national projects and programs for their districts and states, with the expectation that national government spending will stimulate the local economy and produce jobs. For example, it is not coincidental that most defense installations were sited in the South when congressional leadership was dominated by southerners. Members of Congress will also try to defend their states and districts when a federal project is not seen as favorable. Through their political representatives, the states are frequently successful in vetoing national actions, such as nuclear missile basing or nuclear waste disposal, that pose a potential threat to the state.

THE MX MISSILE: THANKS, BUT NO THANKS

The ability of states to defend themselves is well illustrated by the difficulty encountered by President Carter in finding a politically acceptable basing mode for the MX missile. Originally intended to be less vulnerable to a first strike owing to its mobility and wide geographical distribution, the MX was effectively vetoed by the several western states in which its silos would be located. Legislators from these states objected that the interests of their constituents were damaged by the MX scheme, since the missiles were not only inherently dangerous but their positioning would make the states targets of a potentially massive nuclear attack in the event of war. The basing scheme was repeatedly modified to involve fewer and fewer states. Under President Reagan, the plan was reversed entirely in the "dense pack" scheme, which would have placed the missiles close together rather than far apart. This notion was rejected for technical reasons. Finally, Congress voted to place a greatly reduced number of the missiles in already existing silos. This solution had the advantage of satisfying the constraints imposed by the politics of federalism, but the disadvantage of defeating the purpose of building the MX in the first place— to have a weapon less vulnerable to attack.

In addition, legislators act as overseers of the national bureaucracy and often as agents on behalf of individual constituents within their states and districts. An increasingly important part of the congressman's job, such "casework" typically involves solving constituents' problems with national executive agencies. Assuring their constituents fair treatment is important to reelection and also helps members of Congress to check the power of the national government in their states and districts.

The Politics of Federalism: Intergovernmental Relations

This section explores two dimensions of intergovernmental relations. One is the relationship between the states and the national government, or "vertical federalism," the other the relations among the states, or "horizontal federalism." As we shall see, both dimensions involve the essential ingredients of politics—conflict and cooperation.

Vertical Federalism

The relationship between the subnational governments and the national government centers on federal financial grants to the states and cities. There are three basic types of federal grants, each having a different degree of national government control over the manner in which the money is actually spent. By far the most common type, accounting for nearly 80 percent of federal grants-in-aid to states and localities, is the **categorical grant**. A categorical grant is a federal payment to a state or local government for a specific purpose only. The national government determines the purpose of the grant and establishes often extensive guidelines and standards for implementing the funded programs. Categorical grants also contain a matching provision, requiring the states and cities receiving the grant to match the federal grant with some funds of their own. The amount of matching funds varies but is usually from 10 to 50 percent of the cost of the program or project for which the grant is made. Through the use of categorical grants, the national government can induce the states and cities to carry out its policy ends and retain great control over the process.

State and local officials often complain about the strings attached to categorical grants and the complicated and difficult process of applying for them. Others worry that categorical grants give the national government too much power to influence the policy agendas of the states and cities. The lure of federal money is nearly impossible to resist, and states and cities are usually eager to adopt programs simply because they will receive federal aid, rather than because such programs are specifically demanded by their constituents.

In response to such concerns, Congress initiated a second type of grant called the **block grant**. A block grant can be used for a wider variety of purposes than a categorical grant and has far fewer federal guidelines and standards for implementation. In block grants, federal funds are allocated for use in broadly defined functional areas, and their specific use is largely at the discretion of the recipient government, allowing greater choice, flexibility, and policy control for the states and cities. Most existing block grants were formed by consolidating several specific categorical grants. For example, the Reagan administration converted about seventy categorical programs in such areas as health, education, transportation, and urban aid into nine block grants. Block grants have the added advantage to the recipients of greatly reduced or no matching requirements.

Another response to state and local criticism of categorical grants was **revenue sharing**. The general revenue sharing program turned federal funds over to the state and local governments to use entirely at their own discretion. Although the recipient governments were required to show that they did not discriminate against minority groups and women in the programs funded by revenue sharing, there were virtually no other strings attached. The amount allocated to each recipient government was determined by a complicated formula based on population but designed to give more aid to poor urban areas with high levels of taxation.

Criticism of programs such as revenue sharing and block grants, which entail less federal control over the disposal of funds, centers on the administrative competence of state and especially local units of government and on the lack of creativity and the bias often reflected in the spending choices made by these governments in using such funds. The availability of federal money in the form of block grants tends to draw city and county governments into areas where they lack technical and bureaucratic expertise. This results in administrative inefficiency and wasted dollars, which in turn often causes the national government to tighten guidelines associated with the grants. When this happens, the grants become less flexible and more like the categorical grants they were designed to replace.

Hopes for revenue sharing have also been higher than the results. This "no strings attached" program was intended to give state and local governments the resources needed to support innovative new policy approaches to their most pressing problems. Instead, states and cities spent revenue-sharing money largely as they spent their own revenues, often just substituting federal funds in existing programs rather than increasing local taxes to meet

"TOY GOVERNMENTS"

About one-fourth of the local governments that received revenue-sharing funds are so small that they have few if any employees and provide few of the services that are normally associated with local government. They are sometimes called "toy governments" by critics of general revenue sharing, who argue that they have no real needs. One student of state and local government cites Lone Jack, Missouri, as a typical toy government. Lone Jack is a village of 350 people that "has no village hall, no full-time employees, and no telephone listing." [4] Despite the fact that Lone Jack's basic services, such as police protection, public health, and water are supplied by other governments, it received about $700 dollars a year in revenue-sharing funds. In all, about 11,000 such toy governments received some aid under the general revenue-sharing program.[5]

increased costs. The money has also often gone for luxuries rather than basic needs, for example, parks, golf courses, or renovating city hall, especially in small communities not plagued by major urban problems. Whereas about half the money went to cities over 50,000 in population, four-fifths of the cities receiving revenue-sharing aid had 5,000 or fewer people.[3]

Federal grants can also be categorized according to their method of distribution. In this case, *formula grants* are distributed automatically to eligible governments on the basis of a formula established by Congress. As we have seen, revenue-sharing grants were formula grants, as are some categorical grants, such as the interstate highway program. On the other hand, *project grants* require a specific grant application by the recipient government and approval by the federal agency making the grants. As a result, they are not automatically or equally distributed among all potential recipients. Though the greater percentage of money is distributed according to formula grants, the greater number of grants are project grants. Project grants also account for most of the federal aid received directly by local governments.

The distribution of project grants depends largely on the skill of the state and local government in "grantsmanship." Most states and larger cities have established full-time intergovernmental relations staffs to identify federal programs for which they may be eligible and to ensure that they make an application that maximizes their chances of approval. They have also hired their own lobbyists and often set up full-time staffs in Washington to monitor their interests and take advantage of opportunities. The state or local government that does not take part in such grantsmanship and does not professionalize their grant-seeking efforts is likely to be left far behind in the competition for federal money.

Grantsmanship and its associated activities raise two serious criticisms of the federal system. First, some argue, federal money often does not go to the local governments with the greatest need for aid but to those most adept at grantsmanship. Hiring a large staff of grant experts is only affordable to governments that are already relatively well off financially. A second criticism is that the search for federal aid money leads state and local governments to allow their budget-making process and program priorities to be dominated by the requirements of grants. State and local policy making shifts from meeting local needs and responding to local demands to meeting the requirements to obtain federal grants and then providing such programs as are funded by grants, whether or not there is a pressing

"Isn't it wonderful, Orville? And after we thought he'd be whisked off to Washington forever?"

local need or demand for them. The national government, rather than local politics, tends to determine local governmental priorities.

In response to such concerns, the Reagan administration proposed a "New Federalism" designed to return control of budget priorities to the states and localities. Two major changes were proposed. First, as mentioned earlier, more than seventy categorical grants were to be consolidated into nine block grants to be administered by the states with few federal strings attached. Second, there would be what was popularly called the "great swap." In the great swap, the national government was to assume all responsibility for the very expensive and rapidly growing Medicaid program, which provides financial aid for health care to the aged and poor. In return, the states would acquire full responsibility for the Food Stamp program, Aid to Families with Dependent Children (AFDC), and more than forty other smaller categorical programs. To pay for these new responsibilities, the states would be allowed to draw from a New Federalism trust fund of federal monies until they could provide for such programs from their own tax sources.

Congress quickly approved Reagan's proposals for the creation of the block grants, but the great swap idea has met with great resistance. Much of the opposition has come from local officials themselves, who are not anxious to take on new responsibilities or institute the tax increases to finance the programs. Like other attempts to reallocate power in the federal system, Reagan's New Federalism also foundered over the basic question of what are national and state functions. In this case, many state officials viewed poverty and welfare as national problems that should be financed and administered by the national government, and they lobbied vigorously to avoid taking full responsibility for such programs as Food Stamps and AFDC. At present, Reagan's version of New Federalism appears to be a dead issue.

The proper distribution of power between the levels of government in the federal system is a political as well as a theoretical question, for it affects the power of various interests in politics. The issue can be seen as a conflict between those whose interests are benefited by power in the hands of the states and those whose interests are advantaged by national power. Business groups and developers, for

NEW FEDERALISM: MONEY, YES; RESPONSIBILITY, NO

The Reagan administration is not the first to try to return power to the states; indeed, it is not even the first to use the term *new federalism* for its federal reforms. The Eisenhower administration created a national committee to find programs that could be returned to the states. After two years, the committee came up with only two programs— one providing money for sewage-treatment plants and the other for aid to vocational education. Not a single state wished to accept responsibility for such programs, however, and the grants were not dropped. The Nixon administration's new federalism involved the first extensive block grants and the introduction of general revenue sharing. These programs gave the states and localities money with fewer strings attached, allowing greater local control, but did not require the local governments to assume responsibility for funding programs. These programs have been generally popular and successful. Reagan's new New Federalism included both returning money with fewer strings attached, as did Nixon's, and returning responsibility for some programs to the states, as did Eisenhower's. Interestingly, only the part that did not require increased responsibility for the states and localities has ever been instituted. The record clearly suggests that despite rhetorical concern for states' rights, state and local governments are less worried about federal dominance than they are about the prospect of having to take over federal programs. Such responsibility would give them the difficult choice of raising taxes to fund programs or canceling them. Raising taxes is never popular and always politically hazardous. In many cases, the programs are popular and supported by powerful interests, so cutting them is also politically dangerous. Faced with such a dilemma, it is little wonder that state and local officials tend to say yes to the money and no to the responsibility when offered proposals for a new federalism.

example, are likely to feel they have greater influence with state government and thus will benefit if power is returned to the states. Labor groups, consumerists, and environmentalists, on the other hand, perceive themselves at a disadvantage at the state level and prefer federal power for regulation of the activities with which they are concerned. These organizations often seek regulations that would put any state adopting them at a competitive disadvantage in attracting new industry. Labor might desire strict occupational safety legislation, for example, or environmentalists might be seeking antipollution regulations. A state that adopts such laws makes itself less attractive to businesses looking for a place to locate than states with less strict standards. As a result, the states are predisposed to be unwilling to adopt such legislation and to be responsive to business interests. There is no such disadvantage working against these groups at the national level, however, for national regulation would apply equally to all states. How any group feels about the proper distribution of power in the federal system is thus likely to depend on where the group feels its influence and control are greatest.

Horizontal Federalism

Relations among the states are also characterized by both cooperation and conflict. The cooperation is in large part required by the Constitution. The conflict arises largely over the allocation of scarce resources. Both contribute in important ways to the character of our national politics.

The Constitution requires interstate cooperation in several ways. First, in Article IV, Section 1, the Constitution says that the states are to give "full faith and credit" to the laws and official acts of other states. For example, contracts for the purchase and sale of property and for marriages and divorces made in one state must be recognized as valid in the others. Second, states are to give to residents of other states the same "privileges and immunities" that are granted to their own residents. The privileges and immunities clause means that the residents of a different state will not be discriminated against because they are nonresidents. They have the same rights afforded residents. Third, states are to return fugitives to the state from which they fled. Governors control this "extradition" process, however, and have occasionally refused to comply with extradition requests. The Supreme Court has ruled that it is a matter of executive prerogative and a governor may legally refuse extradition. Fourth, a mechanism that has become increasingly popular

for resolving interstate problems is the interstate "compact," an agreement made by two or more states. The states may enter into compacts provided they are ratified by Congress. These agreements usually address problems that cross state lines such as transportation, environmental protection, the management of natural resources, and so forth. One of the most famous and successful interstate compacts resulted in the creation of the Port Authority of New York and New Jersey in 1921. Transportation facilities in greater New York City have been developed and controlled under this authority, which is also responsible for the construction of the World Trade Center.

Conflict is at least as common in interstate relations as cooperation. State and local governments compete with one another in their effort to attract the economic activities that produce revenue, jobs, and new resources for the local economy. States and cities spend a great deal of money each year advertising in publications likely to be read by executives who determine the location of new factories and businesses. They also recruit industry by offering to provide such advantages as land on which to locate, greatly reduced or eliminated taxes for a period of years, job-training programs, minimal regulation of the environment, and right-to-work laws that make it difficult for unions to organize.

When economic conditions are poor, as in the early 1980s, the pressure for economic growth makes the competition for resources among states very intense. In such circumstances, there is a danger that such competition might descend to a more or less unbridled bidding war for private economic investment. Because this involves making revenue and public policy concessions, state and local governments tend to lose control of the process of setting their budgetary and program priorities. Thus state and local budgetary and policy independence is threatened not only by the desire for national grants but by the desire for private economic investment as well. States may find themselves played off against one another, afraid of taxing or forcing industry to stop polluting because the industries may threaten to move to a neighboring state. Tax concessions to attract new industries may also ultimately make it difficult for a state or city to balance its budget and provide adequate public health, safety, and welfare services.

WHAT IF GM'S SATURN WAS A HOAX?

In 1984, General Motors announced it was planning to build an entirely new automobile called the Saturn. It would be built by a new corporate division in a new plant facility. The site for the new plant had not been chosen, however, and that produced a most embarrassing display of state bidding for the favor of GM. Every major industrial state had several sites for GM to choose from and was offering an array of incentives to influence GM's decision. The governors of these states were scheduled into a long series of interviews with Saturn decision makers, each coming hat in hand to plead the special virtues of his state.

At about the same time, the auto makers were attempting to encourage the passage of mandatory seat belt laws in the states to help head off pressure gathering in Congress for legislation requiring them to provide automatic, passive restraint systems, or airbags, in all of their cars. This requirement would not only be technologically complex but would also make cars more expensive.

Given the willingness of the states to curry GM's favor and the fact that the auto makers were seeking this seat belt legislation, one student demonstrated a good grasp of the politics of federalism by suggesting, in jest, that the entire Saturn project was just a hoax. By dangling the prospect of so many jobs and so much investment before the states, he argued, GM was trying to provide the stimulus for the states to pass the mandatory seat belt law. This would demonstrate to GM the favorable business climate available for the auto industry in the state. After the laws were passed, GM would simply wait a few years and let everyone forget about Saturn. Of course, this isn't what GM had in mind, but if it had been ...?

On the positive side, poor economic conditions and competition among the states have sometimes led to innovative new policies and improvements in basic services. The potential of state government to serve as a source of innovation and a political laboratory for the testing of new policy ideas is well illustrated by the case of Massachusetts. During the recession of the early 1980s, faced with unemployment above 10 percent and a large state budget deficit, Massachusetts, under Governor Michael Dukakis, adopted a tax amnesty program that gave citizens an opportunity to pay delinquent taxes without fear of legal punishment. The program produced nearly $300 million in additional revenues for the state, almost enough to wipe out the state's budget deficit. Massachusetts has also chosen to compete economically by fostering the growth of high-tech industries, working actively with business and universities. Nor has Massachusetts cut back on social programs. Instead, to provide a solid human resource base for economic development, the state has pioneered an innovative, nonpunitive approach to workfare for welfare recipients and has increased spending for human services programs such as education and job training.

Similar stories of innovation and improvement have been written in several other states, most notably by Gov. Thomas Kean in New Jersey, Gov. Bruce Babbitt in Arizona, and Gov. Lamar Alexander in Tennessee, in addition, new policy ideas initiated and tested in the states are often borrowed later by the national government, the states thereby influencing national policy choices. This not only limits the general nationalization of power but also assures that the viability and dynamism of state and local government is retained in our evolving federal system.

Conclusion

Federalism clearly expresses the basic American values of limited government, distrust of distant political power, and individual political participation. The division of power inherent in the federal system was intended to limit government and bring political power closer to the people, where individual participation could be effective and meaningful. Federalism is both an important historical and contemporary issue in American politics, and the nature and functioning of the federal system has profound implications for the policy-making process.

As the nation has grown and become more economically and socially interdependent, the national government has become more influential in the federal system. It has been able to expand its power largely because of Court interpretations of key constitutional clauses that have favored a broad definition of national governmental powers. The power to regulate interstate commerce and the power to tax have greatly extended the reach of the national government.

Despite the growth in influence of the national government, the states retain substantial political power in the federal structure. The states and localities are politically represented in Congress, and thus the national government is unlikely to use its expanded powers in ways damaging to their vital interests. The federated structure of the party system, moreover, assures that congressional representatives owe their political position to local interests and will often place those interests before national interests when considering issues in which the two conflict.

The politics of federalism today is characterized by an extensive system of federal grants-in-aid to state and local governments. These grants include categorical grants, which carry many federal regulatory strings; block grants, which are for broad functional areas and allow considerable state and local discretion as to their specific use; and revenue shar-

ing, which returns money to the states and cities with virtually no strings attached. The result of the availability of so much federal money has been that grantsmanship has become an extremely important function of state and local government.

The Constitution requires cooperation among the states in several ways, but their relationships are also characterized by intense competition for federal grants and private investment that can contribute to economic development. Because of the states' efforts to attract and retain industry, businesses are sometimes able to resist regulation by the states and to strongly influence state policy making. The federal division of power thus generally weakens public authority in the United States and the autonomy of governments as policy-making institutions. On the other hand, federalism provides the United States with badly needed flexibility in making policy responses appropriate for a large, heterogeneous society and serves as a vital source of policy innovation and experimentation for coping with newly emerging problems.

 ## Glossary

---

Block grants   Federal grants to state and local governments that are designed to support broad program areas such as community development or health services. This form of federal grant-in-aid allows the recipient government discretion as to how funds will be spent within a broad program area.

Categorical grants   Federal grants to state and local governments that can only be used for specific purposes determined by the national government. This form of federal grant-in-aid provides the national government with maximum control of how grant money is used.

Confederative system   A political system in which the constituent states or provincial governments possess the supreme power and the central government limited and inferior powers.

Cooperative federalism   A political system in which the constituent state or provincial government and the national government share powers, functions, and responsibility for delivering services to the citizens.

Dual federalism   A doctrine, dominant until the 1930's, that the national and state governmental spheres of authority were functionally distinct and separate, each level absolutely sovereign within its own area.

Enumerated powers   Powers expressly granted to the national government by the Constitution.

Federal system   A political system having a legal division of power between national and constituent governments (states, provinces, and the like), in which each level of government has independent powers.

Grants-in-aid   Funds made available to state and local governments by Congress to be used in accordance with prescribed standards and conditions.

Implied powers   Powers possessed by the national government that are inferred from powers expressly given to it in the Constitution. Implied powers are based on the Constitution's grant of authority to do those things "necessary and proper" to carry out powers expressly granted to Congress.

Intergovernmental relations The various interactions of governmental units and levels of government in the federal system.

Reserved powers Powers reserved to the states or the people by the Tenth Amendment to the Constitution. The reserved powers are not specifically enumerated in the amendment, but are described as those neither delegated to the national government nor denied to the states by the Constitution.

Revenue sharing A program in which federal tax revenues were automatically returned to the states and localities to be used entirely as they saw fit. Established by Nixon, revenue sharing was eliminated under the Reagan administration.

Unitary system A system of government in which all power resides in the national government. Constituent governments exercise only those powers granted them by the national government.

 ## Suggestions for Further Reading

Elazar, Daniel. *American Federalism: A View from the States.* 2d ed. New York: Thomas Y. Crowell, 1972. A generally sympathetic account of the development, present nature and condition of federalism.

Graves, W. Brooke. *American Intergovernmental Relations: Their Origins, Historical Development, and Current Status.* New York: Scribner's, 1964. Intergovernmental relations are surveyed in general in this massive treatment.

Haider, Donald H. *When Governments Come To Washington.* New York: Free Press, 1974. A good discussion of a process little recognized by the average citizen, the intergovernmental lobby.

Hale, George E., and Martin Lief Palley. *The Politics of Federal Grants.* Washington D.C.: Congressional Quarterly Press, 1981. A clear account of who gets what from federal aid.

Nathan, Richard, et al. *Monitoring Revenue Sharing.* Washington, D.C.: Brookings Institution, 1975. One of the very best books on how revenue-sharing funds have been used by local governments.

Reagan, Michael D., and John G. Sanzone. *The New Federalism.* 2d ed. New York: Oxford University Press, 1981. A widely read discussion of what federalism has become in the United States.

Riker, William H. *Federalism: Origins, Operation, Significance.* Boston: Little, Brown, 1964. A classic critical analysis of federalism both in the United States and in other nations.

Sale, Kirkpatrick. *Power Shift: The Rise of the Southern Rim.* New York: Random House, 1975. A good discussion of the rise of southern influence in the American federal system and politics.

Wheare, K.C. *Federal Government.* London: Oxford University Press, 1953. The classic study of the general principles of federalism and the institutions and social, economic, and political conditions associated with this form of government.

Wright, Deil S. *Understanding Intergovernmental Relations.* 2d ed. Monterey, Calif.: Brooks/Cole, 1982. Excellent and widely cited treatment of federalist politics from the intergovernmental perspective.

The United States is the only great and populous nation-state and world power whose people are not cemented by ties of blood, race, and original language. It is the only world power which recognizes but one nationality of its citizens—American . . . .
Dorothy Thompson

Chapter 6

Political Socialization, Public Opinion, and Electoral Behavior

Introduction

Every generation in every political system learns prevailing political values and norms from a very early age. After all, how do we know we are Americans? We speak English, but so do the British. We have a presidential system of government, but so do the French. And even though we operate under a federal system, so do the West Germans. What makes any nation distinct is its indigenous **political culture.** Each generation must be taught what the components of the political culture are and what forms of political behavior are acceptable.

Political socialization is at best an uneven process and is never fully successful. In the case of some individuals, it seems to fail completely. Political socialization in the United States is structured to create a citizenry that acts on democratic ideals. Yet American society has also produced communists, neo-Nazis, anarchists, religious fanatics, survivalists, and several other varieties of racial, religious, and ideological extremists. However we may deplore this, such exceptions must be tolerated as inevitable in a society, founded on democratic values such as ours. Indeed, of the basic distinctions between the democratic and **totalitarian state,** none is more important than that political socialization in a democracy is relatively unstructured and tolerates diversity of political values and ideas among the citizenry.

What does it mean that the socialization process in a democracy like the United States is less formal or structured than in a totalitarian state? Try to remember when and where you acquired your political values, opinions, and identity. It can be a difficult exercise. We aren't taught political values and beliefs in the same way we are taught reading or algebra. Unlike totalitarian states, we have no formal education in political values per se. Usually, we acquire our political orientations indirectly from our parents, older siblings, teachers, clergy, editorial commentators, peers, and often simply from notions that are popular or fashionable at the moment.

In fact, political socialization in a democracy is so informal that we often fail to fully understand the possibilities of this process for good or for harm. In all countries, the teaching of common political values is vital for the establishment and maintenance of the social order and for the stability

If you have ever participated in this exercise, you have experienced the political socialization process.

necessary for personal security and societal progress. But political socialization is also a powerful instrument of social control. It can be used to create and maintain the people's support (or at least tolerance) for governments where power is concentrated in the hands of a small elite group, as in a communist state. It also contributes to a government's ability to persuade their people to do things we might consider strange or even harmful, for example, in Iran, to the ability of the army to recruit twelve-year-old boys to fight and die in pursuit of a holy war against Iraq.

Although political socialization in a democracy is largely an informal process, formal education does play a role. National values are inculcated through the public school system that educates most American children. National values are taught in a context of national pride and loyalty. It is difficult, for instance, to find an American eleventh- or twelfth-grade civics class that even implies much wrongdoing on the part of the United States in its two-hundred-year history.

But in the United States as in all countries, personal experience modifies the messages delivered in the socialization processes, both formal and informal. For instance, in the United States, a fifth of all children in the 1980s are growing up in poverty. They are seeing sooner than their better-off contemporaries that the "American Dream" is only a dream for many people. Childhood itself, then, does not always mean a naive acceptance of the political and social values that tend to be espoused by parents or in the classroom. Thus we see the incompleteness of the socialization process from very early stages.

Political Socialization and Political Culture

Political socialization is the process through which individuals learn about politics and the political culture in which they live. This process profoundly influences people's sense of community and common heritage, helps them to appreciate the nation's past, and impresses on them the significance and obligations of citizenship.[1] Yet human beings are not born with a political culture imprinted on their brains. Nor is any individual born with political opinions fully developed. Children, adolescents, and adults learn about the political culture from peers, parents, and other adults. In that learning process, people form political opinions that affect the manner in which they are likely to participate in political activity.

A nation's political culture gives an individual a sense of community, that is, a sense of identity and belonging. When asked, "Who are you?" many people would respond, "I am an American" or "I am a Russian" or "I am a South African," indicating that part of their identity is political. A sense of community thus lends itself to feelings of patriotism and nationalism. In the Soviet Union, the Communist party has fostered the notion that the obligations of Soviet citizenship take precedence over any obligations arising from a person's national or ethnic identity. By contrast, in the United States, people are free to express their ethnic and racial heritage as well as their citizenship by identifying themselves as Asian American, Italian American, Mexican American, and so on. This identification of self and community is reinforced by a set of shared values. For the American political culture, the values of natural rights or human rights, limited government, and popular sovereignty are an important part of the American credo.

During the course of the United State's development, other values grew from the nation's historical experience and now comprise a vital part of our political culture. Economic individualism and anticommunism are two values that shape the thinking of many Americans about the proper role of the national government in the economy and in world affairs. Any nation's political culture is also reinforced by a set of shared symbols and rituals. Uncle Sam gives many Americans a sense of belonging to the same "family;" whereas the Ayatollah Khomeini does the same in Iran. In the Soviet Union, November 7 and 8, the dates of the Bolshevik Revolution of 1917, are national holidays. The French celebrate Bastille Day on July 14 with the same sentiments Americans express on the Fourth of July. Every country makes ritualistic use of national holidays to strengthen feelings of patriotism and nationhood. Flags and national anthems are powerful reminders of a nation's heritage. Statues, monuments, and other memorials to national heroes will be found in the capital cities of virtually all countries. Finally, in important respects, the political culture gives legitimacy to the means and ends of political activity. Such forms of political activity as lobbying, collective bargaining, and electioneering are regarded as appropriate in the United States, but would not be in some countries.

The Stages of Political Socialization

Childhood   Not surprisingly, the primary agents of socialization during childhood are the family and the schools (Figure 6.1). As children grow older,

Powerful symbols such as these are important elements in the political socialization of citizens of every nation.

Figure 6.1
Political Socialization

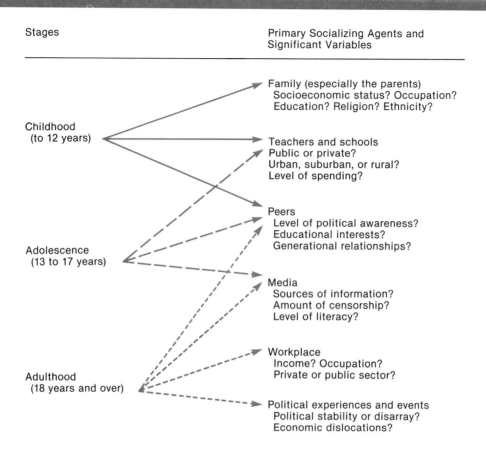

Stages

Primary Socializing Agents and
Significant Variables

Childhood
(to 12 years)

Adolescence
(13 to 17 years)

Adulthood
(18 years and over)

Family (especially the parents)
Socioeconomic status? Occupation?
Education? Religion? Ethnicity?

Teachers and schools
Public or private?
Urban, suburban, or rural?
Level of spending?

Peers
Level of political awareness?
Educational interests?
Generational relationships?

Media
Sources of information?
Amount of censorship?
Level of literacy?

Workplace
Income? Occupation?
Private or public sector?

Political experiences and events
Political stability or disarray?
Economic dislocations?

peers come to play an increasingly important role. Their parents' ethnic heritage, social class, religion, education, occupation, and income also affect how a child perceives the political culture. In the Soviet Union, where it is customary for both parents to work, day care centers are important socializing agents. Muslim clergy in Iran teach youngsters a respect for Shiite Islamic traditions.[2] In other instances, children of a given ethnic or racial background within a state or region or even neighborhood may develop a strong sense of "us" different from "them." A Hispanic Catholic whose parents are migrant laborers will experience a very different socialization process than an upper-class Protestant whose well-educated parents live in an affluent suburb.

Teachers also contribute to the socialization process by imparting, however casually, at least some

of their values to the youngsters in their classrooms. The choice of subject matter, the interpretation given to political and economic developments, and treatment of contemporary controversies such as school prayer are only the most obvious ways that teachers affect the socialization of young people.

Since children learn in an essentially passive, undirected, and uncritical fashion, most of them emerge from childhood with very positive attitudes about the political culture. As learning becomes more active, directed, and critical, political attitudes become more sophisticated, and a person becomes more discriminating in judging political acts. Most people, however, retain as adults many of the political attitudes they formed as children. For example, few individuals change their party identification. Those who viewed themselves as Democrats when they were young remain Democrats as adults.

Adolescence As children approach the teen years, peers become a more significant factor in socialization, often mutually reinforcing political attitudes and orientations different from those of their parents. The attitudes and values learned from parents and the schools do not disappear, but the teenager is much more likely to question them. In the 1960s, when many young people were at odds with their parents over the Vietnam war, such questioning led to the formation of a distinct counterculture. Even in college, the informal influence of peer groups may have a greater impact on the political outlook of an individual than a student's formal coursework. As teenagers become adults, peers continue to exert an influence on political attitudes and behavior.

The close association, similarity of interests, and camaraderie of the adolescent years reinforce one another and provide the emerging generation with a sense of identity. The "silent" generation of the 1950s can be easily distinguished from the political activists of the 1960s and 1970s and the more vocationally minded students of the 1980s in terms of dress, hair styles, and language. Thus a generation gap can exist not only between parents and adolescents on a single issue but also between generations that espouse different sets of values. This is especially true in a period of rapid change or instability.

Over the past several decades, the media's role in adolescent socialization has grown considerably.

Like all college students, these university of New Mexico students are in an important phase of their political socialization.

The media, recognizing the economic impact of adolescents, have created numerous television and radio programs and magazines to attract their dollars. Music videos, for example, are specifically designed to appeal to teenagers. The lyrics and visual interpretations often contain subtle but powerful suggestions about basic political values, authority relationships, and the existing order of things. One study of music videos reported that despite their unusual stylistic images, music videos basically support rather than challenge existing political values, lending indirect support to the "establishment".[3]

Adulthood Adults (and adolescents) are frequently aware of the contradictions between the ideals they have learned and the sometimes unpleasant reality that many individuals must confront in their day-to-day life. Racial prejudice, male chauvinism, job discrimination, and poverty are cruel reminders to many people that the American ideals of equality, economic opportunity, and fairness have yet to be achieved. Adolescents and young adults who are economically disadvantaged may come to look very cynically on such ideals. They may also become alienated from politics if they perceive the government as either uninterested in, or hostile to, their aspirations.

The media continue to exert considerable influence on the socialization of adult Americans. Nearly two-thirds of adults cite television as their major source of news. A little less than half of all adults claim a daily newspaper as an important source for news. Politicians have long recognized the mass media's importance, spending huge sums on television ads in political campaigns to persuade the undecided. Nor has the importance of the media escaped the attention of nondemocratic regimes. They regulate the media closely, either through censorship or outright control, to manipulate the process of political socialization to their advantage.

For adults, the workplace, where adults spend a large portion of their lives, is also significant in the socialization process. Coworkers can exert a subtle influence on one another's political attitudes, although this is difficult to measure. Many nondemocratic regimes such as the Soviet Union and the communist countries of Eastern Europe recognize the value of the workplace in their socialization efforts. They frequently use part of the working day for political indoctrination, replacing the casual contacts of the workplace with a structured effort to influence political attitudes.

Political events and experiences, especially those current at the time an individual reaches the late teens or early twenties, can also influence political socialization. Such events create political generations. The **Great Depression** was one event that stamped, seemingly for life, the political orientations of a generation. The Democratic party took effective advantage of the Depression and the political beliefs and values it engendered to build a majority coalition that lasted at least a full generation. The Vietnam war left its imprint on another, more recent, generation of young people. Watergate was a similar event, though more limited in impact. Most recently, Jimmy Carter's failure to effectively manage the economic uncertainties of the late

1970's and early 1980's and his inability to deal with the hostage crisis in Iran not only contributed to his defeat in 1980 but also helped to produce a more **conservative** and Republican political generation of young people.

Implications of Political Socialization

By its nature, the political socialization process ensures a certain level of support for an existing regime. A child's socialization by parents and teachers tends to reinforce positive attitudes toward the political culture and enhance affirmative feelings of nationhood and patriotism. Both democratic and nondemocratic regimes recognize that political socialization is a critical process, and both use the schools as an instrument of political socialization. Instruction in the nation's history and its contribu-

Hitler's Nazi regime was masterly at the manipulation of powerful symbols and at turning the process of political socialization to political advantage.

tions to the world, political exercises such as mock elections, party conventions, and model United Nations, and national holidays celebrating important political figures and historical events all inculcate appropriate political attitudes and foster stability. In the absence of political upheavals and economic dislocations, most people will support only minimal changes in their form of government and in the kinds of public policies that government uses to address the nation's problems.

Political socialization also builds support for existing values and attitudes. As the level of support and consensus in views among the people become greater on matters of politics, public debate is constrained and limited. There is no point in debating what everyone (or nearly everyone) believes to be true. As a result, some questions are never seriously discussed. The retention of the present structures of government, election of public officials, and adherence to capitalist as opposed to socialist economic principles are examples of such "nonissues" in American politics.[4] So certain are we of the nation's preferences on such matters that they are virtually never included in political opinion **polls.** As a consequence, political socialization acts as a brake on social change. No change in popular opinion can occur on issues that are not raised, are not debated, and on which the public remains unaware of possible alternatives.

The impact of socialization on ideology appears particularly vulnerable to political events and experiences. Socialization processes normally support the dominant ideology, but political upheavals and economic dislocations can dethrone an orthodox ideology. Before the Great Depression, for instance, most Americans believed the national government should not intervene in the nation's economy. After the economic collapse of the 1930s, many people changed their minds and were willing to accept such intervention. Although many Americans continue to identify themselves as conservatives, few people are willing to dismantle existing programs such as government guarantees of bank deposits, Social Security, federal farm programs, and unemployment benefits. In a very short time, socialization processes can build support for government policies that were considered dangerously radical only a few years earlier.

Political socialization also has a marked impact on political participation (Table 6.1). In the United

Table 6.1
Involvement in Different Forms of Political Participation

Form of Political Participation	Percentage
Vote regularly in presidential elections	72%
Always vote in local elections	47
Active in at least one organization involved in community affairs	32
Worked with others in trying to solve community problems	30
Sought to persuade others to vote as they intended to vote	28
Actively worked for a party or candidates during a campaign	26
Contacted local government officials about some problem or issue	20
Attended at least one political rally or meeting in last three years	19
Contacted national or state officials about an issue or problem	18
Organized a group to try to solve some local community problem	14
Donated money to a candidate or party during an election campaign	13
Presently a member of a political organization or club	8

Source: Sidney Verba and Norman Nie, *Participation In America* (New York: Harper, 1972), p. 31.

States, involvement in political life is directly related to socioeconomic status. Americans who enjoy high socioeconomic status tend to participate more in political affairs than do those with low socioeconomic status. Children of parents from low-income groups undergo a socialization process that places less value on political participation. As a result, many of them do not seek to improve their lot in life through political action. On the other hand, parents with high incomes teach their children the value of political involvement and encourage them from an early age to participate politically. The Kennedy and Rockefeller families are prime examples of this phenomenon.

The impact on American politics of this pattern of political socialization has some disturbing consequences. One-third or more of all adult Americans do not vote, join interest groups, or enlist as an active member of a political party. In effect, one-third of the electorate has disenfranchised itself. **Liberal** critics of American democracy contend that if this one-third were a cross section of the adult population, we might have less cause for concern. But as we have seen, nonparticipants are concentrated near the lower end of the socioeconomic scale. If the health of this nation's form of government is measured by the level of political participation from all socioeconomic strata, some way must be found to improve the socioeconomic status of the less fortunate. Studies from other countries confirm that the political attitudes of the lower socioeconomic strata are strikingly different from the attitudes of middle- and upper-income groups. Oscar Lewis's long-range study of a Mexican family, for example, reveals how the "culture of poverty" instills feelings of fatalism about life and resentment towards all political institutions.[5]

Public Opinion

The goal of socialization is to create a consensus among the people about basic values and beliefs that reflects agreement on the nation's basic political institutions. Absence of such consensus may result in political violence such as riots, civil war, or revolution. In the democratic state, however, it is not the goal of socialization to erase all differences in public opinion. In the United States, for example, great room remains for disagreement and conflict over specific political matters. This conflict in public opinion, based on people's different experiences, backgrounds, and interests, generates the political issues that are the focus of most of our attention in politics. The expression of an opinion is the most basic, widespread, and perhaps the most cherished form of political activity in a democracy. It is important, moreover, because it serves as an important guide to decision makers in making public policy. Many of our political institutions and practices are designed to communicate public opinion to the decision makers. Public opinion can reach governmental officials through a variety of channels: interest group activities such as lobbying, electoral activity in support of a party or a candidate, or in mass demonstrations that voice support for or opposition to public policies.

The Dimensions of Public Opinion

There are three principal characteristics of public opinion: First, public opinion has a certain degree of *stability.* Even over long periods of time, some opinions change very little; opinions contributing to a person's party identification are a prime example.

Figure 6.2
Significant Dimensions of Public Opinion

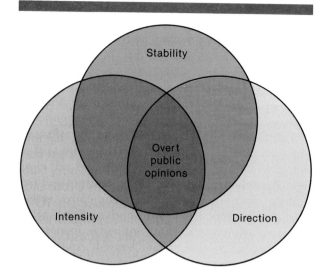

Undeveloped public opinions

As we have seen, still other opinions, such as attitudes about the appropriate kind of economic system, are so basic that people are rarely aware of them. Not surprisingly, such attitudes are the most stable of all.

An opinion may change over time as an individual learns more about a given subject. Many people opposed the recognition of the People's Republic of China before Richard Nixon's historic visit to that country. Since Nixon's visit, public opinion has changed so much that a majority of Americans now favor a closer relationship with China, especially if it will aid the United States in its dealings with the Soviet Union. Public opinion polls also revealed that support for Ronald Reagan's interventionist policies in Central America eroded as the government's covert operations against Nicaragua became more widely known.

The second characteristic is *intensity* of opinion, which refers to how strongly a political opinion is held. If a public issue impinges on an individual's religious beliefs, for example, the political opinions of that person will tend to be more intense. Witness the fervency of opinion of a number of religious groups on the issue of abortion. The intensity of opinion and the likelihood that an opinion will be expressed publicly and acted on politically normally depends on the *salience* of the issue, or the extent to which it is perceived by individuals as directly affecting their life-styles, interests, or deeply held values. The issues that are salient will vary from person to person and even for the same person over time. For example, we worry about the adequacy of Social Security benefits more at sixty-five than at twenty-five.

On many public issues, individuals will not have strong opinions because the issues do not directly affect them or pose any threat to deeply held beliefs. In other instances, certain individuals and groups may be completely unaware of an issue and hold no opinion whatsoever. For example, families on welfare may not know of a struggle to adopt tax provisions that would speed up the depreciation schedule for capital equipment. Occasionally, however, an issue becomes salient for the great majority of the population at the same time. Nearly everyone holds an opinion on such an issue and the level of intensity in public opinion on the issue is inordinately high. Moreover, these opinions are often diverse, even polarized, as opinion on abortion seems to be. Such issues are among the more interesting aspects of politics for the observer, and among the more dangerous aspects of politics for politicians.

Generally speaking, public officials prefer to support public policies that are not the subject of intensely held views. Politicians often see controversial issues as a threat to their reelection, because taking a clear position on the issue is likely to make many ardent political foes as well as generate political support. Because it is such issues that motivate people to vote and tend to determine how they will vote, officeholders are as interested in the intensity of their constituents' views of a public policy issue as in how many express support or opposition to the policy.

The third characteristic of public opinion, *direction,* is simply where a person stands on a particular issue, problem, or policy. By using sophisticated scales, pollsters can ascertain where a person's opinion is located on a continuum between two extremes and in what direction that individual's opinion is likely to move. For example, public opinion on Reagan's tax reform proposals ranged from strong support to vigorous denunciation, with many gradations between.

Political upheavals, economic dislocations, or other sudden changes in the political and economic fortunes of a group can have a dramatic impact on the direction of the group's political attitudes. In the 1930s, the Great Depression altered significantly the direction of the attitudes of many Americans concerning the proper role of the national government in the economy. In more recent times, the failure of the Democrats to reduce inflation and restrain interest rates changed the direction of the attitudes of enough voters to elect Ronald Reagan and a Republican Senate in 1980 and to reelect them in 1984.

Patterns of Public Opinion

On any issue, we may find as many shades of opinion, variations in position, and subtle differences in views as there are opinion holders. Moreover, there is a wide variety of issues that may be related to one another in complex ways. To make sense of something as complex as the "public opinion" of nearly 250 million Americans, we must try to make accurate generalizations about the welter of opinion. Reducing the complex range and variation of public opinion to simpler, more easily understood general categories is one way of "getting a handle" on public opinion. The most commonly used and widely recognized device for categorizing opinions on a variety of issues is the liberal-conservative ideological continuum.

Everyone hears the terms *liberal* and *conservative* used on the television news and in the course of everyday political conversation to describe political personalities and characterize issue positions. President Reagan is described as "conservative" in his desire to cut back social programs, whereas "liberals" in the House of Representatives are seeking to protect programs designed to aid the poor from budget cuts. These terms help us to sort out the political players and label them other than by party. But what do they really mean? What issue positions are associated with each label, and what cluster of opinions is properly considered "conservative" or "liberal." Opinion on these questions is varied as well, but we can offer a couple of guidelines that should help clarify the differences in the two ends of the ideological continuum.

A useful and widely accepted approach to defining *liberal* and *conservative* focuses on the role of government in society. Each view argues for the active use of government in some issue areas and its strict limitation in others. In the area of regulation and direction of the economy, a liberal views government as a positive force for improving the economic well-being of the nation. Thus the liberal tends to support government programs to provide minimum support for the poor, to protect consumers against unfair business practices, to provide health care and retirement income, to improve the health and safety of the workplace, and generally to soften the sharp edges of the free market. By contrast, a conservative places great emphasis on individual initiative and believes it should not be hampered by governmental intervention. The proper role of government is simply to provide the conditions that support the operation of the free market, not to regulate the marketplace. Thus government's role is properly limited to maintaining public order and providing defense and essential economic infrastructural services like highways, education, and a sound currency. In sum, liberals see an active government with extensive involvement as a force for good, whereas conservatives believe that maximum good is achieved by private initiative.

When we turn to moral and social issues, however, we tend to find that the position of the two ideological viewpoints on governmental activity is reversed. It is the liberal who emphasizes individual choice rather than governmental regulation in social and moral matters. For the liberal, the individual, not the state, should determine whether a speech should be heard, a movie viewed, a book read, and what private sexual choices and behavior are appropriate. Conservatives, on the other hand, feel that government should be used to protect traditional moral values. Conservatives tend to support government efforts to maintain the integrity of the traditional family structure and ensure such individual character traits as patriotism and respect for authority, sexual restraint, and religious faith. As a result, conservatives tend to be more willing to use government to restrict the availability of abortion, to forbid the expression of "deviant" sexual preferences, and to use legitimate force (police or national guard, for instance) for the promotion of social order. On matters of social morality, conservatives see the government as a force for good, enforcing the maintenance of cherished values, whereas liberals see government unduly meddling in people's lives, abusing its authority, and posing a threat to cherished individual freedoms and rights.

Table 6.2
Liberal and Conservative Self-identification

Label	Percent* 1980	Percent* 1984
Extremely liberal	2.5	2.3
Liberal	9.3	10.4
Slightly liberal	13.5	12.9
Moderate, middle of the road	30.6	33.4
Slightly conservative	21.0	20.1
Conservative	19.2	18.5
Extremely conservative	3.3	2.3
Haven't thought much about it	33.4	31.1

* Percentages are of those who indicated an ideological identity.
Source: Center For Political Studies, University of Michigan.

The foregoing describes both ends of the liberal-conservative continuum in very general terms. Our next question concerns the distribution of liberal and conservative opinion in the United States. As Table 6.2 reveals, if Americans are simply asked with which ideological label they identify, a greater proportion choose conservative than liberal. The clearest pattern, however, is the tendency of Americans to select moderate labels and to avoid the more extreme labels. More than 65 percent of respondents selected the three central positions, whereas less than 30 percent were willing to accept the straightforward label of liberal or conservative. Significantly, about one-third of the respondents hadn't thought enough about their politics to have an ideological identification.

We can also see the extent to which people actually take liberal or conservative positions on key issues. Figures 6.3 through 6.6 present data collected by the Center for Political Studies (CPS) for four questions likely to clearly divide liberals and conservatives. Taken as a whole, these data suggest that Americans are somewhat more liberal than they are willing to label themselves but that they are neither greatly liberal nor conservative. Figure 6.3 indicates a fairly even distribution of opinion about the desirable extent of government services and spending, with only a slight advantage for the liberal preference for increasing services and spending.

Figures 6.4, 6.5 and 6.6 further suggest the diversity of opinion in the American public. Figure 6.4 indicates Americans still tend to support the

Figure 6.3
Positions of Americans on Government Services vs. Reduced Spending

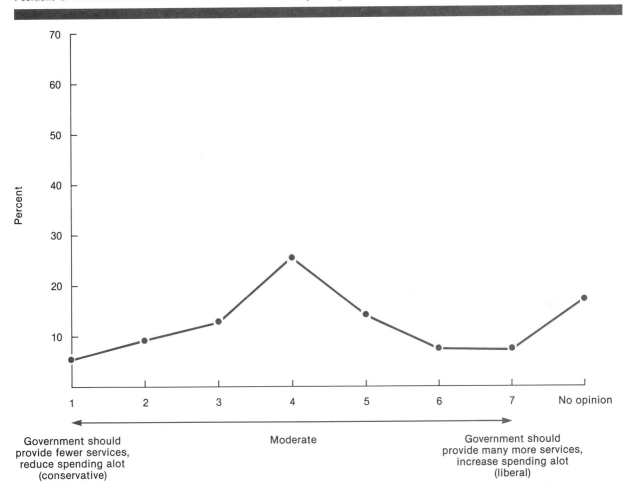

*The question was "Some people think the government should provide fewer services, even in areas such as health and education, in order to reduce spending. Suppose these people are at one end of the scale at point number 1. Other people feel that it is important for the government to continue the services it now provides even if it means no reduction in spending. Suppose these people are at the other end, at point 7. And, of course, some other people have opinions somewhere in between at point 2, 3, 4, 5 or 6. Where would you place yourself on this scale, or haven't you thought much about this?"

Source: Center for Political Studies, University of Michigan.

more liberal, "activist" government role in the area of regulation. A large majority would support the maintenance of environmental regulations, even if it means limiting energy sources. Figure 6.5 shows much less enthusiasm for liberal efforts to have government guarantee jobs and a good standard of living. There is a clear tendency toward the conservative position on this issue. As Figure 6.6 indi-

cates, the liberals have been most successful in winning acceptance for the idea of government jobs to aid the unemployed. People favor increased spending for such jobs (the liberal position) rather than decreased spending (the conservative viewpoint) by a ratio of nearly 4 to 1.

Still another way to look for patterns in American public opinion is to ask *who* tends to take liberal

Figure 6.4
Positions of Americans on Government Environmental Regulation

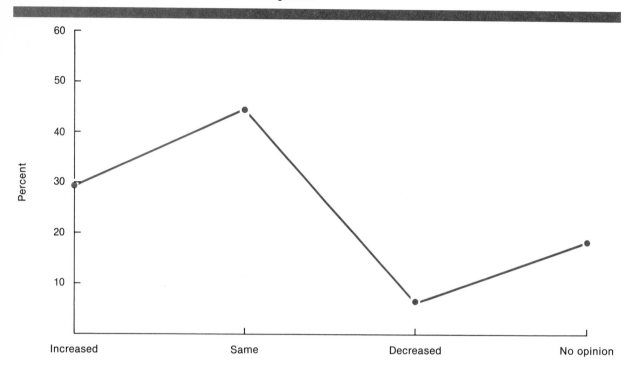

*The question was "Should federal spending on improving and protecting the environment be increased, decreased, or kept about the same?"

or conservative issue positions. Different groups with different backgrounds, experiences, and interests are likely to have distinct liberal or conservative preferences. Factors such as income, education, race, religion, age, and sex contribute to interesting variations in the distribution of political opinion in the United States. It is not surprising that on issues concerning economic regulation and distribution, the lower-income groups tend to be quite liberal, supporting government welfare and consumer protection policies. On noneconomic issues such as civil rights and liberties, the higher-status groups are more liberal. It has been shown that the liberal attitudes of support for minorities and tolerance for diversity are strongly related to educational level. The relative conservatism of lower-status groups on noneconomic matters has less to do with their incomes than with their relative lack of formal education.[6]

Another clear pattern in public opinion in the United States is the consistently greater liberalism

of blacks compared with whites. This racial division of opinion remains intact even when economic and educational variations are held constant for the two groups. Blacks support the larger role of government in the economy and have the liberal concern for fairness and redistribution. On civil rights issues such as tolerance for peaceful protest and civil disobedience, blacks show much more liberal attitudes than do whites.

Religion is also related to variations in public opinion. Historically, Catholics have tended to take liberal positions on most economic issues, perhaps owing to their generally lower average economic status relative to that of Protestants. Until recently, they have been relatively liberal on many social issues as well. One analysis suggests this may be due to their minority status in the United States, making them particularly sensitive to civil liberties issues.[7] In the 1970s and 1980s, with the rise of the abortion issue, Catholics have become somewhat more conservative on social issues generally. Jewish

Figure 6.5
Positions of Americans on Government Guarantee of Jobs

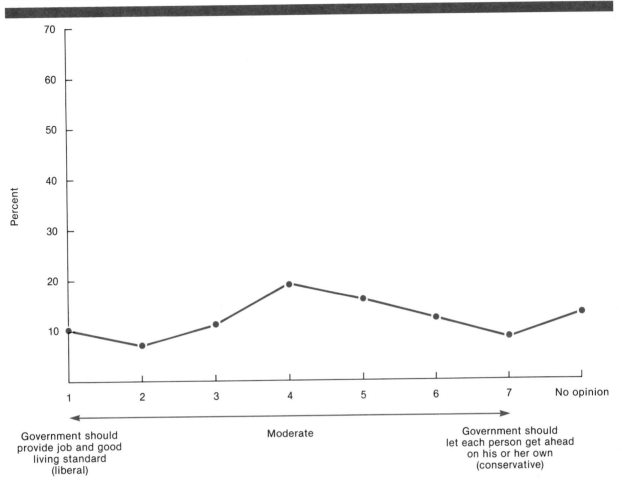

*The question was "Some people feel that the government in Washington should see to it that every person has a job and a good standard of living. Others think that the government should just let every person get ahead on his (or her) own. Where would you place yourself on this scale?"

Source: Center for Political Studies, University of Michigan.

voters are the most liberal religious group in the United States, despite also being the wealthiest religious group. Judaism's stress on social issues and the group's history of persecution have been cited as factors in this orientation.

On a number of issues, differences in opinion are shown to be related to age. We expect that as individuals grow older, they also grow more conservative. On a number of important issues such as foreign aid, the rights of the accused, acceptance of political dissent, racial integration, and the equality of women, the young are indeed significantly more

liberal than older people. But there is little evidence that people actually become more politically conservative as they get older. Although people may dress more conservatively and become more attached to the status quo with age, studies show a strong consistency in opinions over time. The generational difference is due to each new generation's being socialized with somewhat more liberal values than its predecessor. Though the evidence is not clear as yet, this too may be changing. Today's young people seem to be adopting noticeably more conservative views—a trend that may force us to

Figure 6.6
Positions of Americans on Federal Spending for Jobs

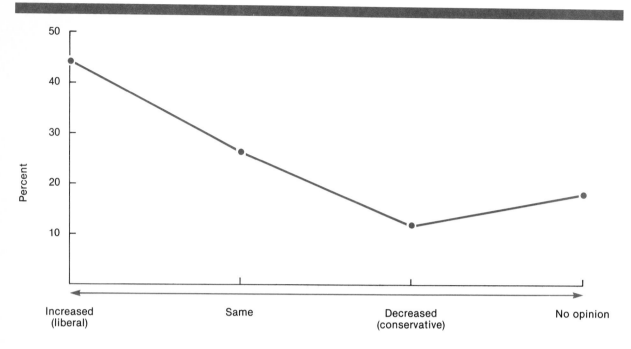

*The question was "Should federal spending on government jobs for the unemployed be, increased, decreased, or kept about the same?"

Source: Center for Political Studies, University of Michigan.

reexamine our conventional expectations if it continues.

Another recent development is the emergence of a distinct difference in the political opinions of men and women. Until recently, the only significant difference in opinion between the sexes had to do with the greater reluctance of women to favor the use of force. Women were more opposed to the Vietnam war and have been more in favor of arms control and more likely to support nuclear disarmament talks and proposals for a nuclear freeze. These differences still exist, but have been supplemented by a host of opinions on other economic and social issues. The source of this change has been in the attitudes of women less than forty-five years of age. They are more liberal than young men and more liberal than older women as well. The greater participation of young women in the labor force may account for this change. This increase in participation has been largely at the lower levels of the work hierarchy and has often included subtle and not-so-subtle forms of discrimination. Consequent-

ly, young women tended to support the Equal Rights Amendment, whereas a majority of older women were opposed. They have also adopted more liberal positions on such issues as equal employment opportunity and abortion rights.

With their more liberal orientation, women have been among the least supportive and most critical of President Reagan (Table 6.3), a development that was dubbed the "gender gap" during the 1982 elections.[8] (Table 6.4 shows how the gender gap has developed since 1976 and its impact on the 1984 presidential race.) The various polls differ somewhat, but indicate a gender gap of from 4 to 9 percentage points. The effect was even greater in some states' senate and gubernatorial races. Unlike the presidential race, in which majorities of both men and women voted for the same candidate, in several state races the sexes voted in majorities for opposing candidates.

Whether these recent developments portend a permanent division between the sexes probably depends on the positions taken by the Republican

Table 6.3
Differing Views of Men and Women on Major Issues*

	Women, aged 18–44	Men, aged 18–44	All Women	All Men	Men and Women
Those approving Reagan's job performance	44%	54%	41%	50%	45%
Those fearing Reagan will get U.S. into war	57	42	52	38	46
Which party is best on unemployment:					
Republicans	21	30	19	26	22
Democrats	51	46	54	50	51
Which party is best on inflation:					
Republicans	32	44	29	42	35
Democrats	39	29	37	31	34
Which party is best on Social Security:					
Republicans	21	35	22	31	26
Democrats	55	46	54	49	52
Which party is best on defense:					
Republicans	32	46	29	41	35
Democrats	41	29	37	30	33

* Responses to the first two questions represent combined percentages from polls conducted in January, March, and May; results for the third and fourth questions are combined from January and May polls; all others are from individual polls.

Source: *The New York Times*, June 1982. © 1982 by The New York Times Company. Reprinted by permission.

party in the post-Reagan years. The development of the gender gap coincides with the Republican party's withdrawal of support for passage of the Equal Rights Amendment in 1980 and the increasing influence of "prolife" forces within the party, culminating in a 1984 platform plank advocating total prohibition of abortion. The party's increasing conservatism has also made it even less willing than in the past to seek legislative or judicial relief for discrimination against women in hiring and pay rates. With women increasingly involved in the working world, many as heads of households, it seems likely that the gender gap will remain as long as the Republicans maintain these issue positions.

The Measurement of Public Opinion

Since the polls called the 1948 presidential election in favor of Thomas E. Dewey rather than the actual

winner, Harry S. Truman, the measurement of public opinion has grown increasingly sophisticated.[9] Professional pollsters, political scientists, and other social scientists now have methods that can reduce the margin of error in opinion polls to a range of less than 5 percent. Such methods ensure that a sample (a subset of the entire population) is representative of the whole population. Because of its reliability, the **random sample,** also known as a probability sample, is perhaps the most widely used. A random sample is one where every person has an equal chance to be included in the sample. If a random sample is properly drawn, only a relatively small number of people need to be interviewed to produce accurate results. In the United States, with a population of approximately 240 million, for example, a properly drawn random sample of only 1,500 individuals will provide results accurate to within a range of plus or minus 3 percentage points.

Because the attributes, or variables, that influence public opinion are uncertain, public opinion polls must be carefully constructed. The wording of the questions is particularly important in ensuring accuracy. Pollsters seek to phrase their queries in such a way that the questions are clear, do not employ emotionally loaded language, and are neutral with regard to possible responses. To eliminate the possibility of unreliable or biased results, pollsters may pretest questions on a portion of the sample they intend to poll before carrying out the poll

Table 6.4
The Emergence of the Gender Gap

		Reagan-Bush	Mondale-Ferraro	
1984 CBS News/New York Times	Men	61	39	

		Reagan	Carter	Anderson
1980 CBS News/New York Times	Men	54	37	7
	Women	46	45	7

		Ford	Carter
1976 CBS News/New York Times	Men	48	50
	Women	48	50

WHAT IS THE PUNISHMENT FOR NONRANDOM POLLING?

The punishment for nonrandom polling is usually not very severe. Many people have fun conducting nonrandom polls, especially during presidential election years. Some movie theaters have taken to selling blue (Republican) and red (Democratic) tickets and keeping track over a period of weeks which party's candidate is ahead. Newspapers may take straw polls of the citizens passing by on a street corner, or a radio station may do a phone-in poll to stimulate conversation and perhaps listener interest and ratings. In each case, the poll is really just a promotion gimmick that the organization takes care to identify as an unofficial or nonscientific poll.

One of the reasons unofficial pollsters make such disclaimers and hazard no predictions based on their polls may be recollection of what happened to the *Literary Digest*. The *Literary Digest* was a popular magazine that decided, in part to promote magazine sales, to conduct a poll before the 1936 presidential election. The poll surveyed a huge number of people (nearly 2.5 million) drawn from lists of telephone and automobile owners. Of course, if the sample is nonrandom and unrepresentative, the results will remain inaccurate no matter how many people surveyed. It isn't surprising that surveying only people who owned cars and telephones in the midst of a depression in 1936, would produce a decidedly upper-class bias in the poll. But apparently the people at the *Literary Digest* did not sufficiently appreciate that fact. With its dramatic overrepresentation of the relatively well-to-do, their poll led them to predict that Alf Landon, the Republican candidate, would not only unseat President Franklin D. Roosevelt but would do so in a crushing landslide. They were right about the landslide in 1936, but it went in favor of Roosevelt rather than Landon, and the magazine's public humiliation was followed shortly by its complete demise. In this case, the punishment for unsophisticated polling methods was severe indeed.

interviewer gets: mood of the interviewee, time of day, and the manner, linguistic ability, and appearance of the interviewer. To enhance the accuracy of their polls, the larger polling organizations have developed a cadre of trained professional interviewers that gives them and their clients greater confidence in the results of their polls.

As the reliability and accuracy of polls have increased, ever-larger numbers of politicians have used public opinion polls as a tool to plan overall campaign strategy and tactics. If polls reveal a candidate is doing well in a certain area or on a particular set of issues, he or she can allocate campaign resources accordingly. The use of polls is by no means restricted to electoral politics. Even in nonelection years, politicians use polls in an effort to reduce the uncertainty surrounding potentially explosive issues, divisive problems, or controversial policies. A wide range of interest groups also use polls to assess popular attitudes on particular issues.

Opinion sampling is not only here to stay but also, with the development of ever more sophisti-

VIETOR'S **FUNNY BUSINESS**

OPINION POLL INC.

VIETOR

"Thank you for seeing me. Would you mind answering a few loaded questions?"

on a random sample drawn from the entire population.

In addition to the wording of questions, the interviewers themselves can influence poll results. Any number of factors can affect the responses an

GEORGE GALLUP (1901–1984) AND PUBLIC OPINION POLLING

Perhaps no other person is so closely identified with public opinion polling as George Gallup. For years, the Gallup poll was easily the most respected poll in American politics. His clients ranged across a broad spectrum: academic social researchers, including political scientists; the news media; various political groups; political parties; candidates for public office; and private individuals. It is not too much of an exaggeration to say that he founded a whole new industry.

So pervasive are polls today that it is difficult to imagine the political scene without them. Yet public opinion polling is little more than a half-century old. Indeed, 1986 marked the fiftieth anniversary of Gallup's founding of the American Institute of Public Opinion. His organization was among the first to apply in a rigorous

fashion market research techniques to the study of public opinion. Gallup's venture succeeded in part because he very quickly established a reputation for reliability and predictability.

Gallup's entry into public opinion polling came only after he had

earned a doctorate in journalism in 1928. He worked for a short while as a reporter, but soon joined a market research firm. While honing his market research skills, Gallup's interest in the political aspects of polling began to grow. Soon he was applying the techniques he had learned to political campaigns. The rest, as the saying goes, is history.

In later life, Gallup began to devote more attention to Gallup-International, which did business in more than fifty countries. As he had in the United States, Gallup introduced public opinion polling in some of them. Gallup's reputation earned him the esteem and the respect of his clients. When he died in 1984, he left behind a flourishing industry and a generation of politicians who would feel handicapped if they did not have their own pollster.

---

cated technology, will almost certainly become less expensive and still more commonplace. One recent technological advance that has had this effect is random digit dialing (RDD). No longer is surveying done by a person going door to door. With RDD, calls are made on a random basis to phone numbers within a neighborhood or area code. Polls taken through the use of RDD cost only about 20 percent as much as those using the old-fashioned, shoe leather method, and bring opinion polls within the budgets of candidates for even minor offices.

Public Opinion as a Guide for Public Policy Making

With public opinion polls becoming more common and more reliable, the role of public opinion as a

decision-making guide for public officials is an increasingly important question. Government by public opinion is an alluring notion to those wishing to maximize the democratic character of the nation's government. Moreover, we seem to be technologically capable of a form of direct democracy through the use of two-way cable television systems such as the "Qube" system already available in several cities. With the use of satellite communication technology, people could vote on even national issues from their living rooms. The question is no longer can we, but should we, use polls or some form of electronic democracy to have government by public opinion.

This notion, though it may be attractive at first glance, has problems that should give us pause. First is the quantity and quality of the information

Table 6.5
Political Knowledge of Fundamental Political Facts

Question	Percentage Responding Correctly
Name the current vice president.	79%
Name the current secretary of state.	34
Name one senator from your state.	59
How many senators represent each state?	52
How many years in a U.S. representative's term?	30
Which party has the most members in the House?	69

Source: National Opinion Research Center (Chicago, 1978).

on which public political opinion is based. Does the general citizenry have access to the information it needs to develop informed opinions and rational policy choices? Further, if it could be made readily available, would the general citizenry avail itself of such information? Existing evidence strongly suggests it might not. Even on matters where information is readily available, most citizens are relatively uninformed Table 6.5.[10] The increasingly complex, specialized nature of much information further removes it from the understanding of the mass of people.

Unfortunately, ignorance has never been a strong deterrent to the expression of an opinion or the casting of a ballot. If much public opinion is likely to be based on little or no relevant information, it is questionable if government by public opinion would serve the interests of the people. This raises the question whether government should serve the people's interests or simply reflect their preferences. The two are not always the same, especially in a world of imperfect information. In short, on complex matters of public policy it can be expected that people do not always know what is good for them. For example, they may favor cuts in taxation but oppose cuts in beneficial spending programs, leading to a spiraling budget deficit not in their long-term interest.

Citizens are often well informed on highly salient, close-to-home, or close-to-the-pocketbook issues such as racial integration of schools through busing or tax increases to finance public works. A broader defense of government by public opinion argues that even uninformed opinion is important.

Broad support or opposition to a policy, even if the details of the policy are not well understood, indicates its likely acceptance and therefore its likely success or failure. This view casts citizens in the role of political consumers who, like most buyers of automobiles, for example, may not fully understand how something works but nonetheless know what they like.

Granted that government in a democracy cannot be insensitive to public opinion, important reasons remain why government should not act solely on public opinion. First, government by majority public opinion would require a fundamental change in the Constitution and its provision for separation of powers and checks and balances designed to prevent simple majorities from deciding policy. Majority public opinion as a governing principle implies entirely different institutions of government. Is there any use for the Supreme Court, for example, in such a system?

Second, can we trust public opinion to protect our most basic political freedoms? Though supportive of such rights as freedom of speech, press, religion, and association when stated as abstractions, polls have consistently shown a lack of support for such principles among the public when applied to specific cases. As Table 6.6 indicates, though the public is apparently becoming more tolerant in recent years, a substantial proportion of the public

POLITICAL LITERACY

Despite the availability of nearly inescapable media, a startling proportion of Americans cannot name their congressional representative or two United States Senators. The Greek word for political illiterate was "idios," meaning an individual who takes no interest in or has no knowledge of public affairs. It would not even be fair to say that such a person has simply been turned off by politics, since being turned off assumes a sufficient amount of information about politics to be disgusted with it. Nor should we assume that political illiterates are either stupid or uneducated. Most are neither. Rather, they have long considered politics to be outside their interests. Probably a good number regard politics as beneath their interests.

Table 6.6
Support for Freedom of Expression

	Percent Tolerant		
	1954	1977	1982
Willing to allow a speech by:			
Atheist	37%	62%	65%
Socialist	59	—	—
Communist	27	56	58
Racist	—	59	61
Militarist	—	51	61
Homosexual	—	62	68
Willing to allow to teach in college:			
Atheist	12	39	47
Socialist	33	—	—
Communist	6	39	46
Racist	—	41	44
Militarist	—	34	—
Homosexual	—	49	57

Source: Michael Corbett, *Political Tolerance in America* (New York: Longman's 1982), p. 36.

continues to be quite willing to revoke such rights for unpopular political and religious groups in specific situations.[11]

Third, as we have noted, the results of a poll depend on the alternatives the respondent is given. How the issue is framed, even the order in which choices are presented, is important to the outcome. For example, if a poll asks simply whether the public approves or disapproves of a president's performance in office, it is likely to get a different set of results than if it asks how people feel about specific presidential actions and programs. Thus no matter how "scientific" the polls or how sophisticated our electronic communications technology, the process will remain subject to inaccuracies in representing the preferences of the people. Worse, the process will also remain subject to subtle manipulation by unscrupulous polltakers who might engage in intentional deception.[12]

Finally, we must ask who would gain in power under a government fully controlled by public opinion? Those who support strengthening the role of public opinion in government often expect it will dilute or eliminate the political power of those who presently wield it. These are usually envisioned as a small elite ruling in their self-interest rather than that of the people. Expanding the role of public

opinion might well weaken the elite, but political power when reduced or eliminated in one place often just ends up somewhere else. In a government controlled by public opinion, it seems likely that power would tend to accumulate in the hands of those whose business is communicating information, packaging ideas, and measuring opinion. People in the mass media (especially television), people skilled in advertising and public relations, and the polling experts themselves would likely become the new political elite, able to determine what issues will be on the public's mind and to shape what it thinks about them. Worse, none of these new elites would be elected power holders, accountable to the people. Is democracy really served under such circumstances?

We have substantial evidence that, with some notable exceptions such as U.S. involvement in Vietnam, public health assistance, and gun control[13], government responds to public opinion most of the time.[14] Moreover, on questions concerning the nature of the political and economic system, the socialization process clearly has been successful, both citizenry and those in positions of political power sharing a consensus. This suggests that our electoral process, though more indirect than government by public opinion, works to make government reason-

"Do you realize that choice puts you in the 2% lunatic fringe?"

From the Wall Street Journal—Permission, Cartoon Features Syndicate

ably, if imperfectly, responsive. How do citizens participate in this process?

Electoral Behavior

In the United States as well as in other Western democracies, voting is one of the most basic forms of political participation. But voter participation rates have been rather low in the United States compared with other democracies (Table 6.8), and since 1960 participation in elections has fallen still further. In the late 1800s, 80 percent or more of the citizens eligible to vote in elections did so. By 1924, the percentage participating even in presidential elections had dropped to around 50 percent. Since then, participation has remained fairly steady,

Table 6.7
Percentage of Voter Turnout in Selected Democracies, 1945–1979

Rank Order	Country	Number of Elections	Average Turnout in elections	Compulsory Voting
1	Australia	14	95.4%	Yes
2	Netherlands [a]	10	94.7	Yes then No
3	Austria	10	94.2	3 provinces
4	Italy	9	92.6	Almost
5	Belgium	12	92.5	Yes
6	New Zealand	12	90.4	No
7	West Germany	8	86.9	No
8	Denmark	14	85.8	No
9	Sweden	10	84.9	No
10	Israel	9	81.4	No
11	Norway	9	80.8	No
12	France	11	79.3	No
13	Finland	10	79.0	No
14	United Kingdom	11	76.9	No
15	Canada	12	76.4	No
16	Ireland	9	74.7	No
17	Japan	13	73.1	No
18	Switzerland	8	64.5	Mostly No
19	India	6	58.7	No
20	United States [b]	8	58.5	No

a Had compulsory voting 1946–67, did not after 1967

b Presidential elections only

Source: Ivor Crewe, "Electoral Participation," in David Butler, Howard R. Penniman, and Austin Ranney, eds., *Democracy at the Polls* (Washington, D.C.: American Enterprise Institute, 1980), Table 10–5, pp. 254–255.

reaching a peak in the 1960 presidential election of 63 percent and dropping to about 53 percent in 1984. If voting is so important, why do so many people choose to stay away from the polls and why is nonparticipation increasing?

Why Many Do Not Vote

Many factors contribute to nonparticipation in American elections, some of which also help to explain why the phenomenon is worsening. First is the makeup of the electorate. We have made the ballot available to more and more groups throughout the twentieth century: women in the 1920s, blacks and other minorities in the 1960s, and younger people in the early 1970s. New groups tend to participate at lower rates than longer-established voters. As a result, average rates of participation have dropped. Though women now vote as frequently as men do, participation rates for minorities and young people remain well below average.

Why do young people and minorities participate far less than others in the political process? One answer for the young is that at their stage in life they are simply more interested in other aspects of life, such as choosing mates and getting started in jobs and careers. They also are often highly mobile with few roots in or ties to their communities. In the case of minorities, the most important factor explaining lower participation levels is socioeconomic status. Political participation appears to be a class-biased activity. Those with higher incomes and education levels are substantially more likely to vote than people lacking these attributes. The most important reason that blacks and Hispanics are underrepresented among voters is that they tend to occupy a lower socioeconomic status. Indeed, blacks and other minorities with high levels of income and education actually vote in higher proportions than high-status whites.[15]

People who vote have a stronger sense of civic duty and political efficacy, both of which are associated with increasing levels of education and income. Civic obligation is the notion that voting is part of being a good citizen. **Political efficacy** is a feeling that one can influence political events. People lacking political efficacy perceive politics as entirely beyond their control; they feel powerless to affect political events and conditions that shape their lives. Moreover, these feelings are likely to be passed on to children through the family in the socialization process. People of lower economic status are particularly likely to be lacking in political efficacy and thus see little reason to participate in elections.[16]

Both logical and legal reasons also account for much of the tendency to stay at home on election day in America. When is it logical not to vote? Here is one example. In the presidential election of 1984, some 92 million people cast ballots, and one candidate won by nearly 14 million votes. This was an outcome that anyone who had been paying any attention at all to the media would have been sure of weeks in advance. Obviously, your chance of affecting such an outcome is, to say the least, not very great. To say the most, under such circumstances voting is a highly irrational act. After all, voting has its costs. You have to spend time and effort to register and to go to the polls, and besides, where you live the weather may not be too great in November. Maybe it makes sense not to vote.

Political scientist Anthony Downs argues that rational people will vote only under certain conditions. First, they must see important policy differences between the parties and their candidates. If they feel the parties offer no real choice or that their differences are unimportant, it is rational not to vote. It seems likely such indifference is an important source of nonvoting in the United States. Second, they must see the direct impact of political decisions on their lives. Government employees, for example, are one group likely to have a high stake in electoral outcomes. For some, their jobs depend on the outcome of elections, but for nearly all, the future of the programs and agencies in which they work will be affected by who wins elective office. Not surprisingly, more than three-fourths of government workers regularly go to the polls.

Third, people are far more likely to be moved to vote if the election is a competitive one in which it can be more credibly said that every vote counts. Our system of elections does little to promote such conditions. For example, under the electoral college winner-take-all system, the losing presidential candidate in any state receives no electoral votes. The votes for this candidate are, in effect, thrown out. Also, in many states, the local outcome is a virtual certainty, reducing the reason for the weaker candidates' supporters to bother to vote, even if the race

is competitive nationwide. The impact of low levels of competition is even greater on state and local races. A Democrat in a largely Republican state or district has little reason to bother to vote.[17]

Finally, a rational person might still vote even if none of these conditions are met. If someone truly feels that voting is a civic duty—a responsibility of citizenship in a democratic political community—then avoiding the guilt that would attend nonvoting would in itself make voting logically worth its costs.

If the decision to vote is a logical and rational matter subject to a calculation of costs and benefits, as Downs would suggest, then one way to increase voting would be to reduce its costs. We have erected several legal barriers to voting that have the opposite effect. Most important among these are registration requirements. Specific requirements vary from state to state, but typically they call for the prospective voter to go to the local registration office at least thirty days before the elections and show proof that he or she meets residency and other requirements. In the United States, knowing the requirements and getting registered is entirely the responsibility of the individual. In Great Britain and Canada, the government actively seeks to register citizens by conducting house-to-house enumerations. As indicated in Table 6.7, election turnout in these countries is substantially higher.

Getting registered will not stop highly motivated voters, but for those with only a slight interest in the election or who find contact with any government bureaucracy distasteful or whose poverty makes the material costs of such efforts prohibitive, it may well make the difference. According to a Gallup poll conducted after the 1984 election, 31 percent of nonvoters gave not being registered as the reason. Few states even make an effort to reduce the costs of registration by making it convenient for working citizens. Registration places are often closed evenings and weekends when most workers are free. Closing registration a month before the election is also inconvenient and confusing for the prospective voter and, in this computerized age, is no longer necessary. States that allow citizens to register up to the day of the election (Minnesota, Wisconsin, Maine, and Oregon) tend to have substantially higher voting levels than the rest of the nation. Studies show clearly that once registered, people tend to vote—even those in low

Uncrowded polling places such as this one in New York's upper west side are too common in America on election days.

turnout categories. In 1984, 87.7 percent of all those registered, 79.4 percent of registered young people eighteen to twenty-four years old, and 79 percent of those registered with less than eight years of education voted.

We also have made the act of voting more difficult than it need be. The date of national elections is constitutionally mandated, but it is a barrier to participation. We vote on a weekday, and election day is not considered an occasion for a holiday from normal work activities. As a result, hourly wage earners must either rise early to vote or stop at the polling place after a tiring day at work. These are the busiest times at the polls, often requiring a wait in line to cast one's ballot. Polling places are often small with insufficient room inside to wait, so the voter must stand outside at a time of year when the weather is far from comfortable in much of the nation. Is it any wonder that under such conditions many people would find the costs too high and

decide, "Well, my vote won't make the difference anyway"? In comparing U.S. turnout with those of other countries, we should remember that most of those nations hold elections on weekends when all are equally free to participate.

How We Vote

Once an individual has decided to vote rather than stay at home, he or she is still faced with the decision of *how* to vote. Many factors influence an individual's political behavior, but when it comes to casting a vote, political scientists have identified three factors of primary importance: the voter's party affiliation, the voter's evaluation of the candidate's character and personality, and the extent to which the voter perceives the candidate's issue positions as similar to his or her own.[18]

Most voters have a long-held identification with one of the major political parties. For most, party identification is acquired early in life from parents in the socialization process, in much the same manner as we acquire other basic identities such as nationality and religious affiliation. As a result, we often have developed a loyalty to the Republican or Democratic party before we understand any issues or know where our party stands on them.

Early party identification and loyalty suggest that party affiliation may help to shape our perceptions of issues and candidates rather than the other way around. Since most of us do not sit down and analyze politics before we acquire a party loyalty, it seems probable that our loyalty colors our evaluation of political issues and personalities when we first encounter them. Party affiliation, along with parental values, thus acts as a guide to tell us what our positions should be and who we should most admire in politics. In time, we forget the order in which our political orientations were acquired and feel that we identify with a party because it basically agrees with our views.[19]

Such perceptual biases tend to be self-reinforcing and are strong motivators for people to vote for the candidates of their own party. Even in the landslide election of 1984, during which the Republicans made an overt and well-funded effort to lure Democrats away from their party, fully 73 percent of Democratic identifiers voted for Walter Mondale.[20] Party affiliation is difficult to abandon, and people rarely make a permanent switch in parties.

Nonetheless, the importance of party as a guide to voting choice has been weakening in recent years, largely because deeply felt affiliation to party has itself been on the wane. Since the early 1970s, young first-time voters have been less willing to identify firmly with either party. By the early 1980s, these independents had surpassed the Republicans to become the second largest "party" in terms of identification, claiming more than 35 percent of the electorate. The weakening of party ties in the electorate has been accompanied by an increase in **split-ticket voting** in which the voter casts ballots for candidates of both parties for different offices. Though recent studies suggest that party remains the single most important determinant of voting choice in most elections, clearly factors other than party identification are at work.[21]

The electorate's attitudes about the candidates also influence voting behavior. Among voters with weak party identification, such attitudes become a powerful predictor of voting behavior. Candidates for public office, regardless of their position on issues, seek to project an image or style that transcends party lines—an image of trustworthiness, decisiveness, confidence, command, and ability to lead. Of these, the quality of leadership seems to be most important and least easily created. Some personalities, like John F. Kennedy and Ronald Reagan, project it, and others, like Lyndon Johnson and Walter Mondale, do not.

Other presidential candidates have nurtured other sorts of images with varying degrees of success. In the 1950s, Dwight Eisenhower was the classic example of the candidate whose appeal reached well beyond his own party. He ran in 1952 as a military hero who was trustworthy and in command and left the presidency with a superimposed image of the kindly and fatherly statesman. In the 1976 elections, Jimmy Carter attempted to project an image of honesty ("I will never lie to you"), and though generally viewed as a weak leader, he was still perceived as an honest man when he left in 1980. In the 1984 Democratic presidential primaries, Gary Hart argued that he, not Walter Mondale, possessed the personal characteristics that could attract voters outside the Democratic party. But he developed image problems of his own concerning honesty, trustworthiness, and stability when it was revealed that he had changed his name and possibly fudged the truth about his age. In 1980 and 1984, Ronald Reagan certainly attracted voters beyond traditional Republican constituencies, owing in large part to his cultivation of an image as a sincere, trustworthy, "nice" person. With the increased importance of television in electoral campaigns and generally weaker party affiliation among voters, it seems likely that candidates' personal characteristics will become still more important to how people vote and that candidates will be encouraged to focus less on issues—the third factor that influences voter choice.

If people engage in issue voting, they are selecting candidates who most nearly match their own issue preferences. This is perhaps the most logical and defensible basis for voting. It gets a substantial amount of attention from the media in their attempt to explain the outcome of the vote. But the extent to which the American people actually engage in issue voting is a matter of some debate.

People who have selected a candidate largely on the basis of personal attractiveness or party affiliation may justify the choice in terms of issue positions. Also, a voter may prefer one candidate on some issues and the other candidate on other issues. When the voter makes a choice, have issues made the difference or has the determining factor had more to do with party affiliation or personality?

Issue voting is probably not as common as the media and campaign rhetoric might suggest, because it demands a lot of the voter. To have engaged in issue voting, the voter must, at minimum, (1) have an opinion on a current political issue, (2) have an accurate idea of where the candidates stand on the issue, (3) perceive a difference between the candidates on the issue, and (4) vote for the candidate whose position is most similar to his or her own. Abramson, Aldrich, and Rohde attempted to determine whether people satisfied these conditions during the 1980 presidential election.[22] They found that although the great majority of people had an opinion on key election issues, less than half of these knew where each candidate stood on them. For example, 83 percent had an opinion on the issue of cutting government spending, but only 48 percent knew that Reagan rather than Carter favored spending cuts. Further, those that did know where the candidates stood on the issues didn't always vote for the one most in agreement with their own stand. On two issues, government spending and welfare aid, people voted their issue position; but on others, specifically women's rights and abortion, there was no relationship between a person's issue opinions and choice of candidates. In sum, issue voting is clearly more important than it was twenty or thirty years ago, as is evidenced by the rise of numerous single-issue-oriented groups. But issue voting remains less important to candidate choice in the United States than either party identification or the candidate's personal characteristics.[23]

Conclusion

Political socialization is a complex process. Political culture, education and economic status of family members, racial and ethnic characteristics of the so-ciety, and openness of the political system are all factors that shape an individual's socialization and influence that person's inclination to participate in politics. The political socialization process can build support for existing values and the existing form of government. Socialization, however, is vulnerable to political upheavals and economic dislocations. During less tumultuous periods, individuals enjoying a high socio-economic status recognize the value of political participation, whereas persons with a low socio-economic status tend to be alienated from the political system.

The principal forms of political participation are the expression of political opinions, membership in interest groups and political parties, and activities surrounding the electoral process, especially voting. Political scientists and politicians alike are interested in the characteristics of public opinion, how such opinion develops and changes, how the media affect popular attitudes and opinions, and what techniques can most accurately measure public opinion. The impact of public opinion polls and the influence of the media on campaigns and elections and on the success or failure of public policies ensure that professional pollsters and political commentators have a secure future.

Despite the importance of political participation and the ubiquitous presence of polls and media coverage, many people do not involve themselves in any form of political activity. Alienation, apathy, other interests, and the legal structure of our elections are among the factors that account for the relatively low voter participation over the last several decades. For those who do vote, party identification remains the single best predictor of voting behavior, though voters' attitudes toward the candidates' personal characteristics and positions on the issues have become more important in recent years.

Elections continue to offer the citizenry the opportunity to express their opinions and meaningfully engage in democratic self-rule. But the electoral process has become the center of important contemporary controversies. The escalating costs of political campaigns and the increasing influence of the mass media are two important concerns that we address in Chapter 7.

 ## Glossary

Conservative A political ideology characterized by belief in a gradual approach to change and traditional social values and institutions and opposes government involvement in the economy or regulation of business or a person holding such beliefs.

Great Depression In modern times, the worst economic upheaval in the West. The United States in the early 1930s suffered nearly 25 percent unemployment.

Ideology A set of political and social ideas that are both structured (limited) and coherent (fit together logically).

Liberal A political ideology characterized by belief in strong protections for civil liberties and positive government action to remedy economic problems and injustices, or a person holding such beliefs.

Political culture Broadly shared ideas, values, and attitudes about the role of government and politics in society and in the nation's economy.

Political efficacy A feeling or belief that one has power in the political system, that one's views and actions count.

Political socialization The process through which political identities and preferences are acquired.

Poll A systematic effort by political scientists and professional pollsters to measure public opinion and to forecast election results.

Random sample A selection of people to be polled from a large group in such a manner that all have an equal chance of being selected. A truly random sample should be an accurate representation of the whole group.

Split-ticket voting Casting a vote for candidates of more than one party on a single ballot; for example, voting for a Republican for president and a Democrat for a Senate seat.

Totalitarian state A state in which all means of communication and production are controlled and monopolized by the government.

 ## Suggestions for Further Reading

Abramson, Paul. *Generational Change in American Politics.* Lexington, Mass.: Lexington Books, 1975. Interesting analysis of the changes in attitudes and values across generations.

Altschuler, Bruce E. *Keeping a Finger on the Public Pulse: Private Polling and Presidential Elections.* Westport, Conn.: Greenwood, 1982. Takes a close look at the role of polls in presidential campaigns beginning in 1968.

Asher, Herbert. *Presidential Elections and American Politics.* Rev. ed. Homewood, Ill.: Dorsey, 1980. Examines the factors that influence voting behavior and explores the reasons for changes in voting patterns.

Corbett, Michael. *Political Tolerance in America.* New York: Longman's, 1982. A good recent study of the attitudes of Americans toward basic political rights and the expression of diverse life-styles.

Erikson, Robert S. and Norman R. Luttbeg. *American Public Opinion: Its Origins, Content, and Impact.* New York: Wiley, 1973. Careful study of this complex subject that explores how public opinion influences the policy process.

Gallup, George. *The Sophisticated Poll Watcher's Guide.* Princeton: N.J.: Princeton University Press, 1972. A leading pollster talks about such issues as the accuracy of polls and their use in forecasting elections.

Greenstein, Fred I. *Children and Politics.* New Haven, Conn.: Yale University Press, 1965. Important study of the development and expression of political attitudes among children.

Hess, R.D., and J.V. Torney. *The Development of Attitudes in Children.* Chicago: Aldine, 1967. A classic introduction to the basic issues involved in political socialization.

Milbrath, Lester W. and M.L. Goel. *Political Participation,* 2d ed. Chicago: Rand McNally, 1977. Useful summary of a number of studies that explore why and how people participate in politics.

Parkes, Henry Bamford. *The American Experience: An Interpretation of the History and Civilization of the American People.* New York: Random House, 1959. A brilliant analysis of the origins and development of the enduring characteristics of American political culture.

Weissberg, Robert. *Political Learning, Political Choice, and Democratic Citizenship.* Englewood Cliffs, N.J.: Prentice-Hall, 1974. Good introduction to the exceedingly complex process of political socialization.

Wheeler, Michael. *Lies, Damn Lies, and Statistics.* New York: Liveright, 1976. A lively account of the uses and misuses of quantitative data and public opinion polls.

Chapter 7

The Electoral Process: Elections, Campaigns, and the Media

Chapter Outline

Introduction
The Structure of Elections
Election Trends and Prospects
Campaigns and The Media
Conclusion

Introduction

Elections give the citizenry opportunities to engage in democratic self-rule. By voting, individuals can demonstrate their support for, or opposition to, the current officeholders and their policies. Competitive parties make it possible for voters to choose whether to retain a party in power. In Great Britain, the people chose the Conservative party in May 1979 and again in June 1983 as the party to lead the nation to economic recovery. By contrast, French voters chose the Socialist party to restore the health of the nation's economy. Even nondemocratic governments recognize the symbolic value of elections. In elections in communist countries, where there is no opposition to the Communist party's candidates, the people are still required to vote. Communist leaders see voting as a way to lend legitimacy to their regime and their policies.

Campaigns and elections are also important because they enhance the level of political participation by engaging individuals and groups in the discussion of political issues. Such discussion can influence elected officials and have an impact on the kinds of public policies enacted. In the absence of competition for public office, the electorate has no opportunity to choose among alternative allocations of the nation's resources. Without competing political parties, elected officials cannot accurately assess the public's reaction to governmental policies. In extreme cases, the suppression of political dissent may lead to violence and instability. The assassination of President Anwar Sadat in October 1981 has been attributed in part to his refusal to permit the representation of certain religious groups in the Egyptian parliament.

Elections are one of the least disruptive ways of deciding who will govern and for how long. In democracies, elections are a substitute for the revolutions and power struggles that wrack nondemocratic regimes. Periodic elections, when combined with competitive political parties, provide a peaceful, legal, and routine means of either legitimating the party in office or transferring power to another party. Countries that lack these features frequently experience power struggles whenever one group of leaders replaces another. Only after the power struggle is completed and the new regime is firmly in control do the leaders agree to hold elections.

This chapter first discusses the major features of the U.S. system of elections and their implications for political outcomes. We also take a brief look at recent electoral trends and their possible implications for the future. Then we examine two of the most important issues surrounding the contemporary campaign process—money and its impact on the electoral process and the "packaging" of candidates. Finally, we turn our attention to the media, its role in politics and its impact on the electoral process.

The Structure of Elections

Elections can be organized in many ways, and every electoral system has built-in biases that shape the nature of the competition and affect the electoral outcome. The American electoral process is no different in this respect. In pointing out some problems of our system and how it biases the process of selecting leaders, we do not suggest that the American electoral system is a poor one or fundamentally inferior to other systems, but only that our system is unique in many ways and its distinct characteristics have definite consequences. Among the characteristics of American elections we consider are (1) multiple and complex elections, (2) staggered fixed-interval elections, (3) single-member district plurality elections, and (4) the electoral college mechanism for election of the president.

Multiple and Complex Elections

If we are only semienthusiastic about voting as a nation, we seem to be absolutely in love with the idea of elections. We are true believers in elections, electing nearly a half million public officials to their offices nationwide. The very commonality of elections may, in fact, help to explain the tendency of Americans not to take part in them. Elections in the United States are routine, ordinary, and conventional. Their frequency tries the patience of many citizens and exceeds the bounds of their sense of civic duty. They become easy to ignore.

Contributing to the frequency of elections is the decentralized character of the electoral system. Although we have national elections in which officers of the national government are selected by all parts of the nation on the same day, it is the states, not the national government, that are responsible for elections. In a sense, we really have no national elections, for all national officials are elected by statewide constituencies or within districts of the states. As long as the states do not violate the Constitution and a few federal election laws, they are free to organize and conduct elections as they see fit.

The decentralized character of elections in the United States also contributes greatly to the complexity of our electoral process. The rules pertaining to elections have become more standardized in recent years, but considerable variation remains from state to state. Registration procedures, residency and other requirements, the offices that are filled by election rather than appointment, the dates and frequency of elections, and even the kinds of elections vary among the fifty states.

Although the election that gets the most attention is that in which we select from among candidates for office, other elections allow voters to engage directly in policy choices. Presently, in twenty-three states, the citizens are able to place an issue on the ballot for consideration directly by the voters through an **initiative** petition. The petition must be signed by a certain percentage (the exact proportion varies from state to state) of the state's voters. The proposed law can then be voted on by the citizens in the general election, bypassing the state legislature. The "tax revolt" of the late 1970s aimed at property taxes was carried out principally through the initiative process in several major states, most notably California and Massachusetts. Another, more common, example of direct legislating is the **referendum**. In a referendum, voters are asked to approve or disapprove of a law already passed by the legislature. Only one state (Delaware) does not have at least some provision for the use of the referendum.

By far the greatest number of elections in the United States, however, are for the selection of leadership—people to represent us and do our policy making for us. Two important kinds of elections of leadership are **primary elections** and **general elections**. General elections are what come most readily to mind when we think of elections. These elections pit candidates of the different parties against one another in contests for public offices. But before these contests, we have primary elec-

tions to select who will be the parties' candidates. Most states use the *direct primary* to select the candidates for public office from each party. Although these contests among members of the same party for the party's nomination for the U.S. Senate, U.S. House, governor, and other state offices are sometimes hotly contested, they typically attract far fewer voters than do general elections. This lack of attention is often justified, for many primaries go uncontested. Typically, no competing candidates are on the ballot in a majority of congressional primary elections, and this is true of most lower-level state and local elections as well.

Adding to the complexity of the American electoral process is the fact that three types of primaries are found in the fifty states. Most states (thirty-eight) use what is called a **closed primary**, which requires that the voters indicate a party affiliation when registering to vote, so they can be limited to voting in the primary for candidates of their own party. Voters are free to change party affiliations, but this must be done before the election by registering again.

By contrast, in an **open primary** (used in nine states), voters never need to indicate a party affiliation. Instead of being given the ballot of their preferred party at the polling place, as in the closed primary, voters will be given ballots for each party. They can then select one of the party's ballots to vote on and discard the others. The advantage of this type of primary is that it ensures the privacy of the voter's party identification. The problem with open primaries is that they allow crossover voting or "raiding" of a party's primary by the opposing party, especially when only one party's primary is hotly contested.

Finally, the **blanket primary**, used by just two states (Alaska and Washington), allows voters not only to keep their party loyalties to themselves, but also to vote in the primary of more than one party. They may choose among the Republican candidates for Senate, for example, among the Democratic candidates for governor, and return to the Republican candidates for state attorney general, and so on. The blanket primary is often criticized for confusing the purposes of the primary (designed to be an internal party election) and the general election. One state, Louisiana, dispenses with considerations of party altogether and has a nonpartisan primary.

A RAID THAT BACKFIRED?

A raid by one party on the other's primary is something frequently suspected but rarely proven. That was the case in Illinois' Democratic gubernatorial primary of 1970. Far more people voted in the Democratic primary in heavily Republican downstate (outside Chicago) Illinois than there were Democrats. Whether this was due to a coordinated effort to raid the Democratic primary or occurred simply because there was a hot race among the Democrats whereas the incumbent Republican governor was unopposed is not entirely clear.

What gave rise to the raid suspicions was the fact that the downstate vote went for Daniel Walker, the more liberal of the Democratic candidates. This seems odd because downstate voters are more conservative, especially Republicans who must have been participating heavily in the election. Walker was widely believed to be the weaker of the two Democrats, however, which to some suggested a motive for Republicans' voting for him. If he won the election and captured the Democratic nomination, he would be more easily defeated by the Republican governor.

An alternative explanation for the downstate voting behavior lies in the peculiarities of Illinois politics. In addition to liberal versus conservative and Republican versus Democratic divisions is a rural versus urban division. Chicagoans (Cook County) and downstaters regard each other with mutual suspicion. Walker's opponent in the primary, Paul Simon, was a popular, established Democrat endorsed by and associated with the Chicago Democratic machine. Walker campaigned hard in the traditionally Republican downstate areas and stressed his independence from and opposition to Mayor Daley's machine. The downstate votes may have simply reflected hostility to the Chicago machine rather than an organized raid.

If a raid was in any part responsible for Walker's narrow primary win, it backfired. Walker went on to defeat the Republican governor in the general election. The result was that conservative Republicans, rather than retaining a Republican governor, wound up with the candidate least attractive ideologically. Whatever happened, Walker's election demonstrates that open primaries can result in strange and unpredictable outcomes.

Staggered Fixed-Interval Elections

The Constitution provides for staggered elections of national officeholders, and most electoral arrangements at other levels of government have followed suit. Staggered elections simply mean that not all governmental offices are elected at the same time. For example, only a third of the U.S. Senate is elected every two years, and the president is elected every other time the House of Representatives is selected. Elections for state offices are often staggered in a similar fashion. Many local elections are held in April of odd-numbered years rather than in November of even-numbered years when federal and state elections occur, further adding to the staggered effect.

Staggered elections have several important political implications. Most obviously, staggering elections adds to the multiplicity of elections in the American system, especially with primaries and such special elections as for school boards, and the like. As we discussed, the frequency of elections may contribute to the relatively low electoral participation in the United States. Participation rates also vary depending on which offices are being contested in an election. Turnout is generally higher in elections where an important, competitive, and highly visible office is being contested than when the most important race is a relatively minor or local one. In presidential election years, the vote in congressional elections is normally about 10 percent higher than in nonpresidential (off-year) elections. Clearly, if all elections were held at the same time, the turnout for the important offices would result in higher levels of voting for the lower level and local races as well. Moreover, since the size of the turnout can affect the ultimate outcome, holding elections at the same time would also alter the results of some lower-level races.

The Founders did not opt for staggered elections just to make things difficult for future generations, but to make it difficult for voters to radically alter the makeup of government in a single election. They placed this electoral brake on governmental change out of fear that rapid change in response to the transient issues of any one election would make for too much instability. Clearly, the arrangement forces the citizens to wait relatively long periods of time to completely change the political leadership.

At the national level, such a process would require at least six years. Of course, *majorities* in Congress can be altered by the voters much more quickly, so the braking effect is not as severe as it may at first appear.

For similar reasons, the Constitution provides for fixed-interval elections. This means simply that elections for any given office will be held every "x" number of years, and only every "x" number of years. In the United States, we elect the president every four years and only every four years. If citizens should want to be rid of a particular president, they could do little about it until the next election. This is not true in many other nations. In Great Britain, for example, major issues may become parliamentary votes of confidence which, if they go against the prime minister, oblige the prime minister and his or her cabinet to resign and call for new elections. The prime minister can also call early elections before the five-year legal limit and will

often do so to seek voter approval for the manner in which an important matter was handled. Prime Minister Thatcher did just that in the wake of her successful handling of the Falklands war in 1982.

Whereas the use of fixed-interval elections undoubtedly makes for more stable and predictable electoral politics, they have some drawbacks as well. Most important, fixed-interval elections prevent even an overwhelming popular majority from removing discredited officeholders until their terms are up. The Watergate crisis of 1973–1974 involving the Nixon administration is a case in point. The crisis began to emerge just three months into Nixon's second term, and it quickly brought government to a virtual halt as both Nixon and Congress became preoccupied with the issue of impeachment. Nixon could not command the public support he needed to govern effectively, the government was deadlocked, and no electoral means was available to quickly end the crisis. If he had not chosen to

President Nixon after announcing that he would provide transcripts of the White House tapes (shown in background) to the House Judiciary Committee. The heavily edited transcript failed to satisfy the committee or deflect its investigation of Nixon's administration. Nixon resigned just 3 months later.

resign, the nation's government might have been tied up in impeachment proceedings for much of his second term. As it was, the crisis lasted more than a year.

Single-Member District Plurality Elections

Most United States elections are designed to select only one individual for an office based on a geographically defined district (**single-member districts**), using as a selection rule the largest number of votes (**plurality**). Elections based on geographical districts in which the candidate with the most votes wins may seem so natural and reasonable that it hardly deserves mention, but it is not the only way to structure elections. Also, although it has the advantages of simplicity and clarity of result, it has some significant problems as well, primarily a systematic bias against minority representation, owing to the **winner-take-all** character of the system.

Most importantly, the single-member plurality system tends to exaggerate the representation of the majority in legislative bodies. We can focus on the competition between our two major parties as an example. Imagine that support for the Republicans and Democrats were evenly distributed throughout all the election districts in the United States. Since the Democrats enjoy the plurality of support, they would win every election and 100 percent of the seats in Congress. Of course, support for the Democrats and Republicans is not equally distributed, but because their support is far from perfectly concentrated in separate districts, the majority Democrats tend to win, with relatively narrow pluralities, a disproportionate number of the winner-take-all elections. Figure 7.1 illustrates the result of this bias in the single-member plurality system.

Clearly, how interests and partisan support are distributed among districts is very important to aggregate electoral outcomes in our system of elections. This in turn depends on where the district lines are drawn. The boundaries of electoral districts are determined by such political entities as state legislatures and courts. The partisan politicians that make up such institutions understand well the biases inherent in a single-member plurality system. As a result, the process of drawing district lines, called **reapportionment**, that follows each new census is considered so important that it produces some of the most bitter partisan struggles of each decade.

Thus the electoral advantage accruing to the Democrats, shown in Figure 7.1, is due not only to the effects of the laws of mathematical probability but also to the politics surrounding the drawing of electoral district boundaries and the advantage the Democrats have had in that process. Majorities in the state legislatures have an opportunity to manipulate the district lines to protect their majority and assure the election of the maximum number of their fellow party members to the national Congress. Democrats have enjoyed such majorities in more of the states for much of the past fifty years, but neither party would pass up the chance for the electoral advantage that reapportionment presents.

The practice of drawing district lines for the advantage of one party or group is called **gerrymandering** and is nearly as old as the republic itself. The term originated when Elbridge Gerry, an early governor of Massachusetts, contorted district lines for political advantage in such a way that one district looked (at least to his opponents) like a salamander. They dubbed the district a "gerrymander," and the term has been used to describe partisan sleight-of-hand in districting ever since.

In Elbridge Gerry's day and up until the 1960s, legislative districts, once established, tended to remain the same election after election, decade after decade. With the passage of time and the movement of people, maintaining the old district lines produced a sort of "silent" gerrymander as urban districts became much more heavily populated than those in rural areas. For example, by 1962 the rural community of Stratton, Vermont, with just 24 people had the same representation in that state's legislature as the city of Burlington with 35,531.[1] By the 1960s, it was common that only 10 to 15 percent of the people in a state, located in its rural areas, were electing 50 percent or more of the state's legislators!

In a series of decisions between 1962 and 1964, the Supreme Court ruled that all state and congressional legislative districts must be as nearly equal in size as possible to ensure that each citizen would be afforded equal representation. Owing to shifts in the population, this requires frequent reapportionment of legislative districts. The census taken at the beginning of each new decade is the basis for determining the new districts.

Figure 7.1

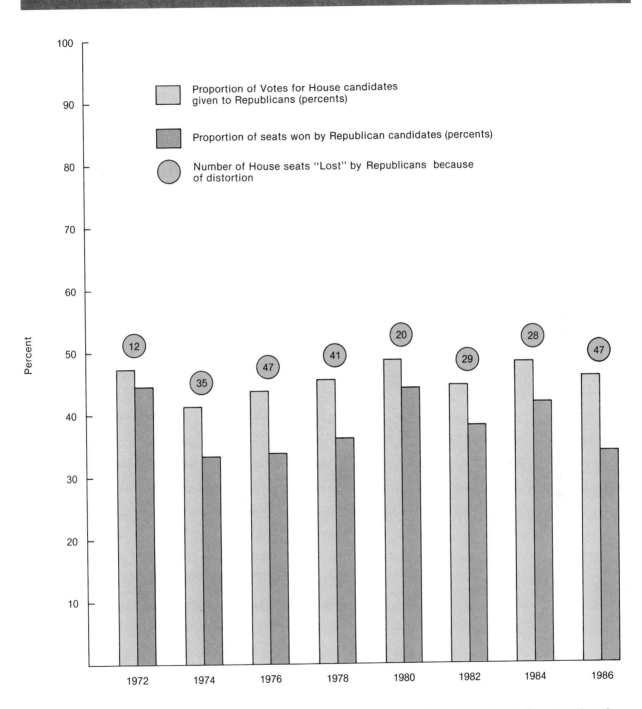

Sources: *Statistical Abstract of the United States, 1960, 1964, 1968, 1974, 1977, 1978, 1982-83, 1984.* The proportion of the total House vote received by Republicans in 1984 comes from David W. Brady and Patricia A. Hurley, "The Prospects for Contemporary Party Realignment," PS 18 (Winter 1985), p. 65. Figures for 1986 compiled from data reported in Congressional Quarterly Weekly Report, Nov. 8, 1986 for 370 contested House races.

ELBRIDGE GERRY (1744–1814): SWIMMING AGAINST THE TIDE

Although Elbridge Gerry earned immortality by having his name attached to the practice of apportioning legislative districts for partisan advantage, he was merely doing what he had done for most of his life, swim against the tide. In this respect, he belongs to a long tradition of maverick politicians.

During the revolutionary years, Gerry was opposed to continuing British rule in America. As a member of the Second Continental Congress, he proudly affixed his signature to the Declaration of Independence. While serving in that body, Gerry also signed the Articles of Confederation.

When the call went out for a Constitutional Convention, Gerry was quite naturally elected one of the delegates from Massachusetts. However, as an advocate of states rights, he vigorously opposed the effort to strengthen the national government. Ultimately, he left the convention without

signing the Constitution and led the fight against ratification in Massachusetts.

His opposition to the Constitution, however, did not prevent him from serving two terms in Congress as an independent-minded Federalist. By 1796, Gerry had been won over to the Democratic-Republican party. He returned to Massachusetts and ran for gover-

nor five times, finally winning in 1810. What few know is that Gerry's famous Gerry-mander led to his defeat by Caleb Strong in 1812.

In that same year, James Madison selected Gerry as his vice presidential candidate. New England had opposed the War of 1812, which they dubbed "Mr. Madison's War." Gerry once again was swimming against the tide. He was a vigorous supporter of the Democratic-Republican party and a firm friend of Madison. The Democratic-Republicans failed to carry Massachusetts but still won the presidential election.

Gerry died while serving as vice president in 1814. By the time of his death, more than half of the delegates to the Constitutional Convention had also died. If his final words had been recorded, Gerry probably would have voiced his opposition to going wherever they had gone.

The equal-size requirement makes gerrymandering for partisan advantage somewhat more difficult, but it in no way makes it impossible. Moreover, the need for new district lines to be drawn every ten years has greatly increased the opportunity for such political mischief. In most states, electoral maps are drawn up by each party, varying in strategic ways to maximize the likelihood of success for its partisans. The idea is either to concentrate your opponent's partisan strength in a few districts, allowing them to win these few by wide margins while losing the majority, or to disperse your opponent's support among the districts in such a way that it constitutes a plurality in few or none.

The problems of gerrymandering and biased and unequal representation among districts that attend a single-member plurality system are largely avoided in the **proportional representation** (PR) electoral system employed widely in Europe. Most PR systems function on an at-large basis, meaning there are no subnational districts whose boundaries can be manipulated. Rather than voting for individual candidates within geographical units, in the PR system voters cast their ballots for a list of candidates offered by a party. Seats in the legislature are allotted to each party in proportion to the popular vote the party receives, and the individuals who occupy the seats are selected from the party's list in rank order from the top of the list. The PR system, much more than ours, ensures fair and equal representation, stresses party as a guide to voting, and encourages minority participation in the electoral process.

Before we decide that we should switch to a PR system, we should consider some of its disadvantages. Because even rather small minorities can win a share of power under PR, it discourages the formation of broad party coalitions and encourages

GERRYMANDERING IN OKLAHOMA IS "OK"

Designed to protect and extend the Democrats' five to one advantage in Oklahoma's U.S. House delegation, the Congressional district map places widely separated Republican-dominated cities into a single district and divides Democratic strongholds among the remaining districts so as to secure the seats of existing Democratic incumbents.

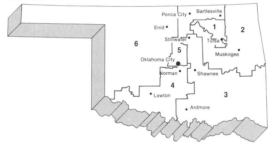

Three aspects of the map clearly indicate the Democrats' effort to neutralize growing Republican strength. First is the shape of the Fifth district, which previously was a compact district around Oklahoma City. The new, irregular L-shape lumps Republican voters in the northern part of Oklahoma City, Ponca City, and Bartlesville into one district so they can do little harm to Democrats in other districts. Second is the finger of the Second district that extends out to cut away a portion of Tulsa from the First district, splitting heavily Republican Tulsa to prevent it from tipping the First to the Republican side. Third is the finger of the western rural Sixth district that extends into downtown Oklahoma City, bringing the portion of Oklahoma City that includes most of the city's 60,000 blacks into a largely rural district.[2]

political fragmentation. PR often results in many small parties contesting elections, each appealing to a relatively narrow set of interests. The political bargaining and compromise necessary for political success in a winner-take-all system are made less necessary in the PR arrangement, allowing greater opportunity for political extremism. Extremist groups like the American Nazi party or the Socialist Workers party must, in the American system, choose either to moderate their principles and join a major party coalition in hopes of gaining a share of power or to adhere to their views and be completely excluded from power. In a PR system, it is much more likely that such an extreme group would be able to win some representation without modifying their views.

The failure of PR to encourage political compromise and moderation also contributes to the relative instability of such systems. Because of the fragmentation and multiple parties, often no one party can capture a majority in the legislature. As a result, the parties must form legislative coalitions to achieve the majority necessary to form a government. Normally, the largest party will secure the cooperation of several smaller parties that share similar ideological leanings. But such cooperation, allowing the largest party to dominate government, does not come without a price. Often, even very small parties can demand and receive policy influence and power far out of proportion to their size in return for the votes needed to form or maintain a governing coalition. Moreover, these small parties are often those most given to extremist views. If their demands are not met, their withdrawal of support may result in the absence of a governing majority, leading to new elections in the hope of producing a more workable balance of power among the parties.

PR has never caught on in the United States because, contrary to American political tradition, it deemphasizes regional-based political loyalties in favor of loyalties based on political ideologies. Most Americans feel more comfortable with political representatives that take care of the local interests, rather than those that defend an abstract ideology or represent a national party. But another electoral mechanism, with its roots in the Constitution itself, has been the focus of great debate; it concerns no less than the manner in which we elect the president.

The Electoral College

How the president should be chosen was a matter of great contention at the Constitutional Convention. Members advocated many different systems of election, and agreement on this important issue was slow in coming. Finally, a special committee appointed to consider the question arrived at a compromise that included nearly all the various suggestions in one way or another—the **electoral college** system. Under this system, each state, in a manner to be determined by the individual state, would select a number of electors equal to the total number of senators and representatives it sent to Congress. The electors in turn would choose the president by majority vote. If no candidate received a majority of the votes, the election of the president would fall to the House of Representatives, with each state having one vote. Again at this stage, a majority would be required for election.

The president is still legally elected by electors in the electoral college today. Owing largely to the development of political parties, however, the system works differently than originally designed. When we vote for a candidate for president in November, we are actually voting for a slate of electors who, if elected, will vote for that candidate in the electoral college in December. In each state, the entire slate of electors loyal to the winning candidate will be sent to the electoral college.[3] The losing

New Jersey's 16 Electors meet to cast their electoral votes for John Kennedy in 1960. The Electoral College remains today as a reflection of the founders' suspicions of popular suffrage.

candidate will get no electoral votes, even if the loss is by a very narrow margin.

This application of the winner-take-all system to the presidential vote is called the **unit rule** and is the source of much of the criticism of the electoral college system. One problem that results from the states' casting their electoral votes as a bloc is that each person's vote in the more heavily populated states (with larger numbers of electors) becomes much more important than the vote in small states. For example, in California a voter helps to elect 47 electors to the electoral college, whereas in neighboring Nevada a voter helps to elect only 4! In a close election, a shift of only a few thousand votes in California could cause a swing of 94 electoral votes! It is no wonder that candidates for president focus their attention on these large states. Indeed, it is possible to collect the 270 electoral votes needed to win the presidency by winning in just the twelve largest states.

We might expect the large urban states to be pleased with this arrangement, but this is not universally the case. Because all states have at least two senators and one representative, no matter how small its population a state will have at least three electors. So the way the electoral college system distributes electoral votes actually results in an overrepresentation of the less populous states. For example, the thirteen smallest states in the union together cast one more electoral vote (48) than California, the nation's largest state. Yet these thirteen states have less than 40 percent of California's more than 25 million citizens! If the approximately 10 million citizens in the thirteen smallest states were all in one state, that state would have only 22 electoral votes!

The manner of electoral college vote distribution not only results in skewed representation but also raises the possibility of a candidate who loses the popular vote nationwide winning in the electoral college. The most likely scenario for this is if a candidate should win the large states by small margins and lose in the small states by large margins. Hypothetically, a candidate could win each of the twelve largest states by 5,000 votes and lose in each of the thirty-eight smaller states by 50,000 votes. The candidate would receive more than 1.8 million votes less than the opposing candidate, but would be elected president by virtue of a majority of electoral college votes. The American electorate would

POPULAR LOSERS

Three American presidents have been elected without receiving the greatest number of popular votes. In 1824, the House selected John Quincy Adams over Andrew Jackson despite a clear popular vote advantage for Jackson. In 1876, in a close and very controversial election of questionable legitimacy, Rutherford B. Hayes won the presidency from the popular vote winner, Samuel Tilden. It happened again in 1888 when incumbent Grover Cleveland won the popular vote but lost in the electoral college to Benjamin Harrison.

More recently, the electoral college has threatened to disrupt presidential election outcomes in 1960 and 1968. The 1960 election was extremely close in both the popular and electoral vote count. John F. Kennedy won by about 100,000 votes nationwide, but a change in just a few thousand votes in very close elections in just two states, Illinois and Missouri, would have swung all their electoral votes, and the majority in the electoral college, to Richard Nixon. As a result, Nixon would have won the presidency while losing the popular vote by about 85,000 votes.

In 1968, it was the presence of a strong third party candidate, George Wallace, that was the source of concern. Up until the week before the election, it appeared that Wallace might get enough electoral votes from southern states to deny a majority to either Republican Richard Nixon or Democrat Hubert Humphrey. If so, the advantage in the House of Representatives would have belonged to Humphrey, despite the fact that Nixon was expected to gain a larger number of popular votes. Fortunately for the system, Nixon was able to win enough states to secure a majority in the electoral college. Such examples suggest, however, that an electoral legitimacy crisis due to the electoral college is just a matter of time.

likely perceive such an election as highly illegitimate, making it difficult for a president elected under such circumstances to govern effectively.

Like all election systems, the electoral college has its advantages as well as its disadvantages. The unit-rule system in electoral college voting acts much like winner-take-all systems at lower levels to encourage moderation in a two-party system. It is very unlikely that a third party would be capable of challenging the Democrats and Republicans effectively, for to do so requires attracting not just significant support but also pluralities in numerous states. It also allows the states an important role in the election of the president, expressing of the federal character of the nation in this most important election. Finally, it may act to further the interests of some minority groups, as it exaggerates their impact on the election. Blacks, for example, constitute only 11 percent of the population but often hold the balance of power in close elections in several large competitive states like California, New York, Pennsylvania, Illinois, and New Jersey. The electoral vote of such states constitutes far more than 11 percent of the votes needed to be elected president.

Election Trends and Prospects

Elections are essentially struggles among party and group leaders who go to the electorate for support of their programs and policies. The competition for public office usually favors the incumbent, the individual already holding office. For nearly three decades, 92 percent of all incumbent representatives have retained their seats, and 77 percent of all incumbent senators have won reelection. Yet elections also furnish voters with opportunities to record shifts in party affiliation and fundamentally alter the direction of political events. The presidential elections of 1800, 1828, 1860, 1896, and 1932 were *critical* elections that produced a dramatic realignment in the pattern of support for the major political parties. Also known as *realigning* elections, they shaped the future of American politics for decades. (Figure 7.1).

Most elections are not nearly so portentous, though those who are elected in them will do their best to make us think they are. Political scientists also have terms for these less notable elections. In a *maintaining election,* by far the most frequent type historically, the majority party wins the election on the basis of essentially the same pattern of support as in previous elections. In the *converting* election, the majority party is victorious, but the supporting coalition has changed significantly. This change may be reflected in either a significantly greater or narrower majority for the dominant party. A *deviating* election finds the minority party winning

Table 7.1
Critical Elections and Party Realignment

Year	Candidates	Parties	Electoral Result
1800	John Adams	Federalist	
	Thomas Jefferson	Democratic-Republican	Elected for two terms
	Impact: Established the Democratic-Republican party's dominance.		
	Federalist party declines and eventually disappears.		
	Agrarian philosophy in the ascendant.		
1828	John Quincy Adams	National Republican	
	Andrew Jackson	Democrat	Elected for two terms
	Impact: Established the Democratic party's dominance.		
	Inaugurates era of Jacksonian democracy.		
	Jackson destroys the Second Bank of the United States.		
1860	Stephen Douglas	Democrat	
	Abraham Lincoln	Republican	Elected for two terms
	Impact: Established the Republican party's dominance.		
	Strengthened the national government and destroyed slavery.		
	Opened an era of rapid industrialization.		
1896	William J. Bryan	Democrat	
	William McKinley	Republican	Elected for two terms
	Impact: Established laissez-faire capitalism as the dominant ideology.		
	Crushed the Populist party and the last vestiges of agrarianism.		
	National government ends efforts to protect civil rights of blacks (*Plessy v. Ferguson*, 1896, declares separate but equal doctrine.)		
1932	Franklin Roosevelt	Democrat	Elected for four terms
	Herbert Hoover	Republican	
	Impact: Reestablished the Democratic party's dominance.		
	Revolutionized the relationship between the national government and the states and legitimized government intervention in the economy.		
	Dethroned laissez-faire capitalism as the dominant ideology.		

the election based on short-term conditions or issues, while the basic pattern of support for the two parties remains the same. Finally, in the *realigning* election, the previous minority party wins owing to a shift in the pattern of support that results in its becoming the new majority party on a permanent basis.

The presidential election of 1984 was a landslide of historic proportions in favor of President Reagan and the Republicans. Reagan won 59 percent of the vote and a record 525 of 538 electoral votes. Does this victory signal a realigning election in American politics? Since one of the key indicators of a realignment is an enduring change in the dominant party, we really cannot tell yet. Our application of the term to past elections benefits from years of reflection and the insight that comes with time. What we can do here is look at the evidence as it stands today and let you draw your own conclusions.

By definition, a realigning election involves a significant and enduring change in the patterns of support for the two parties. We can find some evidence of such a change in the pattern of loyalties and some indication of continuity as well. One change is clear. The Democrats have lost the allegiance of southern whites, once a secure part of the New Deal coalition of 1932. Southern whites have been drifting away from the Democrats for some time and have not voted a majority for the Democratic candidate for president since 1964. In 1984, for the first time, a majority of southerners identified with the Republican party. This is very important because the South represents a crucial bloc of electoral votes, without which any Democrat will find it difficult to capture the presidency. Also, this new identification can be expected to be reflected in greater numbers of Republicans being sent to the Congress from this region, making it more difficult for Democrats to maintain control of the legislature.

A second important positive sign for the Republicans in 1984 was the shift in loyalty of younger voters. Polls showed a majority of voters under the age of thirty identifying with the Republican party, a sharp change from past patterns. This change, however, may not be permanent, but simply a reaction to recent events and a popular president. Young voters do not have long political memories, and we can expect they will be most influenced by recent and transient conditions.[4]

Some factors suggest that the election of 1984 will not be viewed as realigning. First, past critical elections have been attended by major issues and events that have forced a new division of the electorate. In 1984, there did not seem to be such an issue or event. Nothing like the Civil War issues or the Great Depression shook the politics of 1984, not even an issue of the magnitude of "free silver" as in 1896. Instead, in 1984, the parties still seemed to be debating the questions that have divided the parties since 1932. Certainly, many of the basic social voting patterns have remained the same since the 1930s. Higher socioeconomic status groups still form the core of the Republican coalition. Organized labor, Jews, blacks, Hispanics, Catholics, and the poor remain more likely to vote Democratic than nonunion workers, whites, and Protestants. Though only Jews and blacks voted majorities for the Democrats in 1984, there is no evidence that the other groups have abandoned their Democratic loyalties permanently.

The continuing strength of the Democratic party in electoral levels below the presidency also deviates from the pattern of past realignments. In 1932 and 1936, Franklin Roosevelt swept large majorities of Democrats into both houses of Congress with him, clearly establishing them as the majority party in the nation. Reagan's victory in 1980 was accompanied by Republican control of the Senate and substantial gains in the House, but the 1984 landslide did not extend to Congress. The Republicans actually lost two seats in the Senate and gained only a modest fourteen seats in the House, leaving the Democrats with a seventy-one-seat advantage. Some see this tendency of voters to split their tickets between the presidential and congressional races as indicating a general decline in the importance of party identification in voting, especially in the highly visible presidential race. This view leads to the conclusion that 1984 does not indicate realignment, but a further dealignment of the American electorate.[5]

Though the pattern and direction of change is not yet clear, it is clear that things are changing in American elections. The electorate has become more volatile and unpredictable. We find it difficult to classify the 1980 and 1984 elections today for two reasons. If they are deviating elections, what are they deviating from? Though not entirely destroyed, the old Democratic coalition is changed and its loyalties are soft. If 1980 and 1984 are realigning elections, what is the new coalitional pattern? Nothing clear has yet emerged. Perhaps this condition of relative dealignment is itself the permanent new condition.

REAPPORTIONMENT: THE KEY TO A REALIGNMENT?

A great deal of attention has been directed at the battle for control of the Senate in 1986 in hopes of determining whether its capture by the Republicans in 1980 was a deviation or the start of something big. Control of the Senate may be a less important indicator of things to come than the outcome of the 1986 elections at the level of state government, however. If a major realignment is to be completed during the 1980s, a key to it will be the reapportionment of legislative districts following the 1990 census, and that is the job of the several state legislatures.

Republican inroads in Congress and many state legislatures have been limited in part by district boundaries drawn by the majority Democrats. This has helped the Democratic party to retain control of the House of Representatives and many state legislatures in recent election years in which the Republicans were favored for higher offices. If the Republicans can capture a majority of state legislatures by 1990, it will be a powerful indication of major party realignment and would allow them to redraw district lines more to their advantage for the decade that follows. This would remove a major obstacle to their capturing control of the House and completing their dominance of government.

Both major parties are aware of the significance of the 1986, 1988, and, especially, 1990 elections at the state level and are trying to make the most of them. The Democrats realize that even temporary minority status at reapportionment time in 1990 could, with the establishment of unfavorable district boundaries, be frozen out of power for a long period. The Republicans see the possibility of breaking out of the disadvantage that the electoral system has placed them in for years and an opportunity to use the system to their benefit for a change. Republicans hope that their gain of eight governorships in the 1986 elections, three of which were in the politically vital South, is an indication of things to come for the party. Despite the fact that the Democrats gained eight seats and control of the Senate in 1986 and no matter what their fortunes in the 1988 presidential race, further gains by the Republicans at the state level would bode well for the party's future.

The 1986 elections also gave mixed signals concerning the likelihood of realignment. The Democrats' success in recapturing the Senate, despite an extraordinary effort on the part of President Reagan on the behalf of many Republican candidates, clearly suggests that Reagan's 1984 victory was largely due to his personal popularity and is not transferable to the party. On the other hand, the Republicans captured eight new governorships in 1986 bringing their total to 24 of the 50 states. This show of vitality at the state level may be a sign of an important shift in partisan strength, especially because several of the new Republican governorships were won in the traditionally Democratic South.

Campaigns and the Media

The mass media, especially the broadcast media, have become an extremely important part of our electoral process. The purpose of election campaigns has always been to advertise the virtues of the candidates and to inform the public about the issues and the candidates' views on them. It is essentially a communication process. Today, the new technologies of communication have made central the media's role in this effort. One need not look far for evidence of this. For example, in addition to the traditional campaign manager, fund raiser, advance logistics staff, and speech writers, campaign organizations now include media consultants and press secretaries to tend the candidate's image and manage the press. The modern media have altered the nature of campaigns in many important ways. In this section, we discuss the role of money in campaigns and the packaging of candidates, two particularly important issues associated with the contemporary media-centered campaign.

Money and the Media

The cost of running for office in the United States has increased dramatically in the last thirty years. All the candidates running for public office in 1956 spent only about as much as the cost of a single candidate's campaign for the presidency today. Nor is this increase significantly explained by inflation. The costs of campaigns have increased by more

than 750 percent since 1952 whereas inflation has pushed costs up a little more than 200 percent. Moreover, much of the increase in cost has come in just the last few years. In 1974, for example, only one candidate for the House of Representatives spent more than $500,000. By 1982, more than forty spent at least that amount, and ten candidates spent more than $800,000. Eighteen senatorial candidates each spent $2 million or more in the 1982 elections. Overall, we now regularly spend well over $1 billion on elections during presidential years.[6]

Much of the increase has been used for expanded and more sophisticated media advertising, especially on television, the most effective but also the most expensive means of getting a candidate's message to the people. During the 1984 election, the average cost of a one-minute network television spot was $50,000.[7]

But the cost of air time is only a fraction of the expenses of the media campaign. Campaign managers have to hire consultants to dream up and produce the advertisements for fees that can run to $500 a day or more. They also have to pay the production costs for the spots, whose costs increase as they become more elaborate and sophisticated. A simple "talking head" spot may be cheaper, but it does less for image creation than those including action and more elaborate sets. A sophisticated media campaign, just like any marketing effort, also requires knowledge of the market. Knowing what the voter's mood is and what the response to various advertising approaches has been is central to shaping the candidates' image and to targeting spots for particular audiences. Collecting such information is also expensive, requiring professional pollsters to conduct surveys and to tabulate and analyze the information.

So we spend a lot of money on campaigns and for media exposure for candidates, but are elections really too expensive? The answer, as with so many political questions, is "it depends." It depends on which perspective and with what values we approach the question. When compared with what we spend on other things as a society, our investment in democracy seems rather small. We spent about as much for all elections in 1984 (about $1.2 billion) as we did on telephones, for example. We spent more for video games ($1.7 billion), for styling our hair ($8.9 billion), and much more for fixing our cars

The media in America is varied and diverse rather than unified and monolithic.

($39.1 billion).[8] Perhaps we should be spending more on politics. It is certainly more important than video games. Perhaps with a greater investment, we could become better informed and improve the quality of our participation and our government.

Perhaps, but unlike votes, money is not equally distributed among the citizens. This is the real, underlying problem with the increasing importance of money in a time of rapidly rising campaign costs. If we value political equality, as we do in a democracy, the role of money in politics is inherently disturbing. To the extent that money (unavoidably unequal in distribution) is effective in influencing political outcomes, the importance and meaningfulness of the vote (equally distributed among citizens) is reduced. If it is money rather than votes that makes the difference in politics, the attitude of those without much money toward the vote and the political process is likely to become cynical. Indeed, they are likely to choose not to participate in such a process. The perception by most of the citizens that politics is a "rich man's game" is damag-

ing to the operation of democracy. The high cost of campaigns contributes to this perception.

One problem with the high cost of campaigns is that it puts running for office out of the financial reach of all but a few. A person must be relatively wealthy or able to draw contributions from those who have money to make a run for any but lower local offices. Even a direct mail fund-raising system, designed to reach many small contributers with letters asking for a few dollars, requires a large initial investment as well as the assumption of risk. When running for the House can cost two or three million dollars and races for the Senate, eight or nine million, it is difficult to argue that politics at this level is truly open to the average citizen.

Another problem with the high and rising cost of running for office is that it increases the dependence of all but the very wealthiest office seekers on outside funding. This is a problem for several reasons. First, it implies that only those individuals acceptable to the monetary sources in society will be candidates for office. If money determines who

MAKING A CONTRIBUTION TO A GOOD CAUSE: YOUR OWN ELECTION

If you have several hundred thousand dollars lying around not doing anything, you might want to contribute them to your own campaign for national office. The Supreme Court has ruled that it is unconstitutional for legal restrictions to be placed on a candidate's using personal money for his or her own election campaign. This makes it possible for wealthy individuals to mount effective campaigns for public office regardless of their outside funding support. Several have taken advantage of this opportunity. Jane Eskind "lent" her campaign for the senate in Tennessee $425,000 and contributed an additional $200,000, a sum that accounted for nearly all the funds her campaign received. Similarly, Robert Short spent just over $1.4 million running for the senate in Minnesota, of which almost $1.3 million was his own money. Another Minnesotan, Mark Dayton, spent about $5 million of his department store fortune running for the U.S. Senate. Interestingly, none of these candidates was elected to office.

becomes candidates, the choice of the people is narrowed to only those candidates acceptable to interests that have money. Certainly the poor, and even the working class, may feel this choice provides little opportunity for representation of their interests. Second is the question of the impact of money on the policy choices of officials once elected. Most officeholders want to be reelected. They know that to accomplish that goal they will need money. Thus they may be reluctant to take positions or cast votes contrary to the interests of significant past or potential future contributors. Few observers feel there is much out-and-out vote buying in Congress. But at the very least, money buys access to the decision maker. Significant contributors are much more likely than noncontributors to be granted the opportunity to talk directly to the representative and to attempt to influence his or her thinking on an issue.

Is it necessary to spend a lot of money to get elected to a major office in the United States? The answer seems to be a qualified "yes." Large-scale campaign expenditures do increase the probability

of success, and candidates are at a disadvantage if funded less than their opponent. Spending is particularly important to candidates who are challenging an incumbent, as challengers must overcome the built-in advantage that incumbents have in name recognition and record of accomplishment in office. Incumbents also tend to receive greater amounts of campaign contributions than do challengers, and normally outspend their opponents as a result. This financial advantage itself further helps to explain the high rate of success for incumbents' seeking reelection.

Spending more money and dominating the media with even the most sophisticated campaign will not assure victory, however. Each election provides examples of candidates who have outspent their opponents, sometimes by large amounts, and have still been defeated at the polls. Governor Cuomo of New York was outspent by his opponent by about $5 million in 1982, yet won a narrow reelection victory. Similarly, Senator Durenburger of Minnesota was reelected despite being outspent by almost $3 million. Incumbency undoubtedly helped both these candidates in overcoming the disadvantage in campaign spending. Indeed, some incumbents are so popular they need spend very little to gain reelection. The most notable example is Senator William Proxmire of Wisconsin who spent nothing at all on his 1982 reelection, yet was reelected by a wide margin.

Incumbency is not the only defense against a better financed opponent. It is also possible to structure a campaign to maximize *free* media exposure. In 1970, for example, a candidate for governor in Illinois, Daniel Walker, and a candidate for senator in Florida, Lawton Chiles, each used long walking tours of their states to draw media coverage as "news" events, reducing their need to buy political advertising. Neither was an incumbent, yet both were successful in defeating better-financed opponents.

Finally, campaigns will not convince people to vote against their own well-understood, basic interests. No amount of money is going to elect an American Nazi in a heavily Jewish district, a segregationist in a black district, an opponent of farm price-supports in a rural district, or a supporter of heavier taxes on the wealthy in an upper-class suburb. But all other things being equal, money may make the crucial difference in closely competitive elections. Moreover, there are many closely competitive elections, and they tend to be for the more important national and statewide offices. Money may not be a sure ticket to success, but it has always been important; and it is clear that it is becoming more important in today's media-centered politics.

Who has the most money to spend? As we noted, incumbents tend to receive more contributions and outspend their opponents. Campaign contributors want their money to be politically influential, and the only way it will be is if it backs a winner. Proven past winners are a safer bet than challengers, so incumbents often attract money even from interests that are not strong supporters. Conservative business organizations that strongly support the Republican party, for example, have been giving about one-third of their money to incumbent Democrats in the past few elections. Nonetheless, Republicans are also normally much better financed than Democrats. Business and conservative groups that back Republican candidates simply have far more to give than the labor, minority, and liberal groups that back Democrats. The Democrats are nearly always fighting to pay off old debts, whereas the Republican party often finds itself with a surplus.

Where all this political money comes from was once a fairly easy question to answer. It came largely from very wealthy individuals, and it came in very large sums. In 1972, for example, the Nixon campaign received about 150 contributions of $40,000 or more—sometimes much more. Almost sixty people contributed more than $100,000 and a few more than $1,000,000. Even the McGovern campaign, though successful in attracting many small donations through direct mail solicitation, depended heavily on the large contributor. Nine people contributed more than $100,000 to the liberal Democrat, and one gave nearly $750,000.[9]

It was the financing irregularities of the Nixon reelection campaign of 1972 that finally touched off serious demands for reform of campaign financing. The influence of large campaign contributions on elections at all levels had been a growing public concern for some time. The investigation of the Watergate scandal simply raised the issue by revealing the Nixon administration's bigger and bolder abuses. In the wake of the Watergate revelations, the Congress passed the **Federal Election Cam-**

MONEY, ELECTIONS, AND "FREE SPEECH"

The courts have been an effective way around (or, in this case, through) the election laws for those who wish to weaken them. By striking down various provisions of the election laws, gaping new loopholes have been opened by the Supreme Court. The 1974 law originally limited total contributions by individuals to $25,000 dollars per year. In the case of *Buckley v. Valeo*, however, the Court argued that limiting individual spending not coordinated with a particular campaign was an unconstitutional restriction of the right to free speech. The decision also struck down provisions limiting how much an individual could spend on his or her own campaign and all spending limits on congressional campaigns.

To these three major loopholes, the Court added a fourth in 1985. In the case *FEC v. NCPAC* (pronounced "nickpack," for the National Conservative Political Action Committee), the Court again employed the free speech argument to strike down limits on PAC spending in presidential general elections. These limits had been ignored during the 1984 elections by NCPAC and several other conservative PACs that together independently spent more than $15 million on behalf of Reagan. Similar PAC spending for Mondale totaled $621,000. With the legal lid off such "independent" PACs, the cost of free speech can be expected to amount to many more dollars in 1988.

In defense of the decision in *FEC v. NCPAC*, Justice William Rehnquist argued that limiting such expenditures was "like allowing a speaker in a public hall to express his views while denying him the use of an amplifying system." Others disagree and are concerned that the weakening of the election laws by the Court threatens to put the United States back on the path to "dollar democracy" rather than true "electoral democracy." Using Justice Rehnquist's analogy, it might be argued that taking the lid off spending is like letting everyone have the amplifying system but turning the volume down for those without dollars and turning it up for those with dollars. In dissent, Justice Byron White argued that with this decision, the Court had "transformed a coherent regulatory scheme into a nonsensical loophole-ridden patchwork." Obviously, there is no consensus as yet on whether or how money in campaigns should be regulated.

paign Act of 1974 (FECA). To reduce the influence of wealthy contributors that had been so central to campaign financing in past elections, the law established strict limits on the amount of money that an individual could contribute to any candidate ($1,000 in the primary and $1,000 in the general election), to **political action committees (PACs)** ($5,000 per election year), and to party organizations ($20,000 per election year). The amount contributed to all organizations could total no more than $25,000 per election year (Table 7.2). The FECA has been amended several times, and some of its provisions have been found unconstitutional by the Supreme Court, weakening its effect somewhat.

Table 7.2
Basic Facts About Campaign Finance Regulation

Major campaign finance laws were enacted in 1971, 1974, 1976, and 1979. The laws have been modified by court decisions, the most recent coming in early 1985. The laws are enforced by the Federal Election Commission (FEC), created by the FECA of 1974. Though constantly evolving, the major provisions of campaign finance regulation deal essentially with three areas—contributions, expenditures, and reporting. More details can be obtained by writing or calling the FEC, 1325 K Street, N.W., Washington D.C. 20463, (800) 424–9430. The major facets of the law as it stands today are as follows:

Contributions

By individuals:

Per candidate for each election	$ 1,000
To PACs each annually	5,000
To party national committee annually	20,000
Total annual contributions not to exceed	25,000
Independent contributions on behalf of candidate . .	unlimited

By PACs and parties

Per candidate for each election	$ 5,000
Total annual contributions	unlimited
Independent contributions on behalf of candidate . .	unlimited

By candidate for own campaign

In all elections except presidential	unlimited
In presidential election (if publicly funded)	$50,000

Expenditures

In all elections except presidential	unlimited
In presidential election (if publicly funded)	Amount of public funding *

Reporting

Candidates must file with the FEC if they receive or spend	$ 5,000
Records must be kept of contributions over	50,000
Violations carry fines of up to	50,000

* Amount of public funding changes in each election. In 1984, each candidate was given about $40 million to contest the general election.

KNOWING YOUR WAY AROUND THE FEDERAL ELECTION CAMPAIGN LAWS

Several loopholes in the present election laws allow for the collecting and spending of more money than that actually reported to the FEC. One is simply the formation of many separate PAC organizations with different names and different staff but with essentially the same goals. Since spending by each PAC is limited, the way around such limits is more PACs.

Another simple tactic is to delay the official declaration of one's candidacy. Not surprisingly, campaign contribution and spending limits do not apply to noncandidates. Of course, there are limits to this strategy. Candidates can delay only until the official filing deadlines, and for many important races a late start would do more harm than the extra money would do good. But when you hear someone expected to run for office say, "I have made no decision yet" or "We will cross that bridge when we come to it," you will know one of the reasons he or she is being evasive.

Some areas of campaign activity are beyond the reach of the federal regulations. Since such regulations do not apply to state and local election activity, for example, an increasingly used device is to channel money through state party organizations. Another area not covered by the federal laws is the donation of services. Unions and corporations can donate "volunteers" and other services to their respective favorites. A free concert given by a rock group can generate thousands of dollars for a candidate, but as a service it does not count against contribution limits.

In its present form, the FECA alters the character of campaign contributions but does little to limit the amount of money spent below the presidential level, nor does it reduce the importance of money in campaigns. Certainly, the reforms have reduced the direct impact of wealthy individual contributors in campaigns. But in their place has arisen a multitude of PACs that contribute directly to campaigns (up to $5,000) and can spend unlimited amounts independently on behalf of a candidate. Also, restrictions on independent individual expenditures on behalf of a candidate, no longer exist, so the wealthy individual can still influence political outcomes.

Clearly, the most important result of the campaign finance reform laws has been the proliferation of PACs and the rapid increase in their total contributions of money to the campaign process. In 1984, the **Federal Election Commission (FEC),** created by the FECA to enforce the act, reported no less than 3,803 PACs. Together, in 1984, they contributed around $104 million to the races for the House of Representatives, and accounted for nearly 30 percent of the total contributions for the Senate races. Some senators derived more than 70 percent of their money from this source, whereas for others, PACs accounted for less than 10 percent. The top recipient of PAC money was Texas Republican Phil Gramm (of Gramm-Rudman fame [see Chapter 12]) who received just under $1.4 million in PAC money in his successful campaign for the Senate.[10]

Despite the fact that receiving PAC money has taken on a negative connotation and even became a campaign issue in the 1984 Democratic presidential primaries, the role and influence of PACs and their money is likely to become still greater in the years to come. One reason for this is the recent removal of some restrictions on their spending activity by the Supreme Court, but the fundamental reason is simply that candidates need PAC money to pay the cost of high-tech, media-centered campaigns and the PACs wish to help shape policy by influencing who holds office and by having access to those who do. PACs provide for the needs of both.

The Media and the Selling of Candidates

Candidates have always attempted to sell themselves to the American voter. But gone are the days of speeches from the back of a campaign train. Today, candidates have at their disposal a far more powerful and flexible mechanism for reaching the people. Television consumes about half of the budget of the average campaign for major office and is the only source of experience most voters have with the candidate. The candidate's screen image is more important than the impression he or she conveys in person.

Image creation is not new in American politics. Indeed, it dates at least as far back as the first politician who kissed a baby in hopes of being perceived

Image-making in American elections is not a new phenomenon, but has acquired greater impact with the advent of mass media.

as warm and caring. Many of our early presidents employed images to appeal to the public. Perhaps the most famous was *honest* Abe Lincoln, the *rail-splitter* from Illinois. An honest man of the people is still a good image to run on today. Others have traded on their success, sometimes wildly exaggerated, as generals. William Henry Harrison parlayed a minor battlefield success at Tippecanoe into one of the most famous political slogans in American electoral history, "Tippecanoe and Tyler Too," and won the presidency in 1840. Teddy Roosevelt also drew his image from military experience, though his background as a rough rider certainly was more genuine than Harrison's claims for military prowess.

Image making, then, has always been a part of American campaigning. What is different today is that the mass media have made it easier to create an image not based on fact and have it reach more people more effectively and, with modern polling techniques, to learn what people want and to target the image accordingly.

The use of the media for the purpose of image creation often is at odds with thorough treatment of the issues. It is often lamented that this powerful

In the role of party leader, presidents are called upon to campaign for party members. Here, President Reagan makes a campaign stop in support of Senator Jeremiah Denton of Alabama.

instrument of communication, with its potential for political education, is largely wasted. Most political advertising campaigns are built around the thirty-second spot. Candidates cannot seriously address an issue in that length of time, so most such ads focus on the candidate as a person. When issues are brought into the advertising, it is often as part of the image being created for the candidate. Advertising the candidate's stand on Social Security, for example, may take the form of showing the candidate with a group of smiling and attentive elderly people. We learn nothing about the candidate's views on the complex problem and its alternative solutions, only that he seems concerned and that old people seem to approve. Television tends to focus the attention of the voter on the character of the candidate to the virtual exclusion of other issues.

The nature of television advertising and image making also tends to make the candidate a performer. The media-centered campaign rewards candidates that can look good in what are essentially acting situations on television. Being able to communicate effectively on television is an important modern political skill, but personal attractiveness and a "mediagenic" personality may be overemphasized in our leadership choices. Certainly, some of our greatest leaders of the past would have fared poorly in a modern television campaign. Television's tendency to reduce elections to "beauty" contests robs them of much of their meaning and purpose.

Focusing on a candidate's attractiveness also has implications for the type of candidates likely to be recruited to run for office in the future. The actual candidates for office may tend to become mere figureheads, chosen by political parties and groups for their personal appeal and media skills, whereas the real decision-making and policy choices are made by others less visible to the public. Some observers fear that real power will come to rest in the hands of the unelected professional campaign consultants and advisers who will determine what issues the officeholder will raise, what the officeholder will say about them, and how the officeholder will vote on them.

But it seems unlikely that all candidates will ever be willing to allow themselves to be fully packaged and sold by their consultants. Also, the consultant's ability to control political events and the candidate's response to them is limited. The candidate's real knowledge of and position on the issues is likely to slip out somewhere along the way, as are indications of his or her genuine character. Imagine the consternation of Jimmy Carter's image makers when he admitted in an interview with *Playboy* magazine that he had "lusted in his heart" after many women or those of President Reagan when he insists on repeating a factual error

at a press conference. The media may provide the inducement for image making, but they also scrutinize candidates and report such public relations blunders. The media's hunger for news is a potent check on the potential power of the candidate-packaging professionals.

Media News Coverage and the Campaign

Candidates and their media professionals have relatively little control of the coverage of the news. That the news media largely decide for themselves what is going on in a campaign is reflected by the tension that is often present between the press and the campaign organization. Campaigns do their best to manage the news, creating media events designed to play to the visual needs of the media, create a newsworthy episode, and show the candidate in a favorable light. Campaigns also give reporters canned press releases to save the press the job of finding its own news and to allow the campaign to decide what will be reported. But the news media have an interest in reporting the troubles of the campaign and the problems of the candidate as well. Such things are interesting, and attracting readers and viewers is at the heart of the media's business. The news media are also sensitive to being used by campaigns and will often label a staged media event as such for the information of their readers or viewers.

The business demands of the competitive news media help explain another prominent feature of campaign coverage. It is often noted that the news media tend to focus on the "horse race" aspect of the campaign (who is ahead, who is gaining or losing in the polls, what are the strategies, and so on) rather than the substantive issues in the campaign. In the broadcast media, time is quite literally money, whereas for the print media the key commodity is space. Both must be used to maximum effect. Covering the issues adequately requires a lot of time and space and is less effective in drawing viewers and readers than the more colorful matters of candidate personality, strategy, and standing in the polls.

News coverage of campaigns is often criticized for being shallow, but few would charge that the media fail to wield tremendous power in the cam-

FOILING A MEDIA EVENT: "SO, WHAT'S GOING TO HAPPEN NEXT, DAVID?"

A good example of media coverage undoing a media event occurred during the 1972 Republican National Convention. With the coming of television coverage, each party's national convention has become a gigantic media event kicking off the presidential campaign season. In 1972, the Republicans met with little to do except renominate Richard Nixon. Nixon's campaign organization had arranged everything for a calculated media effect. The choreography was laid out in detail in a book distributed to key campaign workers at the convention. It was a carefully planned show, but part of the show required the display of "spontaneous" outpourings of support for the president and his running mate. The book made clear when these spontaneous demonstrations should occur and exactly how long they should last! Unfortunately for the Nixon campaign, one of these books fell into the hands of NBC. Viewers were then treated to David Brinkley and John Chancellor's gleefully reading from the book what was about to happen on the convention floor. Brinkley would predict that a spontaneous demonstration would erupt in a couple of minutes—and it did. Then he would announce that it will last for exactly twelve minutes—and it would. The convention remained a marvel of organization, but thanks to the news media, it conveyed a rather different image than its managers had planned.

paign process. Citizens receive virtually all their information about the campaigns from the media, mostly from television news and advertisements. The media are positioned not only to shape the public's perception of the candidates but also to play the role of agenda setters in a campaign. Since it is the media that decides what is news, their choices of what candidates to cover and what issues to mention tend to determine what is perceived as important.

An example of this power is the active part the media play in the process of winnowing out candidates during the presidential primary season. The candidates compete in a series of primary cam-

QUICK "CALLS": CAN THE MEDIA AFFECT THE OUTCOME OF ELECTIONS?

Competition among the media is intense. Success, many media executives believe, depends on offering the public information that is unique, useful, and important. But being *first* with the news is of paramount concern. Newspapers vie to break major stories, while television networks contend to find the most interesting and photogenic stories to attract viewers. Such competition normally functions to produce better and more entertaining news coverage.

One aspect of this competition has produced considerable controversy, however. Since the development of sophisticated polling techniques in the 1960s, the television networks have competed to be the first to call or project the outcome of major elections. The problem arises when, in their desire to be first, the networks have called a winner in the presidential election before the polls have closed in the West. The fear is that knowing the outcome of the election, many potential voters in the West will not bother to vote or will be swayed to vote for the projected winner.

Networks base their projections on the voting trends in a few key precincts in the East or on the data collected in exit polls—surveys of voters leaving the polling place. With the three hours' difference between the East Coast and the West Coast, enough early returns are available from eastern precincts to enable the networks to project a winner while westerners are still voting. The use of key precincts and exit polling allows the networks to identify voting trends even with as little as 1 percent of the vote actually counted. If a normally Democratic precinct is going Republican, for example, a Republican landslide is indicated.

Concern with early projections and their impact on election outcomes reached a high in the 1980 election. Not only did the networks project Ronald Reagan the winner quite early, but Jimmy Carter believed the networks' (and his own) polls and conceded the election on national television before the voting was over in the West! This triggered the fear that many Carter supporters in the West would not bother to vote because the election was already over. Although such Carter supporters could not change the outcome of the presidential election, their votes for lower offices in which the race was close might have made a difference. For a time, Democrats blamed the defeat of a number of western senators and representatives on the media and Carter's early concession.

Some political scientists have tried to determine whether early projections actually affect voting behavior in the West. Although the studies are not conclusive, media projections appear to have relatively little impact on the decision whether to vote and for whom. These studies suggest that media projections probably did not affect the election outcomes for lower level offices in 1980, but they have the potential to do so in extremely close races.[11] Recognizing this potential, the media have informally agreed not to make projections in the presidential race until all the polls have closed.

---

paigns in various states in the spring of presidential election years. The media, based on poll results, will have identified a leader in this primary horse race and will assess the results of each election and later polls to identify the front-runner. As a result, candidates begin to run against the expectations created by the media rather than one another. This greatly complicates the determination of the winner of a primary, for winning means doing better than the expectations created by the media rather than finishing first! It isn't exciting news if everything comes out as expected. The big news is if it doesn't. And the big newsmaker is the candidate who con-

founds the polls. Thus it may be the candidate who finishes second in the primary but was expected to finish fifth who actually has won in terms of media attention. Candidates know this and may actually begin to predict a low finish for themselves in hopes of doing better than expected.

It is also dangerous to be the front-runner in such a game, for even winning by a narrower than expected margin may mean projecting the image of a defeat. This happened in 1968 when President Johnson beat Eugene McCarthy in the New Hampshire Democratic primary by about 8 percent of the vote. This was a narrower margin than was expected for an incumbent president, and the media interpreted the election as a defeat for the president and his Vietnam war policies. Johnson subsequently withdrew from the race. Months later, a majority of the people thought that McCarthy had actually won the primary. Front-runner Edmund Muskie suffered a similar fate in the 1972 New Hampshire primary after failing to defeat George McGovern by the expected margin.

The power of the media in campaigns is not unlimited, however. A number of studies have indicated that the impact of the media is not as great as might be imagined. Research suggests that despite extensive media campaigns, for example, some candidates still fail to penetrate the public consciousness. A big media budget may be a necessary, but not sufficient, condition for success.[13] Other studies have indicated that media campaigns are not very successful in changing votes. Once someone has developed a favorable or unfavorable attitude toward a candidate, the candidate's television ads appear to simply reinforce the preexisting orientation. Rarely will voters actually change their voting preferences.[14]

The media's power is limited by two important factors: one having to do with the character of the people the media serves, the other with the actual character of the mass media. The foregoing research reminds us that the people served by the media are not empty vessels waiting to be filled with ideas, attitudes, and information that will determine their political choices. Instead, citizens come to each campaign with preexisting political values, attitudes, opinions, and orientations. These act as a built-in filter that is an effective defense mechanism against the messages of the media. People afford the media only **selective attention,** paying heed only to those messages they want to see or hear and avoiding or ignoring messages that do not agree with existing beliefs.[15] For some, it is easier to tune politics out altogether. Others carefully choose to read and view only material that reinforces rather than challenges existing views.

The media's diversity helps make selective attention possible. In the United States, citizens have a great many choices from which to garner their political information, and there exists a range of opinions and viewpoints in the media wide enough to satisfy the selective attention of virtually any political taste. The media are also becoming more,

rather than less, diverse in important ways, especially television, which up until recently has been the least diverse. The growing phenomenon of narrow casting via cable television, allowing this medium to profitably target specific audiences, is the most important aspect of this growing diversity. Before, television had been limited to general mass

THE MAKING OF A CANDIDATE

Even more than the print media, television can make or break a candidate for political office. No one knows this better than the candidates themselves. How they look, sound, and even smile can decide an electoral outcome in the most powerful country in the world. The campaign and subsequent election of Jimmy Carter in 1976 illustrates this point. He was ''Jimmy Who?'' until the media discovered presidential candidate Carter. Part of the reason for Carter's emergence had to do with the career interests of a portion of the media. Younger journalists saw that the leading candidates in 1976 were already fully covered by their more well-established colleagues. An unknown Carter began to be covered by equally unknown members of the press:

> Then *we* found someone *they* didn't know—an outsider. We began touting Jimmy Carter in 1976; they began mocking him. ... We were already committed to Carter. We knew him, we had forecast his triumph, we had checked out our new desks at the White House and we had begun our Carter books—the books we expected to take us into the first rank of our business ... I'm not saying we liked Carter. Liking was never part of it. Our lives and ambitions happened to come together—to mutual benefit.[12]

This doesn't mean that the press decides who will occupy the presidency or any other office. Obscure candidates are covered by ambitious young journalists every election year, usually without the candidate's enjoying any success. But the press has interests of its own in political campaigns and is in a position for such interests to powerfully affect political outcomes.

audiences and thus had been pushed toward general, noncontroversial, middle-of-the-road presentations to attract and maintain audiences. In seeking to offend no one, television tended to display a bias toward moderation. Cable and satellite technologies have freed television to provide offerings as varied as the print media have always done.

Media diversity makes it very unlikely that the media will present views to the public reflecting only one or a very few viewpoints. The media do not have a single bias to impose on the people, for they reflect many biases, and subtle shades of opinion tend to influence people in differing directions. Also, the competition among the news media helps to keep them relatively objective. If one of the networks is slanting the news or if a newspaper has targeted a particular candidate for defeat, the other networks and newspapers are likely to see this behavior itself as newsworthy and report it to the public. Major news organizations find it difficult to abandon their objectivity completely and retain their credibility for any length of time. So diversity also serves to discipline the press and helps to keep it trustworthy.

Conclusion

Elections are important for several reasons. They provide for political accountability, they are symbols of political legitimacy, and they provide a fundamental avenue for political participation. Perhaps their most fundamental contribution is a peaceful alternative to the more violent and unstable means of selecting leadership prevalent in much of the world.

All electoral systems have biases and help to shape political outcomes. In the United States, our complex system of multiple, staggered elections may discourage participation for a number of reasons. It is not only somewhat difficult to participate in elections but also elections are so frequent and of so many types that they may come to be taken for granted and seen as unimportant. Holding elections at fixed intervals prevents the people from

making sudden, major changes in the makeup of government and the direction of public policy. Single-member district plurality elections result in skewed and unequal representation in legislative bodies and lead to efforts to manipulate political outcomes in the form of gerrymandering. Finally, the unit-rule custom in the operation of the electoral college misrepresents the electorate. The misrepresentation is great enough that the election of a president who has not won the most popular votes is a distinct possibility.

The electorate itself has recently become volatile and unpredictable in their voting, though the pattern and direction of change is not yet clear. We may be entering a period of realignment in loyalties to the major parties that will result in a new majority for the Republicans. In any case, the pattern of electoral competition in the United States seems permanently altered from that of the decades before the 1970s.

The cost of elections has expanded dramatically in the last few years, due in large measure to the increased use of the media to sell candidates. With the rising costs, money has become more important than ever in electoral politics and the influence of those who contribute the money has also increased. Donations are limited by a number of federal election laws, but the laws have loopholes and court decisions have opened several other avenues for money to flow into and influence elections. Although money and the media exposure it buys cannot always determine electoral outcomes, they may be decisive in close elections.

In sum, the media are a powerful force in our lives and our politics. They shape how we see and understand the world around us, and as a result they can affect our politics and electoral outcomes. They are not all-powerful, however. They are not in a position to exercise coordinated control over political outcomes or to manipulate them in a consistent manner. The media do not achieve their full potential for contributing to the electoral process through educating the electorate on the issues, but they also do not destroy the integrity of the democratic process.

 **Glossary**

Blanket primary An election to select the candidates of a party for government office that allows the voters to cast ballots in both party primaries for different offices.

Closed primary An election to select the candidates of a party for government office that is limited to registered party members. This limit prevents members of other parties from crossing over and helping to select the nominee of an opposing party.

Electoral college A group of people called electors, selected by the voters in each state when voting for president, that officially elects the president and vice president. The individuals that serve as electors are chosen by the parties, usually as an honor for past service and loyalty.

Federal Election Campaign Act of 1974 A law that created the Federal Election Commission (FEC), established limits for campaign contributions and spending in presidential elections, provided for some public financing of presidential primaries and general elections, and required disclosure of all sources and uses of campaign funds.

Federal Election Commission (FEC) A six-member, bipartisan commission created by the Federal Election Campaign Act of 1974 to administer and enforce campaign finance laws.

General election An election held to fill government offices. In the United States, general elections are contests between the candidates of the two major parties.

Gerrymandering Drawing legislative district boundaries in such a manner as to advantage one party, interest, or candidate (usually the incumbent).

Initiative A law proposed by a petition of citizens and then submitted to a popular vote.

Open primary An election to select the candidates of a party for government office that allows voters to choose the party primary in which they will vote. Voters may cast votes for the candidates for nomination of only one party.

Plurality A number of votes received by a candidate that is more than that received by any other candidate, but less than a majority of votes cast.

Political action committees (PACs) Organizations created by unions, corporations, and citizen groups for the purpose of collecting and contributing campaign funds. The groups may also spend on behalf of causes and candidates independent of candidate campaign organizations.

Primary election (direct primary) An election in which voters select the candidates of each party for the general election.

Proportional representation A system of election in which seats in the legislature are allocated to each party contesting the election in equal proportion to its percentage of the popular vote.

Reapportionment (redistricting) Alteration of the pattern of representation among electoral districts in accordance with changes in the population that occur over time. Reapportionment assures that all electoral districts will remain roughly equivalent in population.

Referendum An election in which an issue before the legislature or a law passed by the legislature is voted on by the public for approval or disapproval.

Selective attention A psychological process whereby a person tends to read and view only material that reinforces preexisting, favored attitudes and views.

Single-member district An electoral district from which a single legislator is selected, resulting in a winner-take-all electoral system. Selection is usually by plurality vote.

Unit rule The customary practice of a state casting all its electoral college votes for the candidate with the largest number of popular votes. The unit rule expresses the winner-take-all principle in voting for president.

Winner-take-all An electoral procedure whereby only the candidate receiving the most votes gets elected.

Suggestions for Further Reading

Alexander, Herbert E. *Financing Politics: Money, Elections and Political Reform.* 3d ed. Washington, D.C.: Congressional Quarterly Press, 1984. An authoritive discussion of the role of money in politics.

Atherton, Christopher F. *Media Politics: The News Strategies of Presidential Campaigns.* Lexington, Mass.: Lexington Books, 1984. A thorough discussion of how campaigns are reported and the influence of the mass media in politics.

Burnham, Walter Dean. *Critical Elections and the Mainsprings of American Politics.* New York: Norton, 1970. A thorough historical tracing of electoral trends in the United States, focusing on explaining the decline in voting participation and the importance of critical elections.

Clor, Harry M., ed. *The Mass Media and American Democracy.* Chicago: Rand McNally, 1974. A series of essays that presents competing viewpoints about the influence of the media on politics.

Drew, Elizabeth. *Politics and Money: The New Road to Corruption.* New York: Macmillan, 1983. A good and entertainingly written discussion of money and politics.

Goldenberg, E.N., and M.W. Traugott. *Campaigning for Congress.* Washington D.C.: Congressional Quarterly Press, 1984. Provides an interesting and thorough discussion of various campaign strategies.

Krause, Sidney, and Dennis Davis. *The Effects of Mass Communication on Political Behavior.* University Park: Pennsylvania State University Press, 1976. A general introduction to the media's influence on political activity across a wide spectrum of issues.

McGinniss, Joe. *The Selling of the President, 1968.* New York: Trident Press, 1969. A modern classic that first drew wide public attention to the "packaging" of candidates in presidential campaigns.

Paletz, David, and Robert Entman. *Media, Power, Politics.* New York: Free Press, 1981. A good general treatment of the influence of the media in politics.

Pierce, Neal R., and Lawrence D. Longley. *The People's President: The Electoral College in American History and the Direct Vote Alternative.* Rev. ed. New Haven, Conn.: Yale University Press, 1981. A comprehensive treatment of the way the electoral college operates and the political implications of proposed alternatives.

Pomper, Gerald M., with Susan S. Lederman. *Elections in America: Control and Influence in Democratic Politics.* 2d ed. New York: Longman, 1980. Discusses several important election-related issues including the justification of elections in a democracy, the influence of elections, and the behavior of voters.

Rae, Douglas W. *The Political Consequences of Electoral Laws.* Rev. ed. New Haven, Conn.: Yale University Press, 1971. A thorough and sophisticated treatment of the impact of electoral laws on the nature of political structures, institutions, and competition.

Sundquist, James L. *Dynamics of the Party System: Alignment and Realignment of Political Parties in the United States.* Rev. ed. Washington D.C.: Brookings Institution, 1983. Excellent historical analysis of realigning elections from 1860 to the present. Includes a discussion of why the 1980 election did not signal a realignment.

Thayer, George. *Who Shakes the Money Tree?* New York: Simon and Schuster, 1973. Provides a close look at the process of financing politics.

Who lobbies? Everybody.
Nicholas Henry
John Hall

I belong to no organized political party—I am a Democrat.
Will Rogers

Chapter 8

Interest Groups and Political Parties

Chapter Outline

Introduction
The Functions of Interest Groups and Political Parties
Interest Groups: Organizing for Influence
Political Parties: Organizing for Political Power
Contemporary Trends and Prospects
Conclusion

Introduction

In this chapter, we explore the two most important extraconstitutional institutions that affect both the operations of the national government and the policy process. Because interest groups and political parties play such a complementary role in these operations, they are best examined together. After identifying the key similarities and differences between interest groups and political parties, we turn to an analysis of the contributions each of these institutions makes to America's democracy. Finally, we discuss the contemporary condition and prospects for groups and parties.

The Functions of Interest Groups and Political Parties

Interest groups and **political parties** link the individual citizen and the government. Through this linkage, interest groups and political parties function as alternate forms of representation. Despite the absence of constitutional provisions for interest groups and political parties, they are the principal nongovernmental institutions that shape the policy process. Indeed, no major public policy emerges from the national government that has not been affected by interest group pressure and party considerations.

Though both are important links between the individual and the government, interest groups and parties perform this vital function in distinct ways. Interest groups attempt to *influence* the policy-making process and produce policy outcomes favorable to the central concerns of their members by gaining access to key governmental decision makers. Gaining access means to assure that the group's concerns, demands, and wishes are heard by decision makers and that the group has ample opportunity to present its case. Interest groups aid in the process of articulating the claims of competing groups— liberals versus conservatives, labor versus management, environmentalists versus developers, prochoice versus pro-life groups on the abortion issue, and so on.

In a democracy like the United States, political parties endeavor to build popular support sufficient to capture public office through the electoral process, gain control of the government, and *formulate* public policy. To win support at the polls, political parties strive to aggregate various groups—agriculture, business and professional, trade, labor, racial, ethnic, religious—into an electoral coalition large enough to win elections. A successful party may gain control of the government and seek to enact its programs and policies into law.

In short, interest groups and parties serve distinct representational purposes. An interest group represents a specific minority and endeavors to influence government in order to protect, maintain, and enhance the interests of its members. A political party, in contrast, is an aggregative, coalition-constructing, majority-building institution that strives to gain governmental power and enact its policy preferences into law.

Interest groups and political parties, then, organize the pursuit of influence and political power in a democracy. They are the basic vehicles for articulating and aggregating the concerns and demands of the people. As such, they are central to maintaining peaceful, democratic means of conflict resolution. Conflict resolution is a basic, perhaps the primary, function of government. In providing a peaceful means for substituting political and legal competition for the use of force, interest groups and parties are of immense importance to the stable functioning of the political system. Moreover, interest groups and parties are the principal means through which people participate in government. As we noted in Chapter 2, the extent and quality of participation is central to the democratic character of the political system. Thus, interest groups and parties play a central role in determining the quality of democracy itself.

Interest Groups: Organizing for Influence

Groups of citizens, rather than isolated individuals, are central to the expression of political interests in the American political system. Such groups of citizens are represented in nearly seven thousand formal organizations in Washington, D.C. That so many of them exist and that their number is so rapidly expanding (about 70 percent have established their Washington offices since 1960) testifies to their success in accomplishing their public policy goals.[1]

The kind of government created by the Constitution explains the utility and political success of organized interest groups. In our government, political authority is distributed among separate institutions. The sharing of power in the policy process by the two houses and numerous committees and subcommittees within Congress, by the president, and by the federal courts ensures that important policy decisions are made in many places. Such a policy process also ensures a multiplicity of "pressure points" or "veto points" where interest groups can attempt to influence decision makers. The more active the government becomes and the more areas of life it significantly affects, the more groups will find it in their interest to organize for influencing governmental policy.

Today, few industries or occupational groups are not organized to represent and defend their interests with government. Though generally less influential, there are also active groups representing noneconomic interests. These include groups organized around broad racial and ethnic identities; around the environment, urban areas, civil rights or women's rights, or the possession and use of firearms; and around single issues such as a nuclear freeze, abortion, or school prayer.

Busy volunteers at Common Cause Headquarters. Such public interest or "consumer" groups are particularly vulnerable to incentive problems.

Still other groups are organized to represent the public interest. These groups work for goals that benefit all society rather than the members of one group. Such groups include consumer groups (the Consumer's Union or the Consumer Complaint Research Center), good government groups (Common Cause or the League of Women Voters), and social protection groups (the Children's Foundation or the American Horse Protection Association).

Institutional and Membership Interest Groups

The type of interests around which groups organize is the most common way to categorize groups. Another useful way to categorize organized interests is to distinguish between "institutional" and "membership" groups.[2] Although we usually think of an interest group's membership as consisting of individuals, as with the PTA or League of Women Voters, many of the most powerful and influential interest organizations represent other organizations rather than individuals. These institutional interest organizations are often law firms or public relations firms that make a profession of representing the interests of their client organizations and institutions. A great many corporations have hired professional representatives in Washington on a full- or part-time basis, paying them very high fees for their services but reaping the benefits of professional, on-site expertise in the lobbying process.

Just one example of an institutional interest organization

Another important type of institutional interest organization is the trade association. Formed as permanent organizations to represent the interests of a particular business or trade, their large number includes some of the most influential and familiar interest groups, such as the American Medical Association (AMA) and the American Petroleum Institute, as well as a great many groups representing smaller and less familiar businesses, such as the American Mushroom Council or the Fatty Acid Producers Council.

Institutional interest organizations represent not only business organizations but also governments and even universities. The American Council on Education speaks for the interests of institutions of higher learning like the one you are attending. Organizations such as the National Association of Counties and the American Public Transit Association represent the interests of lower levels of government with the national government.

Membership groups, by contrast, are usually noneconomic in orientation and represent the interests of individuals. They are what most people think of when they think of political interest groups. They are also the organizations through which the average person may take part in political and civic affairs. Despite the fact that membership groups tend to be less powerful (see Table 8.1), Americans join them in part because they are convinced that organized activity is an effective way to influence government—even a government as seemingly remote as that in Washington D.C.

Some people join membership groups because they deeply and passionately believe in the goals or purposes of the organization. These people usually form the core organizers and activists of the organization, but are too few in number to provide a mass membership. Most people who are sympathetic to the goals of a membership organization, in fact, do not join the organization. Most blacks are not members of the National Association for the Advancement of Colored People (NAACP) or any other civil rights organization, nor does the Sierra Club attract a majority of those sympathetic to preserving the environment.

It is quite rational for sympathetic individuals not to join such groups. As Mancur Olson points out in his classic study, *The Logic of Collective Action,* membership involves such costs as membership dues, and perhaps more important, the time devoted to group activities. Moreover, any given individual knows that he or she is unlikely to affect in a significant way the ultimate success or failure of the group to attain its ends. Moreover, if the organization succeeds the individual will reap the benefits regardless of membership. Thus, it makes sense to sit by and save the personal costs of money and time that membership entails.

Membership groups clearly need some incentive beyond their stated purposes to persuade people to join. Many organizations employ material incentives to attract members, typically goods and services that have a clear and significant monetary benefit that is available only to members, such as the opportunity to buy certain goods at discount prices, take trips at group fares, or purchase relatively low-cost insurance. The American Association of Retired Persons (AARP) is such an organization. Another kind of incentive to join membership-based interest groups is "solidary" incentives. Such incentives involve the sense of belonging, the companionship, and the general pleasures derived from associating with like-minded others in a small group.

To offer solidary incentives, membership groups must furnish the opportunity for face-to-face contact in relatively small local organizational units. Even national interest groups seeking national goals through influence on the national government are usually organized at the grass-roots level in small local units capable of providing such benefits to their members. This sort of organizational structure can be seen in the NAACP, the League of Women Voters, and the PTA, to mention a few prominent examples. The local chapters pursue local goals and furnish voting and financial support for the national organization, which presses for national goals.

Many political scientists have argued that interest group activity is the key to understanding political power and policy in the United States. In short, "who gets what, how, and when" depends on the outcome of the clash of competing organized political interests. Let us turn now to the group characteristics and activities that tend to bring a group power, influence, and success in American politics.

Requisites for the Success of Interest Groups

Interest group success depends on several factors, the most important of which are leadership and

Table 8.1
Points of Access for Interest Groups in the National Government

Interest Group	Congressional Committee	Executive Agency
MORE POWERFUL GROUPS: Agriculture 　American Farm Bureau Federation 　Associated Milk Producers 　National Farm Organization 　National Farm Union	House: 　Agriculture Senate: 　Agriculture and Forestry	Agriculture Department, Farm Credit Administration
Business, Trade, and Professional Groups 　American Bankers Association 　American Medical Association 　American Petroleum Institute 　Iron and Steel Institute 　National Association of Realtors 　National Small Businessmen's Association	House: 　Banking and Currency, 　　Interstate and 　　Foreign Commerce Senate: 　Commerce	Commerce Department, Export-Import Bank, FDIC, FSLIC, Small Business Administration
Organized Labor 　AFL–CIO 　National Education Association 　Seafarers International Union 　Teamsters 　United Auto Workers 　United Mine Workers	House: 　Education and Labor Senate: 　Labor and Public Welfare	Education Department, Labor Department, Federal Mediation and Conciliation 　Service, National Labor Relations Board
LESS POWERFUL GROUPS: Civil Rights Groups 　American Civil Liberties Union 　American Indian Movement 　American Jewish Congress 　La Raza 　National Association for the Advancement of 　　Colored People 　National Welfare Rights Organization	House: 　Commerce, 　Judiciary Senate: 　Commerce, 　Judiciary	Civil Rights Division of the Justice 　Department Civil Rights Commission Equal Employment Opportunity 　Commission
Environmental Groups 　National Audubon Society 　National Wildlife Federation 　Resources for the Future 　Sierra Club 　Wilderness Society	House: 　Interior and 　Insular Affairs Senate: 　Interior and 　Insular Affairs	Agriculture Department Energy Department Interior Department Council on Environmental Quality Environmental Protection Agency
Urban Area Groups 　International City Managers Associations 　National Conference of Mayors 　National League of Cities	House: 　(none) Senate: 　Banking, Housing, and 　Urban Affairs	Health and Human Services, Housing and Urban Development, Transportation

organization, resources, support from underlying values, and access.

Leadership and organization: A small, internally cohesive group with stable and effective leadership, well-defined goals, and support from the people most likely to vote will tend to be much more influential than groups that lack these characteristics. Among the best organized and most effective groups are business interests generally, some professional associations like the American Medical Association (AMA) and the American Bar Association (ABA), some agricultural commodity associations such as dairy farmers and tobacco growers, and a few special interest groups like the National Rifle Association (NRA). Organized labor also tends to have cohesive and coherent leadership and organization.

The NRA has been one of America's more successful membership groups.

By contrast, consumer groups and other broad-based, mass membership interest groups are often poorly organized and lack stable, united, and effective leadership. Those from the lower socioeconomic strata, such as the homeless, are also unlikely to be members of well-led and well-organized associations.

Resources: The most important resource is the ability to attract financial support. Such support enables a group to communicate its message effectively to governmental officials and to the public. Groups that lack this resource often cannot wage the lengthy campaign necessary to reach their political and economic goals. Other valuable resources include prestige or status, expertise, critical skills, talent, moral commitment, patriotism, and name recognition. The Air Line Pilots Association (ALPA), for example, is an influential group partly because it combines several of these resources. Groups that are unable to accumulate such resources are unlikely to develop more than a very modest amount of political influence.

Support from underlying values: Interest groups often attempt to draw support from the underlying values held by the people most likely to vote, by trying to universalize the importance of their objectives. In other words, interest groups seek to link their special interests to the broader public interest. If an interest group cannot reconcile its purposes and goals with the dominant values, the level of resistance the group experiences is likely to be high and its chances for success will be greatly reduced. For example, welfare recipients have been relatively unsuccessful, partly because the notion of welfare runs counter to the strongly and widely held value of economic individualism.

Access: Basic to any interest group's success is the ability to communicate effectively with governmental decision makers. A group that can't make its case with public officials is hopelessly handicapped in its efforts. Indeed, gaining access to governmental decision makers is the most fundamental instrumental goal of all interest groups (Table 8.1). As mentioned earlier, such groups are not lacking for access points in the federal government. Depending on their goals and purposes, organized interests will also seek access to state and local governments and the major political parties. In some cases, even such national and international political organizations as the Council of State Governments and the United Nations can provide the necessary access.

Regardless of the access point or points, *effective* access depends largely on the possession and skillful use of the requisites mentioned earlier—leadership and organization, consistency of goals with underlying cultural values, and plenty of money. Indeed, money may be the single most important requisite for success because it can be helpful in acquiring others. For example, money can be used to hire and retain a professional staff for strong leadership and organization or for linking a group's special interest to broader cultural values through expensive advertising and public relations techniques of mass propaganda.

Tactics of Interest Groups

The tactics used by interest groups can be placed on a continuum, with the tactics employed by the more successful groups at one end and the tactics used by the less successful groups at the other. In the following pages we explore the factors that di-

The homeless poor are one group clearly lacking representation
in the interest system.

vide the more successful from the less successful groups and describe the tactics used by each.

More Successful Groups: The most influential interest groups include agriculture, business, professional, trade, and labor organizations. Three principal factors account for their past and continuing success. First, these groups enjoy support from the people most likely to vote because their goals are largely in harmony with underlying cultural values. The business community, for example, is sheltered from serious threats to the notions of private property and free enterprise by the strongly held value of economic individualism. Nor is it an accident that this value continues to be strongly held. Business organizations, among others, reinforce it constantly through advertising and other mass media messages.

Second, successful groups have established close working relationships with executive agencies or legislative committees serving their interests. Such a relationship is a key goal of organized interests, and the creation of such an agency or a committee is a clear indication of their success and a formidible instrument for future use. For example, a central goal of the National Education Association (NEA) in the 1970s was the creation of a department of education. After their support helped elect Jimmy Carter in 1976, they realized this goal. Despite strong opposition to the department by the Reagan administration, the NEA has been able to maintain the department's existence.

Finally, the more established groups have their economic interests protected by government policies. Of course, this is the ultimate aim of all interest organizations and thus is both a measure of their success and an important tool for gaining further successes. Organized labor, for example, can count on numerous government policies to protect its status and power in the collective bargaining process, and midwestern farmers stand to benefit from a policy of uninterrupted grain sales to the Soviet Union.

Lobbying: The more powerful interests engage extensively in **lobbying,** as they seek to influence the

Successful groups often use professional lobbyists like Charles Walker, pictured above.

timing, content, and even the need for legislation. Established and powerful interests instinctively prefer a stable legislative environment since any change means uncertainty and unpredictability.[3] Aspiring groups, on the other hand, are more likely to prefer a fluid legislative environment where the likelihood of change is greater.

Lobbying, if successful, tends to minimize change and enhance stability and predictability. Although much lobbying is informal in nature, lobbyists are most active at the committee stage of legislation. They will often appear before a committee and testify as to the probable impact of proposed legislation. Such testimony furnishes the committee with factual data as well as expert opinion that can influence the provisions of the legislative bill under consideration. If the legislature passes a bill that is perceived as harmful to a group's interests, that group will then pressure the executive agency to interpret and implement the legislation in a way less damaging to their interests.[4]

Political Campaign Activity: Interest groups support candidates who appear to be favorably disposed to their interests. The most common form of support is a financial contribution. Although there

is nothing new in this, in recent years, the quantity of contributions has reached unprecedented proportions. Many reasons for this growth exist, including the need for great sums of money to wage a modern mass-media-based campaign. But, as we noted in Chapter 7, most observers agree that the

WILL CONGRESS KICK THE PAC HABIT?

In late 1985, the Congress, at the insistence of Democratic Senator David Boren of Oklahoma, began to formally consider the controversial financing of congressional campaigns by political action committees. Boren's anti-PAC proposal is viewed as a long shot even by Boren himself, but it attracted early support from a surprising number of his colleagues, including such heavyweights as Republican Barry Goldwater of Arizona and Democrat John Stennis of Mississippi. Boren says PAC money is "like a drug and everybody's hooked." Characteristically even more dramatic, Barry Goldwater sees PACs as "the primary threat" to our political system.

There is no question that congressional candidates are becoming more reliant on PAC money. *Newsweek* magazine reported that in 1984 more than 150 members of the House received more than 50 percent of their funds from PACs. In 1986, PACs provided about one-third of money spent by House candidates, and about one-fourth of that spent by candidates for the Senate. Members of Congress certainly do not wish to be dependent on PACs or have to spend time and bruise their pride begging for PAC largess. But campaign costs, driven by the expenses of television advertising, continue to rise rapidly, and many in Congress are not likely to support reforms like Boren's that would cut this lucrative source of funds nearly in half.

The problem also exists of what would become of this money if it is not given to congressional campaigns. The PACs will still raise and spend it in pursuit of their objectives. The money would probably be redirected into "independent expenditures" not under the control of any campaign. Such expenditures have often been used for negative campaigns by PACs in the past, and might make elections even more unruly and unpredictable. Like other finance reforms that had unintended effects (such as the PAC problem itself), these reforms might create new and even more serious long-term problems.

Table 8.2
Biggest Givers Among Political Action Committees to Congressional Candidates in 1984

PAC	Contribution
1. National Association of Realtors	$2,429,552
2. American Medical Association	1,839,464
3. National Association of Home Builders	1,652,539
4. National Education Association	1,302,519
5. United Auto Workers	1,405,107
6. Seafarers International Union	1,322,418
7. International Association of Machinists and Aerospace Workers	1,306,497
8. Food and Commercial Workers Union	1,271,974
9. Letter Carriers Union	1,234,603
10. Retired Federal Employees	1,099,243

Source: Federal Election Commission.

dramatic increases in contributions can be traced to the legal reforms that were designed to correct the campaign finance abuses uncovered in the Watergate scandal. These reforms sought to regulate how money is given and, ironically, limit the amount of money that could be donated. By providing for the formation of legally regulated political action committees (PACs), however, the reforms created an avenue for a massive growth in political contributions. Table 8.2 lists some of the largest recent contributors to the campaigns of congressional candidates. As the table makes clear, business groups give by far the largest amount of money to political campaigns through PACs. Corporate, trade, and professional PACs taken together accounted for $62.2 million in contributions to con-

gressional races in 1984, or nearly 60 percent of the total. As might be expected, their contributions favor Republicans, but as incumbents, Democrats also attract substantial contributions.

The contributions made through PACs are not evenly distributed among the members of Congress. Such contributions vary in size between the House and the Senate, among the candidates of the two major parties, and especially according to whether the candidate is an incumbent or a challenger in the race for office. Table 8.3 summarizes the distribution of PAC contributions among the members of Congress.[5]

One important trend in PAC activity that is not reflected in Table 8.3 is the rapid growth of ideological PACs in recent years. Their numbers have increased at a rate far greater than that for business or labor groups. Also, since 1980, they have consistently raised more money than either business or labor. These groups spend substantially less on campaign contributions, however.

There are two important reasons for this. First, unlike business or labor PACs that solicit money from within their organizations, ideological PACs usually raise money by means of direct mail campaigns. This is expensive, usually costing at least $.50 for each $1.00 raised, and often much more. Second, ideological PACs have chosen to direct a larger proportion of their spending into campaign activities and media advertising independent of any candidate's organization.

Spending on campaigns and media is perfectly legal, and the amounts are not limited by the Campaign Reform Act. The negative tone and provoca-

Table 8.3
The Distribution of PAC Contributions to Congressional Candidates in 1984

PACs sponsored by	Contributions (in millions)						
	By election		By party		By incumbency		
	Senate /	House	Dem /	Rep	Incumbent /	Challenger /	Open
Corporations	$11.9	$23.4	$13.5	$21.8	$27.5	$3.7	$4.1
Labor unions	4.9	19.9	23.5	1.3	15.9	5.7	3.2
Trade and Professions	6.3	20.3	13.1	13.4	20.9	3.0	2.7
Single issue and ideological	5.4	9.1	7.7	6.8	7.3	4.9	2.3
Other	0.8	2.9	2.2	1.4	4.1	0.2	0.3

Source: Federal Election Commission.

THE RISE OF THE NEW RIGHT

Among the ideological PACs that have become active in politics in recent years, about two-thirds have been conservative in their orientation, and none have been more important than those journalists have grouped under the label "New Right." Leaders of the New Right groups, such as Jerry Falwell of the Moral Majority and Terry Dolan of the National Conservative Political Action Committee (NCPAC), have been able to put together a loose alliance of organizations that form a potentially potent political force. In addition to the organizations, the New Right alliance includes groups like Phyllis Schafly's Stop ERA, Citizens for the Republic (founded by Ronald Reagan), the Committee for the Survival of a Free Congress, Howard Phillips's Conservative Caucus, the Fund for the Conservative Majority, and the American Conservative Union.

Falwell and a few other political evangelists project the New Right's media image and attempt to wield the weapon of mass propaganda for the movement's causes. Broadcasts like Falwell's "Old Time Gospel Hour" also have the more practical purpose of raising money for political activities, and are quite successful at it. The "Old Time Gospel Hour" earned about $70 million in 1980, for example, much of which went for lobbying, education, and campaign efforts. In addition, they have been very successful in the use of direct mail solicitations. These efforts, directed by Richard Viguerie, raised millions of dollars for sympathetic candidates like Jesse Helms of North Carolina and Ronald Reagan himself. Campaign efforts are largely in the hands of Terry Dolan and NCPAC, which actively recruits, finances, and trains conservative candidates and their staffs, as well as targets liberal and moderate members of Congress for defeat. NCPAC and its New Right allies have been effective in the view of many observers who credit these organizations with playing an important role in the election of Ronald Reagan and a Republican Senate majority in 1980. Though they have been less successful in eliminating targeted politicians since, in 1980, of six liberal senators that NCPAC selected for defeat, only Alan Cranston of California survived the election.

tive character of some of these independent efforts has prompted concern and criticism by many legislators, however. The association of negative campaigns with ideological PACs is one reason PACs and their money remain controversial actors in American electoral politics.

Mass Propaganda: Mass propaganda is a public relations effort of the more successful groups to foster a favorable image of themselves and their goals. By developing positive public opinion, established groups seek to enhance the level of support they already enjoy. Corporate underwriting of public television programs is one way in which business interests seek to demonstrate their sense of responsibility to the larger community.

Mass propaganda has also been used very effectively by ideological interests, particularly those from what has come to be called the "New Right." The most prominent leaders of the New Right are highly skilled in the use of the electronic media and the art of communication. Jerry Falwell of the Moral Majority is one such leader of a rather complex network of organizations that seek to further their conservative social agenda through mass persuasion.

Less Successful Groups: Groups in this category are less likely to use the tactics examined earlier. Among the many interests in this category, perhaps the most well known are civil rights groups, racial and ethnic minorities, environmentalists, consumers, and the economically disadvantaged. In many respects, these groups are less powerful because they do not share the three principal factors we have identified as contributing to the success of the more established interests.

First, the less powerful groups often espouse political and economic goals that run against the grain of the underlying values held by large numbers of people. Demands for racial equality by blacks, for example, run counter to strong feelings of racial hostility on the part of many Americans.

Second, whereas the established groups have an executive agency or a legislative committee serving their interests, the less successful groups often do not. Consumers, despite many attempts, have yet to be successful in securing an executive agency at the cabinet level to shield their interests. Nor have they fared any better with the Congress. No major standing committee has as its primary responsibility the protection of consumer interests.

Finally, the more powerful interests are the beneficiaries of numerous governmental policies, whereas important economic and noneconomic interests of the less successful groups are inadequately protected by public policies. When Chrysler Corporation was experiencing difficulties, they were successful in securing several hundred millions of dollars of federal loan guarantees. The economically disadvantaged, on the other hand, have been unable to secure a comparable level of federal support.

Direct action in the form of protests can serve to draw attention to less powerful groups.

Litigation (Legal Action): The less powerful groups, especially civil rights groups and religious minorities, have successfully vindicated their interests in the federal courts, the most notable instance being *Brown v. Board of Education* (1954), where the NAACP challenged the separate but equal doctrine that provided legal justification for segregated public schools in many southern states.[6] The Warren Court's unanimous decision declared segregation laws unconstitutional and an abridgement of the equal protection clause of the Fourteenth Amendment.

Although less spectacular, religious minorities, such as the Amish, have had their right to establish parochial schools upheld by the Supreme Court despite state attempts to regulate such schools. The American Civil Liberties Union (ACLU) is a prominent interest group that has used litigation to defend religious freedom as enunciated in the First Amendment.

Grass Roots Pressure: The less powerful groups also attempt to influence the actions of legislators and executive officials by bringing pressure to bear in their home districts or in the local office of an executive agency. For example, environmentalists seeking to protect wildlife have found that telephone calls to the home office of a legislator is more effective than mere news releases detailing their position. Welfare groups have likewise discovered that concerted pressure, such as a mass meeting with a local administrator, may produce more favorable results than individual recipients challenging adverse interpretations of welfare regulations.

Direct Action: Direct action can be either nonviolent or violent. Almost without exception, violence is regarded as illegitimate in a democracy. Boycotts, demonstrations, strikes, "blue flu," job actions, and picketing are some of the more important forms of nonviolent direct action. The Reverend Martin Luther King, Jr., during the 1960s, for example, made nonviolent civil disobedience the keystone of his civil rights efforts. A strike or the threat of a strike is one of the oldest direct action techniques and remains organized labor's most powerful weapon against a recalcitrant management.

Violent direct action can range from an isolated assassination of a political figure to civil war and revolution. The use of violence raises several disturbing issues. Under what conditions does a minority group have a right or an obligation to resist majority oppression? Is violence a direct and natural consequence of a political regime that denies basic human rights to certain groups and individuals? In a democracy, what principles should be employed to assist in defining the relationship between majority rule and minority rights?

From one perspective, democracy is a search for peaceful answers to the most troubling political questions. Given the complexity of modern society, it is not surprising that some people are willing to turn to violence in the hope of finding an easy answer.

NEGATIVE CAMPAIGNS

"Negative campaigns" is a new term for a rather old and time-honored practice in American politics—vilifying your opponent. Formerly called "dirty" campaigns, or more graphically "mudslinging contests," negative campaigning has become a concern in the 1980s, probably because the modern version is threatening to become more pervasive and institutionalized than the occasional mudslinging contest of the past. Today, the source of the negative campaign is usually not the other candidate, but an independent PAC that acts outside the control of the candidates. As a result, the natural, often tacit, agreements between candidates not to start rattling the skeletons in each other's closets or encourage the other to get nasty by getting nasty oneself fail to operate. Modern attacks on political opponents also may seem more pervasive and be more damaging, because they are often carried out in provocative, attention-grabbing mass-media campaigns.

The concern over negative campaigning has accompanied the growth of ideological groups, especially those of the New Right, with whom these tactics are associated. But the New Right, as they did with direct-mail fund-raising techniques, did not invent the negative campaign, but only improved on and extended its techniques. Nor are they alone in its use. Liberal ideological PACs that have formed to counter the influence of the New Right have also conducted negative campaigns. Such liberal organizations as the Fund for the Democratic Majority organized by Edward Kennedy, Walter Mondale's Committee for the Future of America, John Anderson's Independent Action, and the National Progressive Action Committee, have used many of the tactics the New Right found successful—direct-mail fund-raising campaigns and providing public relations services to candidates, as well as media attacks on conservative candidates.

One of the problems with negative campaigning is thus its tendency to spread. In the elections of 1986 negative tactics were extensively used and became a focus of the media's attention and a hallmark of the elections. If such pervasiveness continues, it could contribute to further cynicism among citizens about elections and the entire political process. If the process loses legitimacy in the eyes of the people, the stability of the system itself may ultimately be threatened.

Criticisms of Interest Groups

A serious criticism of interest groups in the United States' democracy is that not all interests are equally represented. Some groups—agriculture, business, and organized labor—have a decided advantage over other interests. Racial and ethnic minorities have far less influence in the policy process. Other interests, such as the economically disadvantaged, lack effective organization and leadership. Such defects guarantee political weakness. When interests are not equally represented, or represented ineffectively, the democratic ideals of fairness, equality, and justice are less likely to be honored. This nation's women have suffered both political and economic discrimination. Their efforts to overcome this discrimination and to secure their rights has been a painfully slow process.

A second criticism, (derived from Roberto Michel's "Iron Law of Oligarchy") is that elites inevitably dominate the most powerful interest groups.[7] An entrenched leadership hinders a healthy rotation of office and thus widens the gap between leaders and the rank and file. To some critics, the absence of competition within interest groups is even more damning. Virtually none of this nation's labor unions, for example, has a "two-party" system. A slate of candidates chosen by the leadership often runs for union office unopposed. Interest groups in a democracy, these critics claim, should adhere in their internal operations to the same standards of electoral competition found elsewhere in the political system.

Compounding the problem of elitism in entrenched leadership is the presence of "interlocking directorates" among the top institutional interests. The existence of such directorates suggests that elites are not only entrenched but far narrower and more exclusive than the number of institutional interests and positions would seem to indicate. Political scientists such as Thomas Dye and sociologists such as G. William Domhoff have shown that elites tend to occupy more than one powerful political or economic position.[8] In one study, Dye found that nearly forty institutional positions, such as corporate and foundation boards and university trusteeships, were held by individuals holding more than one such position. The narrowness of this elite raises serious questions about the extent and quality of competition among supposedly distinct interests.

Third, interest groups are criticized for their self-interestedness and lack of accountability. Obviously, the chief objective of most economic interest groups, whether they be farm, business, or labor, is to defend or improve the economic position of their members. This emphasis on economic concerns means that interest groups are mostly organized for narrow political advantage. These groups are not seeking the public interest, the common good, or the general welfare.

Some argue that the public interest can only be meaningfully defined as the sum of all individual interests; therefore, the self-seeking of interest groups is necessary and healthy for the realization of the public interest. But others maintain there is a clear clash between the public interest and special interests, which is growing more intense and threatening as we become more interdependent on a planet with finite resources.

Finally, interest groups are criticized because they wield too much power in our policy-making process. Concern about the power of interest groups stems, in part, from the *informal* structures within which their influence is wielded. Group competition and contact with government tends to occur largely in "subgovernments" or "iron triangles" of reciprocal influence. These subgovernments are composed of three key sets of political actors, including (1) interest group leaders concerned with a particular policy area, (2) the government agency responsible for the administration of the policy area, and (3) members of the congressional committee, and especially subcommittees, responsible for the formulation of legislation in the policy area.

The fundamental interests of the three corners of this policy-making triangle are often quite similar. Government policies regulating economic enterprises or industrial production are good examples. Normally, the interests, the bureaucrats in the agencies, and the legislators on the subcommittees all share a basic interest in promoting the particular enterprise or industry. Without that enterprise or industry, the three actors have no role to play.

Perhaps the most often-cited example of such a cozy subgovernment arrangement is the tobacco industry (Figure 8.1). Organized interests include the Retail Tobacco Distributors of America, the American Tobacco Institute, and the tobacco growers. The House Tobacco Subcommittee handles most government policy concerning the industry and is com-

HEARD OF THE IRON TRIANGLES?

No, Iron Triangles is not a new rock group or nickname for your favorite football team's defensive line. It is the name political scientists have dreamed up for the often cozy personal relationships of reciprocal influence that tend to develop in the highly decentralized national policy-making process. Lobbyists that are successful will attempt to establish close working relationships with both the members and staffers of relevant congressional subcommittees and the relevant agencies of the executive bureaucracy. Once such relationships are established for a particular interest, the three actors form the sides of the iron triangle within which policy on the issue of interest to the lobbyist will be made and implemented. Also called policy subsystems or subgovernments, these triangular relationships are formed around fairly specific clusters of policy interests, such as environmental controls, insurance regulation, energy regulation, or a particular agricultural commodity such as dairy products or tobacco.

Iron triangles exist because each of the three sides benefits from membership in the triangle. To the bureaucratic agency, the lobbyist can provide support for the budget requests that are its lifeblood. To the congressional subcommittees, the lobbyist can give support in the form of campaign contributions and information about the issue or industry represented that is useful for intelligent legislative decisions. In return, the lobbyist receives favorable consideration on legislative decisions from the subcommittees and favorable rulings on implementation regulations from the bureaucratic agency. Of course, the subcommittees and agencies are also linked directly in the triangular relationship. The subcommittee receives important policy information from the agency and often help with specific complaints of their constituents—the casework so valuable for a member of Congress' reelection. In return, the agency receives favorable consideration of its requests for higher budgets.

The iron triangle is thus an arrangement of mutual advantage in which the actors scratch one another's backs. No one knows for sure how many iron triangles are operating, but given their usefulness, the number must be nearly as high as the number of interests seeking to influence the policy process.

**Fig. 8.1
An Example of an Iron Triangle**

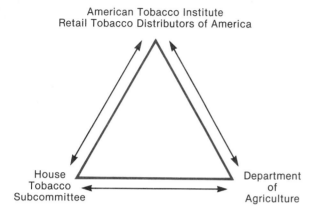

American Tobacco Institute
Retail Tobacco Distributors of America

House Tobacco Subcommittee

Department of Agriculture

prised of members knowledgeable about the industry, who also come from tobacco-growing states. Several agencies within the Department of Agriculture administer the various tobacco policies.

All three actors in the triangle clearly have a common interest in maximizing tobacco sales. Where their interests may diverge, as between growers and retailers over wholesale prices, their close relationship within the subgovernment allows them to resolve differences without major battles and without involving external interests that may be hostile to the industry as a whole.

Similar group-subcommittee-agency subgovernments exist in hundreds of other policy areas. The political and economic consequences of this network of subgovernments can be quite disturbing. Such a system can permit "public" policies to be formulated by the interested parties and the job of governing to become the promotion of the interests of powerful and well-organized groups. If this happens, to paraphrase Lincoln, what we have is government of the interest groups, by the interest groups, for the interest groups, and the unorganized people are effectively excluded. Interest groups become so powerful when policy is made within subgovernments because a natural check on their power is eliminated. We expect our many and conflicting interest groups to check each other—to compete and accept compromise in governmental policy. Policy subgovernments allow interest groups with largely similar interests to operate in

isolation from their major competitors, thus avoiding the direct conflict and competition that serve to limit their influence.

As a result, instead of choosing between environmentalists and polluters, the tobacco industry and anticancer forces, business and labor, highways and mass transit systems, and so on, the government can favor all of them through subgovernments that limit direct conflict between competing interests. The absence of direct confrontation and the need for compromise tend to lead to contradictory policies characterized by conflicting programs and regulations, a proliferation of bureaucratic agencies, and a rapidly increasing budget.[9] Growth in government spending is unlikely to be brought under control until the power of interest groups isolated within subgovernments is checked.

Clearly, problems exist with the role of private interest organizations within the policy process. But when contemplating reforms that might alter that role, increase popular or democratic control of groups, or restrict their activities, we must keep the First Amendment in mind. That amendment includes a constitutional right to assemble and to petition the government for a redress of grievances. In one sense, participation in interest groups can be perceived as an exercise of First Amendment rights. Thus laws that would more stringently regulate the activities of interest groups would be subject to Supreme Court scrutiny as possibly infringing on constitutionally protected rights.

Political Parties: Organizing for Political Power

Although both interest groups and political parties function as forms of representation, they do so in different ways. Whereas interest groups organize for influence, political parties seek political power. By mobilizing individuals and groups, parties strive to create a majority, win elections, control the government, and make policy. In representative democracies, almost without exception, two or more political parties compete for political power.

By contrast, nondemocratic regimes are often characterized by a single party that holds a monopoly on political power or by a ruling military elite

CHECKS ON THE POWER OF INTEREST GROUPS

COMPETITIVE GROUPS:

There are more than forty thousand groups seeking to protect their interests. Naturally, they often come into conflict with one another. The United Auto Workers, for example, competes not only with management but also with other labor unions for jurisdiction and membership. Likewise, Chrysler's management comes into conflict with several different unions and with other domestic and foreign auto manufacturers.

OVERLAPPING MEMBERSHIP AND CONFLICTING LOYALTIES:

Large numbers of people are members of several groups with conflicting interests or goals that result in cross-pressure. A teacher, for example, may belong to a union that is seeking higher salaries. At the same time, that teacher as a property owner will be opposed to the higher property taxes necessary to pay for increased salaries for educators.

POLITICAL PARTIES:

Political parties may check the interest groups that normally support the opposing party. The Democratic party, for example, may oppose tax policies favorable to large corporations.

GOVERNMENTAL INSTITUTIONS:

Legislatures may pass laws contrary to the interests of a broad array of groups. Executive agencies may interpret rules and regulations in such a way that they frustrate the interests of certain groups. Courts may decide cases in a fashion that impairs the interests of affected groups. In the American federal system, an interest group may be successful at one level and unsuccessful at another level.

THE PEOPLE AS A POTENTIAL GROUP:

If people become aroused, they can constrain the power of even well-established groups. The nuclear accidents at Three Mile Island in the United States and Chernobyl in the Soviet Union have strengthened popular opposition to nuclear energy. By buying smaller, more fuel-efficient cars, consumers influenced domestic auto manufacturers to match the efforts of Japanese auto producers.

that outlaws all party organizations. The Communist party, whether we are talking about the Soviet Union, China, or Cuba, allows no opposition. The same was true of the Nazi party in Germany (1933–1945) and of the Fascist party in Italy (1922–1945).

Surprisingly, given the important role that political parties play in our form of government, there is no mention in the Constitution (or in the twenty-six amendments) of political parties. By the beginning of George Washington's second term of office in 1793, however, the Federalist and (Anti-Federalist) Democratic-Republican parties had emerged as the two leading contenders for the votes of the American electorate.

During Washington's administration, the Federalist party was led by the able, often brilliant, Alexander Hamilton. He fashioned the party's philosophy, which called for a strong, positive role for the national government in the development of the American nation. Government policy was directed toward strengthening the national government in relation to the state governments and to foreign governments. Hamilton sought to achieve these goals through policies that would encourage the growth of a balanced economy of farming, commerce, and most important, manufactures. These policies would also have the beneficial effect of binding the propertied classes to the national government by making the public interest of the nation largely identical with the financial interests of the wealthy, creditor classes.

By contrast, the Democratic-Republicans led by Thomas Jefferson, the foremost agrarian, saw the national government playing only a minimal role in the nation's development. The central government would wield only those powers and functions that could not be performed by state and local governments. Rather than centralize power, Jefferson sought to decentralize it in so far as possible. His vision of America was that of a nation of small, independent yeoman farmers. Since such farmers were largely self-sufficient, there was little need for a positive role for the national government. Nor did such farmers require governmental policies to bind them to the national government through mere self-interest. Farmers were the chosen people of God, and their patriotism did not need to be purchased by governmental policies that would enrich them at the expense of the other producing classes. Table 8.4 traces party changes from 1800 to 1980.

Table 8.4
Changes in the Dominant Ideology, Party, and Branch of Government

Year	1800	1830	1860	1890	1930	1960	1980
Dominant Foreign Policy Ideology			Isolationism			Internationalism	
Dominant domestic ideology			Frontier individualism	Industrial individualism		Welfare capitalism	
Hero of the age			Frontiersman Daniel Boone Davy Crockett Jed Smith	"Self-made" businessman Andrew Carnegie J.P. Morgan Henry Ford		Common man (working class) Archie Bunker Organization man (middle class)	
Dominant political party			Democratic	Republican		Democratic	
Dominant party presidential election victories			13 of 15	13 of 17		8 of 14 (including 1984)	
Dominant branch of government			Legislative	Judicial		Executive	

Persistence of Political Parties

Once established, political parties, in this country as well as others, continue to exist for a number of reasons. Political parties help to define alternative futures for a nation. The election of Ronald Reagan in 1980 and his reelection in 1984 can be cited as evidence that the Republican party has communicated its vision of what the future of the United States should be like much more effectively than have the Democrats.

Political parties also persist because they offer differing answers to certain fundamental questions. How extensive should government intervention in the economy be? What is the responsibility of the national government for the resolution of social problems? Under what conditions should the president be able to intervene militarily in the affairs of another country? How should the division of power between the national and state governments be determined? What is the proper role for each of the branches of the national government?

A third reason that political parties persist is because some institution is needed to organize the competition for public office, especially in a nation of the size and population of the United States. Parties recruit candidates, mobilize the electorate through campaigns, and outline policy positions. They also play a vital role in building a consensus on issues that are dividing the nation.

Finally, political parties persist because those unwilling or unable to organize as special interest groups must be represented in a democracy. In this sense, political parties are institutions concerned with the public interest rather than with narrower, more parochial interests. Distributional issues, that is, matters pertaining to the allocation of a nation's resources, are almost always subject to influence by special interest groups. If political parties do not offset this influence, no other institution in a democratic society is likely to be able to do so.

The Characteristics of Political Parties

Political parties are first and foremost power-seeking organizations. A political party seeks public office through the electoral process for the purpose of capturing control of the government. Such control enables a party to have its policies enacted as law. However, if one party controls the Congress and the other the presidency, policy making is not as easily accomplished.

With the growth of executive power, parties have increasingly focused their attention on capturing that office. Since policy initiation now rests principally in the hands of the president, parties that seek power must necessarily seek control of the executive branch. Both George Wallace's American Independent party in the presidential campaign of 1968 and John Anderson's Independent party candidacy in 1980 are examples of this phenomenon. Parties have thus become executive-centered organizations.

Parties have also become executive centered because the executive, who is chosen by the entire electorate, is able to capture the leadership of the party, is the focus of attention during campaigns, and is the chief dispenser of patronage. Nor can we overlook the executive's ability to dominate the media. We need only to contrast the attention presidential campaigns receive in comparison with congressional campaigns for evidence of executive dominance in a party's electoral efforts.

Next, political parties to some degree provide an ideological position around which individuals and groups can gather. The working class and liberals tend to gather around the Democratic party, whereas the middle class and conservatives tend to gather around the Republican party. Neither major party, however, is committed to an ideologically inspired program in the same way that many European parties are. Although the more leftist parties in France, and to a lesser extent in Britain, have begun to adopt a more pragmatic (Americanized?) economic and social outlook, most European parties have an ideological program they seek to implement if they gain power.

American political parties are best characterized as decentralized parties where the constraints of ideology are often less important than the interests found in any given legislative district. As a consequence, a Republican in a highly urbanized area and a Republican in a farm state may take opposite positions on price supports for dairy farmers. A Democrat from a northern city and a Democrat from the Deep South may take opposite positions on civil rights legislation.

The decentralized character of American parties is also reflected in the variation of interparty competitiveness from state to state. As indicated in Table 8.5, in some states the two major parties are closely competitive, in others one party tends to be dominant.

Finally, political parties are characterized by support from a conglomeration of diverse interest groups. Parties not only articulate demands, as do interest groups, but they also aggregate demands by drawing diverse interests together behind a more unified issue agenda. Democrats tend to draw support from liberals, organized labor, the working

Table 8.5
Party Competition in the States, 1974–1980

ONE–PARTY DEMOCRATIC

Alabama (.9438)	Mississippi (.8673)	Maryland (.8509)
Georgia (.8849)	Arkansas (.8630)	Rhode Island
Louisiana (.8762)	N. Carolina (.8555)	(.8506)

MODIFIED ONE–PARTY DEMOCRATIC

S. Carolina (.8034)	Hawaii (.7547)	California (.7081)
W. Virginia (.8032)	Florida (.7524)	Oregon (.6954)
Texas (.7993)	Connecticut (.7336)	Missouri (.6932)
Massachusetts	New Jersey (.7330)	Minnesota (.6680)
(.7916)	Virginia (.7162)	Tennessee (.6648)
Kentucky (.7907)	New Mexico (.7113)	Wisconsin (.6634)
Oklahoma (.7841)		
Nevada (.7593)		

TWO–PARTY COMPETITIVE

Montana (.6259)	Illinois (.5384)	Indiana (.4145)
Michigan (.6125)	Nebraska (.5166)	N. Hampshire
Ohio (.5916)	Maine (.5164)	(.3916)
Washington	Kansas (.4671)	Idaho (.3916)
(.5808)	Utah (.4653)	Wyoming (.3879)
Alaska (.5771)	Iowa (.4539)	Vermont (.3612)
Pennsylvania	Arizona (.4482)	S. Dakota (.3512)
(.5574)	Colorado (.4429)	
Delaware (.5490)		
New York (.5390)		

MODIFIED ONE–PARTY REPUBLICAN

North Dakota
(.3374)

Note: 1.000 = complete Democratic success; .000 = complete Republican success.

Source: John F. Bibby et al., "Parties in State Politics," in Virginia Gray, Herbert Jacob, and Kenneth Vines, eds. *Politics in the American States*, 4th ed. (Boston: Little, Brown, 1983), p. 66.

class, lower-income groups, the white South, racial and ethnic minorities, center cities, Catholics, and Jews, although several of these groups have seen many of their members defect to the Republican party in the 1980s.

By contrast with the Democratic party, the Republicans tend to draw support from conservatives, industrialists, small businesses, white collar workers, the middle class, upper-income groups, suburbs, small towns, and rural areas. The 1980 and 1984 elections also saw the Republicans make significant inroads into a former Democratic stronghold, the white South. The shift in voting allegiance in the South to Republican candidates for national level offices can clearly be seen in the election outcomes reported in Table 8.6, although the Democratic party continues to dominate at the state and local levels. Though they have made gains in the South, the Reagan administration's failure

Table 8.6
Voting Patterns in the South, 1960–1986

Year	Number of Representatives		Number of Senators		States Voting for Presidential Candidate		
	Dem.	Rep.	Dem.	Rep.	Dem.	Rep.	Ind.
1960	99	7	22	0	8	2	1
1962	95	11	21	1			
1964	89	17	21	1	6	-5	
1966	83	23	19	3			
1968	80	26	18	4	1	5	5
1970	79	27	16*	5			
1972	74	34	14*	7	0	11	
1974	81	27	15*	6			
1976	82	26	16*	5	10	1	
1978	77	31	15*	6			
1980	55	53	11	10	1	10	
1982	80	33	11	11			
1984	72	41	12	10	0	11	
1986	76	37	17	5			

* Harry Byrd, a former Democrat, served as an independent from Virginia.

to respond adequately to the farm debt problems of the mid–1980s caused many farmers to shift allegiance to the Democrats, weakening Republican strength in the agrarian Midwest, and resulting in the loss of Senate seats in both North and South Dakota in the 1986 elections.

These shifting alliances among interest groups are a distinctive feature of American political parties. European political parties are far less likely to divide along interest group lines. In Great Britain, France, and Italy, class and ideology rank ahead of interest group coalitions in determining how a party will seek support from the electorate. Nonetheless, even in these countries the parties do seek support from a broad array of interests and voters.

Despite their efforts to draw support from a diverse set of interests, the major parties in the United States have suffered a decline in voter identification. After the 1984 elections, 37 percent of the electorate identified itself as Democratic, 27 percent as Republican, and fully 35% as Independent or as having no preference.[10] The Democrats in the postwar era reached a high of 51 percent in 1964, and the Republicans topped out at 29 percent in 1956. In contrast with the major parties, independent voters represent an increasing percentage of the electorate, growing from 22 percent in 1952 to 35 percent in 1984.

The decline in voter identification has affected the nominating and campaign strategies of both the Democratic and Republican parties. Given the size of the independent vote and the need to attract voters from the opposing political party, many candidates have downplayed their party affiliation. In their media efforts, candidates may use ads that do not carry the party label, or if used, give it a minor place. Such a practice may lead to a further decline in voter identification. At some point, candidates who have won office without strong party support may feel they have few obligations to that party. However, nominating procedures ensure there will be some ties between the candidate and the party.

In the nomination process, both parties seek to identify candidates that will unite their respective party coalitions. With the decline in voter identifi-

TEN SURE WAYS TO TELL A DEMOCRAT FROM A REPUBLICAN

1. Democrats buy most of the books that have been banned somewhere. Republicans form censorship committees and read them as a group.
2. Democrats give their worn-out clothes to those less fortunate. Republicans wear theirs.
3. Republicans employ exterminators. Democrats step on the bugs.
4. Republicans have governesses for their children. Democrats have grandmothers.
5. Republicans tend to keep their shades drawn, although there is seldom any reason they should. Democrats ought to, but don't.
6. On Saturday, Republicans head for the hunting lodge or the yacht club. Democrats wash the car and get a haircut.
7. Republicans raise dahlias, Dalmatians, and eyebrows. Democrats raise Airedales, kids, and taxes.
8. Democrats eat the fish they catch. Republicans hang them on the wall.
9. Republicans study the financial pages of the newspaper. Democrats put them in the bottom of the bird cage.
10. Republican boys date Democratic girls. They plan to marry Republican girls, but feel they're entitled to a little fun first.

cation, this is more critical than ever. A party nominee that does not unite the party coalition will be soundly defeated. Barry Goldwater in 1964, George McGovern in 1972, Jimmy Carter in 1980, and Walter Mondale in 1984 did not unite their parties and all lost by wide margins.

Although much derided in recent years, the party's national convention must hammer out a party platform that takes into account the outer limits of the party's coalition; that is, the platform must be formulated in such a way that it does not drive people out of the party, while at the same time providing the maximum and most consensual attractiveness. If the national convention fails to accomplish this vital task, the party almost certainly will suffer defeat at the polls.

In addition to uniting their party coalitions, both parties must nominate candidates that will attract support from independent voters and from members of the opposing party. Since more of the electorate considers itself Democratic, Democratic candidates do not need to attract as many "other" voters as Republican candidates. With only 27 percent of the electorate identifying itself as Republican, the Republican party must seek the support of large numbers of independent voters and Democrats if it is to win elections. Ronald Reagan and the Republican party succeeded in 1980 and 1984 because they gained the necessary outside support. Republican success in 1980 was especially stunning because Jimmy Carter was the first elected incumbent president since 1932 to lose a presidential election.

Finally, political parties must capture the support of the moderate majority to win elections. If a party appeals only to liberals or only to conservatives, it is in trouble at the polls. The majority of American voters are not ideologues, and the successful candidate and the successful party will have taken this into account in both the primary and general election campaign. Ronald Reagan tempered his appeal to conservatives in 1980 to attract the support of moderates. This had a devastating effect on John Anderson who had sought the support of moderates in his efforts to drive a wedge in between Jimmy Carter on the left and Ronald Reagan on the right. Reagan's success in 1980 and also in 1984 can be traced to the fact that he was able to unify his party, attract the necessary outside support, and appeal to a broad spectrum of voters.

Party Reform

The decline in voter identification and voter confidence in the major parties during the past two decades has made the process of building and maintaining majority coalitions much more difficult. This is particularly true in the nationwide contest for the presidency. The personality and individual characteristics of the candidates are the single most important determinant of most voters' choice, whereas party loyalty has declined as a guide to the voter for candidate selection. This is clearly reflected in the increased reluctance of voters to vote a straight party ticket—all Democratic or all Republican—for every office on the ballot. Instead, ticket-splitting (which occurs when a voter casts a ballot endorsing candidates from both parties for a variety of offices) has become the norm. The change has been dramatic. In 1960, nearly two-thirds of the voters cast **straight-ticket** ballots. Just twelve years later, in 1972, two-thirds of the voters engaged in **split-ticket** voting, and this trend has continued.[11]

This more independent-minded voter has made it more difficult to find candidates capable of uniting the various elements of the party coalition while attracting large numbers of independents. At the same time, the increase in independent voters has made it even more vital to have such a candidate if a party is to succeed in building a majority coalition. One response has been reforms in party rules about the nomination of candidates.

Though party conventions still formally nominate the presidential and vice presidential candidates, due to reforms in the delegate selection process the real decision has usually been made before the convention meets. Today conventions are largely media events kicking off the presidential campaign.

THE BEST CONGRESS MONEY CAN BUY?

Interest groups spend many millions of dollars attempting to gain access to political leaders or influence who will be the political leadership. The question of the influence of special-interest money in the national legislature in not new—it was Mark Twain who first suggested we had the best Congress money could buy. But the phenomenal growth of the spending of PACs has given the issue a special urgency in recent years. Some observers feel that congressional voting is on the auction block because of the dependence of members of Congress on interest group money for political survival. Others argue this notion is greatly overstated.

Proponents of the auction block view cite examples like the hospital cost containment measure that would have placed ceilings on hospital charges for specific services. The measure was killed in committee by a one-vote margin, twenty-two to twenty-one. Later it was found that of the twenty-two representatives who voted against the bill, nineteen had received a total of some $85,000 in campaign contributions from the American Medical Association, a group adamantly opposed to the measure. They argue that such contributions can't help but color a representative's thinking and voting behavior and on close issues like this one have a pivotal effect on the outcome.

Others point out that political scientists have not been able to find any systematic evidence that PAC contributions affect how members of Congress vote. Other factors, like their ideology, party identification, and the makeup of their constituency, play more important roles. Moreover, despite the rather large total of contributions, no one PAC contributes a very large amount to individual members of Congress, nor accounts for a significant proportion of their total campaign fund. PACs can contribute no more than $5,000 to a candidate for public office, and the average donation to a candidate for the House of Representatives is still less than $1,000. Even in the AMA case cited here, the $85,000 averages out to only about $4,500 for each of the nineteen members of Congress involved—not a lot of money in an era when running for Congress can cost hundreds of thousands or even millions of dollars.

Even those who believe the impact of money on congressional voting is exaggerated do not argue that money has no effect, however. Virtually everyone agrees that what money does buy is access. Members of Congress are almost certainly more willing to set aside time in their busy days to speak with the representatives of a group that has contributed money than for one that has not. Money opens the door so that one's case can be made, which is at least necessary if not sufficient for having influence.

The reform spirit has been particularly strong in the Democratic party. Party leaders attributed the unrest and disunity at its 1968 convention and subsequent defeat at the polls largely to the closed and undemocratic character of the candidate selection process. To avoid a repetition of these disasters, Democrats instituted a number of reforms before the 1972 presidential election. The most important of these reforms sought to assure proportional representation for women, the young, and racial minorities at the national convention, which nominates the presidential candidate. The hope was that a more open, representative convention would produce candidates more acceptable to the various factions of the party and to the independent electorate as well.

The Republican party has also sought greater representation for women and minorities at its national conventions. But party leaders have pursued these goals with less commitment and enthusiasm and out of greater concern for national image than for representativeness. It was not until 1984 that women achieved a significant increase in convention representation, and even then their numbers remained far below their proportion in the party as a whole. Republican reforms have focused on strengthening the national organization. Specifically, the national committee was developed into a much more substantial service agency for the state Republican parties.

Whereas the Republican party has had greater electoral success since the reforms, it is the representational reforms spearheaded by the Democrats that have had the greatest impact on the presidential election process, both positive and negative. On the positive side, they have led to a substantial increase in the representation of women and minorities in the presidential selection process. They have also led to the greatly increased use of the presidential primary as a means for the selection of delegates to the national conventions, substantially increasing citizen participation in selecting presidential nominees. At the same time, the reforms have had the negative effect of contributing to the decline of the parties, as the party organization has been losing control of the nominating process to the party membership—and this at a time when loyalty to the party has been falling. Selection of nominees is at the core of a party's reason for existing. Yet the primaries have become so important in determining the delegate vote at the nominating convention that the party leaders no longer choose or reject the nominee.

When all these factors are coupled with the parties' declining significance as financial conduits for campaign funds (which the PACs have largely appropriated), it is clear that the role of the party system in the electoral process has been eroded. Indeed, in the view of one political observer, parties have become mere "shells" without a significant function in the electoral process.[12] In a more conventional view, political parties in our system of government still have several functions.

Functions of Political Parties

Political parties are a link between the American people and their government. Since a direct democracy is not feasible in a nation of more than 240 million people, some institution must provide a bridge between the governors and the governed. Under our form of government, parties have functioned as that institution for nearly two centuries. Parties also function as a reference group by helping citizens to organize their political opinions. Competitive parties make it possible for voters to narrow their choice of candidates and policy preferences to understandable and workable alternatives. For the politically sophisticated, party platforms outline alternative policies and alternative allocations of the nation's resources.

The recruitment of candidates is also a function of political parties. Candidates are usually selected through either a party convention or a primary election. Party officials can exert more influence over the recruitment process at party conventions. Voters play a more important role in candidate selection in primary elections. In either case, as we have noted, the party seeks to recruit candidates that will unite the party coalition and attract independent voters and voters who may identify with the other major party. As a consequence, many candidates are compromise choices, that is, acceptable to a large number of voters, but actually the first choice of a much smaller group.

Political parties also furnish a mechanism of accountability. When the people are dissatisfied with the government's policies, elections are a means of peacefully removing one party from power and replacing it with another party. In 1976, voters held Gerald Ford and the Republican party responsible for the Nixon Watergate scandal in 1972–1974. Four years later, Jimmy Carter and the Democratic party suffered the wrath of the voters because of the ailing American economy and the Iranian hostage crisis. The Democrats were still feeling that wrath in 1984.

Finally, political parties structure and institutionalize political conflict. Competitive parties help to identify the critical issues and offer alternative policies that will resolve peacefully the problems confronting a nation. By institutionalizing political conflict, parties reduce the chances that violence will break out. From one perspective, the most important function of political parties is to aid in the peaceful transfer of power following an electoral victory by the opposition party.

Given the relative youth of this country, it is somewhat surprising that the United States has the longest history of unbroken elections in the world. Even in the midst of the Civil War and World War II, the presidential elections were held as scheduled. Nondemocratic regimes, even in less tumultuous times, often experience a power struggle whenever the ruling leadership dies or is ousted from power. In China, for example, the death of Chairman Mao was followed by extensive infighting over who would be the next leader. Yet no one can predict whether a transition will be troubled or not. The elevation of Mikhail Gorbachev to the top leadership post in the Soviet Union in 1985 was a smooth if somewhat secretive transfer of power from one individual to another.

The American Two-Party System

The United States uses an electoral system of single-member legislative districts, which means only one representative can be elected from each legislative district. When combined with plurality elections, single-member districts tend to produce two-party systems.[13] This makes sense from both a logical and a strategic point of view: If only one person can be elected, the chances of a candidate winning are greatest when there are only two parties.

A second factor accounting for the two-party system is that the central divisive issues in American politics can be perceived as essentially two-sided. A sketch of this nation's history reveals patriots versus loyalists in the revolutionary era, large states versus small states at the Constitutional Convention, Federalists versus Anti-Federalists in the struggle over the ratification of the Constitution, North versus South during the Civil War era, laissez-faire capitalists versus economic interventionists from the Populists to the New Deal, and **Keynesian economics** versus **supply-side economics** in recent times. To this list, we might add liberals versus conservatives, labor versus management, prolife versus prochoice, and doves versus hawks.

Custom and tradition have also enhanced the two-party system. The Democratic party traces its origins from the election of Thomas Jefferson to the presidency in 1800, whereas the Republican party emerged in the 1850s. We saw in Chapter 6 that voter behavior is shaped in very significant ways by the socialization that individuals undergo early in their lives. In the absence of major upheavals, most people will continue to identify with the same political party throughout their adult years.

The Civil War and the Great Depression were pivotal events in American politics that changed the party preferences of large numbers of people. Before the Civil War, the Democratic party attracted the most support. From the Civil War to the Great Depression, the Republican party prevailed in most elections. From the Great Depression to (perhaps) the 1980s, the Democrats were again the dominant party.

The Failure of Third Parties: Considering the electoral strength of the Democratic and Republican parties, it is a formidable task for a third party to challenge or displace one of them. Their appeal is also limited by the fact that third parties usually concentrate on a few issues. The Free Soil party in the 1852 presidential election, George Wallace's American Independent party in 1968, and John Anderson's independent candidacy in 1980 are all examples of this phenomenon (Table 8.7).

Because third parties tend to focus on a narrow range of issues, they typically do not attract support from a broad spectrum of voters. Without that electoral base, third parties are often unable to contest more than the presidential election.[14] Third parties as a rule have minimal success in fielding candidates for Congress or for state and local offices, partly because the states have historically made it difficult for third parties or independent candidates to gain a place on the ballot.

Such parties and candidates must usually demonstrate their popularity by collecting a substantial number of signatures on petitions before their candidates' names will be placed on the ballot. Sometimes that is not enough. George Wallace in

THE AMERICAN OR "KNOW–NOTHING" PARTY: NATIVISM AND PREJUDICE

A short-lived political party competed with the Democrats and the Republicans in the 1856 presidential election. The American party was often referred to as the "Know-Nothing" party because the Know-Nothings were an early expression of the native resentment toward an increasingly numerous influx of immigrants. The former were primarily of English or Scottish descent and Protestants whereas the immigrants of the 1840s and 1850s tended to be Irish or German Catholics. The dynamics of the country's demography had already changed dramatically since the 1780s. Then as now, the United States was a pluralistic society. Now as then, the United States produced fringe political movements. Today, the philosophical descendants of the "know-nothings" are represented by such groups as Christian Identity, the American Nazis, and the Ku Klux Klan.

Table 8.7
Significant Third Parties in Presidential Elections, 1880–1980

Year	Candidate	Party	Popular Vote	Percentage of Vote	Electoral Vote
1880	James B. Weaver	Greenback-Labor	308,578	3.4% *	0
1888	Clinton B. Fisk	Prohibition	249,506	2.2	0
1892	James B. Weaver	People's (Populist)	1,029,846	8.5	22
	John Bidwell	Prohibition	264,233	2.2	0
1904	Eugene V. Debs	Socialist	402,283	3.0	0
1908	Eugene V. Debs	Socialist	420,793	2.8	0
1912	Theodore Roosevelt	Progressive	4,118,571	27.4	88
	Eugene V. Debs	Socialist	900,672	6.0	0
1916	A.L. Benson	Socialist	585,113	3.2	0
1920	Eugene V. Debs	Socialist	919,799	3.4	0
1924	R.M. LaFollette	Progressive	4,831,189	17.1	13
1932	Norman Thomas	Socialist	881,951	2.2	0
1936	William Lemke	Union	882,479	2.0	0
1948	J. Strom Thurmond	States' Rights	1,169,063	2.4	39
	Henry Wallace	Progressive	1,157,172	2.4	0
1968	George Wallace	American Independent	9,906,141	13.5	46
1980	John Anderson	Independent	5,551,551	7.0	0

* Includes candidates receiving 2 percent or more of the popular vote.

Source: U.S. Bureau of the Census, *Historical Statistics of the United States.*

1968 and John Anderson in 1980 had to go to court in several states to secure a place on the ballot. Such efforts consume much time, energy, and money, which might otherwise be used in the election campaign itself.

Inability to attract adequate financial support also accounts for the limited success of third parties. Even with federal matching funds available if a presidential candidate can obtain just 5 percent of the vote, third-party candidates must operate on meager budgets. Since most American voters prefer to cast their ballot for winners, their financial support goes almost exclusively to those candidates who have a chance of winning. The ability of third parties to raise money is also hampered by the fact that the leadership of third parties is usually perceived as occupying the extreme ends of the political spectrum. With the two major parties occupying the political center, third-party candidates are often characterized by the major parties as eccentric or radical or simply "unelectable." George Wallace was seen by many voters as a dangerous radical, whereas John Anderson had to contend with the unelectable label.

Notwithstanding these other factors, the principal reason for the failure of third parties is very simple. Whenever the issues raised by a third party gain enough popular support, the major parties will either modify their positions or actually adopt the third party's position. The direct election of senators, the eight-hour workday, minimum wage legislation, and Social Security are all examples of issues first raised by third-party candidates and later embraced by the major parties and ultimately adopted into law.

We should distinguish between third parties and minor parties. Third parties usually focus on a single issue or a narrow range of issues, whereas minor parties typically espouse an ideology of some sort. Given the issue-oriented nature of third parties, they tend to be short-lived. By contrast, the ideological nature of minor parties tends to ensure that they persist. Thus both George Wallace's American Independent party and John Anderson's Independent party quickly disappeared from the political scene, whereas the American Communist party endures, but without any chance of electoral success.

Contemporary Trends and Prospects

Interest groups and political parties clearly reflect the dominant political conditions of the 1980s in their organizational disaggregation, that is, their inability to line up supporters behind a unified issue agenda. The rapid proliferation and growing importance of interest groups based on narrowly defined single interests and the dealignment and decomposition of stable national party coalitions reveal an aggregation process in an advanced state of disarray. Such a condition is likely to be associated with a political process that is less predictable, less stable, and possibly less effective in meeting the needs of the people.

As their name suggests, the members of single-interest groups tend to be unconcerned about the wide range or complexity of issues with which the American political system must contend. Because of their focus on one issue, single-interest groups may lack an appreciation for the art of compromise or the broader purposes of government.

Most political scientists would agree that it is the interplay among interests in the form of bargaining and compromise that holds the politics of interest groups together. Such interplay is central to the proper functioning of our form of government, for it assures policy moderation and relative fairness. It also gives legitimacy to the policy process because interaction of interests contributes in the long run to the public interest.

Single-issue groups are often made up of people relatively new to politics who are uninterested in or unaware of the traditional rules of the game. They depend on ideological or religious fervor, rather than bargaining skills, in the pursuit of their goals. Their activities are therefore separate from interest group politics and add to the disaggregating tendencies all too prevalent today.

Single-issue groups are not a new phenomenon in American politics, but only recently have they become so important. Anti-Vietnam war activists of the late 1960s and early 1970s might be considered the first of the modern single-issue groups. Opponents of nuclear power plants or supporters of the nuclear freeze could be cited as leading examples of single issue groups of the 1980s.

It is no accident that the increase in the activity and influence of single interests has coincided with the decline of the political parties. When party orga-

nizations were strong, candidates owed their nominations more to party activists and professionals than to specific interest groups. As a consequence, the parties insulated the members of Congress and other elected officials from the demands of single-issue groups. As the role of the parties in the nomination and electoral process has weakened, candidates and officeholders have become more dependent on the support of single-interest groups. Such groups often control significant amounts of campaign contributions that are crucial to electoral success. Also, though single-issue groups do not normally command extremely large blocs of votes, in a highly competitive race, a group with as little as 1 or 2 percent of the electorate can effectively threaten the defeat of a candidate it opposes.

From the politician's point of view, the central problem is that these groups exert pressure on candidates and elected officials to take issue positions that are fundamentally incompatible with one another. Single-issue groups thus make it difficult if not impossible to forge legislative compromises and construct the broad coalitions of support needed to govern effectively.

The decline in party alignment among the electorate and the resulting evaporation of the Democratic majority coalition makes it apparent that the American political system is no longer successfully performing its aggregative function. The party system seems to be at an important crossroads in its history, but what sort of transformation is in store cannot be foreseen. Scholars who have attempted to peer into the future disagree on whether the parties will find a way to form new stable coalitions or will continue to disintegrate. There is also much debate about whether a new majority coalition would belong to the Democratic or Republican party.[15]

If the Republicans are to become the majority party, they must broaden their appeal and win converts from some voting groups they have conceded to the Democrats in recent years. One of these groups is the black community. As recently as 1960, more than one-third of black voters identified themselves as Republican. Owing to the great expansion of the number of largely lower-income black voters enfranchised by the Voting Rights Act and the Democratic leadership on civil rights and social issues important to blacks, only about 10 percent of this often pivotal group identifies with the Republican party today.

By ignoring the black vote, Republicans have picked up substantial support, especially in presidential elections, among conservative southern whites. But if the Republicans sought to appeal to a somewhat larger proportion of blacks, it seems unlikely that their support among southern whites would be greatly diminished. Although Republicans probably cannot hope to gain a majority of the black vote, even a marginal increase would seriously hurt the Democrats.

Another, more likely source of new support for the Republicans is the upwardly mobile white ethnics—Jews and Italian, Irish, and Polish Catholics. The traditional assumption is that with increasing affluence, such groups may increasingly identify themselves as Republican. In addition, in the 1980 and 1984 elections, the Republicans were able to make some inroads among Catholics because of conservative stands on social issues like abortion.

JESSE JACKSON (b. 1941) AND THE FUTURE OF THE DEMOCRATIC PARTY

In 1984, Jesse Jackson discomfited the Democratic party establishment by running as a Democratic candidate for president in the primaries. Jackson, frustrated by the unwillingness of the Democratic leadership to champion the cause of the disadvantaged, meant to ensure that the constituency he spoke for could not be safely ignored. Besides his campaign efforts, Jackson led a voter registration drive that enrolled millions of black voters across the nation.

Although active in civil rights since his college days, Jackson had for a number of years downplayed political goals in favor of economic gains for blacks. His activities, whether in the Congress on Racial Equality (CORE), the Southern Christian Leadership Council (SCLC), or his own People United to Serve Humanity (PUSH), focused on bettering the economic conditions of blacks and other disadvantaged people. Rather than strive for school desegregation, for example, Jackson sought to pressure businesses to hire more blacks, to promote

blacks within an organization, and to do more business with minority-owned enterprises.

A powerful speaker, Jackson had emerged as a leader of the black community by following in the footsteps of other prominent black leaders. Like Martin Luther King, Jr. and Ralph Abernethy, Jackson was an ordained minister. He had joined King's SCLC and had worked closely with him. Indeed, Jackson was with King when he was assassinated. After King's death, Jackson returned to Chicago and renewed his efforts

to improve the economic status of blacks.

By the late 1970s, Jackson had come to value the ways in which public policies could be used to better the economic conditions of minorities. At the same time he became increasingly unhappy with Democratic leaders who he saw turning their backs on the disadvantaged. This led to Jackson's political activism and ultimately to his presidential candidacy in 1984.

Jackson has vowed to be a candidate again in 1988 if the Democratic party does not listen to his appeals. Although his Rainbow Coalition in 1984 remained largely black, he did put the Democratic leadership on notice that the party could not move too far to the right without losing a substantial number of black supporters. Party realignment may be occuring, but Jackson is determined to ensure that the Democratic party does not ignore one of the most important segments of the Democratic coalition—blacks and other minorities.

This conservative appeal also entails one of the principal challenges to the Republican party. As Everett Carl Ladd has noted, this challenge involves the choice of whether the party will become a coalition or a church. By "church" Ladd refers to those Republicans who are strong ideological conservatives, and wish to see the party embrace conservative ideology, candidates, and policies to the exclusion of all others.[16] Other, more moderate party members wish to broaden the party's appeal to form a coalition of diverse ideologies and interests and select candidates with the pragmatic goal of winning elections. This is the main split in the Republican party today, and it threatens to be a serious problem for the next generation of Republican leadership.

The success of Ronald Reagan and the Republican party during his tenure as president has been in no small part due to his ability to stand astride this ideological split in the party, appealing to both factions and uniting them in their support of him. There is no heir apparent among the Republican leadership at this time that is not perceived as a representative of one faction or the other. Such leadership is quite likely to be less able to provide the party unity needed to contest elections successfully. Moreover, if the party should choose the "church" alternative, it might drive away the less ideologically motivated voters the Republicans need to establish a majority coalition.

The Democratic party also faces a problem of unity. The split between those who are more liberal on social issues and less liberal on economic ones, dubbed "Yuppies" (young, upwardly mobile, professionals) by the press, and the older New Deal economic liberals has been growing wider during the last several years. They too need to find a candidate at the presidential level who can successfully appeal to and mobilize both factions.

In recent years, the Democrats have been unable to do so, and the dissatisfied faction has tended not just to stay home at election time but also to vote in large numbers for the Republican presidential candidate. In 1984, this split was represented by the candidacies of Walter Mondale (New Deal economic liberals) and Gary Hart (Yuppie social policy liberals). Polls showed that when Mondale won the nomination, more than one-third of the Hart supporters subsequently voted for Reagan. Clearly, this split is very deep and damaging to the electoral chances of Democrats.

The Democratic party has several other problems it must confront. Chief among them is the need to devise a program that is both true to their traditional philosophy and concerns and yet appeals to a nation in a more conservative mood. In brief, Democrats must define a positive role for government that is more consistent with the prevailing values of the electorate.

The Democrats have also been slow to adopt the new organizational techniques of the 1980s. This is partly owing to their lack of financial resources but also to a lack of attention to organizational maintenance and development. To compete effectively in elections, they must emulate the innovations introduced by the Republican National Committee in servicing state and local candidates, in direct mail fund raising, and in candidate preparation and packaging.

Conclusion

Although the traditional functions of interest groups and political parties are undergoing some fundamental changes, these institutions still make an important contribution to our form of government. Interest groups remain an effective form of representation for minority interests. Whether those interests are economic, religious, racial or ethnic, issue oriented, or geographic, interest groups express to public officials the concerns of significant number of people.

Effective interest groups employing a wide variety of tactics can ensure that their voice is heard when the government is considering competing public policies and alternative allocations of the nation's resources. Although powerful interests are the subject of legitimate criticism, interest groups have a vital role to play in the constant struggle to produce public policies that are widely perceived as legitimate. Only when minority rights are fully protected can a majoritarian system achieve such a goal.

Equally important to the American form of government is the health of the party system. Competitive political parties have been a hallmark of this nation for nearly two centuries. The decline in voter identification of the major parties over the last three decades strikes some observers as a sign of a lack of vigor in the party system. During the remaining years of this century, both Democratic and Republican party leaders must seek to renew and revitalize their respective parties.

Both parties have shown remarkable resiliency when confronted with political upheavals and economic dislocations. Yet the parties today face even greater challenges. The organizational disaggregation and disarray that characterize contemporary electoral politics presents difficulties of an extremely subtle nature. Whether the major parties can forge innovative responses to the problems of party dealignment and decomposition will determine what role parties can be expected to play in the years ahead.

 ## Glossary

Interest groups   Groups of individuals (membership groups) or organizations (institutional groups) organized to gain specific economic and political goals through access to and influence on political officeholders.

Keynesian economics   The theory that government spending can be used to regulate the economy, especially as a tool to counter economic slumps.

Lobbying   Attempting to influence the passage or content of legislative and administrative decisions of government. Usually done by a person acting as an agent for or representing an interest group.

Political party   A group of individuals and interest groups organized to win elections and operate the government to implement a set of public policy programs.

Split-ticket voting   The practice of voting for candidates from different parties for a variety of offices.

Straight-ticket voting   The practice of voting only for candidates of a single party for all the offices contested in an election.

Supply-side economics   The theory that reducing taxes, government spending on social welfare, and public sector regulation of the economy generally will restimulate the economy owing to the increase in the supply of resources in the private sector.

 ## Suggestions for Further Reading

Bauer, Raymond A., et. al. *American Business and Public Policy.* New York: Atherton, 1963. A careful examination of the efforts of business lobbyists to influence foreign trade legislation, which found that, at least in this policy area, they can be quite ineffective.

Berry, Jeffrey M. *Lobbying for the People.* Princeton, N.J.: Princeton University Press, 1977. The major study of public interest groups, focusing in detail on two such organizations.

Cigler, Allan J., and Burdett A. Loomis, eds. *Interest Group Politics.* Washington, D.C.: Congressional Quarterly Press, 1983. An excellent set of readings including discussions of the nature and growth of interest groups and essays on a number of currently important groups such as prolife groups, the Christian right, and the National Organization for Women.

Fritschler, A. Lee. *Smoking and Politics: Policymaking in the Federal Bureaucracy.* Englewood Cliffs, N.J.: Prentice-Hall, 1983. An entertaining account of subgovernment policy-making.

Greenwald, Carol S. *Group Power: Lobbying and Public Policy.* New York: Praeger, 1977. Takes a close look at the public policy effects of interest group activity.

Lowi, Theodore J. *The End of Liberalism,* 2d ed. New York: Norton, 1979. One of the most influential critiques of the role and impact of interest groups in American democracy.

Malbin, Michael J. *Money and Politics in the United States.* Chatham, N.J.: Chatham House, 1984. An extremely interesting and highly readable recent treatment of PACs and the influence of money in the electoral process.

Michels, Roberto. *Political Parties.* New York: Free Press, 1966. Classic statement of the thesis that political parties are inevitably oligarchist in nature, even in representative democracies.

Moe, Terry M. *The Organization of Interests: Incentives and the Internal Dynamics of Political Interest Groups.* Chicago: University of Chicago Press, 1980. Employs economic analysis of individual self-interest to explore the motivations for joining and the internal politics of interest organizations.

Olson, Mancur. *The Logic of Collective Action: Public Goods and the Theory of Groups.* Cambridge, Mass.: Harvard University Press, 1971. Influential analysis of why groups and individuals behave as they do.

Schattschneider, E.E. *The Semi-Sovereign People.* New York: Holt, Rinehart, and Winston, 1960. A standard reference work in American politics that documents the bias of the interest group-based policy process.

Truman, David B. *The Governmental Process.* New York: Knopf, 1971. The classic analysis and defense of interest group politics.

Wilson, James Q. *Political Organizations.* New York: Basic Books, 1973. The most influential treatment of the incentives interest groups use to attract members.

It could probably be shown by facts and figures that there is no distinctly native,
American criminal class, except Congress.
Mark Twain

Chapter 9

The Legislative Branch:
Forging Policy from Conflict

Introduction

For two hundred years, the Constitution has proven to be a very flexible framework for policy making. All three branches of the national government have interpreted the language of the Constitution so as to encompass a wide array of policies without the need for frequent amendment. In the economic arena, for example, public policies have ranged from laissez-faire measures prescribing minimal governmental regulation of the economy to welfare capitalism where the government funds a broad array of social programs.

Constitutional provisions establish few real limits to the scope of permissible public policies. Instead, it is the values held by the most politically active groups that constrains public policy making. For example, cost and resource allocations, particularly the taxing and spending policies found in the federal budget, are seldom limited by specific constitutional language, but are heavily influenced by the values of the most active political groups. The strongly held value of anti-communism is an important base of support for national defense expenditures, whereas the value of economic individualism limits spending for social welfare programs.

Within this context of a flexible Constitution, strongly held values, and active political interests, Congress, the president, and the federal courts carry out their policy-making activities, reconciling competing ideas, values, and interests. The end result is a pattern of public policies that determines the nation's priorities and allocates costs and resources.

Each of the branches, Congress, the president, and the federal judiciary, has a distinctive role to play in the policy-making process. Whereas the Constitution shapes the role that each branch plays, it is the interaction of public officials, political interests, and values of the American people that is critical. Policy making is more a response to certain factors arising from the political environment than to specific constitutional provisions.

Policy Making in the Congress

Congress is composed of two houses, the House of Representatives with 435 members (elected for two-year terms) and the Senate (one-third of which is elected every two years for a six-year term) with 100 members (Table 9.1). As we would expect, power is not divided equally among the members in either house. The roughly 40 to 50 individuals who have more power than most members of Congress occupy key positions reached through their position in the party and seniority on committees.

These individuals hold power in two different, yet approximately equal, echelons of leadership. First are the party leadership positions in both houses. In the House of Representatives the speaker

Table 9.1
Differences Between the House of Representatives and the Senate

House of Representatives	Senate
Two-year terms	Staggered six-year terms
435 members	100 members
Represent equal population districts formed by state legislatures	Represent states
Tends to be more responsive to suburban and rural interests	Tends to be more responsive to urban interests
Less prestige	More prestige
Less media attention	More media attention
22 major committees	15 major committees
Committees and committee chairs more important	Committees and committee chairs less important
Rules Committee very important	Rules and Administration Committee less important
Less flexible rules	More flexible rules
Limited debate on bills	Unlimited debate possible; cloture difficult to invoke
Tax and appropriation bills originate in the House	Advice and consent of the Senate on appointments and treaties

Jim Wright (b.1922):
The New Speaker of the House

Ten years ago, Jim Wright of Texas would not have been expected to be the man to follow Tip O'Neill to the speaker's chair. His decision to seek the post of majority leader in 1976 was a surprise, and he was not expected to seriously challenge the odds-on favorite, Phillip Burton of California. He managed to edge Richard Bolling of Missouri by two votes on the second ballot to finish second to Burton and beat Burton on the third ballot by a single vote 148–147. Since that time, he has slowly consolidated and strengthened this originally insecure margin of support for his leadership.

Wright's surprising rise to the leadership of the Democrats may be attributed to several factors. First, he is a centrist within a party divided between a conservative southern wing and a liberal northern wing. Perhaps the most liberal of Texas Democrats, he remains less liberal than most of the northerners. As a result, both factions at times regard him with suspicion, but he is ideally placed to moderate party disputes, find compromises, heal wounds, and

generally play the role of party leader. Moreover, he has proven himself to be a skilled legislative tactician, an eloquent and persuasive orator, and a generally adroit politician who usually wins when he sets his mind to it.

Wright's legislative record shows him to be a strong supporter of national defense programs and a fairly dependable friend of federal social programs. He has supported programs in the areas of health care, education, housing, and consumer protec-

tion, and has been a strong advocate of welfare reform. His support for national defense fits in well with his ever-present efforts on behalf of his constituency in Texas. His Twelfth District is home to important areospace installations, and he has always been a strong proponent of that industry, securing important government contracts in both defense and nondefense areas. Like most Texans, he has also consistently supported the oil industry, so important to that state. As a result, he enjoys a secure political base at home. Wright seems to possess both the political and personal talents to be an effective and successful speaker. Certainly, his political foes do not take Jim Wright's talents lightly. One such opponent, David Stockman, characterized Wright as possessing "frightening rhetorical powers" and "more energy" than his predecessor O'Neill. It seems certain that Wright will relish the opportunity that the speakership will provide.

is the most powerful leadership position in the majority party. The speaker works closely with the **majority leader** and **majority whip** to secure the passage of the party's legislative program. The minority party is lead by the **minority leader** who is aided by the **minority whip** in an effort to provide legislative alternatives to the majority party's program. Minority party leadership positions become quite important when a member of that party is president, as has been the case during the Reagan

years. Minority leaders then have the responsibility of defending and attempting to secure passage of the president's legislative program.

The Senate has no leadership position equivalent to the Speaker of the House, which makes the position of majority leader especially important. The minority leader and majority and minority whip positions in the Senate are quite similar to the equivalent positions in the House. One part of the party leadership's job in both houses is to work with each other to plan a strategy that will assure passage of the party's program in each house. Between 1981 and 1986, this process was complicated by the fact that the Democrats had a majority in the House while the Republicans narrowly controlled the Senate. The Democrats regained control of the Senate in the 1986 elections and thus should find the job of legislative coordination between the two houses greatly simplified.

The second echelon of leadership is lodged in the chairs of the standing committees of both houses. Committee chairs are always members of the majority party in their respective houses. Whether in the House or in the Senate, the committee chair exercises considerable influence over the legislative activity of each committee. As the head of the committee, the chair is largely responsible for scheduling meetings, deciding which bills to consider, holding hearings, establishing subcommittees, guiding floor debate on committee bills, assigning members to conference committees, and supervising the committee's professional staff. Since all legislation must pass through a standing committee, the disposition of the committee chair toward a particular legislative bill will have a marked impact on its chances of passage.

Not all committees or the members of Congress who chair them are equal in power and influence.[1] In the House, the Rules, the Ways and Means, and the Appropriations Committees rank among the most powerful; in the Senate, the Foreign Relations, the Finance, and the Appropriations Committees are widely regarded as most influential. These committees are significant because they deal with the rules that govern debate on the floor of the House, with the taxing and spending policies that pay for federal programs, and with the foreign policies of the American government. Little major legislation emerges from Congress that has not been closely examined by one or more of these committees.

The separate organization of committees in the two houses ensures that legislative bills are scrutinized from differing viewpoints by legislators responsive to different constituencies. Given the technical aspects of most legislation, the committee structure permits members of Congress to develop expertise in certain subject areas. By specializing, committee members are better able to perform their oversight responsibilities; that is, congressional

THERE ARE COMMITTEES AND THERE ARE COMMITTEES

Both houses of Congress overwhelm their members with committee assignments. These assignments are not always the most politically desirable (Defense and Foreign Affairs, for example, are more prestigious than a committee formed to investigate whether the snail darter should be on the endangered species list). Moreover, a member of Congress can belong to several different types of committees:

Standing — permanent committees such as Agriculture, Foreign Relations, and Judiciary.

Conference — a combined committee from the House and the Senate that is appointed to resolve differences in legislation passed in different forms by the two houses.

Joint — a combined committee, such as the Joint Economic Committee which receives the Economic Report of the President.

Temporary — a committee convened for a specific purpose and for a limited time.

committees not only draft legislation but also ensure that administrators in the executive branch are properly implementing legislative intentions.

This dispersion of power and influence among party leadership positions and committee chairs has three significant effects on Congress as a policy-making body.[2] First, neither house is very responsive to change. As a consequence, Congress tends to be the brake in the federal system. Next, the decentralization of power allows legislation to be blocked at many points. Third, the dispersion of power in Congress furnishes the president with many opportunities to exercise leadership in making public policy. Although Congress may occasionally check presidential policy making, the legislative branch usually cannot compete with the president as a policy initiator. Instead, its modern role in the policy process is to oversee the operations of the federal bureaucracy and to legitimate presidential policies.

Contemporary Developments in the Policy Process

Congress has not been unaware of its problems and limitations as a policy maker. In response it has changed in significant ways in the 1970s and 1980s. We will examine two of the most significant developments in Congress—the reforms of the committee and party leadership arrangements and the emergence of informal caucuses.

Congressional Reform

In the 1970s, members of Congress pursued a number of reforms intended to enhance the legislature's effectiveness. Not all the reforms have had their intended effects, however, and some may have actually harmed congressional policy-making efforts. Because the reform movement was particularly strong and significant in the House, we will focus our attention on that body.

Over the years, legislative power had come to be centered in the committees in Congress. This trend was accompanied by a decline in the power of the party leadership positions. As a result, the committee chairs had emerged as the dominant figures in the policy process. They were able to wield virtually unlimited authority over their committees if they so chose. The chairs could assign the committee's professional staff, create or abolish subcommittees, appoint subcommittee chairs, schedule committee meetings, determine the agenda of such meetings, and decide who would act as floor manager of legislation reported out of their committee.

Individuals held these powerful positions because of **seniority rule**. According to seniority rule, the committee member who had served longest on the committee and belonged to the majority party automatically became the chair. This system obviously makes leaders of those persons able to get reelected time and time again. Whenever Democrats enjoyed a majority, this practice favored members from the noncompetitive one-party Democratic South. It also often meant that committee chairs were much more conservative than most other Democrats in Congress. Younger, more liberal Democrats chafed under this dominance by conservative southerners.

In the late 1960s and early 1970s, the number of liberal members elected to Congress grew substantially. This gave them an opportunity to institute a number of reforms to weaken the autocratic power of the committee chairs and hopefully make Congress more responsive to social changes and progressive legislation.

These reforms tended to weaken the standing committees and their chairs by increasing the number and autonomy of subcommittees and by strengthening party leadership positions, especially the speaker of the House. The measures that strengthened the power of the subcommittees at the expense of the full committees and their chairs are perhaps the most important. The reformers accomplished their goals by (1) establishing *permanent* subcommittees with *fixed* legislative jurisdictions (2) providing the subcommittees with an *independent* professional staff and (3) securing an adequate budget for the subcommittee staff.

In today's Congress, the subcommittees conduct most of the real legislative business. It is there that most of the testimony is heard, the bills are rewritten or "marked up," and the critical votes are taken. The decisions of the subcommittees tend to be routinely accepted by the full committee.

This does not mean that once out of the subcommittee, a bill has smooth sailing into law. The legislative process is such that a single bill might have to find its way through several subcommittees and committees on its journey to enactment. The job of communication, compromise, and agreement among all the actors necessary for passage of a bill has become even more difficult with the dispersal of power into a large number of subcommittees. In this respect, the reforms have made the policy process more complicated and difficult to coordinate, and has increased the number of points at which the process can be blocked. As one author puts it: "The net result [of power dispersal] is that the tools of obstructionism have been made more widely available in Congress than in the past. That is to say, obstructionism has been dramatically democratized."[3]

Significantly, this dispersion of power within Congress tends to enhance the ability of interest groups, the president, and the federal bureaucracy to influence the congressional policy process. Subcommittees are likely to have as members individuals interested in a relatively narrowly defined subject matter. These smaller, more narrowly focused legislative units are easier targets for penetration and influence by special interests than were the more broadly defined full committees.

Subcommittees are tailor-made for the development of narrow policy subsystems called "iron triangles" or "subgovernments," discussed in Chapter 7. Such subsystems are based on close personal relationships among the legislators, lobbyists, and bureaucrats involved in a particular policy area. If these relationships are abused, it can reinforce the popular image of Congress as a tool of the special interests and damage the legitimacy of Congress as a national policy maker.

Despite (and partly because of) the reforms, Congress remains an institution better designed for delaying, diluting, or killing legislation than producing it. Today, Congress is largely incapable of becoming a formidable policy initiator. This role falls, almost by default, to the president, who wields tremendous influence in the legislative process due to his ability to shape the legislative agenda.

Informal Organization in Congress: The Caucuses

Congress is formally organized in a complex maze of party leadership positions, committees, and subcommittees. Informally, organizational structures called caucuses are becoming increasingly important.

A **caucus** is simply a grouping of members of Congress that is based on some common interest, identity, belief, or characteristic. Their membership thus often cross-cuts the other organizational structures of Congress, bringing together members of both chambers, both parties, and individuals with disparate legislative responsibilities. They can, as a result, constitute powerful forces for the legislative concerns they seek to promote, helping to overcome some of the problems associated with the extreme decentralization and fragmentation of congressional power just discussed. On the other hand, there are a great many of them—about seventy in the current Congress—and they are often pitted against one another, lending more political complexity to the legislative process.

Caucuses have formed around a number of distinct types of legislative concerns. Members of Congress from a particular state, regardless of their partisan and ideological differences, have long banded together to defend the interests of their state. Recently, entire regions of the country with similar general economic interests have done the same. For example, more than two hundred members of the House from sixteen states have come together to form the Northeast-Midwest Economic Advancement Coalition in an effort to protect the interests of the industrial Snowbelt. Of course, a Sunbelt Caucus has also been organized to see to the interests of the South and the West.

Economic interests are not always related to geography, however, and other caucuses have formed around more specific occupational and professional interests, for example, the interests of the steel, travel and tourism, textile, auto, jewelry, and even mushroom industries, as well as a small, blue-collar caucus made up of representatives from heavily unionized districts.

Caucuses have also formed around the background characteristics of the members. One of the best-known caucuses is the Congressional Black Caucus. The Congresswomen's Caucus is fast increasing its influence as well. There is also a small Hispanic Caucus largely composed of individuals of Hispanic heritage. Some caucuses are based not only on similar background characteristics of the members but also shared experiences, as with the Vietnam-era Veterans Caucus.

Other well-known caucuses include those that are essentially ideological in nature. The Democrat-

Members of the Congressional Black Caucus

WILLIAM PROXMIRE (b.1915) AND THE GOLDEN FLEECE

During the course of each year, Democrat William Proxmire, the senior senator from Wisconsin, will bestow his "Golden Fleece" award on some unhappy recipients. For Proxmire, this award helps him call attention to what he regards as the most wasteful recent expenditure of taxpayers' dollars. These awards almost always capture the attention of the media and give the senator valuable press.

Not that he actually needs media coverage to bolster his popularity. In an age when even some incumbent senators spend millions on their reelection campaigns, Proxmire typically spends less than several hundred. His report to the Federal Election Commission for the 1982 election noted that he had spent about $100!

First elected to the Senate in

1957 to take the place of the notorious Joseph McCarthy, who had died, Proxmire has won every succeeding election by a larger margin than the previous one. His populism, his consumer rights advocacy, and his ethic of hard work have earned him the admiration of his constituents. He has

in addition been a vigorous critic of wasteful military spending.

Proxmire is also widely regarded as somewhat of a health nut. He often jogs to his office from his Washington home, can do an amazing number of pushups for a man his age, and follows a rather strict diet. Coupled with his usually liberal stance on most issues, Proxmire is a gadfly for both the nation's political and physical health.

Yet his wit and his humor ensure that he does not convey an air of moral righteousness. Nor does Proxmire project an image of aloofness. Nearly every weekend, the senator can be found back in Wisconsin at some fair, shopping center, factory gate, flower show, or dairy farm exhibit, doing what he appears to like best, shaking the hands of all those who pass by.

ic Study Group, perhaps the oldest and best known of the ideological caucuses, was instrumental in the movement for congressional reform discussed earlier. Several others have since been formed, including the Democratic Forum, made up largely of conservative southern Democrats, and an organization of conservative Republicans called the Republican Study Committee. In addition, a number of groups have formed to promote particular causes or issues such as environmental protection, international peace, and even the fine arts.

Although caucuses form for a variety of reasons, they share certain goals and pursue similar strategies. Caucuses seek to assure that their particular issue or concern will be given a prominent place on Congress's agenda. They press for committee hearings on their issues, promote particular pieces of

legislation, and attempt to influence the vote on bills they favor. In all these respects, caucuses function much like private interest groups. But because their members serve in Congress, caucuses are in a position of potentially even greater influence in the policy-making process.

Members of Congress: Their Backgrounds and Activities

In this section, we examine the backgrounds and behavior of the members of Congress. The values they hold, the interests they seek to protect, the **constituents** to whom they must respond, all shape the policy-making activities in which Congress engages.

Table 9.2
An Average Day for a Representative

Activity	Average Time	
In the House chamber	2:53 hours	
In committee/subcommittee work	1:24 hours	
Hearings		26 minutes
Business		9 minutes
Markups		42 minutes
Other		5 minutes
In office	3:19 hours	
With constituents		17 minutes
With interest groups		9 minutes
With others		20 minutes
With staff aides		53 minutes
With other representatives		5 minutes
Answering mail		46 minutes
Preparing legislation, speeches		12 minutes
Reading		11 minutes
On telephone		26 minutes
In Other Washington locations	2:02 hours	
With constituents at capitol		9 minutes
At events		33 minutes
With leadership		3 minutes
With other representatives		11 minutes
With informal groups		8 minutes
In party meetings		5 minutes
Personal time		28 minutes
Other		25 minutes
Other activities	1:40 hours	
Total average representative's day:	11:18 hours	

Source: U.S. House of Representatives, Commission on Administrative Review, Administrative Reorganization and Legislation Management (95th Congress, 1st Session, 1977, H.Doc. 95–232): pp. 18–19.

Background Characteristics

Who are the senators and representatives, and what do they do? Common popular perceptions of Congress offer clear but contradictory images of the members and their work. The notion that Congress is made up of a high-minded group of national policy makers who spend their days considering reasoned arguments on the floor of their chamber, debating the critical policy issues of the day, and directing the course of the nation through their votes has long existed in uneasy conjunction with the image of members as at best a group of parochial, self-interested promoters of narrowly construed special interests and at worst a group of corrupt and incompetent bunglers and bickerers primarily concerned with their own reelection.

It is not surprising that such conflicting images exist. The first is one that some members tend to promote and seems implied by the constitutional role of the Congress. The second is a view that is often encouraged by a president who is a member of the party opposite that of the majority in Congress. Both images are, of course, gross oversimplifications and distort the true nature of the members and their activities. Moreover, most legislators are simply too busy to conform to either stereotype.

The average day of a representative or a senator is so crowded that he or she has relatively little time for contemplation of key policy issues or the study and formation of a personal judgment on each of the enormous number of bills considered by Congress. Instead, much of this work must fall to top staff aides. Nor do legislators spend much time actually listening to debates on the floor. Instead, most of the genuine debate and decision making occur within subcommittees focusing on particular types of legislation. As Table 9.2 suggests, most legislators have scant time for lofty reflection or an unhurried pace as they carry out their responsibilities.

Although some spectacular exceptions exist, Congress is not predominantly peopled by rogues interested only in personal enrichment and power. Most members of Congress are honest, and most try to discharge their responsibilities conscientiously. Despite the occasional graft and a salary and job benefits high by the standards of the average citizen, there are certainly easier, safer, and more dependable routes for those primarily interested in amassing great personal wealth. Indeed, one of the ways in which members of Congress differ from the rest of the nation is that a rather large number of them already possess substantial wealth.

The disproportionate wealth of the members of Congress reflects their backgrounds in high-status or elite professions (Table 9.3). The overwhelming dominance of those in law and business/banking is quite clear. Conspicuous by their absence are individuals from blue-collar or working-class occupations. On the other hand, racial minorities and women, who are also underrepresented in the elite occupations in the private sector, have made some progress in Congress. Though their numbers remain small, given the proportion of minorities and women in the total population, their representation in the Congress today reflects a substantial increase over earlier years.

Does this pattern of disparate representation mean that Congress is unrepresentative? Some commentators say yes, arguing that the fundamental job of a member of Congress—representation—involves sharing experiences, attitudes, viewpoints, and even deeply held feelings with the majority of their constituents, which can only be gained through a shared background. A Congress without members from a particular group, they contend, leaves those individuals unrepresented in the legislative halls. Other scholars argue that perfect demo-

A NATIONAL FLOWER AND A COUNTRY LAWYER

The American Congress has included thousands of members in the two centuries of its history. Most of them are not universally remembered, even though as a rule they did their jobs to the best of their abilities. As with most professional populations, both abilities and interests were wide ranging. One-term Whig Representative Abraham Lincoln, for example, highlighted his brief congressional career by opposing the Mexican-American War. He was defeated in a bid for reelection (1848) and did not win office again until 1860 when he was chosen president.

In more recent times, Everett Dirksen, the Republican minority leader in the Senate through most of the 1950s and 1960s, sometimes pursued less dramatic causes. He spent a good deal of time, for instance, insisting to his colleagues and anyone else who would listen that the marigold should be officially adopted as the national flower of the United States.

During the 1973 Senate Watergate hearings, the Watergate committee was chaired by an elderly Democratic senator from North Carolina named Sam Ervin. Before that time, few outside his home state of North Carolina had heard of Ervin, who modestly described himself as only a "country lawyer." Both he and his opponents underestimated his abilities. During the Watergate hearings, Ervin gradually revealed himself to be a foremost constitutional lawyer, his folksy ways notwithstanding.

Table 9.3
Demographics of the One-hundredth Congress

	House	Senate	Congress Total
Average Age	50.7	54.4	52.5
Occupation*			
Law	184	62	246
Business or Banking	142	28	170
Public Service and Politics	94	20	114
Education	38	12	50
Journalism	20	8	28
Agriculture	20	5	25
Other	27	7	34
Sex			
Men	412	98	510
Women	23	2	25
Race			
White	398	100	498
Black	23	0	23
Hispanic	14	0	14
Religion			
Protestant	259	69	328
Roman Catholic	123	19	142
Jewish	29	8	37
Other	24	4	28

* Occupational categories total more than the number of members because some indicate more than one occupation.

Source: Congressional Quarterly Weekly Report, Vol. 44, No. 45, November 8, 1986, pp. 2861–2863.

graphic representation in Congress is both impossible and unnecessary. The multitude of human groups that make up society cannot all be physically represented in Congress. Further, a member need not necessarily be black to represent blacks nor a woman to represent women. Important legislation (the Civil Rights Act of 1964, for example) has been passed by past Congresses favoring these and other groups such as the handicapped who have not been historically well represented in the national legislature.

Although Congress cannot reflect perfectly the demographic makeup of the nation, it does seems likely that a Congress with greater numbers from such groups as women and minorities would bring different issues to the national policy agenda and such a Congress would make somewhat different policy choices as well. Several years ago, an outspoken leader of the women's movement, Representative Bella Abzug (Dem. N.Y.), graphically raised this point with respect to women in government as follows:

DO YOU REALLY WANT TO GO TO CONGRESS?

The experiences of Congressman Marc Lincoln Marks aren't all that unusual, but Marks did something unusual (and unusually rational) about them—he quit. After three terms as a congressman from northwestern Pennsylvania, he had had enough and decided not to seek reelection in 1982. As he described it to a group of students after his retirement, there are really four big problems in being a congressman. First, you are constantly running for reelection. Because congressmen are elected every two years, they are campaigning in one sense or another every day of their lives. The costs of reelection are also constant, and thus a big part of the job is seeking money from interest groups. The pressure from groups is heavy, as are the financial consequences of ignoring their wishes. Marks said he refused to vote the way some large contributors wanted, and their contributions went to his opponents in subsequent elections.

Second, the pay is not as good as it appears. Indeed, it is hard for someone with a family to get by at a reasonable standard. The cost of maintaining two homes, one in the district and one in Washington, is great. Renting in Washington is expensive, decent housing often costing more than $1,000 a month. The job also calls for doing a great deal of entertaining of visiting groups and individuals from the home district. It is not uncommon for a congressman to entertain three or four times a week, and the costs are not reimbursed. In Marks' case, he finally was forced to sell his home in Pennsylvania, renting a small apartment to maintain an address in his district. Nonetheless, he was charged by a political opponent with having "abandoned" his district.

Third, the job puts considerable strain on family relationships. Often it means an absent spouse and parent as the congressperson decides to leave the family home and take an inexpensive apartment in Washington. Even though Marks took his family with him, he found little time to spend with his children. Few in Congress do find the time. Most return to the district two or three weekends a month, and week nights are crowded with mandatory social events and legislative homework.

Finally, there are the constituents themselves. Marks complained of cranks and critics who seemed to view congressmen as fair game for all manner of advice and verbal abuse. It comes in visits home, over the phone, and through the mail. It is an accepted and expected part of the job, but congressmen need an extremely thick skin to put up with it and keep their cool over the years. Marks admitted to not having such a thick skin and to enjoying making some rather pointed responses to cranks after having decided not to seek reelection. Perhaps it should be no surprise that voluntary retirement is a rapidly rising cause of turnover in Congress.

Would we rank 14th in infant mortality among the developed nations of the world? Would we allow a situation in which thousands of kids grow up without decent care because their mothers have to work for a living and have no place to leave their children . . ., or else that condemns women to stay at home when they want to work, because there are no facilities for their children? . . . Would women allow the fraudulent packaging and cheating of consumers that they find every time they shop? Would they consent to the perverted sense of priorities that has dominated our government for the past few decades, appropriating billions of dollars for war and plunging our cities into crises of neglect? Would they vote for ABM's instead of schools, MIRV's instead of decent housing or health centers? And does anyone think they would have allowed the war in Vietnam to go on for so many years, slaughtering and maiming our young men and the people of Indochina? [4]

The greater representation of women may not have these policy implications but the questions Ms. Abzug raised do serve to make the point that different people might, based on their backgrounds, choose alternative policies that would result in very different cost and resource allocations.

Roles

Regardless of their demographic background characteristics, all members of Congress have one thing in common. They share a difficult job made up of many roles, and their first task is to manage their time and to balance these roles. As policy makers, members of Congress are expected to do legislative homework so they can vote intelligently on bills. Because of the number of bills considered and the shortage of time available for careful study, this is a difficult job for even the most conscientious member. As a result, legislators often rely on "cue givers" or outside experts rather than on personal study to arrive at a decision on how to vote.

Cue givers are usually other members of Congress in whose judgment the legislator has confidence. Quite often, these cue givers have served on the committee that gave the piece of legislation its form. Outside experts may include lobbyists, agency administrators, or the legislator's own staff. Cue givers and experts tend to have inordinate influence on particular pieces of legislation. The more complicated, technical, and esoteric the legislation, the greater the influence such sources of information are likely to exert on each stage of the policy process and on the policy outcomes.

Each legislator has the opportunity to develop into a powerful cue giver through involvement in another key congressional role—that of committee member. It is in committee, and increasingly in subcommittees of the larger committees, that most policy formulation occurs. Because committees and subcommittees consider legislation within a relatively narrow range of subject matter, work within these bodies tends to result in members becoming specialists, and they are soon recognized by their colleagues as experts in these subjects.

As an expert member of Congress, a legislator on a subcommittee, on a committee, and on the floor can wield considerable influence. As cue givers, legislators may be able to influence the actual content of legislation important to their constituents. And within their specific area of expertise, they may be able to cue other votes to secure passage of the legislation.

To be an effective representative, members must serve on a committee dealing with legislation that is of concern to their home districts. From a strategic point of view, a legislator from a farm district is

Congressman Bill Frenzel of Minnesota meeting with a group of senior citizen constituents—a group important both in his role as politician and in casework.

more likely to want to serve on an agriculture committee than one dealing with urban affairs. Farmers who see a legislator working on behalf of their interests will tend to vote for that member, whereas they may have little interest in legislation that affects urban centers.

Representing constituents is not confined to legislative work in committee and voting on the floor of Congress, however. Direct constituent service, or casework, is an important aspect of a legislator's job. Casework often includes helping to solve a problem a constituent is having with the federal breaucracy. If a member can help ensure that a Social Security check arrives on time or straighten out a mix-up in Medicare, he or she can earn good will invaluable for the next election.

Another form of constituent service involves benefits to larger groups of constituents or even the district as a whole. Long called the **pork barrel**, this variety of constituent service takes the form of securing federal projects, contracts, or grants for cities, businesses, and other institutions in the district. The pork barrel will provide money, jobs, and usually some lasting physical evidence of the legislator's service to the district that can be pointed to at election time, such as a community sewage treatment plant, a regional water project, or the construction of a new federal installation of some kind.

This leads us to another of the roles of the member of Congress—that of politician. All legislators are politicians because they have to be, and

ROBERT PACKWOOD (b. 1932) AND TAX REFORM

Tax reform has been a top priority item on President Reagan's agenda for his second term, but Senator Robert Packwood, Republican of Oregon, seemed an unlikely candidate to champion the cause in the Senate. Indeed, Packwood had made it clear earlier that the tax system seemed fine to him just the way it was. The tax reform bill under consideration in the powerful Senate Finance Committee, which Packwood chairs, was well on its way to being shot full of loopholes for special interests when Packwood engineered a dramatic change in direction.

Packwood's sudden and successful maneuver was spurred by both pragmatic political considerations and growing revulsion with the multitude of insistent lobbyists for special interests. Though considered a popular senator, Packwood had never won election in Oregon by impressive margins. With his seat up for election in 1986, he almost certainly did not want to be seen as a lackey of the special interests or as the senator most responsible for al-

lowing the initiative on tax reform to slip to the Democrats in the House of Representatives. Moreover, both Packwood and his colleagues on the committee were distressed with the unseemly extent and intensity of the lobbying efforts to secure special treatment for special interests in the tax code. Packwood complained it was as if "assassins" were after him and observed that it was a "ridiculous way for government to run things."

Packwood's role in tax reform

might have been unexpected, but it is not entirely out of character. He has always been a maverick and independent-minded Republican, ardently defending progressive policies such as environmental protection, population control, and family planning. He continues to be the Senate's most eloquent defender of federal funding for abortions. Nor has he been shy about advocating significant reforms in the past. He had an immediate impact on the Senate on his arrival in 1969, advocating reform of the seniority system for selection of committee chairs.

It may be that Packwood will be best remembered for his role in advancing a radical restructuring of the tax code, however. His contribution undoubtedly contributed to his reelection in Oregon, to his growing influence in the Senate, and his increasing visibility on the national political stage. It is of such legislative accomplishments as Packwood's tax reform measure that outstanding careers in the Senate are made.

they must be successful politicians if they are to have the opportunity to continue to play the other roles required of members of Congress. Their every move and thought may not be guided by their concern for reelection as they engage in the other aspects of their jobs, but, to be reelected, they must and will play the instrumental role of politician.

Fortunately, members of Congress already possess the most valuable resource for being reelected—incumbency. Many factors, of course, contribute to electoral success, including having access to the money needed to campaign, being personally

photogenic or charismatic, being a member of the majority party in a district or state, taking policy positions popular with the voters, and so on. But nothing is more important than already holding a seat in Congress, that is, incumbency. Since the end of World War II, about 90 percent of the incumbents who have sought reelection have been successful. The percentage has been somewhat higher for the House (94 percent between 1956 and 1978) than for the Senate (83 percent).[5]

Why is incumbency such a powerful electoral advantage? After all, many people do not hold

Congress as an institution in high regard, and others frequently appear to be dissatisfied with the government of which these incumbents are a part. It would seem that incumbents must often be in the position of trying to defend a less than perfect record, while challengers, unburdened by past voting records, are free to make popular promises.

Part of the reason is that the factors often assumed to be important determinants of voting behavior are not really significant. Voters do not return a member of Congress to office because they agree with his or her policy positions on important pieces of legislation. In fact, very few people know how their senators and representatives vote. Nor are they elected or thrown out because of fluctuations in the economy.[6] Instead, such simple advantages of incumbency as being well known and having the opportunity to provide service to their constituents seem to be central factors.

Incumbents seek to ensure that their names are recognizable to the average constituent, and the evidence reveals they are quite successful in establishing this visibility. One study has shown that about 90 percent of the population claims to have some form of contact with their representative or senator. They have seen them on TV (50 percent), received mail from them (71 percent), seen them at a meeting (20 percent), or even met them personally (23 percent).[7]

Stressing constituency service is an effective way to enhance visibility through contact with constituents and to build good will. Unlike the strategy of taking and publicizing policy stands, which will always be popular with some voters and unpopular with others, casework and pork barrel activities produce positive images with virtually all the public. Thus getting reelected has more to do with how many of the voters know a legislator and how they

"I propose legislation. I do my best to aid in the process of government.
And I try like hell to keep my name out of 'Doonesbury.'"

feel about the quality of constituency service.

Members of Congress have taken several steps to enhance the advantage of incumbency. They have dramatically increased the volume of mail sent out from congressional offices during the last twenty years. House members have increased the budget for district travel allowances, as well as allowances for office equipment, stationery, constituent communications, and other official expenses. Both houses have also increased the monies available to support district offices. All these actions are clearly designed to increase constituent contact and the member's visibility.

The Functions of Congress

In addition to being a body composed of individuals playing a variety of roles, Congress is also a policy-making structure. As such, Congress has five basic functions—representation, issue clarification, lawmaking, **administrative oversight**, and the legitimation of presidential policies. Each of these contributes a distinct element to the policy-making process. Each also has an impact on the types and kinds of policies that emerge from the legislative branch.

Representation

Congress is frequently called the people's branch because its members must in some way express the diversity of the citizenry they represent. Legislators must articulate the conflicting views and the competing interests, whether economic, social, racial, or ethnic, that make up this nation. These articulations furnish a context for policy making that legislators must use when determining cost and resource allocations. Public policy will be perceived as legitimate only if the people believe they have had the benefit of what Chief Justice Earl Warren, in *Reynolds v. Sims* (1964), characterized as "fair and effective representation."[8]

Thus one of the most crucial tasks for legislators is to determine how to represent the people that elected them.[9] Should a member of the House of Representatives, for example, seek merely to speak for the narrow interests of the congressional district? Or does such a representative have a duty to

THEORIES OF REPRESENTATION

These theories attempt to answer two fundamental questions concerning the nature of representation. First, to whom is a member of Congress responsible? Second, how should the mandate-independence dilemma be resolved?

DELEGATE THEORY:

This theory, which stands at the mandate end of the continuum, argues that a representative should simply record the wishes of the majority of the district's constituents. The principal difficulty with this theory is how does a member of Congress ascertain the wishes of the majority. Being human, majorities tend to shift frequently on the issues.

RESPONSIBLE PARTY THEORY:

A second theory also emphasizes a mandatory feature of representation. Since a member of Congress wins election under a party label, this theory argues that the representative should follow the party leadership. The most serious problem here is that American political parties are far less responsible than their European counterparts; that is, American parties are decentralized and exercise far less control over party members and are less likely to adhere to a consistent ideological program.

BROKER THEORY:

This theory stresses the group nature of politics. Broker theory insists that a representative should seek to facilitate compromises among the competing and often divergent interests in a legislative district. An important problem with this theory is that individuals unable or unwilling to organize as interests are effectively excluded from the policy-making process.

BURKEAN THEORY:

This theory stands at the independence end of the continuum. Edmund Burke, an eighteenth-century English statesman, argued that the people elect a representative to exercise reason and judgment and not merely to record the desires of constituents. The principal difficulty with Burkean theory is the legislator's lack of responsiveness to the electorate or to significant segments of it.

speak for his or her party or an even larger responsibility to seek the public interest, whatever or however unpopular that may be? An opportunistic legislator may answer these questions by simply gauging which actions will contribute most to future chances of reelection, but that simply begs the question.

Britain's failure to provide representation in Parliament for the American colonists gave revolutionary leaders one of their most powerful slogans: "No taxation without representation." The issue of representation in the new Union was also one of the most nettlesome problems at the Constitutional Convention. Only after a long and difficult struggle were the convention delegates able to reach a compromise that called for a bicameral Congress with the House representing the people and the Senate representing the states. With the exception of Nebraska, the states have all adopted this bicameral mode of representation. After more than two centuries, they have become a fixed institutional feature of American representative government.

Issue Clarification

Congress has a responsibility to identify and clarify issues of concern to the public. To carry out this responsibility, the standing committees have a formidable tool at their disposal, the power of investigation. Committees can use this power to gather

CONGRESSIONAL PRIME TIME

Both houses of Congress now have televised sessions. The sessions of the House, though, are more regular and a good deal more open than the limited and carefully prescribed sessions of the Senate. Members of Congress must even more than before "look" like national legislators. With the coming of TV to the chamber, many members are paying more attention to the way they dress: a great many have invested in red ties because they look good on television. There has been a noticeable drop in the practice of reading through the morning newspapers while on the floor or dozing off for a few winks in the afternoon. The concern that television would be abused by congressmen seeking media exposure for political reasons has proven largely unfounded. However, some speeches that never would have been given, but merely "read in" to the Congressional Record are now being delivered for the cameras.

So far, being able to see democracy at work has had little impact on the electorate. Perhaps the real question is whether the drama of congressional politics will be of more interest than the older soap operas millions of Americans habitually watch every weekday afternoon.

Senior citizen testifies at congressional committee hearing. It is in such hearings that congressmen develop much of their expertise on particular policy issues.

information as a basis for possible new legislation. By holding hearings, both committees and subcommittees can assemble a body of expert opinion to determine whether existing policy is accomplishing the ends for which it was formulated or whether new legislation is required. Committee hearings also furnish an opportunity for opposing views to be heard. Such testimony can clarify the issues that members of Congress need to reconcile before legislation can be drafted.

Legislators can also use the power of investigation to discover and to develop public opinion, as did former Senator George McGovern of South Dakota when his subcommittee investigated the problem of malnutrition in the United States. Within a short period of time, his efforts led to legislation that provided for food stamps for the poor. Because the problem of hunger had been widely publicized, the legislation's passage through Congress was greatly facilitated.

Lawmaking

Lawmaking is undoubtedly the most well-known and controversial function of Congress. Yet the major source of the most important legislative bills is not Congress, its committees, or its members. Two-thirds of all bills actually originate in the executive branch. In four major messages—the State of the Union address (the only message mandated by the Constitution), the Budget, the Economic Report, and the Environmental Quality Report—the chief executive presents his most important legislative proposals to Congress.

Presidential leadership in formulating public policy, however, has not negated the fact that it is in the halls (as well as cloakrooms and cafeterias) of Congress where conflicting ideas, values, and interests must be reconciled before legislation emerges. Most legislative bills have little chance of becoming law unless members of Congress are successful in building a consensus through bargaining and compromise (Table 9.4). Subcommittees and standing committees seek to draft legislation that will attract a legislative majority.[10] If they fail to reach an acceptable compromise, their legislative effort is doomed even before it reaches the floor for debate. This process is so hazardous that 90 percent of all legislative bills die in committee. At every step, subcommittee, committee, floor debate, and conference committee, the effort to achieve consensus through bargaining and compromise must be sustained or a bill will never become law.

In addition to taxing and spending powers, Congress wields its most significant legislative powers in the areas of foreign affairs and commerce. In foreign affairs, the Senate must ratify treaties and approve all presidential appointments of ambassadors and cabinet secretaries. Without congressional support or authorization, the president would be handicapped in undertaking such actions as sending American advisers to El Salvador, occupying the

In his State of the Union address, the president reveals his legislative agenda in broad outline for the year to come.

Table 9.4
The Politics of the Legislative Process

Legislative Steps	Political Decisions
INTRODUCTORY STAGE	
A legislator introduces a bill in one of the houses of Congress. If the bill is a tax bill, it must originate in the House of Representatives.	Who should introduce the bill? Is the timing of the bill appropriate? What provisions should be included? What groups will oppose/support the bill? Who should lead the legislative effort? Will the public need to be educated?
COMMITTEE STAGE	
The bill is referred to the appropriate committee.	Which committee is the appropriate committee?
The committee decides if a bill is to be reported to the floor for debate.	Who will testify at committee hearings? What compromises must be reached for the bill to be reported out of committee? What political considerations bear on the committee's decisions?
FLOOR STAGE	
After floor debate the bill is voted on by the entire house.	Who should guide floor action? How will a legislative majority be mobilized? What provisions will be voted on? When? Will amendments to the bill be permitted?
If the bill receives a favorable vote, it is sent to the other house. The same legislative steps and political decisions ensue. If the other house acts favorably, the process continues to the next stage.	
CONFERENCE STAGE	
A conference committee is selected to work out a compromise of the versions passed by the two houses.	Who will be selected for the conference committee? Which compromises will be acceptable to both houses?
Both houses vote on the conference bill.	Should the conference bill be supported? Does the conference version satisfy the bill's backers in both houses?
PRESIDENTIAL ACTION	
The bill is signed or vetoed in its entirety by the president.	What political considerations will affect the president's decision? If he vetoes the bill, are the legislative majorities large enough to command the two-thirds vote necessary to override the veto? Will the president return the bill to Congress with a veto message?

Beirut Airport in Lebanon, or invading Grenada in the Caribbean.

The commerce power has proven, over the course of American history, to be the most flexible and potent grant of authority possessed by Congress. On numerous occasions, the Supreme Court has upheld congressional use of this power to regulate interstate commerce, to ban the interstate transportation of women for immoral purposes, to establish a framework for labor relations and collective bargaining, and to protect the civil rights of minorities through such legislative efforts as the comprehensive Civil Rights Act of 1964.

During the last two decades, Congress has increasingly used its lawmaking authority to overturn regulations issued by executive agencies. The 1970s saw the number of laws passed by Congress far surpassed by the number of executive regulations. In 1974, for example, Congress passed a little over 400 public laws, whereas executive agencies issued nearly 7,500 regulations. To counteract the possible abuse of executive authority, or simply to ensure that congressional intentions are followed, Congress has had to enact laws that supersede executive regulations. Although this type of legislation is basically negative in nature, such laws appear to be

The Senate Foreign Relations Committee holding confirmation hearings for George Schultz—nominated by Ronald Reagan to be Secretary of State.

the only way to effectively check the exercise of executive authority.

Administrative Oversight

Congressional responsibility does not end with the passage of legislation. The legislative branch must also oversee the administration of government programs. Executive oversight is lodged primarily in the standing committees of Congress. They are given the responsibility to ensure that the federal bureaucracies are correctly implementing congressional intentions.[11] For example, the House Agriculture Committee is charged with the responsibility of ensuring that the Agriculture Department is adhering to congressional mandates for farm programs. The president, however, can hinder congressional oversight by claiming executive privilege, that is, by instructing his subordinates not to appear before Congress, nor to release certain information to its members.

In numerous instances, Congress has felt the need to create a new agency to carry out the congressional will. Under its directive and supervisory power, Congress can create, alter, or abolish any executive office except that of the president and the vice president. Since the turn of the century, Congress has created at the cabinet level the Departments of Commerce, Labor, Health and Human Services, Housing and Urban Development, Transportation, Energy, and Education. The latter five departments have been authorized since 1950. During this same period, Congress created a host of lesser executive offices such as the Commission on

Civil Rights, the Environmental Protection Agency, and the Nuclear Regulatory Commission.

Oversight also entails the evaluation of federal policies and programs. To ensure that executive agencies are spending tax dollars properly, the General Accounting Office (GAO), the principal agency assisting Congress, audits all federal spending. A GAO audit of an executive agency can give Congress information to help determine whether a program is cost effective. If a program is not cost effective, Congress must decide whether other (political) benefits of the program outweigh economic considerations. For example, in an attempt to limit farm surpluses, Congress has authorized the president to substitute in-kind payments for cash payments. Congress could not afford to antagonize farm groups by abolishing a program that is not cost effective. But it did seek to modify the existing program in a way that was more effective, yet did not upset farmers.

Legitimation of Presidential Policies

The formal endorsement of presidentially initiated policies is the most significant function of Congress in terms of a policy-making relationship with the president. Although this too is a negative function, it ranks as the most important role played by Congress today. The federal budget and other economic policies, treaties and trade agreements, civil rights and voting rights legislation, environmental policies, and the appointment process are all initiated by the president.[12] Congress must respond to these presidential initiatives. The quality of that response will have a perceptible impact on the power equation between the two branches.

Despite efforts by Congress in the 1970s to reassert itself, the president has many resources that enable him to dominate the American political system. From an organizational perspective, the very nature of the respective branches makes it difficult for Congress to challenge presidential leadership over the long term. Effective leadership also depends on unity. But the Ninety-seventh, Ninety-eighth, and Ninety-ninth Congress were divided along party lines; Democrats controlled the House, whereas Republicans enjoyed a majority in the Senate.

In a world setting of economic interdependence and ideological conflict, the complexities of eco-

ROBERT MICHEL (b. 1923): HOUSE REPUBLICAN LEADER FROM "MIDDLE AMERICA"

Illinois' Eighteenth Congressional District has long been considered representative of the great expanse of nonurban "middle America." The city at its hub, Peoria, has been the butt of jokes as the essence of parochial, uncultured, main street America. Whatever else it is, the Eighteenth has produced interesting and significant politicians. The last three include Everett McKinley Dirksen, senator renowned for his unkempt appearance, sonorous voice, and rhetorical abilities; Harold H. Velde, who chaired the powerful and infamous House Committee on Un-American Activities during the communist witch hunt of the early 1950s; and, since 1957, Robert Michel who, as minority leader in the House since 1980, has been the chief advocate of Ronald Reagan's programs in that Democratic body.

Michel is well suited to the job he prefers to call "Republican Leader" rather than minority leader. He has impeccable conservative credentials, having begun his political career as an administrative assistant to Representative Velde and, as a congressman, becoming a staunch supporter of the U.S. military effort in Vietnam and a vocal critic of LBJ's Great

Society social programs. With his position on the Labor, Health, Education, and Welfare subcommittee of the Appropriations Committee he has made his opposition to social programs felt. Michel's affability enables him to get along, not only with his fellow Republicans, but with most Democrats as well. His approach to issues often attracts Democratic votes, and attracting votes from the opposition is, of course, a key to success for a leader of a minority in Congress.

In a sense, Michel has been a leader for the Republicans almost since the day he entered Congress. He was chosen president of the "Eighty-fifth Club," a group of twenty-two freshmen Republi-

can representatives elected in 1956. His service to the party as cochair of the Republican "Truth Squad" following and rebutting Democratic candidates during the 1964 elections is just one example of his tireless party activity. In 1966, he was elected assistant minority whip, and in 1974 rose to minority whip, the second-ranking party leadership position.

Michel seems to have a secure hold on the Republican leader position. Perhaps his greatest worry is his reelection. He narrowly survived a strong challenge in 1982, when, as legislative point-man for Ronald Reagan, he was perceived as partially responsible for the effects of the recession on his heavily working-class district. Barring similar or even more severe circumstances in the future, however, his seat seems safe. Should the Republicans capture control of the House, he would most likely become speaker. If not, Michel's potential for becoming a truly important national political figure hinges on his ability to forge a relatively permanent voting majority of Republicans and conservative Democrats into an effective conservative coalition. He seems well equipped to take advantage of any such opportunity.

nomic policy and the constantly changing problems of foreign affairs assure presidential primacy for the foreseeable future. Despite this primacy, Congress has shown that it can effectively check abuses of executive power, as President Nixon's forced resig-

nation in 1974 dramatically demonstrated. For many Americans, the political events of the 1960s and the 1970s confirmed the wisdom of this nation's founders in separating executive and legislative power.

OTHER POWERS OF CONGRESS

AMENDING POWER:

Congress plays the dominant role in the amending process. Proposal of amendments is either by a two-thirds vote of both houses of Congress or by a national convention that has been authorized by Congress, Ratification occurs either when three-quarters of the state legislatures or when state conventions in three-quarters of the states approve. The amending power is the most important power of Congress that is not directly related to lawmaking. Neither the president nor the Supreme Court plays any immediate or direct role in the amending process. For the most part, the president is restricted to exhortation. Jimmy Carter, for example, tried to use his office to influence public opinion on behalf of the proposed Equal Rights Amendment. Despite his efforts, the ERA failed to be ratified.

ELECTORAL POWER:

The votes of the electoral college in presidential elections are certified by Congress. If none of the candidates has received an electoral majority (at least 270 out of 538 electoral votes), the House of Representatives, with one vote per state delegation, chooses the president. Under the same circumstances, the Senate chooses the vice president. The elections of Presidents Thomas Jefferson and John Quincy Adams occurred in this fashion in 1800 and 1824, respectively.

ADVISE AND CONSENT POWER:

This power is also known as the confirmation power. For the most part, this is not a power of Congress, but rather of the Senate only. Presidential appointments to virtually all the most important positions in the national government— cabinet secretaries, ambassadors and ministers, and federal judges—require senatorial confirmation. All treaties with foreign nations must be ratified by a two-thirds vote of the Senate. Senatorial courtesy is a practice that restricts the president's appointing power. In turn, executive agreements limit the Senate's advise and consent power. Finally, the Senate shares with the House the constitutional obligation to confirm the president's choice for filling a vice presidential vacancy.

JUDICIAL POWER (IMPEACHMENT):

Executive officials and federal judges are subject to the judicial power of Congress. Impeachment occurs in the House. If that body votes articles of impeachment, the trial for possible removal takes place in the Senate. The chief justice of the Supreme Court presides if the president is being tried. Conviction by a two-thirds vote results in removal from office. (President Andrew Johnson underwent such a trial in 1867, but failed to be removed from office by one vote.) Congress is also the sole judge of its members. By a simple majority, either house can refuse to seat a newly elected member. Either house can expel a sitting member by a two-thirds vote. Or Congress can choose some lesser punishment such as censure. Federal courts have been reluctant to intervene when Congress exercises its judicial power, and since Congress rarely uses this power, the courts have had little opportunity to do so.

The Power Equation Between Congress and the President

During the course of the twentieth century, the balance of power between Congress and the president has tipped decisively in favor of the president.[13] Three principal factors account for this shift in the power equation. Without a doubt, congressional grants of power to the president rank as the foremost factor. In the last half-century alone, Congress has enacted nearly five hundred federal laws that together give the president many powers not found in the Constitution. These grants of power have contributed directly to the decline of Congress as a policy initiator.

In many ways, the most important grant of power was the Budget and Accounting Act of 1921, which enabled the president to exercise leadership in comprehensive policy making. By making the chief executive responsible for the formulation of the budget, Congress reduced significantly its power over how money is raised and spent. President Reagan's budget proposals for each of the fiscal years he has been in office underscore how far a determined president can go in insisting on legislative acceptance of the executive's budget.

The **Congressional Budget and Impoundment Control Act** of 1974 was an effort by Congress to recover some of its budgetary powers.[14] However, after more than a dozen years, there is scant evidence that this statute has put Congress on a budget-making par with the president. Perhaps with still more experience, the congressional budget committees will be able to assume leadership in Congress and eventually make the congressional budget a viable alternative to the presidential budget. As it

now stands, the president's budget proposals are seldom altered significantly by congressional actions. Nor is this likely to change in the near future regardless of which party controls the presidency or the Congress.

Other major grants of power to the president in such areas as tariffs, labor relations, executive organization, and the economy have contributed significantly to the president's ability to dominate the policy process, although the Founders originally assigned responsibility for these matters to Congress. These congressional grants not only shifted power to the president but also revolutionized the relationship between the national government and the economy.

Although Franklin Roosevelt initiated a number

MAJOR STATUTORY GRANTS OF AUTHORITY BY CONGRESS TO THE PRESIDENT

THE FEDERAL BUDGET: THE BUDGET AND ACCOUNTING ACT OF 1921

This act, which placed the responsibility for the formulation of the federal budget on the president, made it possible for the chief executive to exercise the leadership role in virtually all areas of policy making. Congress has attempted to recoup some of its fiscal power by passage of the Congressional Budget and Impoundment Control Act of 1974.

TARIFFS: RECIPROCAL TRADE AGREEMENTS ACT OF 1934
TRADE EXPANSION ACT OF 1962
TRADE REFORM ACT OF 1974

By this series of acts, Congress has given the president wide discretion in the setting of tariffs. Congress has not withdrawn any of this authority.

LABOR RELATIONS: THE RAILWAY LABOR ACT OF 1926
NATIONAL LABOR RELATIONS ACT OF 1935 (WAGNER ACT)
LABOR MANAGEMENT RELATIONS ACT OF 1947 (TAFT–HARTLEY ACT)

In each of these acts, Congress has provided the president with substantial authority in the area of

labor relations and collective bargaining. Congress has not altered these grants of its commerce power.

EXECUTIVE ORGANIZATION: REORGANIZATION ACT OF 1939
REORGANIZATION ACT OF 1949

Within rather broad limits, these acts authorized the president to reorganize the structure of the executive branch. The president has substantial discretion in the organization of the Executive Office of the President. His discretion in reorganizing cabinet departments is more limited. Congress has left these grants intact.

THE ECONOMY: THE EMPLOYMENT ACT OF 1946

Congressional passage of this act marked the official end of a laissez-faire attitude on the part of the national government toward the economy. The president was made responsible for developing economic policies that would ensure maximum employment, maximum production, and price stability. Given the recurrent recessions the nation has experienced since the Great Depression, both Congress and the American people have continued to look to the president for the resolution of the nation's economic problems.

of innovative programs in his efforts to end the Depression, it was Congress who passed the Employment Act of 1946. This act, one of the most significant laws ever enacted by Congress, made the president rather than the legislative branch responsible for initiating economic policies that would foster full employment, healthy economic growth, and price stability.[15] By placing these responsibilities on the president, Congress officially marked the end of a laissez faire attitude on the part of the national government toward the economy.

The second factor accounting for the shift in power to the president is the recurrent political and economic crises that have marked the twentieth century. As a crisis manager, the president has proven better able to respond decisively to both domestic and foreign emergencies. Strong presidents, we should note, have an easier time acquiring power in periods of national crisis. Examples include Abraham Lincoln during the Civil War (1861–1865) and Franklin Roosevelt during the Great Depression (1933–1941).

The emergence of the United States as a world power has also led other countries to look to the American president for answers to international problems. In some instances, the president has become directly involved in negotiating agreements between foreign countries. A recent example is the Camp David accords, which produced a peace treaty between Egypt and Israel. These accords were possible only because President Carter personally intervened.

Military intervention in Vietnam, however, was viewed very differently both at home and abroad. President Lyndon Johnson's actions, and more particularly, President Richard Nixon's, prompted Congress to pass the **War Powers Act** of 1973. So determined was Congress to place limits on the president's ability to intervene militarily in the affairs of other nations that this resolution was passed over the president's veto. In this instance, Congress succeeded in putting the president on notice that presidential authority to use military force is subject to congressional scrutiny and cannot be extended beyond ninety days without congressional approval. Despite President Nixon's assertion that this resolution was an unconstitutional intrusion on the president's authority, there is little evidence that the foreign policies of later presidents

POWER WARS: THE RETURN OF THE PURSE STRINGS

Probably the most important initiative taken by Congress to regain power has been the steps taken to gain control of the budget process. In 1974, amid rising federal budget deficits and President Nixon's attempts to invade some of Congress's traditional budgetary prerogatives, Congress passed the Budget and Impoundment Control Act. This act sought to deal with the lack of coordination within Congress in the budget process by creating new budget committees in each house. The act also created a **Congressional Budget Office** (CBO) staffed by a panel of bipartisan budgetary experts. The purpose of the CBO is to give Congress information on the economy, independent of the executive branch.

Congress probably has no more effective way to enhance its participation in government than to gain some real control of the budgetary process. Budgetary priorities, of course, are ultimately reflected in what government actually does or does not do. Unfortunately, from the experience to date, it appears that the new budgetary process has not been as successful as its congressional backers had hoped. Certainly, it has not been successful in limiting spending to levels balanced with revenues, one of its basic objectives. The CBO has turned out to be the more important element of the new process, providing Congress with a valuable independent source of information on which to draw for the formulation of policy alternatives. It would be difficult to argue that the Congress is not a stronger policy-making institution due to the existence of the CBO, but the balance of domestic policy-making power remains in the hands of the president.

have been impaired to any significant degree. As of the middle 1980s, military actions by presidential order have kept within the time constraints of the resolution.

The third factor that contributed to the shift of power from the legislative to the executive branch has been the transition from negative government (the ensurance of domestic tranquility and protec-

POWER WARS: THE CONGRESS STRIKES BACK

In the area of foreign policy, the Constitution gives Congress only a very limited role to play. Its most important responsibility, the power to declare war, has been eroded since Korea and Vietnam. Ambiguity concerning the roles of Congress and the president in the power to make war are rooted in the Constitution, and has been a problem throughout our history. The issue was brought to a head, however, by the unpopular war in Vietnam. That war was to become the longest in American history and result in 58,000 American deaths and more than 150,000 wounded—all without a formal declaration of war by Congress. In an effort to reassert congressional control over war making, Congress passed the War Powers Act in 1973 over President Nixon's veto.

The War Powers Act has three major provisions:

1. If the president sends U.S. troops into a foreign combat zone, he must report this deployment to Congress within forty-eight hours and explain the reasons for doing so.

2. The commitment of U.S. troops to foreign combat can continue for no more than ninety days, unless the Congress specifically approves an extension or formally declares war.

3. The Congress can end U.S. involvement in a foreign conflict before the end of the ninety days by passing a resolution to that effect, and such congressional action is not subject to a presidential veto.

Many commentators doubt that the act will really be effective in limiting the president's power, as commander-in-chief of the armed forces, to make war. As Vietnam so vividly demonstrated, once troops are committed, it is difficult, strategically and politically, to withdraw them. Since the act's passage, American military intervention in Lebanon, Nicaragua, and Grenada has raised the issue of the legitimacy and effectiveness of the act, and resulted in ad hoc compromises between Congress and the president neither foreseen by nor provided for in the act. Such compromises have led some critics to argue that the act as written probably would not have prevented the escalation of the Vietnam war—the very circumstance that prompted its adoption!

In June 1983, the Supreme Court raised further questions about the legitimacy of the War Powers Act, along with about two hundred other pieces of legislation, when one of its decisions seemed to indicate that the **legislative veto** may be unconstitutional. A legislative veto is a provision in a law that allows Congress to override or veto the actions of the executive. Such a provision is clearly a part of the War Powers Act. Thus it remains to be seen if this effort to reassert congressional power in this area will be effective.

---

tion against foreign invasion) to positive government (the implementation of welfare capitalism). Economic modernization produced a change in the role of the federal government vis-a-vis the states, which perhaps culminated in Franklin Roosevelt's New Deal. Since that time, the president rather than Congress is perceived by the American people as responsible for exercising the leadership role in resolving the nation's problems.

The rise of welfare capitalism as the dominant domestic ideology displacing the ideology of economic individualism has also promoted reliance on the national executive. Welfare capitalism insists that government has the prime responsibility for the efficient functioning of the economy. Although the precise role of the national government in the economy is often the source of bitter disputes between liberals and conservatives, the role of the president as an economic manager is widely accepted. Indeed, Jimmy Carter's inability to manage the economy effectively was one of the major factors that led to the election of Ronald Reagan in 1980. Despite his conservative convictions, President Reagan has endorsed welfare capitalism by pressing for governmental economic policies he believes will promote the efficient functioning of the economy.

Conclusion

The Constitution provides only very general language to guide policy making. The values held by the most active individuals and groups, the influence of competing interests, the goals of the major parties, and the existing policies in a given area are the principal factors that help to determine what types and kinds of policies emerge from the Congress. These factors also shape how the functions of Congress—representation, issue clarification, lawmaking, oversight, and legitimation—are carried out by its members.

With the growth of presidential power, especially in the twentieth century, the functions of Congress have undergone substantial alteration. The role of Congress as a lawmaking body has declined in significance as the president has become an important policy initiator, as the size of the federal bureaucracy has grown, and as the number of regulations issued by executive agencies has increased. Congress has reacted to these changed circumstances by paying greater attention to congressional oversight of the federal bureaucracy and to the legitimation of presidentially initiated policies.

During the 1970s, Congress also took several steps to reassert its authority. The War Powers Resolution of 1973 and the Congressional Budget and Impoundment Control Act of 1974 were among the most significant attempts by Congress to redress the power equation. The limits placed on the president's power to intervene militarily appear to have been effective. However, the budget legislation has not led to a congressional budget that is a viable alternative to the presidential budget. Despite the mixed results of the congressional reform efforts, the imbalance of power between Congress and the president so apparent in the 1960s and 1970s does seem to have been somewhat rectified.

 ## Glossary

Administrative oversight The effort by Congress to ensure that the bureaucracy is implementing legislation in accordance with congressional intentions.

Caucus A group of members of Congress based on some shared interest, belief, or characteristic.

Congressional Budget Impoundment Control Act Legislation enacted in 1974 to strengthen the role of Congress in the process of formulating the budget.

Congressional Budget Office An Office created by the Congressional Budget Act to provide Congress advice on the likely economic effects of its budget decisions and to forecast future revenues. Designed to be an independent counter-weight to the President's Office of Management and Budget (OMB).

Constituents The residents of a legislator's district.

Legislative veto Clause in legislation passed by Congress that allowed Congress to veto executive actions or required congressional consent to an administrative act before being carried out. Found unconstitutional in 1983 by the Supreme Court.

Majority/minority leader The chief spokesman and strategist of the majority and minority party in Congress respectively.

Majority/minority whip An assistant to the majority or minority party leader respectively, whose principal duty is to organize party members and induce them to vote.

Markups Committee or subcommittee sessions at which amendments to bills are offered and voted upon.

Pork barrel The securing of "pork" (federal projects, contracts, grants) from the national government's treasury "barrel", by the members of Congress for their home districts. This form of casework is often perceived as important for reelection.

Seniority rule A method of selecting committee chairs in Congress, used exclusively until the 1970s, whereby the longest-serving member of the committee of the majority party in Congress automatically became chair. It is still the most common, though not exclusive, method of selection.

War Powers Act Legislation enacted in 1973 intended to limit and define the conditions under which the president can send troops into combat situations abroad.

Suggestions for Further Reading

Asbell, Bernard. *The Senate Nobody Knows*. Garden City, N.Y.: Doubleday, 1978. A highly readable and fascinating journalist's account of the workings of the U.S. Senate.

Davidson, Roger, et al. *Congress and Its Members*. Washington, D.C.: Congressional Quarterly Press, 1985. Contemporary examination of the Congress, particularly the establishment of the Republican majority in the Senate.

Dodd, Lawrence C., and Bruce I. Oppenheimer, eds. *Congress Reconsidered*. 2 ed. Washington D.C.: Congressional Quarterly Press, 1981. Recent studies of Congress that provide good explanations and evaluations of the impact of congressional reforms.

Dodd, Lawrence C., and Richard L. Schott. *Congress and the Administrative State*. New York: Wiley, 1979. Excellent treatment of congressional interaction with the bureaucracy in the policy process.

Fenno, Richard, Jr. *Congressmen in Committees*. Boston: Little, Brown, 1973. This leading student of Congress examines the manner in which committees work.

Fenno, Richard, Jr. *Home Style: House Members in Their Districts*. Boston: Little, Brown, 1978. A close look at how 118 members of Congress interact with their constituents.

Keefe, William J., and Morris S. Ogul. *The American Legislative Process: Congress and the States*. 5th ed. Englewood Cliffs, N.J.: Prentice-Hall, 1981. Thorough examination of the legislative process at both the national and state levels of government.

Malbin, Michael J. *Unelected Representatives*. New York: Basic Books, 1980. Worthwhile reading on an important subject—the role and influence of congressional staff.

Mann, Thomas E., and Norman J. Ornstein, eds. *The New Congress*. Washington D.C.: American Enterprise Institute, 1981. Explores what has changed in Congress in recent years and what has stayed the same.

Matthews, Donald R. *U.S. Senators and Their World*. Greenwich, Conn.: Greenwood, 1980. First published in 1963, this work has become a classic study of the mores and unwritten rules that operate in our upper house.

Mayhew, David R. *Congress: The Electoral Connection*. New Haven, Conn.: Yale University Press, 1974. Presents a strong argument that the desire for reelection is the primary factor shaping the behavior of members of Congress.

Redman, Eric. *The Dance of Legislation*. New York: Simon and Schuster, 1973. An insider's description of the way Congress actually works.

Sunquist, James L. *The Decline and Resurgence of Congress*. Washington, D.C.: Brookings Institution, 1981. Traces the gradual decline of congressional power relative to the president and Congress's resurgence after 1973.

*I sit here all day trying to persuade people to do the things
they ought to have sense enough to do without my persuading them.
That's all the powers of the President amount to.*
Harry S Truman

Chapter 10

The Executive Branch:
The Presidency and the
Federal Bureaucracy

Chapter Outline

Introduction
Theories of Executive Power
Roles of the President
Controlling the Federal Bureaucracy
How Powerful The Presidency: A Comparative Analysis
Conclusion

Introduction

The Constitution strongly suggests that the Framers intended Congress to be the dominant branch of the national government. The legislative article, which creates Congress, is the first and longest article and contains the most impressive grant of powers. By contrast, the executive article, the second article, is brief and includes a mere handful of powers. Despite these constitutional provisions, today the president dominates the American government. This dominance rests on an expansive theory of executive power, on the numerous strategic roles the president plays, and on the president's demonstrated capacity to exercise leadership in resolving the nation's problems. Recent events have confirmed, however, that a strong presidency is a two-edged sword; the power to act can be used to advance the public interest or to undermine it.[1] Lyndon Johnson's presidency revealed this dualism in a dramatic way. The **Great Society** programs were accompanied (and to an extent undermined) by massive military involvement in Vietnam.

Theories of Executive Power

Contrasting theories of executive power were developed long before Congress had made any significant grants of power to the president, before the recurring economic and political crises of the twentieth century, and before the proliferation of social welfare programs. Yet it would be inaccurate to conclude that Theodore Roosevelt, who proposed the stewardship theory of the presidency, forged his ideas in the absence of a rich body of historical materials. Roosevelt looked back to earlier strong presidents such as Thomas Jefferson, Andrew Jackson, and Abraham Lincoln, and after reviewing their actions carefully, produced a theory of presidential power that justified the vigorous exercise of executive authority. (Table 10.1 classifies presidents according to attitudes toward politics and energy level.) This, he thought, would enable the national government to address the problems the nation faced at the beginning of the new century. Huge corporations dominated the economy in what he believed was an unhealthy concentration of economic power. The conservation of natural resources was a need that he was among the first to recognize. His views of the presidency also made him eager to project American power into world affairs. Central and South America, the Pacific Islands, and the Russo-Japanese War all furnished him with the opportunities he sought to establish the United States as a major military and political power.

Theodore Roosevelt's stewardship theory rests on a broad construction of the Constitution in its entirety. It is an expansion of the doctrine of inherent power. Inherent power is power vested in a government without a reliance on any specific grant of authority by the Constitution. Broadly speaking, the stewardship theory maintains that the president has not only the constitutional power but also the

Table 10.1
A Classification of Presidential Personality

ATTITUDES TOWARD POLITICS	ENERGY LEVEL	
	Active	Passive
Positive	Franklin D. Roosevelt Harry S. Truman John F. Kennedy Gerald R. Ford Jimmy Carter	William H. Taft Warren G. Harding Ronald Reagan
Negative	Woodrow Wilson Herbert Hoover Lyndon B. Johnson Richard Nixon	Calvin Coolidge Dwight D. Eisenhower

Source: James David Barber, *The Presidential Character: Predicting Performance in the White House*, 3d ed. (Englewood Cliffs, N.J.: Prentice-Hall, 1985).

Theodore Roosevelt (1858–1919):
The Crowded Life

Few other presidents have enjoyed being president, or indeed being alive, as much as Theodore Roosevelt. Besides being one of the foremost politicians of his age, Roosevelt was a Dakota badlands rancher, an award-winning historian, a cavalryman in the Spanish-American War, a South American explorer, an African big game hunter, and a world traveler. And despite his failing eyesight, Roosevelt was a prodigious reader, often finishing a book a day.

His reforming zeal as Governor of New York led the political bosses to try to shunt Roosevelt aside by having William McKinley name Roosevelt as his vice presidential candidate in 1900. When McKinley was assassinated in 1901, Mark Hannah exclaimed in disgust: "That damn cowboy is now President!" Roosevelt reinvigorated the executive office and was easily the most energetic and popular president since Abraham Lincoln.

As the first "Progressive" president, Roosevelt challenged big business and earned a reputation as a trust-buster. He led the fight for the Pure Food and Drug Act, for an end to railway rebates, for federal meat inspection, and for a more effective Interstate Commerce Commission. While he condemned the "muckrakers" on the one hand, he battled the "malefactors of great wealth" on the other.

Roosevelt was also the first president to be concerned with the conservation of the nation's natural resources. He established four major wildlife refuges, quadrupled the acreage of national forests, proclaimed eighteen national monuments (four of which later became national parks), and called the first national conference on conservation. At this conference in 1908, he held the nation's governors virtual prisoners for a week while he lectured them on the virtues of conservation.

In foreign affairs, Roosevelt also established several firsts. He sent the "Great White Fleet" around the world as a demonstration of America's power. He countenanced the revolt in Panama so he could get a treaty to build the Panama Canal. He announced the Roosevelt Corollary to the Monroe Doctrine, which made the United States a policeman for the Western Hemisphere. And he became the first American to win a Nobel Prize when he was awarded the Peace Prize for his intervention and mediation of the Russo-Japanese War. Roosevelt may have recommended that America should walk softly and carry a big stick, but he was not one to walk softly.

Roosevelt's dissapointment with his hand-picked successor, William Howard Taft, led to his reentry into politics in 1912. Denied the presidential nomination by Republican party leaders, Roosevelt ran as the candidate of the Progressive Party, more popularly known as the Bull Moose Party. He polled more votes than Taft, but because the Republican vote was split, Woodrow Wilson, the Democrat, won the election. Roosevelt's days of triumph were over. When he died in 1919, the nation mourned its loss, but Theodore Roosevelt had crowded several lifetimes into the sixty-one years he lived.

constitutional duty to do what is needed to protect the American people, unless such actions are specifically prohibited by the Constitution.

Ironically, Roosevelt's handpicked successor as president, William Howard Taft, who also served as Roosevelt's secretary of commerce, expounded a theory of the presidency diametrically opposed to Roosevelt's. Taft's contractual theory is based on a strict construction of the Constitution, restricting the president to the specific powers enumerated in

William Howard Taft (1857–1930) was a jurist, a legal educator, and twenty-seventh president of the United States.

Roles of the President

Head of State

The president is the ceremonial head of the United States government. He greets representatives of foreign powers, hosts state dinners, and bestows honors and medals on everyone from astronauts to sports figures. Most countries today separate the ceremonial role from the chief executive role. Great Britain is a prime example; the Queen is head of state, whereas the prime minister is the head of the British government. As head of state, the president functions as a symbolic representative of the American people. More important, the presidency is viewed as a nonpolitical, unifying symbol. When the White House announces that the president is making a "nonpolitical" appearance, they are seeking to capitalize on this aspect of the presidential office.

Andrew Jackson was the first president to fully exploit this role. Audaciously proclaiming himself the "voice of the people," he called attention to the

Article II, the executive article. Emphasizing the contractual and limiting nature of constitutions rather than their enabling functions, contractual theory insists on the primacy of the legislative branch. It views legislative power as democratic and popular and executive power as quasimonarchical and nondemocratic.

Theory aside, the question of who should exert leadership in a democracy has been undercut by the recurring political and economic crises of the twentieth century and by the proliferation of social welfare programs. Both have contributed significantly to the growth of executive leadership.[2] Certainly, every president since Franklin Roosevelt has sought to exert leadership, and no president has willingly accepted the view that Congress should lead. Although it has occasionally resisted executive encroachment, Congress has also signaled its acceptance of presidential leadership through its grants of power to the president.

POWER AND POMP: HEAD OF GOVERNMENT AND HEAD OF STATE

The president of the United States has a bewildering variety of responsibilities. Much of his time is taken up by the not unpleasant task of welcoming other (often powerless) heads of state and attending a myriad of social functions. Could he use his time more productively? In Britain, for example, the Queen is the head of state, whereas the prime minister serves as the head of the British government. Since the Queen "reigns but does not rule," she has ample time for social activities. The United States has no equivalent of a royal family. *Punch* magazine, a British publication, has strongly urged us to adopt one and has kindly offered to send several members of their royal family to us. Most presidents, however, have preferred to use their vice presidents and even their wives to meet foreign dignitaries and to attend weddings or funerals. In effect, then, Vice President George Bush became a quasi-head of state when he represented President Reagan in Moscow at the funerals of the two previous Soviet leaders.

fact that the president is elected by all the people, whereas legislators have at best a statewide constituency. In this way, Jackson turned the presidency into a popularly elected office by appealing to ordinary citizens.[3] Historians call this period in American history "the Jacksonian Era," a tribute to Old Hickory's success. Ronald Reagan has also enjoyed great success in this role. His skills as the Great Communicator have become legendary and have helped greatly in his role as a policy initiator as well.

Party Leader

The president is head of his party and head of the party organization.[4] As such, he functions as the chief politician. A popular president can campaign very effectively for a party candidate. Because the president commands the attention of the media in ways that congressional party leaders, Democratic or Republican, cannot, he is the party's most effec-

Andrew Jackson

tive voice. He can as party leader also reward the faithful by dispensing patronage. A newly elected president can appoint friends, campaign workers, and other loyal party members to the several thousand offices that electoral victory brings. Although the federal civil service now limits presidential patronage, Andrew Jackson earned undying notoriety by his wholesale introduction of the spoils system when he became president in 1829.

Thomas Jefferson, however, was the first president to exploit the role of party leader. By working closely with congressional leaders of his own party, Jefferson cemented Democratic-Republican party (now known as The Democratic party) control of the national government. Jefferson's long experience as a legislator made him keenly aware that his effectiveness as party leader would strengthen him in his relationship with Congress. Thus the president's role as party leader assists him in overcoming in a limited way the separation of powers built into the American form of government.

Policy Initiator

Not until the twentieth century did the president become the most significant policy initiator. The process began in 1922 when Congress granted the president the authority to formulate the federal budget. Since that time, the president has dominated the policy-making process. His power to deliver messages to Congress, especially the State of the Union Address, the Budget Message, the Economic Report, and the Environmental Quality Report, gives the president ample opportunity to lay his legislative program before Congress and the American people. In addition to these regularly scheduled major messages, the president can also send special messages to Congress at any time, and can even call a Congress that has adjourned back into special session.

Once his legislative proposals are before the Congress, the president can send any number of executive officials to argue for his programs before congressional committees. If testimony from cabinet secretaries or other high-ranking executive officers is not sufficiently persuasive, the president can personally communicate with legislators by inviting them to the White House or by telephoning them. Presidents Johnson and Reagan used both methods to take advantage of their considerable

Table 10.2
Selected Policy Responsibilities of the President

Types of Functional Leadership	Foreign Policy	Economics	Domestic Policy
Crisis management	Iranian crisis Grenada Terrorism	FDR and the Depression	Enforcing court orders on school desegregation
Symbolic and morale-building leadership	Nixon trip to China	Being bullish on American productivity	Visiting flood and disaster victims
Recruitment of top officials	Selecting chair of the Joint Chiefs of Staff	Choosing the wisest economic advisers	Appointing a Chief Justice
Priority-setting and problem clarification	Defining our relations with the U.S.S.R.	Outlining a tax cut program	Setting priorities in environmental protection
Legislative and political coalition building	Carter's efforts to pass the Panama Canal treaties	Winning approval for a tax cut program	Carter's efforts to pass civil service reform
Program implementation and administration	Making Middle East peace accords work	Shoring up the Social Security program	Seeing that the laws are faithfully executed
Oversight of government performance and early warning detection of possible problems	Evaluating our relations with Japan	Monitoring internal revenue performance	Appraising the impact of federal welfare programs

Source: Thomas E. Cronin, *The State of the Presidency*, 2d ed. (Boston: Little, Brown, 1980), p. 155.

skills as persuaders. (Table 10.2 outlines the policy responsibilities of the president.)

If Congress resists the president's proposals and passes legislation at odds with his policies, he has a powerful weapon in the veto. In the entire history of this country, fewer than one hundred laws have commanded enough votes to override the presidential veto. Often the mere threat of a presidential veto is sufficient to cause potential legislation to be shelved or to be altered in such a way that it becomes acceptable to the president. When the president vetoes a bill, he can return it to Congress with his reasons for the rejection. Andrew Jackson was the first president to choose this course of action. His message vetoing a renewal of the charter for the Second Bank of the United States not only detailed his reasons for the veto but also included a brilliant exposition of Jacksonian political philosophy.

Within the executive branch, the president also has "legislative" power through the issuance of executive orders. Following World War II, Harry Truman desegregated the armed services by executive order when Congress failed to do so. Richard Nixon authorized federal employees to organize and bar-

gain collectively by executive order. The heads of executive agencies and certain independent offices can also issue rules and regulations. Federal rules and regulations now greatly outnumber federal statutes, underscoring the power of unelected bureaucrats.

Chief Executive: The President as Head of the Federal Bureaucracy

In addition to being the ceremonial head of state, the president is also the head of the executive branch (Figure 10.1). As chief executive, the president assumes ultimate responsibility for a federal **bureaucracy** numbering nearly three million employees, 85 percent of whom work outside Washington. This is the president's weakest role when his constitutional responsibilities are measured against his constitutional authority to carry out this duty.[5] Article II charges the president with ensuring that the laws are faithfully executed, yet gives him only the power to appoint officials to see that this responsibility is discharged. By contrast, the chief executives of large corporations and even the presidents of major universities are given a far more impressive set of powers. Even middle-level managers would consider themselves seriously handicapped if their only operational authority were to hire subordinates. This authority is further circumscribed in the president's case by the need to seek the consent of a separately constituted body for many appointments.

The president's effectiveness as chief executive stems primarily from his statutory control over the formulation of the federal budget.[6] Since virtually all federal programs require the expenditure of money, the president has a powerful instrument with which to influence reluctant bureaucrats to comply with his policies. The **Office of Management and Budget (OMB)**, through its analyses and evaluation of government programs, gives the president some control over the federal bureaucracy.

The OMB performs two essential functions. It is responsible for preparing the administration's proposed budget, and it serves as a clearinghouse for any budgetary request a federal agency makes of

Figure 10.1
The Roles of the American President

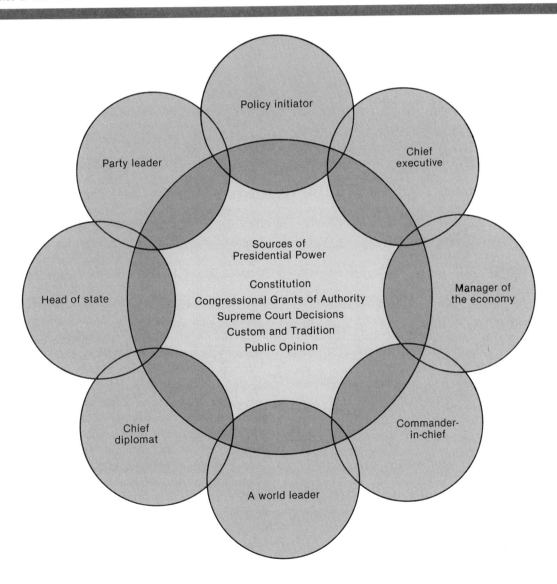

Policy initiator

Party leader

Chief executive

Head of state

Manager of the economy

Sources of
Presidential Power

Constitution
Congressional Grants of Authority
Supreme Court Decisions
Custom and Tradition
Public Opinion

Chief diplomat

Commander-in-chief

A world leader

DONALD REGAN (b. 1918):
FROM TREASURY TO CHIEF OF STAFF

Shortly after Ronald Reagan's re-election in 1984, Secretary of the Treasury Donald Regan and Chief of Staff James Baker agreed to do something very unusual—they traded jobs. It is not publicly known why the swap was so acceptable to both men, but Regan's move to Reagan's inner circle made sense in terms of his personality, ambitions, and relationship with the president. Regan has a reputation for relishing the possession and perquisites of power, and his desire to move from the cabinet to the head of the president's staff reflects a good understanding of where real power resides in the executive branch. Moreover, his influence and prominence has continued to expand since the move, whereas James Baker has slipped deep into the background.

Regan had no previous experience in government before joining the Reagan administration as treasury secretary in 1981. He had developed his skills in political and bureaucratic infighting in the corporate world, rising to the post of chairman and chief executive officer of Wall Street's Merrill Lynch and Co. As secretary of the treasury, his chief job, and ac-

complishment, was the promotion of Reagan's massive tax cut measure. Though he was a late convert to supply-side thinking, Regan became the administration's key economic spokesperson and defender of the tax cut as a step toward eliminating the budget deficit by 1984.

Regan has a reputation as a tough and determined negotiator who is not bashful about displaying his temper on occasion. As secretary of the treasury, he adopted tax policy as his personal "turf" and locked horns with anyone who presumed to trespass in that area, most notably David

Stockman of OMB. He has generally succeeded in securing his way, however. The skills he learned in the corporate wars and serving him well in government. Though enjoying considerable success in government service, he has found the hours long and the work hard for the money. He admitted that such circumstances "really shocks a guy coming from Wall Street."

Though not a personal friend of Reagan's before joining the administration, Regan has reportedly grown quite close to the president over the last few years. This relationship may reflect a genuine confluence of personalities and the trust that develops with consistently sound advice, but David Stockman has raised questions about that. He accuses Regan of building this relationship to enhance his own power, and doing it by playing the yes man to Reagan, telling the president only what he wants to hear. Regardless of the truth of such allegations, Regan's influence is clearly growing, and in trading his position in the cabinet for chief of staff, his opportunity to exercise such influence is greatly expanded.

Congress. In formulating the annual budget proposal, the OMB plays a large role in determining what the rest of the government will be debating and doing in the year to come. As a clearinghouse for budgetary requests from the executive bureaucracy, the OMB is in a position to study the organization and operation of all federal agencies. In this role, it tries to find and reconcile conflicting budgetary claims made by different agencies and to assure that agency requests are within budgetary limits and consistent with the general goals of the administration. Whenever a legislative proposal is at odds with the president's overall program, the OMB simply recommends that the proposal not be funded.

All agency requests for congressional appropriations must receive clearance from the OMB. The OMB thus has a big and important job. The director of the OMB heads a staff of about six hundred and runs one of the most powerful agencies in the national government.

Although the OMB is the most significant, there are a number of critical agencies in the **Executive Office of the President (EOP)** that enable the president to function as an effective chief executive. The Council of Economic Advisers helps the president prepare the Economic Report, which spells out the president's economic policies. The National Security Council assists the president in integrating foreign, domestic, and military policy to protect the national interest. The Office of the United States Trade Representative advises the president on trade agreements and tariff policy. Finally, the Council for Environmental Quality aids the president in preparing the Environmental Quality Report, which details the president's stance on environmental issues. These offices are the most important; several other agencies in the EOP also assist the president in carrying out his responsibilities.

The **Cabinet departments** rank as the major organizations of the executive branch. These departments are the principal line agencies, that is, the agencies that actually administer most federal programs. All thirteen cabinet departments are headed by a secretary appointed by the president and reporting directly to him. Each secretary has the responsibility of ensuring that the department properly implements presidential policy. The United Nations ambassador, who holds cabinet rank, serves as the president's representative to that body. Political observers know that individual secretaries are always more effective in advising the president than is the cabinet as a whole. George Shultz, Reagan's secretary of state since 1982, for example, is one of the most influential secretaries since George Marshall, who served in Truman's administration in the late 1940s. Shultz, as Marshall before him, clearly carries more weight with the president than most other cabinet officers.

As Figure 10.2 shows, numerous independent offices and establishments stand outside the cabinet departments. Most of these do not have important policy responsibilities, and the public is often unaware of their existence. However, events can change public awareness. The accident at the Three Mile Island nuclear reactor in Pennsylvania brought the role of the Nuclear Regulatory Commission to the attention of many concerned citizens. The persistence of high interest rates has also focused attention on the role of the Federal Reserve System in regulating the nation's money supply.

Manager of the Economy

Since the Great Depression of the 1930s, the president has functioned as the manager of the economy. Congress officially recognized this role in the Employment Act of 1946, when it made the president responsible for developing economic policies that would foster full employment, healthy economic growth, and price stability. The Employment Act also requires the president to submit an Economic Report each year to Congress outlining his economic policies. Despite the importance of this report, it is the president's formulation of the budget that is crucial and, in the light of deficits approaching $240 billion per year, increasingly demanding.

The federal budget is much more than a plan of how the national government intends to raise and spend money. It is a key instrument of macroeconomic management. Government taxing and spending policies are the major weapons the

During the Great Depression, President Roosevelt did much to establish and expand the role of the president as manager of the economy.

**Figure 10.2
The Government of the United States**

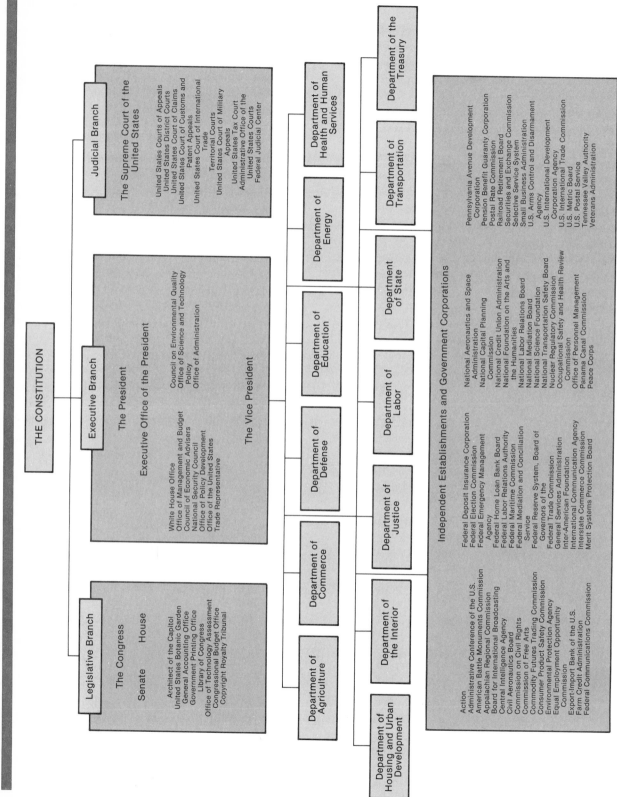

THE CONSTITUTION

Legislative Branch

The Congress

Senate   House

Architect of the Capitol
United States Botanic Garden
General Accounting Office
Government Printing Office
Library of Congress
Office of Technology Assessment
Congressional Budget Office
Copyright Royalty Tribunal

Executive Branch

The President

Executive Office of the President

White House Office
Office of Management and Budget
Council of Economic Advisers
National Security Council
Office of Policy Development
Office of the United States
Trade Representative

Council on Environmental Quality
Office of Science and Technology
Policy
Office of Administration

The Vice President

Judicial Branch

The Supreme Court of the
United States

United States Courts of Appeals
United States District Courts
United States Court of Claims
United States Court of Customs and
Patent Appeals
United States Court of International
Trade
Territorial Courts
United States Court of Military
Appeals
United States Tax Court
Administrative Office of the
United States Courts
Federal Judicial Center

Department of
Agriculture

Department of
Commerce

Department of
Defense

Department of
Education

Department of
Energy

Department of
Health and Human
Services

Department of
Housing and Urban
Development

Department of
the Interior

Department of
Justice

Department of
Labor

Department of
State

Department of
Transportation

Department of the
Treasury

Independent Establishments and Government Corporations

Action
Administrative Conference of the U.S.
American Battle Monuments Commission
Appalachian Regional Commission
Board for International Broadcasting
Central Intelligence Agency
Civil Aeronautics Board
Commission on Civil Rights
Commission of Free Arts
Commodity Futures Trading Commission
Consumer Product Safety Commission
Environmental Protection Agency
Equal Employment Opportunity
Commission
Export-Import Bank of the U.S.
Farm Credit Administration
Federal Communications Commission

Federal Deposit Insurance Corporation
Federal Election Commission
Federal Emergency Management
Agency
Federal Home Loan Bank Board
Federal Labor Relations Authority
Federal Maritime Commission
Federal Mediation and Conciliation
Service
Federal Reserve System, Board of
Governors of the
Federal Trade Commission
General Services Administration
Inter-American Foundation
International Communication Agency
Interstate Commerce Commission
Merit Systems Protection Board

National Aeronautics and Space
Administration
National Capital Planning
Commission
National Credit Union Administration
National Foundation on the Arts and
the Humanities
National Labor Relations Board
National Mediation Board
National Science Foundation
National Transportation Safety Board
Nuclear Regulatory Commission
Occupational Safety and Health Review
Commission
Office of Personnel Management
Panama Canal Commission
Peace Corps

Pennsylvania Avenue Development
Corporation
Pension Benefit Guaranty Corporation
Postal Rate Commission
Railroad Retirement Board
Securities and Exchange Commission
Selective Service System
Small Business Administration
U.S. Arms Control and Disarmament
Agency
U.S. International Development
Corporation Agency
U.S. International Trade Commission
U.S. Metric Board
U.S. Postal Service
Tennessee Valley Authority
Veterans Administration

(Paul Conrad. © 1982, Los Angeles Times. Reprinted with permission.)

Affixing blame for our economic problems

president has at his disposal to affect the overall performance of the economy. Tax policies outlined in the budget can have either an expansive or contractive effect on the economy. Government expenditures can either add to inflationary pressures or counter the effects of a recession. Taxing and spending policies can also be focused on different groups, resulting in quite different costs and benefits to those groups.

Keynesian economics essentially urges the government to manage the economy in a countercyclical fashion. If economic growth is too robust, government policy should restrain economic activity; if the economy is performing sluggishly, government policy should stimulate economic activity. Keynesian policies, adopted during the Depression, are an effort to manage the demand side of the economy. In recent years, Keynesian economic policies have been the subject of intense criticism by supply-side theorists. Supply-side advocates argue that the weak performance of the American economy during the 1970s and early 1980s can be traced directly to Keynesian (demand management) economic policies. The tax burden resulting from such policies has drastically diminished incentives to save, invest, and produce. Supply-side theorists in-

sist that tax cuts combined with reductions in government spending will release the resources the private sector needs for investment and production. The national government has been pursuing this approach, with some success, since 1981. (See Chapter 12 for a fuller discussion of economic theories and policies.)

Supply-side theory has been applied by the Reagan administration in an attempt to curb the rate of inflation and to bring down the rate of unemployment.[7] The catch-all term for this application is **Reaganomics**. By the middle 1980s, the rate of inflation had been cut to approximately 3.5 percent after reaching a terrifying 12 percent a decade earlier. Unemployment remained above 7 percent, but had declined from 11 percent, a figure that had not been approached for more than forty years. Since supply-side advocates maintain it takes from three to six years for supply-side policies to produce beneficial effects, Reagan's administration cannot be given all the credit for the decline in inflation nor held entirely responsible for the high level of unemployment. To the public, however, President Reagan is widely viewed as the individual most responsible for the economic policies that have restored the health of the American economy.

Chief Diplomat

In his role as chief diplomat, the president bears the responsibility for the conduct, successes, and failures of American foreign policy. To carry out his foreign affairs responsibilities, the Constitution gives the president the authority to make treaties and to recognize foreign governments (Table 10.3).

Table 10.3
Treaties and Executive Agreements From 1789 to 1979

Period	Treaties	Executive Agreements	Totals
1789–1839	60	27	87
1839–1889	215	238	453
1889–1939	524	917	1,441
1940–1973	364	6,395	6,759
1974–1979	102	2,233	2,335
	1,265	9,810	11,075

Source: Congressional Research Service, Library of Congress.

The Constitution gives the president broad authority to
conduct foreign policy. Ronald Reagan is pictured here with
Soviet leader Mikhail Gorbachev.

These constitutional grants of power have been
supplemented by executive agreements. Such
agreements are very similar to treaties except they
do not require senatorial ratification. As a consequence, the president has come to rely ever more
heavily on them.

The National Security Council, the United Nations ambassador, and, most important, the State
Department all assist the president when he acts as
the chief diplomat. As the most prestigious of the
cabinet officers, the secretary of state often exerts
considerable influence in the development of foreign policy. During the Truman administration, for
example, Secretary of State George C. Marshall
conceived a plan whereby American aid would help
restore the war-torn economies of Western Europe.
This effort became known as the Marshall Plan.
Henry Kissinger, secretary of state in both the Nixon and Ford administrations, played a key role in

opening relations with China and in negotiating an
agreement with the North Vietnamese to end the
war in Vietnam. Ultimately, however, it is the president who has the final say in determining this
nation's foreign policy. No other individual can
speak authoritatively for the United States in foreign affairs.[8] Even the Supreme Court has recognized the preeminence of the president in this
arena, and the justices have seldom restricted his
power.

Commander-in-Chief

The Constitution makes the president the commander-in-chief of the nation's armed forces. Only
the president can originate military alliances, declare martial law, authorize military governments
for conquered areas, end armed hostilities, and sign
an armistice. The wars in Korea and Vietnam re-

President Kennedy discusses blockade of Cuba with top
naval officers during Cuban crisis

vealed that presidents can commit the nation to prolonged military conflict without congressional declarations of a state of war. To prevent future presidents from intervening with military force without congressional approval, Congress passed the War Powers Resolution Act of 1973. Nevertheless, the fact that the nation allocates more than one-fourth of the federal budget to defense spending assures that the president will not be unduly handicapped in his role as commander-in-chief.

Nor does the president lack an organizational structure to aid him in this role. Both the National Security Council and the Defense Department provide invaluable assistance. A staff agency in the EOP, the National Security Council has the primary responsibility of advising the president on matters affecting national security. The Defense Department is headed by the secretary of defense, who ranks second in the cabinet in prestige and influence. However, the defense establishment's size dwarfs all other executive agencies. In addition to the more than two million people who serve in the armed forces, the Defense Department employs nearly 900,000 civilians. By comparison, the next largest department, Health and Human Services, employs approximately 155,000 people.

A World Leader

Since the emergence of the United States as a nuclear superpower, the president has assumed the role of world leader. Both developed and developing countries look to the American president to exercise this role, from helping developing countries in their quest for economic modernization, to acting as the principal negotiator in troubled regions such as the Middle East.

Despite the absence of either a constitutional or a statutory basis for this role, the first president to

A PRESIDENTIAL HIJACKING

In October 1985, President Reagan ordered American navy pilots to intercept an Egyptian commercial airliner and force it to land at an American air base in Sicily. He had his reasons. The plane's passengers included four terrorists who had commandeered an Italian cruise liner and had killed an American tourist. The president was demonstrating a power and resource few other national leaders possess or could afford to exert. Although the Egyptian government professed humiliation and the Palestine Liberation Organization leader Yassir Arafat pronounced the United States guilty of terrorism, President Reagan had the backing of nearly all Americans and most Western governments. As commander-in-chief, the president could employ force to back up his words that terrorists "can run, but they can't hide." The fact that many legal experts believed the president's actions were inconsistent with international law did not appear to reduce the effect of the American retaliation. Rather, it had the positive effect of warning terrorists that the United States could react swiftly and effectively.

claim a leadership role for the United States in international affairs was Theordore Roosevelt. He helped open Japan to the West, exerted an American presence in Latin America, and pressured the Russians and the Japanese to end their war. Ironically, three-quarters of a century later, American foreign policy concerns are still dominated by these regions of the world.

These various roles give the president a monopoly on the most important strategic positions in the American form of government. Constitutional provisions, statutory grants of authority, custom and practice, the acts of individual presidents, and Supreme Court decisions all underpin and reinforce the president's power.[9] The dispersion of power in Congress and the fact that Congress has delegated certain responsibilities to the president have produced a legitimating rather than a leadership role for Congress. In the absence of dramatic changes both at home and abroad, presidential leadership for the foreseeable future is assured.

Controlling the Federal Bureaucracy

Among the factors limiting the power of the president, none is more problematic than the bureaucracy. Other limitations on presidential power derive from the constitutional plan for checks and balances, originate from beyond our shores and are unavoidable, or, like the independent media and public opinion, are regarded as a vital part of the democratic process. There appears to be no justification, on the other hand, for the bureaucracy serving as a constraint on presidential power. It is not mentioned in the Constitution and was created to help the president carry out the constitutionally mandated responsibility to implement the laws. It is certainly a home-grown creation, but one that is commonly perceived as a threat to democracy rather than a legitimate part of the policy process.

The policy-making role of the bureaucracy allows it to function as a check on the president and draws the most serious concerns about its compatibility with democracy. In a democracy, policy alternatives are theoretically decided in elections, when voters choose between candidates who represent different approaches to policy problems. Those who are elected to public office make policy that reflects the voters' wishes. In our national government, the elected officials are Congress and the president. The function of the bureaucracy is to carry out the policy that is decided by these elected officials. The reality is that rather than being merely an instrument of implementation, the bureaucracy has become a significant source of public policy. Indeed, it is often referred to as the fourth branch of government, which follows its own goals rather than those of the elected Congress and president.

There are three key reasons why bureaucracy has been able to develop as a relatively independent, fourth branch of government. The first is that by leaving the language of the laws rather general and vague, Congress deliberately delegates the policy details to the bureaucracy. Congress has its reasons for legislative vagueness. Two reasons are purely political: It is easier to pass vague legislation, and it distances Congress from institutional responsibility for any unpopular consequences of policy when implemented. Consensus is far broader on general goals than on the specific means to achieve them. Often the means are controversial and involve damage to specific interests. Nearly everyone may support equal educational opportunity, for example, but many strongly oppose busing as a means to that goal. Nearly everyone may support safer products and safer working conditions, but various interests will necessarily be damaged by how the Consumer Product Safety Commission and the Occupational Health and Safety Administration go about achieving these ends. Much of the political heat can be deflected onto the bureaucracy by giving it responsibility for making the specific rules that are objectionable.

In many cases, the matter of legislation is so complex that Congress has neither the time nor expertise to write specifics. Congress knows the results it wishes to produce, spells them out in the legislation, and allows the experts in the bureau-

cratic agency to determine the details of how the legislated end will be brought about. For example, Congress may pass an environmental protection law but leave the technical details of determining what levels of pollution are dangerous and how to clean up the air and water to the agency. This is a useful and necessary process, for Congress cannot acquire expertise in all areas nor keep up with rapidly changing technical standards. By doing this, however, Congress transfers considerable policy power to the bureaucracy.

Another reason for bureaucratic independence in policy making is that bureaucratic officials serve a different constituency from elected officials, and as a result develop different interests and loyalties. Elected officials, especially the president, must deal with a broad range of interests. Much of their job includes finding ways to reconcile conflicting inter-

One of the president's primary roles is commander-in-chief.

ests. Career bureaucrats, on the other hand, deal with a very narrow range of interests, usually limited largely to their agency's clientele.[10] Much of their job involves finding ways to best serve these interests. It is not surprising that an agency and its clients should develop a shared perspective on matters of mutual concern. In most cases, they will have regular contacts with each other and few contacts with groups whose interests and viewpoints differ sharply. Moreover, bureaucrats serving in a particular agency are often drawn from the same institutional background as their clients. The career bureaucrats may be more loyal to the client than to the president.

The final reason the bureaucracy can become independent is that the president and the appointed heads of departments are amateurs and transients compared with career bureaucrats. Few presidents, even if former governors, are really familiar with the workings and complexities of the national bureaucracy. The lawyers and business people normally chosen to head major departments of the government are often even less well prepared. By contrast, career bureaucrats are professionals and, having worked in the bureaucracy for years, intimately know its possibilities and limitations, its ins and outs, and how to use them to best advantage.

Transiency compounds the effect of the relative inexperience of the president and department heads. Presidents will be around only four to eight years, and cabinet secretaries heading departments often for much shorter periods. The average stay in office of eighteen months for Nixon's cabinet officials was only a little shorter than for other presidents.[11] Career bureaucrats know that the political leadership is temporary. Their jobs, however, are permanent, and they have longer-term interests. That is another reason they tend to attach their loyalties to their clientele rather than to elected officials. The clientele will be around long after the people in power are gone.

In sum, the career bureaucrat will usually have greater expertise and experience than will elected officials and their appointees. They will also have long-established working relationships with their clientele and with other parts of the permanent bureaucracy. As a result, rather than controlling the bureaucracy, presidents and cabinet secretaries must often rely on these permanent career bureau-

crats for guidance in formulating and implementing policy.

The bureaucracy is a powerful and independent force in the policy process, but it is not unchecked. As we saw in Chapter 9, Congress has oversight powers and the ultimate power over the monetary appropriations without which the bureaucracy cannot function. The president also has important powers for managing the bureaucracy, especially his authority to prepare the national budget and the role of the OMB, discussed earlier. The president also has the power to reorganize the bureaucracy. This can be a formidable tool for dealing with a recalcitrant agency, for it threatens the comfortable network of supportive relationships, both inside the bureaucracy and with clientele, that the agency has developed. President Nixon, for example, used this power to replace the Bureau of the Budget with the OMB in 1970, significantly strengthening his control of the budget process.

It remains true, however, that no modern president can truly control the national bureaucracy, because of its size, its policy-making authority, and the ability of its agencies to become independent centers of power. It is important to remember that an action by the executive branch is not necessarily a presidential action, or even an action approved of by the president. The bureaucracy is only one constraint on the power of the American presidency, however. A comparison of the presidency, with other forms of leadership will highlight others.

How Powerful the Presidency: A Comparative Analysis

Presidential and Parliamentary Executives

Americans almost fondly regard the presidency as the most powerful office in the world. In certain respects, this is quite true. The president has access to a formidable military establishment that includes a nuclear arsenal. He also possesses the ability to meet with his counterparts anywhere in the world to persuade both adversaries and friends with rewards or sanctions. At the same time, because ours is a democracy, the president must govern within certain constitutional guidelines.

LIMITS ON PRESIDENTIAL POWER

The Constitution:

The Constitution embodies the doctrine of separation of powers. Congress and the federal courts are separate, independent, coequal branches that can check the authority of the president. The Constitution also provides for a fixed term of office and periodic elections that limit the president's tenure of office.

The Federal Bureaucracy:

Presidential policies must be administered by executive agencies that are often beyond the president's immediate control. Cabinet officers and other executive officials, if lukewarm about certain programs and policies, can undermine them.

State and Local Governments:

Fifty state governments and nearly ninety thousand local units of government can limit presidential power. Mayors of large cities can sometimes frustrate presidential programs for urban areas.

The Opposing Political Party:

In addition to resistance from factions within his own party, a president faces a competing party. This opposition can be particularly forbidding when his own party joins with the rival party to thwart parts of his program.

Interest Groups:

The most powerful interests can combine forces either to restrict presidential initiatives or to bring about alterations in policies unwanted by the president.

The Media:

Investigative journalism can exert a powerful influence on public opinion and thus on the presi-

dent's ability to act. Hostile commentators, editorial opinions, and political cartoons can also shape the climate of public opinion.

Opposing World Powers:

The Soviet Union and its allies are the most important obstacle to the president's role as a world leader. Nations in conflict, such as those in Central America and the Middle East, can also frustrate presidential policies.

International Organizations:

A number of international organizations, among them the United Nations, OPEC, and the European Common Market, can limit the president's prerogatives.

Economic Conditions:

Prevailing economic conditions can severely restrict the range of economic policies open to a president. The role of economic manager is perhaps the president's most important role, but it can also lead to his downfall, as the elections of 1932 and 1980 clearly demonstrated.

Public Opinion:

Public opinion, both at home and abroad, can thwart a president. Unrealistic expectations about a president's ability to resolve persistent problems can narrow the options available to a president.

Conscience and Convictions

In the short run, a president's conscience and personal convictions are the most effective constraint on his power. If a president decides to ignore constitutional or statutory limits to his authority, none of the preceding checks would be immediately effective.

The constraints of power in a democratic society are best understood by comparison with another democracy, Great Britain. Despite the fact that we inherited a number of legal and constitutional traditions from the British, our form of government is quite different from theirs. The prime minister, the

head of the British government, has powers that would startle an American president. For example, the prime minister (1) can dissolve Parliament and call for new elections, (2) can fix the date of the elections [12], (3) can serve an indefinite number of terms or years, (4) needs to secure the assent of only one house to pass laws, and (5) relies on party discipline to accomplish legislative goals.

An American president has none of these advantages, except on infrequent occasions when he has a reliable legislative majority in both houses of Congress. In the United States, such a majority is politically helpful, whereas in Britain it is a political necessity. Without a majority, the prime minister loses the right to govern. The president, who has a fixed term of office, will just move on to the next item in his legislative program.

Our form of government can be referred to as a *presidential* democracy. Most other Western democracies are *parliamentary* democracies. Some political scientists have suggested that we adopt a parliamentary form of government to avoid legislative impasses that can result when the presidency is controlled by one party and Congress by the other. In parliamentary governments, such as the British, both the executive and the legislative branches must be controlled by the same party for the following reasons: (1) A government can be formed only by a party (or sometimes by a **coalition** of parties) controlling a majority of seats in the Parliament. (2) If in any significant legislative matter the government loses a vote in Parliament, it also loses the right to govern, since it no longer commands a majority. (3) If the government loses its majority, either new elections must be called or a new party leader chosen who can form a government that does have majority support.

Neither of the last two situations necessarily precipitates new elections. In this respect, **parliamentary government** is both more efficient and less democratic than **presidential government**. The head of government in a parliamentary democracy is not elected separately from the legislature. Rather, as in Britain, the individual who becomes prime minister is one of several hundred legislators who also happens to be the majority party leader. Since the prime minister commands a legislative majority, the legislative process is more efficient because it does not rely on coalition building, as it does under presidential governments. As long as the prime minister and majority party leader retain a numerical majority of parliamentary seats, the government's legislative program is likely to be enacted.

The American president is not so fortunate. As head of the government, the president must frequently deal with a Congress where either one or both of the houses are controlled by the other party. If he lacks the legislative majority he needs to get his legislative program enacted, the president cannot call for new elections in an attempt to secure a majority. The dates for federal elections are constitutionally prescribed, and no legal procedure exists for altering those dates. Even during the Civil War, for example, President Lincoln had to ensure that congressional and presidential elections would be held as required in 1862 and 1864. The risk of such elections was substantial, since the result could have been a congressional majority critical of his conduct of the war or even his defeat as president.

Any American president, then, is stuck with a Congress for two years whether he likes it or not. This arrangement is an inherent part of the balance of powers established by the drafters of the Constitution. In the British scheme, no attempt has been made to separate the executive and legislative branches. Indeed, since British cabinet ministers are also members of the House of Commons, the executive branch can almost be said to function as a high-level committee of the legislature.

Every form of government has its advantages and its flaws. In the United States, a national election determines the individual who becomes the chief executive. In Britain, the choice is left to a party convention. American and British political parties also function in very different ways. British political parties are more disciplined than our own. It is unlikely and politically dangerous for a British parliamentarian to vote against the party leadership, whereas in the United States it is a common practice. The American policy-making process tends to institutionalize compromise and coalition building. The president and the opposition party do not expect to get everything each wants. Neither party can afford to be too committed to ideologically based legislative programs. By contrast, policy making in Britain tends to be more ideological because the party that controls Parliament can be assured of the enactment of its legislative program.

Presidential Democracy and Limitations on Tenure of Office

In 1951, the Twenty-second Amendment was ratified. This amendment limited a president's tenure

Table 10.4
Presidential Terms of Office

Country	Terms and Restrictions *
Costa Rica **	One 4-year term; ineligible for reelection
France	Indefinite number of 7-year terms
Venezuela	One 5-year term; ineligible for reelection
United States	Two 4-year terms or 10 years

* Eligibility for reelection refers to an immediately following or consecutive term. An individual can become president again after having been out of office for one full term.

** Costa Rica's limits are especially severe, since its Constitution even forbids members of an incumbent president's family from running for the office.

of office to two terms or ten years. Two factors contributed to its passage. First, Franklin Roosevelt was the first president to break the two-term tradition established by George Washington. This tradition had become so entrenched that it was almost an unwritten law. Second, the fact that Roosevelt was a Democrat encouraged Republicans to seek a limitation on the president's tenure of office, so no other Democrat could duplicate Roosevelt's feat.[13] The Twenty-second Amendment is far less controversial than it once was. But no easy answer has been found to the question whether such a limitation on the president's tenure of office is consistent with democratic politics. Simply put, why should the American electorate be forbidden to choose a popular president for as many terms as they wish?

As Table 10.4 indicates, other nations similarly restrict presidential terms. Although Costa Rica and Venezuela are more restrictive than the United States, the only other major presidential government among Western democracies, France, does not limit presidential tenure.[14] Costa Rica and Venezuela are among a minority of countries in Latin America that are democratic, although the number is growing. Because these countries are very sensitive to the authoritarianism that is part of their past and is still endemic in their region, stringent restrictions were placed upon the president's term of office.

The French, on the other hand, do not seem worried. They have given their president a lengthy seven-year term (perhaps as a token to their monarchical past) and have made whoever holds the office eligible for reelection. The French Constitution

has only been in effect since 1958, however, and it is possible that the French, who are wont to experiment with a variety of political regimes, may change again. After all, this is their sixteenth constitution since 1792!

Although the two-term limitation is not exactly a high point for the most ardent advocate of political democracy, the American people have come to accept it as a constitutional principle embedded in American history. Thomas Jefferson, James Madison, James Monroe, and Andrew Jackson all followed the precedent established by George Washington and retired after eight years. On average, only one of every three presidents is even elected to a second term. There have been lengthy periods during which no incumbent president served more than one term.[15] If he completes his second term in 1989, Ronald Reagan will be the first president since Dwight Eisenhower in 1961 to complete two full terms.

Every president knows he has only a limited time in office. Almost every president also wants to serve two terms. Because of this, a first-term president tends to be especially concerned with how the electorate views his performance. On the other hand, if a president is reelected, he immediately becomes a lame duck. How much of a handicap this is on presidential effectiveness is debatable. Second-term presidents tend to be mindful of their place in history and are perhaps prone to undertake activities that will enhance that place. President Reagan, for example, began his first term by referring to the Soviet Union as an "evil empire." His views have probably not changed, but he has softened his rhetoric in his second term. Moreover, by the end of his fifth year as president, Reagan joined the Soviet leader Mikhail Gorbachev at a summit meeting in Geneva to discuss arms control, bilateral relations, human rights, and regional conflicts. Despite conservative fears, Reagan has aligned himself with other presidents who wanted to be remembered as doing everything possible to pursue peace.

The Vice President

Of the forty men who have served as president, nine did not complete their terms: eight, including four who were assassinated, died in office, and one resigned. Particularly since John Kennedy's assassination in 1963, we have become painfully aware of the mortality of presidents and the consequent need to choose vice presidential candidates carefully and selectively. We have also had to provide for replacing vice presidents. Before 1967, no constitutional provision existed for filling a vacancy in the vice presidency. President Harry Truman from 1945 to 1949 and President Lyndon Johnson from 1963 to 1965, for example, governed without vice presidents.

For most of American history, the nation's leaders have had little concern with the office of vice president. The first vice president, John Adams, declared that the office was certainly among the most insignificant ever devised by the mind of man. One hundred and fifty years later, one of his successors, John ("Cactus Jack") Nance Garner, graphically observed that the office was not "worth a pitcher of warm spit." [16] When we consider that the only constitutionally prescribed duty for the vice president is to preside over the Senate's proceedings as its president,[17] there does seem to be ample justifica-

LOWI'S "LAW OF SUCCESSION"

Theodore Lowi, a noted political scientist, has developed the interesting if disconcerting theory that "each president contributes to the upgrading of his predecessors" by being inferior to them. This theory raises an intriguing question: Do factors other than qualifications for the office enter into our choice for president? The answer appears to be an unqualified "yes". But what should be the characteristics we look for in a president? Are there factors in a person's background that suggest he or she would be a good president? For example, is Ronald Reagan a better or worse president because he attended Eureka College rather than Harvard University where John Kennedy earned his degree? We have no licensing for politicians as we have for engineers, scientists, physicians, and teachers. It has been said that because they have a choice, Americans get the government they deserve. Given the difficulty of defining and ascertaining the elusive quality of leadership, perhaps they haven't done too badly.

tion for the sentiments expressed by Adams and Garner.

Only when the president dies, resigns, or cannot discharge his duties does the office of vice president become important.[18] Under normal circumstances, the vice president has only those duties that the president assigns. Although many presidents have simply ignored their vice presidents, since Eisenhower's presidency (1953–1961), they have made extensive use of them. One indication of the greater importance of the office is that vice presidents now regularly participate in cabinet meetings.

Thus despite the rather inauspicious beginnings of the vice presidency, the office has become a vital part of the executive branch. At least three factors account for this development. First hard experience has taught us that the president is tragically vulnerable. The assassination of John Kennedy and the attempted assassinations of Gerald Ford and Ronald Reagan demonstrate this vividly. Second, the presidency has become such a burdensome job that logic dictates some sharing of responsibilities (and powers) with the second-ranking executive officer. Third, because of the first two factors, vice presidential candidates are increasingly selected for their qualifications to be president should the need arise.[19]

Jimmy Carter and Ronald Reagan, recent presidents who were Washington outsiders, have used their vice presidents in productive ways. Since President Carter lacked Washington experience (and like Reagan took some pride in this fact), he called on Vice President Walter Mondale's congressional background and expertise. President Reagan has relied on George Bush's knowledge of foreign affairs, gained through serving as head of the Central Intelligence Agency (CIA) and as ambassador to China.

Even with these positive developments, the importance of the vice president rests on insecure grounds. In the final analysis, the president, not the Constitution or federal law, determines the duties and responsibilities of the vice president. The president does not expect his vice president to disagree with him in public, and he may not give the vice president the opportunity to do so in private.

Always in the shadow of the president and always in public agreement with the president's policies, the vice president must cease being his or her own person for four or eight years. At best, the vice

Vice President George Bush

American history, the vice president has rarely been universally accepted as the heir apparent, even within his own party.

As we are aware, the vice president is only a heartbeat away from the presidency. This knowledge and the fact that seven of the first thirty-six presidents died in office finally prompted the adoption of the Twenty-fifth Amendment, clarifying the position of the vice presidency and its relationship with the presidency. In effect, the amendment upgraded and updated the vice presidential office. Ratified in 1967 and applied in 1973 and 1974, it has already demonstrated its worth. In brief, the Twenty-fifth Amendment provides for (1) the succession of the vice president to the presidency whenever a presidential death or resignation occurs (Section 1); (2) a replacement whenever the vice presidential office becomes vacant (Section 2); and (3) the vice president to become **acting president** in case the president cannot discharge the duties of his office (Section 3).

So far, so good. But Section 4 is the most controversial part of this amendment. Its intent is to resolve any discrepancy between a president who believes he is capable of fulfilling the duties of his office versus a vice president who believes the president is unable to do so. Such a conflict has not yet occurred. Hopefully, it never will. As a safeguard, the cabinet secretaries, the president pro tempore of the Senate, the speaker of the House of Representatives, and, if necessary, the entire Congress can be constitutionally involved in deciding the issue of alleged presidential disability.

Clearly, the vice president is now much more than simply a person who adds geographical or ideological balance to the party ticket. The vice president is at all times a potential president and should be viewed as such by the American people. A president has a right to expect the vice president to be loyal and to support and defend presidential policies. At any moment, however, the vice president must be prepared to assume the nation's most important and most powerful political office.

president can be a colleague of the president, but never an equal.[20] If the vice president succeeds in gaining the presidential nomination, he or she must then run on the president's record and in defense of that record. As several vice presidents and would-be presidents can testify, this is far from an enviable task.

Despite the uncertain character of the office, the vice presidency has become a much sought-after position. Many vice presidential candidates harbor presidential ambitions of their own. From the perspective of the vice presidential candidate, the most important factor is that such a candidacy can become a springboard for the presidential nomination. Former vice presidents Richard Nixon, Hubert Humphrey, and Walter Mondale all sought the presidency after winning their party's nomination. George Bush is expected to seek the Republican presidential nomination in 1988. However, Bush is not expected to have an easy time of it. Throughout

Conclusion

The twentieth century has witnessed a dramatic growth in the power of the presidency, to the point where the president now dominates the national government. Congressional grants of authority to the president, recurrent political and economic crises, the growth of social welfare programs, and the dawning of the nuclear age have been the principal factors that have spurred the development of executive power. These factors, combined with a theory of executive power that legitimates a strong presidency, have placed the necessary conditions for presidential leadership on a firm foundation. As a consequence, twentieth-century presidents have come to the executive office well versed in Roosevelt's stewardship theory and with the firm expectation that the nation expects forceful leadership from them.

A variety of roles that overlap and reinforce one another have also contributed to the president's capacity for leadership. Although certain of these roles arise from constitutional provisions (such as chief executive, chief diplomat, and commander-in-chief), two major roles (policy initiator and manager of the economy) result from congressional grants of powers. In many respects, these two roles are the key to presidential dominance of the policy-making process. As policy initiator, the president is able to lay before Congress his version of what is necessary to resolve the nation's problems. As manager of the economy, the president influences the allocations of the nation's resources. The remaining roles (head of state, party leader, and world leader) add still other dimensions to the office of the presidency. Such a combination of roles enables a determined president to overshadow the Congress and the federal courts.

A number of factors limit the powers of the president. Not least among them is the federal bureaucracy that the president heads. Because of its size, congressional grants of authority to its agencies, the support of private outside clientele groups, and its expertise in comparison to elected political officials, the bureaucracy has become a major element in the policy-making process. It has in many ways become a fourth branch of government, not fully under the control of either the Congress or the president.

Predictably, the strong contemporary presidency has proved to be a mixed blessing. The capacity to act can be productive of both good and evil. In a democracy, the key issue is how to foster creative presidential leadership without damage to our form of government and without infringing on the rights of the people. Such leadership must be able to attain, by democratic processes, outcomes that both benefit the people and are consistent with democratic principles. For the president, the challenge is to translate these laudable goals into concrete public policies in a world where the issues are exceedingly complex.

 ## Glossary

Acting president   A position the vice president assumes whenever the president cannot satisfactorily discharge his duties. The conditions and procedures concerning presidential disability are outlined in the Twenty-fifth Amendment to the Constitution.

Bureaucracy   A hierarchically structured organization composed of many subdivisions with specialized functions.

Cabinet departments   The principal line agencies that administer most federal programs. For example, the Department of Health and Human Services is responsible for the delivery of most social welfare programs.

Coalition   A group of two or more political parties that together control a majority of legislative seats.

Necessary to form a government in those countries with multiparty systems such as Italy and Israel.

Executive Office of the President (EOP)   The principal staff agencies that advise the president and help him to function as chief executive, for example, the National Security Council, which advises the president on foreign policy.

Great Society   President Lyndon B. Johnson's name for the social welfare programs he sought to enact that would expand and update Franklin Roosevelt's New Deal.

Office of Management and Budget (OMB)   The agency primarily responsible for the formulation and administration of the federal budget. This office enables the president to implement his fiscal goals for managing the economy and to exert control over the federal bureaucracy.

Parliamentary government   A form of government in which the majority party in the national legislature furnishes the officers of the executive departments.

Presidential government   A form of government in which the electorate, either directly or indirectly, chooses the government's chief executive.

Reaganomics   A series of economic measures undertaken since 1981 to reduce the national government's role in the economy, to lower taxes, and to hold down government expenditures.

 ## Suggestions for Further Reading

Altshuler, Alan A., and Norman C. Thomas, eds. *The Politics of the Federal Bureaucracy*. Harper & Row, 1976. A good basic overview of the federal bureaucracy and its political role.

Burns, James MacGregor. *The Power to Lead: The Crisis of the American Presidency.* New York: Simon and Schuster, 1984. Argues that the separation of powers embedded in the Constitution fragments power too much and impairs coherent policy making.

Corwin, Edward S. *The President: Office and Powers.* 4th ed. New York: Oxford University Press, 1957. A classic study that traces the constitutional, historical, and legal development of the presidency.

Cronin, Thomas E. *The State of the Presidency.* 2d ed. (Boston: Little Brown, 1980). Authored by one of the foremost scholars of the presidency, this work is both readable and revealing as to how the presidency works.

Funderburk, Charles. *Presidents and Politics: The Limits of Power.* Monterey, Calif.: Brooks Cole, 1982. Particularly valuable for showing how cabinet secretaries can thwart the presidential will.

Hamilton, Alexander, John Jay, and James Madison. *The Federalist Papers.* Edited by C. Rossiter. New York: New American Library, 1961. In No. 70, Alexander Hamilton advocates an active and vigorous presidency. A vital source for understanding the intentions of the Founding Fathers.

Hargrove, Edwin C., and Michael Nelson. *Presidents, Politics, and Policy.* New York: Knopf, 1984. Careful study of how presidents achieve their goals through mastery of the policy process.

Lowi, Theodore J. *The Personal President: Power Invested, Promise Unfulfilled.* Ithaca, N.Y.: Cornell University Press, 1985. A provocative investigation of the disillusionment many feel toward the modern presidency and a suggestive analysis of how this situation came about.

Reeves, Richard. *The Reagan Detour.* New York: Simon and Shuster, 1985. A brief but intriguing examination of how Reagan administration policies have affected both the social welfare programs and the foreign policies of this nation.

Rosen, Bernard. *Holding Government Bureaucracies Accountable.* New York: Praeger, 1982. A good, brief review of the techniques to control government bureaucracies and the problems associated with them.

Rossiter, Clinton. *The American Presidency.* New York: Harcourt, 1960. One of the classic studies of the presidential office.

Rourke, Francis E. *Bureaucracy, Politics, and Public Policy.* 4th ed. Boston: Little, Brown, 1986. An excellent and thorough explanation of the role of bureaucracy in public policy.

Schlesinger, Arthur. *The Imperial Presidency.* Boston: Houghton Mifflin, 1973. A scathing indictment of the misuse of presidential authority and how that misuse undermines American democracy.

*It is emphatically the province and duty of the judicial department
to say what the law is.*
Chief Justice John Marshall

*The sword of the law should never fall but on those whose guilt is so apparent as to
be pronounced by their friends as well as foes.*
Thomas Jefferson

Chapter 11

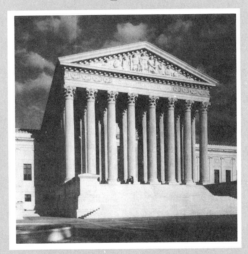

The Judicial Branch:
The Intersection of
Law and Politics

217

Introduction

In our form of government, the judiciary, particularly the federal judiciary, enjoys a unique position. The distinctive quality of American courts was pointed out as early as the 1830s by Alexis de Tocqueville, author of the classic study *Democracy in America,* when he declared, "Scarcely any political question arises in the United States that is not resolved, sooner or later, into a judicial question." [1]

Tocqueville recognized the intersection of law and politics that has characterized the judiciary almost from the nation's founding. Indeed, throughout the course of American history, few if any major issues of public policy have escaped scrutiny by the courts. Although court involvement in public policy issues has on occasion generated fierce opposition, that opposition has never been able to dislodge the judiciary from the policy-making arena.

The Development of Judicial Power

In the next two sections we explore how the Supreme Court became the authoritative interpreter of the Constitution and how the Court has used its authority to make policy. As our analysis reveals, these exercises of judicial power were not specifically provided for in the Constitution. Rather, the Court forged for itself a role that, although often challenged as unwarranted by the Constitution, has never been successfully countered by the president, Congress, or the states.

Judicial Review

Judicial power in the United States does not rest wholly on explicit constitutional grants of power. Article III establishes the judiciary as a separate branch of government, but that article does not ordain the federal judiciary as the guardian of the Constitution. Rather it was the Supreme Court, under the leadership of Chief Justice John Marshall (1801–1835), that claimed for the courts the power of **judicial review.** Judicial review is the power of the courts, especially the Supreme Court, to determine the constitutionality of the acts of the Congress, the president, and state officials. **Constitutional interpretation** and **statutory interpreta-**

tion, which seldom reach constitutional issues, also ensure that the courts are an integral part of the policy-making process. (Table 11.1 gives an overview of Supreme Court decisions declaring federal laws unconstitutional.)

The Founding Fathers clearly had not intended such a role for the courts.[2] Neither Article III, the judicial article, nor Article VI, the **national supremacy** article, grant either federal or state courts the power of judicial review. Rather, as we noted in Chapter 4, John Marshall claimed this power for the courts in the famous case of *Marbury v. Madison* (1803). A lesser judge than Marshall would have been unable to establish so substantial a power in a case that appeared to favor his political rivals. This decision was only the first of Marshall's great decisions in a judicial career that spanned more than three decades.

In the Marbury case, a conflict over judicial appointments between the Federalist party and the Democratic-Republicans gave the newly appointed chief justice the opportunity to lecture the Democratic-Republicans, particularly President Jefferson, on their duties and to lay the groundwork for judicial review. Although the logic of the Marbury decision is deceptively simple, it has never been successfully refuted.

Marshall pointed to Article VI to support his argument that the Constitution is the supreme law of the land. Using deductive logic, he maintained that acts contrary to the Constitution must be void or the notion of supreme law has no meaning. Finally, Marshall cited the language of Article III and Hamilton's argument in *Federalist* No. 78 to support his contention that it was the peculiar function of the judiciary to say what the law was. The chief justice's triumph in this case overshadowed the fact, which was not immediately recognized, that he had established the judiciary as the guardian of the Constitution.

Since Marshall's tenure as chief justice, the Supreme Court has exercised the power of judicial review in three distinct arenas. First, federal judicial review gives the courts an opportunity to determine the contours of federalism. Not surprisingly, the Court's decisions have frequently strengthened the national government in its relationships with the states. *McCulloch v. Maryland* (1819), Marshall's most constitutionally significant decision, established this trend very early in the nation's history. Mar-

Table 11.1
Declarations of Unconstitutionality of Federal Laws by the Supreme Court

Time Span	Chief Justice	Number of Declarations of Unconstitutionality *	Commentary
1798–1801	Jay	0	Weak, placid Court
	Rutledge	0	
	Ellsworth	0	
1801–1835	Marshall	1	*Marbury v. Madison* (1803)
1836–1864	Taney	1	*Dred Scott v. Sandford* (1857)
1864–1873	Chase	10	*Legal Tender Cases* (1870)
1874–1888	Waite	9	*Civil Rights Cases* (1883) **
1888–1910	Fuller	14 (15)	*Income Tax Cases* (1895)
1910–1921	White	12	*Child Labor Cases* (1918)
1921–1930	Taft	12	*Minimum Wage Case* (1923)
1930–1936	Hughes	14	Thirteen came in 1934–1936!
1936–1941	Hughes	0	The New Deal Court emerges after the "switch-in-time that saved nine" in 1937.
1941–1946	Stone	2	New libertarian emphasis
1946–1953	Vinson	1	Abstemious court
1953–1969	Warren	25	High watermark of civil libertarianism
1969–1985	Burger	29	Chiefly First and Fifth Amendment concerns
		130 (131)	

* Statute declared unconstitutional in whole or in part.

** Consolidated five different cases in one opinion (here counted as one).

Source: Henry J. Abraham, *The Judicial Process*, 5th ed. (New York: Oxford University Press, 1986), p. 294.

shall's opinion held that state laws in conflict with federal statutes must give way. In this decision, the chief justice established both the doctrine of national supremacy and that of **implied power.**

Federal judicial review can also include conflicts between the states or conflicts between citizens of different states. Despite the importance of such conflicts, little significant constitutional law has been developed to resolve them.

Determining the contours of the separation of powers constitutes the second arena of judicial review. On numerous occasions and often in difficult cases, the Supreme Court has had to define the boundaries of legislative, executive, and judicial power. The justices faced this issue in *United States v. Nixon* (1974), when President Nixon insisted that he, rather than the courts, would decide the limits of executive privilege. The Supreme Court unanimously rejected the president's position and held that the courts are the ultimate interpreters of the Constitution. As a direct consequence of this opin-

ion, the president was forced to release his tape recordings. Three weeks later, Richard Nixon resigned from office.

In 1986, the justices were called on to decide whether Gramm-Rudman, the deficit reduction act, was constitutional. Representative Mike Synar (D-Okla.) challenged the act on the grounds that it violated the separation of powers by giving the General Accounting Office (GAO) executive authority. Under Gramm-Rudman, if Congress fails to meet strict deficit targets, the GAO is empowered to cut federal expenditures across the board. The central question in the case was whether the GAO, widely perceived as a creature of Congress, can wield executive, budget-cutting authority.

The Supreme Court's response was negative. Congress, the Court held, could not constitutionally delegate executive authority to a legislative agency. This decision was somewhat ironic because the Court accepted the argument brought by a sitting member of Congress that Gramm-Rudman violated

JOHN MARSHALL (1755–1835)

Widely regarded as the greatest chief justice, John Marshall literally created that office while establishing the Supreme Court as a power to be reckoned with. His accomplishment is all the more remarkable considering that before his tenure on the High Court, he had served in a number of governmental offices without really distinguishing himself. Even his appointment as chief justice did not suggest that he would revolutionize the Court. John Adams appointed Marshall in the waning days of his administration to ensure a Federalist majority on the Court. Marshall accepted the appointment to have the time and the money to write a biography of George Washington.

From this rather inauspicious beginning, Marshall led the Court from one triumph to another. He established the doctrine of judicial review in *Marbury v. Madison* (1803) and of national supremacy and implied power in *McCulloch v. Maryland* (1819). In *Dartmouth*

v. Woodward (1819), he held state legislatures bound by the contract clause, and in *Gibbons v. Ogden* (1824), Marshall struck down state regulation of interstate commerce. With these decisions and many others, Marshall established the federal judiciary as a coequal branch of government and laid down the legal foundation for national power vis-à-vis the states.

Marshall's opinions, though deceptively simple, are rhetorical and logical masterpieces that have never been successfully refuted or overturned. Even Thomas Jefferson with his formidable intellect recognized Marshall's skill as a rhetorician when he remarked, "When I am conversing with Marshall, I never admit anything. So sure as you admit any position to be good, no matter how remote from the conclusion he seeks to establish, you are gone."

As chief justice from 1801 to 1835, Marshall stood as a bulwark against the Democratic-Republican party and the presidencies of Jefferson, James Madison, and James Monroe. When John Quincy Adams, a Whig, was not reelected, Marshall refused to retire and stayed on the bench. He finally died in Andrew Jackson's second term of office. No one before or since has done as much as John Marshall to determine the character of our federal system.

the separation of powers. The net effect of the Court's decision was to shift back to Congress the responsibility for deficit reduction.

Limiting the power of government is the third functional arena of judicial review. From 1937 until the early 1970s, this was the most important activity of the High Court. The justices, especially Chief Justice Earl Warren (1953–1969), sought to protect **civil rights** and **civil liberties** against unwarranted intrusion by either the national government or the state governments.[3] In the school desegregation cases, in the reapportionment cases, in cases concerned with the rights of the accused, and in cases

involving church-state relations—particularly prayers in public school—the Court forged new law and made policy that Congress and the president could not or would not undertake.

From the perspective of the civil rights activist, the Supreme Court has done more to protect individual rights and liberties during the last half-century than the people's elected representatives have done. By contrast, conservatives view the Court's policy-making activities as a usurpation of either legislative authority or states' rights. With the ascension of William Rehnquist to the chief justiceship, they hope to see an end to such usurpations.[4]

Judicial Policy Making

The functions of the judiciary, both federal and state, include conflict resolution, administration of the law, and policy making. The last of these is the most important. The power of judicial review, constitutional interpretation, and statutory interpretation gives the courts the requisite authority to be policy makers. Although all courts make policy, the Supreme Court has the greatest opportunity to make policies that will have far-reaching effects. Supreme Court justices make policy by the decisions they reach and by their choice of cases to review.

Supreme Court policy making can be divided into three distinct eras. (Table 11.2) The first great era lasted from 1801 until 1865. During these years, the Court was primarily concerned with federal-state relations. Since federalism was a novel way of allocating governmental power, that allocation required clarification. Two of the greatest chief justices, John Marshall (1801–1835) and Roger Taney (1836–1864), used the national supremacy clause, the commerce power, and the contract clause in their attempts to define the proper sphere of federal and state authority. After more than a half-century of great decisions, the limits of judicial power were reached; a civil war was fought to determine finally the nature of the federal Union.

The second policy-making era dated from 1865 until 1937. During these years, questions about the proper scope of government regulation of business came increasingly to the Court's attention. Three prominent associate justices with laissez-faire attitudes—Joseph Bradley, Stephen Field, and Samuel Miller—interpreted the Fourteenth Amendment's due process clause, the commerce power, and the Tenth Amendment in ways that often frustrated governmental attempts to regulate business.

Supreme Court resistance to government regulation of the economy ended during the Great Depression of the 1930s. Yet that end came only after a major confrontation with Franklin Roosevelt. Although never conceding to Roosevelt, the Court began to reverse itself, and a new majority accepted the argument that the federal government possessed the constitutional authority to determine the government-business relationship.[5]

From 1937 to 1969, the Supreme Court engaged in a third great era of policy making. During these years, the justices turned their attention more and more to civil rights issues. Chief Justice Earl Warren reinvigorated the Fourteenth Amendment due process and equal protection clauses. The Warren Court used the due process clause to protect the constitutional rights of individuals accused of crime. The equal protection clause became the instrument an activist majority wielded to end racial segregation in public schools and to establish the one-man, one-vote principle for both congressional and state legislative districts. Under Warren's leadership, the Court also upheld Congress's use of the commerce power to pass civil rights legislation.

Although a number of important civil rights de-

Table 11.2
Three Eras of Supreme Court Policy Making

Major Issues	Most Interpreted Clauses	Prominent Justices
Nature of the Union 1801–1865	National supremacy Contract clause Commerce clause	John Marshall (1801–1835) Joseph Story (1811–1845) Roger Taney (1836–1864)
Government-business relations 1865–1937	Fourteenth Amendment due process Commerce clause Tenth Amendment	Samuel Miller (1862–1890) Stephen Field (1863–1897) Joseph Bradley (1870–1892) Oliver W. Holmes (1902–1932) Charles E. Hughes (1930–1941) Owen J. Roberts (1930–1945)
Civil rights activism 1937–1969	Fourteenth Amendment due process Fourteenth Amendment equal protection First Amendment Fourth Amendment	Harlan F. Stone (1925–1941) Hugo Black (1937–1971) Felix Frankfurter (1939–1962) William Douglas (1939–1975) Earl Warren (1953–1969)

cisions followed Earl Warren's retirement in 1969, the Court under Chief Justice Warren Burger was far less protective of the civil rights of disadvantaged groups.[6] Indeed, liberal critics of the Burger Court protested what they perceived as the Court's retreat from the landmark decisions of the Warren years.

Yet the Burger Court did not escape censure from the right either. Conservatives complained that Burger was never able to exert the leadership necessary to establish the conservative vision of the Court's responsibilities. They look to William Rehnquist, who succeeded Burger to the chief justiceship in 1986, to do this.

In the area of criminal procedures, for example, conservatives see a need for strengthening the forces of law and order against a rising crime wave. The Court's 1984 limitation on the exclusionary rule, which bans illegally seized evidence from admission in court, is a prime example of what the conservatives seek. Before this decision, even if the police had made a good faith effort to adhere to evidentiary rules, the evidence gained in a search was often held inadmissible because of procedural blunders. Such evidence would now be admissible.

Despite the fact that the Supreme Court has been an important policy maker since John Marshall's tenure, debate continues about the appropriate policy-making role of the Court and its proper relationship with the "other" branches of government. From one perspective, the argument can be stated in terms of judicial activism versus judicial restraint.

Advocates of judicial activism hold an expansive view of Court authority, whereas those who favor judicial restraint insist on a narrow interpretation of Court authority. Whenever the Court comes into conflict with the "political" branches—Congress, the president, and the state governments—judicial activists argue that the Court need not defer to those branches. Proponents of judicial restraint, on the other hand, contend that the Court should defer to the political branches, which are the elected representatives of the people.

Judicial activists perceive the Supreme Court as the guardian of the Constitution, the supreme law of the land, a concept that is challenged by those who insist on judicial restraint in policy making. In their view, the Constitution emanated from the people and should only be changed by their representatives, Congress and the president. Essentially, the proponents of restraint rely on the value of popular sovereignty. Congress and the president are democratic agents because they are elected for fixed terms, whereas justices on the High Court are appointed for life.

Judicial activists note several grounds that can justify the Court's pursuit of its policy preferences.

EARL WARREN (1891–1974)

Although his tenure as chief justice (1953–1969) was often marked by controversy, few scholars would not rank Earl Warren with John Marshall and Roger Taney as among the greatest chief justices. Even those who would not so honor him are compelled to acknowledge the Warren Court as the preeminent, activist Court concerned with individual rights and liberties. In four significant areas—school desegregation, the constitutional rights of those accused of crime, reapportionment, and church-state relations—the Warren Court reached the high tide of civil libertarianism.

As with John Marshall, one could find few hints in Warren's earlier years of public service that he was destined to be a great chief justice. Indeed, one notable piece of evidence might have suggested the contrary. While attorney general in California, he supported the evacuation of Japanese Americans from the West Coast during World War II.

His appointment to the Supreme Court, again like Marshall's, owed more to political considerations than to perceived judicial acumen. In return for Warren's support in the electorally important state of California, Dwight Eisenhower promised him a seat on the High Court. Ike grew to regret this decision, and on one occasion exclaimed that Warren's appointment was the "worst damn-fool mistake that I ever made."

For sixteen tumultuous years, Earl Warren championed the cause of civil rights from his position on the Supreme Court. His vigorous support for the downtrodden led Harry S Truman to remark: "The facts of the case are that Warren is really a Democrat, but doesn't know it." Perhaps, but the fact is that Warren gave Richard Nixon, a Republican president, the opportunity to appoint his successor by retiring in 1969.

Despite the conservative proclivities of the Burger and Rehnquist courts, the great decisions of the Warren years are still largely intact after nearly two decades. These decisions stand as a monument to his life and to his deeply felt humanitarianism.

If Congress or the president fails to address issues of pressing national importance, if the states do not adequately protect individual rights, if minorities are disadvantaged by majoritarian policies, the Court has ample reason to exercise its policy-making authority. Nor should legal precedents deter the Courts. If the need arises, the justices should not hesitate to depart from outdated precedents to make new policy. Changed circumstances may demand a new interpretation of the Constitution, and justices would be neglecting their responsibilities if they failed to forge new law.

By contrast, those who favor restraint argue that policy should be formulated only by the political branches and, where appropriate, the state governments, which are closest to the people, should be closely involved. Proponents of restraint also insist that all courts should adhere to precedent. If precedents become outdated, the political branches should be the initiator of changes in the law.

When measured against activist ideals, the Warren Court stands out as the epitome of an activist Court.[7] Indeed, in the entire history of the Supreme Court, few other Courts can equal the activism of the Warren era. By contrast, even after more than a decade and a half, the Burger Court was difficult to characterize.[8] Part of the reason for this difficulty, as even Burger's supporters admit, was Burger's lack of intellectual leadership. Conservatives are hopeful that William Rehnquist will be able to translate his affability and intellectual prowess into effective leadership. Clearly, the Rehnquist Court will follow a path different from the one Earl Warren had tread. Most important, it can be expected to embrace the philosophy of judicial restraint and to seek to change the substance of Court activism.

The Organization and Structure of the Federal Courts

Article III provides for one Supreme Court and for such inferior courts as Congress shall deem necessary (Figure 11.1). Thus the Constitution empowers Congress to create the lower federal courts and to define their jurisdiction. The judicial article also grants Congress the power to alter the appellate jurisdiction of the Supreme Court while denying it

the authority to modify the Court's original jurisdiction.[9] In an indirect way, the executive branch also shares in creating the courts because it is the president who appoints, with the advice and consent of the Senate, federal judges. The president, however, has no authority to shape the jurisdiction of any federal court.

The word *jurisdiction* can be used in three different ways. Jurisdiction may simply mean the power of courts to determine the law. Jurisdiction can also refer to the boundaries that distinguish the federal judiciary from the state judiciaries. By constitutional design and in actual practice, federal jurisdiction is largely separate from state jurisdiction.

Although appeal from a state's highest court to the United States Supreme Court is possible, the

Figure 11.1
Federal and State Court Organization *

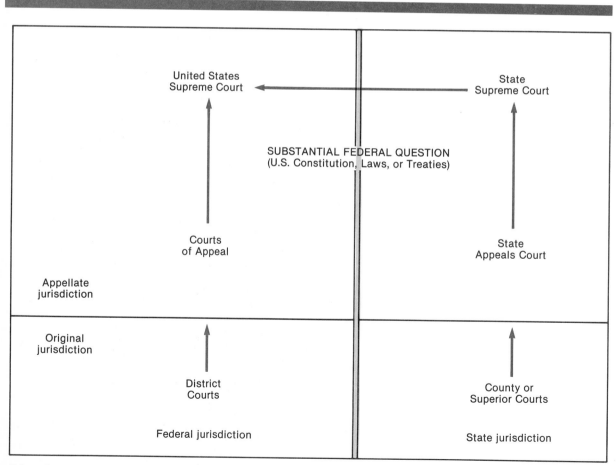

*Minor Courts and Special Courts have been omitted.

Court has limited this path. Only if the Court determines that a substantial federal question, that is, a question concerning the Constitution, federal law, or a treaty, is involved will the Court review a case originating in a state court. However, the Supreme Court must hear appeals from any court that either declares a federal law unconstitutional or upholds state laws against a federal constitutional or statutory challenge. Despite these exceptions, most cases reach the Supreme Court from the lower federal courts. Access to the Supreme Court, even by the lower federal courts, is largely limited to cases involving major policy issues.

Finally, jurisdiction may refer to the level or stage of court activity. The trial level is called original jurisdiction. At this stage, judges and juries determine the law and the facts of a case. Under certain circumstances, a case may be tried in either a federal court or a state court. Jurisdiction in these cases is known as concurrent jurisdiction, which simply means shared, original jurisdiction.

Appellate jurisdiction refers to the review level. Judges hear appeals to determine whether the law was applied properly at the trial in the case at hand and in other similar cases. Since the facts of the case are not under review, there are no juries at this level. Although the Supreme Court is empowered to review both the facts and the law, normally the High Court reviews only legal questions.

PLEA BARGAINING: THE LAW VERSUS JUSTICE?

Part and parcel of the American judicial system is the process of plea bargaining. It is a process that has been severely criticized, yet remains widely used. Cases in which a charge of first-degree murder are reduced to voluntary manslaughter in exchange for a guilty plea, for example, usually have two consequences: (1) the perpetrators spend far less time in jail, and (2) the victim's survivors and much of the public is outraged. Given these negative consequences, why are plea bargains used? There are several reasons. First, without plea bargains, the prosecutors, the courts, and the jails would be quickly overwhelmed. Second, a plea bargain saves taxpayers the expense of a costly trial and the likelihood of numerous appeals. Finally, a plea bargain ensures prosecutors of a conviction, whereas the outcome of a trial is always in doubt until the jury hands down its verdict. In some instances, a jury may be deadlocked, forcing the judge to declare a mistrial, and the process has to start all over again. The uncertainties surrounding the judicial process make it unlikely that the law can guarantee perfect justice. A plea bargain is an attempt to secure an achievable amount of justice in an imperfect world.

An Overview of the Judicial Process

All cases, whether civil (infringing on an individual's rights), or criminal (breaking a law), are adversarial in nature.[10] In either a civil or criminal case, the adversary system pits a plaintiff or a prosecutor against a defendant. A criminal case in Kansas, for example, would be called the People of the State of Kansas versus John Doe. In criminal cases, the prosecution is always some unit of government. By contrast, a civil case in the same state may simply be Smith versus Jones, both of the parties being private individuals.

At the arrest stage in a criminal proceeding, the individuals accused must be informed of their constitutional rights. In 1966, these rights were spelled out in the *Miranda* case. "The Miranda warning," is a prime example of the greater concern with consti-

tutional protections in criminal cases as opposed to civil cases. Indeed, in the Bill of Rights, the Fourth, Fifth, Sixth, and Eighth Amendments include such protections. About one-half of all arrests are dismissed for a variety of reasons at or before arraignment, that is, an appearance before a judge or a magistrate.

The number of cases that actually go to trial is further reduced by the plea bargaining that normally takes place after an indictment has been handed down. An indictment is the formal accusation, drawn up by a prosecutor and brought by a grand jury, charging one or more individuals with the commission of a crime. Plea bargaining is the process during which the prosecuting attorney and the defense counsel negotiate a guilty plea in exchange for a reduced charge. Approximately 40 percent of all arrests are plea bargained. If the trial proceeds and the defendant is found guilty, that individual has the right to appeal the conviction.

Different standards for proof or guilt prevail in civil and criminal cases. In criminal cases, accused individuals must be proven guilty beyond a reasonable doubt, whereas in civil cases a fair preponderance of the evidence is sufficient to determine responsibility. This difference in standards is reflected in the jury's verdict. Most states require that the verdict in a criminal case be unanimous, whereas nonunanimous verdicts in civil cases are not unusual. The reason for the difference is quite simple: Conviction of a criminal offense often entails imprisonment; the verdict in a civil case typically involves a money payment by one party to another. Despite these differences, the losing party in both types of cases has a right to appeal.

Eventually, an appeal from either a lower federal court or a state court of last resort can reach the Supreme Court (Table 11.3). If the Court accepts a case for review, the opposing attorneys file legal briefs with the Court.[11] Other interested parties may file an amicus curiae (friend of the court) brief. As a general rule, affected interest groups are the most important source of such briefs. For example, in a race discrimination case, it would not be unusual for the NAACP and the American Civil Liberties Union to file amicus briefs. When the Supreme Court was considering whether pension plans could pay smaller amounts to women, with their greater longevity, a number of insurance

companies filed briefs because their interests were directly involved.

Oral arguments may be scheduled to explore further the legal issues in dispute. After the oral arguments, the justices meet in private conference to discuss the cases under review and to vote on the outcome. In conference discussions, the chief justice speaks first but votes last. If the chief justice votes with the majority, he may either write the opinion of the Court himself or assign that task to one of the associate justices. However, if the chief justice votes with the minority, the senior associate justice in the majority assigns the opinion. Individual justices may also decide to write either concurring or dissenting opinions.

Supreme Court opinions are essentially instruments of persuasion. Through its opinions, the Court seeks to convince the lower courts, the legal profession, Congress, the president, interest groups, the media, and the public to accept the Court's reasoning and to comply with its decisions.

Since the Supreme Court lacks enforcement powers, complete and rapid compliance with the Court's decisions may be thwarted by political pressures, especially when a decision is controversial or unpopular. This is certainly what happened after the *Brown v. Board of Education* (1954) decision. A number of southern states developed a variety of legal strategies designed to evade or delay school desegregation. Ultimately, the Court relies on the president to commit the executive branch, particularly the Justice Department, to enforcement of the Supreme Court's decisions.

Table 11.3
The Case Load of the
United States Supreme Court

Term Ending in Summer	Cases on Supreme Court Docket	Opinions Issued
1930	984	134 *
1940	1,078	137
1950	1,448	87
1960	2,178	117
1970	4,202	108
1985	5,006	139

* Some opinions decide more than one case. The 129 opinions in 1978, for example, included 161 cases.

Source: Office of the Clerk, the United States Supreme Court.

The Federal Courts and Civil Rights and Civil Liberties

The recent history of the Supreme Court and the progress of civil liberties testify to the emergence of the federal judiciary as a formulator of national policy. By the late 1970s and 1980s, the federal courts were being asked to decide the legality and constitutionality of such matters as abortion, capital punishment, pornography, school prayer, and sexual preferences. Neither the judiciary's critics nor its advocates envied the judges their tasks. Both groups clearly recognized that the courts were being besieged by cases that were testing what many peo-

LIMITS ON FEDERAL JUDICIAL POWER

FEDERAL POWERS THAT ARE BEYOND THE SCOPE OF JUDICIAL POWER:

Some of the most significant federal powers, such as the power to spend money, to hold property, to engage in quasibusiness activity, and to foster certain enterprises, are beyond the scope of judicial power because individuals and groups usually cannot meet the standing requirement necessary to file suit in federal court.

CONGRESSIONAL CHECKS:

Congress can pass laws or use its amending power to overturn court decisions. Although modern instances are rare, Congress can use its power of the purse to limit financial allocations to the courts. With its authority in Article III, Congress could abolish the lower federal courts or alter their jurisdiction. Finally, Congress can bring impeachment charges against individual justices.

PRESIDENTIAL CHECKS:

The most important checks the president possesses are his willingness to enforce court decisions and his power to appoint federal judges. Since courts are passive and must wait for cases to be brought to them, the president can instruct the attorney general either not to prosecute or not to appeal decisions where the federal government is the losing party.

THE LOWER FEDERAL COURTS:

The lower courts are primarily a check on the Supreme Court's power. Most Supreme Court decisions are carried out by the lower federal courts, which can undermine those decisions simply by failing to implement them. The Supreme Court can overcome such resistance, but it takes time and energy.

STATE OFFICIALS:

Many Supreme Court decisions must be enforced by state officials. If they disagree with the Court's decisions, compliance may be extremely slow. State officials can also act in ways designed to evade Supreme Court rulings. Since federal jurisdiction is largely separate from state jurisdiction, state judges can limit the reach of federal court decisions.

PUBLIC OPINION:

Public opinion, especially when courts have made controversial or unpopular decisions, can severely limit the impact of federal judicial power. Such opinion can also be translated into political action that may cause legislators to act or interest groups to bring new suits that may produce a different ruling.

INTERNAL RESTRAINTS:

Courts have developed an array of internal restraints that can limit the reach of judicial power. Some of the more important restraints include the doctrines of substantial federal questions, political questions, and the exhaustion of state remedies. Other restraints, such as the ban on advisory opinions, a presumption of constitutionality, and limiting decisions to the narrowest grounds possible, can also constrain federal judicial policy making.

---

ple viewed as the maximum, legally permissible limits of constitutional guarantees:

Does an unborn fetus have the constitutional protection afforded a person after birth?

Can the state legally deprive even a convicted mass murderer of his or her life?

Are certain "adult" reading or video materials protected by either the First Amendment or a right of privacy?

Should homosexuals be allowed to teach in public schools?

Is a state law prescribing a "moment of silence" at the beginning of the school day a violation of the separation of church and state?

This list does not even begin to exhaust the critical issues that federal courts must confront. In the 1950s, as the civil rights cases produced historically significant (and history-changing) decisions, court critics accused the Supreme Court of implementing sociological ideas rather than strictly legal

Despite the Court's decision in *Roe v. Wade* (1973) granting women the right to an abortion during the first trimester of pregnancy, the issue remains a highly contentious one in American politics.

principles. The school desegregation cases seemed to open the floodgates. Now judges must be lawyers and moralists, physicians and librarians, censors and sexologists.

No matter which way the Supreme Court ultimately rules on such controversial issues, its decisions will offend large numbers of people. Yet the history of the federal courts indicates that people expect judges to bite the bullet and make the hard decisions that Congress, the president, or the states cannot or will not make. Because judges are human, however, their decisions will also reflect the imperfections of human nature. Judicial opinions may be soul-searching exercises, but they cannot always produce clear and unambiguous legal principles. Many opinions express the thinking of Justice Potter Stewart, who declared that he could not give a precise legal definition of pornography, but (like most of us) he knew it when he saw it.

Judges must also grapple with the difficult fact that some civil liberties may actually clash with one another. Do AIDS victims, for example, have a right to attend public schools? Some parents have argued that the rights of their children are being infringed on by forced exposure to the carrier of a dreaded disease. Under what conditions, if any, should the sexual behavior of consenting adults be regulated by the state? Whose rights should come first in the case of a woman with an unwanted pregnancy: the unborn fetus (which clearly has the potential to be a human being) or the prospective mother who asserts a right to decide whether to bear a child?

Modern technology has created other problems. Medical and scientific discoveries are extending the life span, providing better and more effective health treatments, and improving the overall quality of life. In many instances, technology has outdistanced the law. An individual's "life" may be extended indefinitely by a support system, even if that person is and will remain unconscious. Is that individual dead? What is death? When is a person legally dead? Who should decide? Who should make the decision to remove the life support system? Doctors? The next of kin? Clergy? Lawyers? Judges?

Ultimately, the Supreme Court may have to decide these issues. Given their complexity, the moral sentiments held by different people, and the impossibility of securing universally agreed-on scientific determinations, the Court will not have an easy time. The justices will consider testimony on all sides of the issues, but that testimony is unlikely to produce a consensus. In the end, the Court will necessarily render decisions that will displease significant numbers of people. Their displeasure may even be shared by justices on the high court who dissent from the Court's opinions. On the basis of these considerations, we have ample reason to believe that the Rehnquist Court will not escape controversy in the future, nor will Reagan's newly appointed justices find the issues they face any less challenging.

The Supreme Court may be entering an era of policy resolution that the other branches will be understandably reluctant to consider. To appreciate fully what challenges await the Court, we must explore the political rights of American citizens; analyze the meaning of equality, of limited government, and of due process of law; and examine how the Court has protected the rights of individuals accused of crime and how it forged a rationale for the nationalization of the Bill of Rights.

Citizenship Rights and Political Participation

The most basic political rights are found in the First Amendment—freedom of speech, press, assembly, and petition. Since the nation's founding, the trend has been to extend these rights. Other rights, such as a right of association, which includes joining political parties and interest groups, are derived from the First Amendment. Beyond the expression of political opinions, voting and competing for public office are among the most important ways that citizens can participate in the political process. So important is the right to vote that six amendments—the Fifteenth, Seventeenth, Nineteenth, Twenty-third, Twenty-fourth, and Twenty-sixth—have extended this right and thus contributed in a major way to the democratization of the Constitution.

Any infringement on these rights, unless carefully circumscribed, can be a threat to an open society. Democracy flourishes only in a society where the expression of competing political beliefs is permitted, where groups and parties can organize to influence the political system or to control the institutions of government. Without the protection of the civil rights and civil liberties of citizens, political participation is an empty symbol. Critics of the Soviet Union contend that such is not the case in that nation. Soviet citizens are required to participate politically but such involvement does not include realistic possibilities for dislodging the Communist Party from power.

The Meaning of Equality: The Declaration of Independence and the Fourteenth Amendment Equal Protection Clause

The most powerful statement on equality may be that found in the Declaration of Independence. Jefferson's phrase "All men are created equal" does not restrict the meaning of equality to political or economic equality, but clearly implies that individuals are equal regardless of political or economic considerations. If the phrase is read "All are created

equal," then it can be interpreted to mean equality without regard to gender differences.[12]

Jefferson's idea of equality can be contrasted with concepts that would limit the reach of the meaning of equality. For example, a tension exists between equality and a meritocracy, equality and male dominance, equality and racial supremacy, equality and concentrated wealth, equality and the politically powerful. In each instance, advocates for inequality have sought to justify the limits they would place on the meaning of equality. White males have been particularly adept at justifying their dominant position in the American economic and political systems. Feminists have thus far unsuccessfully sought an equal rights amendment to combat this dominance.

Unfortunately for egalitarians, the natural rights philosophy of a prepolitical equality was not written into the Constitution. Indeed, not until the adoption of the Fourteenth Amendment did egalitarians have any language on which to base an argument. Rather than the robust language of natural rights, the provisions of the Fourteenth Amendment require only the equal protection of the laws. Moreover, the Supreme Court has historically been reluctant to give that clause an expansive reading. Despite this handicap, egalitarians have succeeded in removing many of the obstacles to equality. Following is an overview of the most important contemporary meanings of equality.

Equality of rights concerning political participation: Restrictions on the right of ethnic minorities to vote and to participate politically are barriers to political equality that must be dismantled. Indeed, this was a major theme of the Reverend Jesse Jackson during the 1984 Democratic presidential primary campaigns. Although it is difficult to measure, a good share of the success he enjoyed can be traced to his efforts to register large numbers of black Americans.[13] Jackson also vigorously attacked the run-off primary system, which he contended had the effect of diluting the voting strength of southern blacks.

Equality before the law: The Fourteenth Amendment equal protection clause and in certain respects the due process clause forbid unequal treatment of individuals on the basis of race, sex, religion, or

ECONOMIC AND POLITICAL RIGHTS

From one perspective, the United States Constitution is a document designed to guarantee individual and political rights. Remarkably little is said about economic rights. No constitutional provision, for example, guarantees anyone a job or a right to health care. In the last half century, however, the national government has passed legislation that is moving in that direction. Since the 1930s, both Democratic and Republican administrations have adopted policies to foster economic growth, reduce unemployment, compensate for limited periods those who are unemployed, underwrite at least part of the health care costs of older Americans, and establish pensions (social security) for those who are no longer working. Even though these policies and programs are either of limited duration or offer only partial economic relief, some people ask the question: Can the national government, with budgetary deficits in the hundreds of billions of dollars and the national debt approaching the trillions of dollars, afford these measures? No nation, not even an economic superpower such as the United States, has unlimited resources. Yet no nation with an industrialized economy lacks an extensive array of social welfare programs. The Founding Fathers knew it would not be easy to guarantee individual and political rights. But today we know that it is far less expensive to guarantee political rights than economic rights.

Equality of opportunity: Equal access to housing, schools, and jobs have been the most important dimensions of equal opportunity. Federal laws, executive regulations, and court decisions have all been used to end discrimination in these areas. Foremost among these efforts has been the Civil Rights Act of 1964. This act specifically bars discrimination on the basis of race, color, religion, or national origin in public accommodations—restaurants, hotels, theaters, sports arenas, and so on— and in employment. Owing to the sweeping nature of this law, it was quickly challenged in the courts. Just as quickly, the Supreme Court in *Heart of Atlanta Motel v. the United States* (1964) sustained the use of the commerce power by Congress to pass civil rights legislation.

Traditionally, in the United States equality has not meant economic equality. The notions of property rights, economic individualism, and capitalist theory have all justified the continuance of economic inequality. Although many Americans have come to accept the legitimacy of the demands by blacks and women for racial and sexual equality, far fewer are willing to accept the idea of economic equality. Nor have the courts been willing to extend the economic meaning of equality. The wealthy, of course, are also opposed to an equal distribution of the nation's resources and are prepared to defend their interests. Since the economically affluent as a group are better educated and more likely to be involved in politics, they exert an influence far beyond their limited numbers.

national origin. Under Chief Justice Earl Warren in the 1950s and 1960s, the Supreme Court held unconstitutional many state laws that disadvantaged or discriminated against individuals on the basis of race. Foremost among its decisions was *Brown v. Board of Education* (1954), which struck down legal segregation of the nation's public schools. While chief justice, Warren employed the Fourteenth Amendment to review a wide range of state actions that were alleged to discriminate against the nation's minorities. He did not hesitate to use the Court's power to restrain both the states and the federal government when he felt there had been an unwarranted infringement of civil rights and civil liberties.

Limits on Government Intrusion: The Concept of Limited Government

As far back as the ancient Greeks, the natural law tradition has held that limits exist to the legitimate reach of governmental power. This notion was reinforced by the natural rights philosophy that maintained people have certain rights that governments cannot justify invading. Although governments may have the power to infringe on these rights, they lack a lawful authority to do so.

As we noted in Chapter 3, Jefferson argued in the Declaration of Independence that these rights are prepolitical and included, minimally, the rights of life, liberty, and the pursuit of happiness. Many of the Founding Fathers came to the conclusion that a government responsible to the people should be

Thurgood Marshall argued the *Brown v. Board of Education* case before the Supreme Court and later became the first black to be appointed to the Supreme Court.

gained by that search be admissible in court? In *Mapp v. Ohio* (1961), the Supreme Court ruled such evidence inadmissible in state courts.[14] Ever since that decision, law enforcement officials have sought a modification of what has come to be known as the "exclusionary rule." In 1984, a more conservative Supreme Court majority carved out an exception to the exclusionary rule. Where police have made a good faith effort to adhere to the provisions of the Fourth Amendment, a blunder on their part will not be sufficient to cause evidence to be excluded.

For many citizens, issues involving the reach of governmental power do not have a direct impact on their lives. Much closer to home are rights concerned with religion and conscience, privacy, a woman's ability to decide whether to have a child, and property rights. In each of these areas, how far the power of the state should intrude into what are widely perceived as private concerns is a troubling question. Should parents whose religious convictions forbid certain types of medical care for their children be overruled by the courts? Should consenting sexual activity between adults be protected by a right of privacy? Should the state have the power to ban abortions? Especially since 1937, the Supreme Court has been called on to provide the nation with authoritative answers to these and similar questions.

restrained from infringing on these rights. For this reason, they appended to the Constitution a bill of rights containing a specific set of limits on governmental power.

Other limits on governmental authority can be found in Article I Sections 9 and 10, and the Civil War Amendments, particularly the Fourteenth Amendment. Only in the First Amendment, however, is a categorical limit placed on the government. The First Amendment begins, "Congress shall make no law," whereas the Fourth Amendment bans only "unreasonable" searches and seizures. Thus both the Constitution and the amendments place varying limits on governmental intrusion. Owing to these varying limits, courts have had to develop standards to determine whether, for example, a search was unreasonable.

Nor does the problem end there. If a search is held to be unreasonable, should the evidence

Government Intrusion and Due Process of Law

The Fifth and Fourteenth Amendment due process clauses protect individuals and groups against arbitrary deprivation of life, liberty, and property. If, for example, a state government seeks to appropriate a group's property, the Fourteenth Amendment due process clause requires that state officials act in a procedurally fair manner. To ensure that the state does act fairly, both groups and individuals can seek a review by the courts. Such review prevents the state from being the judge of its own actions. (It is, moreover, a good example of separation of powers.)

Government intrusion is also limited by the **writ of habeas corpus**.[15] Essentially, this writ provides for judicial oversight of executive actions. Whenever an individual is deprived of liberty by being arrested by police, that person must be brought before a judicial magistrate to determine whether the arrest was warranted. If the court decides the arrest was not warranted, the police must release that individual because no legal grounds for detention exist. By separating the executive and the judicial functions of government through the provision of a writ of habeas corpus, the Founding Fathers sought to protect the people from a government that might arbitrarily deprive individuals of their lives, liberty, or property.

Constitutional Protections for Those Accused of Crime

The Fourteenth Amendment, and as the following section illustrates, the Bill of Rights contain numer-

ous provisions that protect an individual accused of committing a crime from being subjected to arbitrary procedures. The Fourth, Fifth, Sixth, and Eighth Amendments spell out procedures that governments must follow, set limits to governmental power, and ban outright certain actions by government, and provide for legal processes that accused persons can employ in their defense. Because the language of the Bill of Rights is often ambiguous and the issues involved in depriving a person of life, liberty, or property are complex, the Supreme Court has had a difficult task in determining under what conditions governments can lawfully undertake such deprivations.

From the defendant's perspective, the Sixth Amendment's right to counsel must rank among the

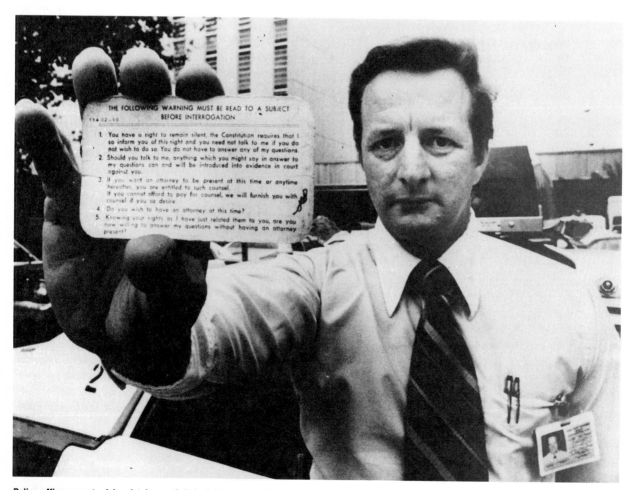

Police officers must advise detainees of their rights as a result of the court's decision in *Miranda vs. Arizona.*

CLARENCE GIDEON AND THE RIGHT TO COUNSEL

At his trial for breaking and entering a poolhall, Clarence Gideon asked the judge to appoint an attorney to represent him because he could not afford to hire one. The judge refused, pointing out that Florida law made no provision for such appointment. Gideon represented himself, but was convicted and sentenced to jail. Although lacking in any legal training, Gideon filed an appeal with the Florida Supreme Court. That court denied the appeal.

Undaunted, Gideon asked the United States Supreme Court to hear his case by filing an *in forma pauperis* writ, a writ available to individuals too poor to use the normal routes of appeal to the nation's highest court. The Supreme Court accepted the appeal and appointed Abe Fortas, one of Washington's most prominent lawyers (and later an associate justice), to represent Gideon. Florida was represented by a relatively inexperienced assistant attorney general.

In handing down its unanimous decision, the Supreme Court held the states bound by the right to counsel provision of the Sixth Amendment. State courts must ensure that all defendants in felony cases are provided with an attorney. If the defendant cannot afford a lawyer, the state must appoint one. Known as *Gideon v. Wainwright* (1963), this landmark decision was hailed from the outset as a vindication of individual rights.

quist Court will overturn or modify to any great extent the Miranda ruling.

The Nationalization of the Bill of Rights

In *Barron v. Baltimore* (1833), the Marshall Court held that the Bill of Rights did not bind the state governments. Marshall's reasoning for this decision was quite simple. The Constitution created the national government, not the state governments. Therefore, the Bill of Rights, which was appended to the Constitution, bound only the national government. He also pointed to the language of the First Amendment, which opens with the phrase "Congress shall make no law . . ." In the absence of specific language to the contrary, these provisions were not intended to include the states. Moreover, many of the state constitutions contained their own bills of rights.

Clarence Gideon

most important of the provisions found in the Bill of Rights. Indeed, a number of legal scholars insist that all the other constitutional rights of accused persons are heavily dependent on the right to counsel.[16] For in the absence of legal counsel, large numbers of individuals who have the misfortune to be arrested would be unaware of the existence of their constitutional rights.

The Supreme Court's decision in *Miranda v. Arizona* (1966) making it a police obligation to inform accused individuals of their rights recognized this very point. Prominently featured in the so-called Miranda warning is the right to counsel. Despite the conservative posture of the Supreme Court in the last decade or so, it is unlikely that the Rehn-

Not until the adoption of the Fourteenth Amendment did the Constitution provide for national protection of civil rights and civil liberties. Yet even this protection was at first limited to blacks freed by the Civil War. In *The Slaughterhouse Cases* (1873), the Supreme Court refused to extend the meaning of the Fourteenth Amendment to include economic concerns. Rather, the Court insisted that the Civil War Amendments displayed a "unity of purpose" which was to protect the freedmen. Unfortunately, even that limited interpretation was emasculated by *Plessy v. Ferguson* (1896), which announced the separate but equal doctrine. This decision made it evident that the Court had surrendered a role for the national government in civil rights.

Turning its back on civil rights, the Court carved out for itself an economic role that was destined to last until 1937. In particular, it fashioned the doctrine of **substantive due process,** which limited the power of both the national and the state governments to regulate the economy and such economic matters as wages and hours, child labor, and hours for women.

Despite growing frustration with the Court's obstructionist decisions, it was not until the Great Depression struck that sufficient political pressure was brought to bear on the Supreme Court to change its attitude about the power of the national government to intervene in the economy. Even then, it took a direct attack by President Franklin Roosevelt on the Supreme Court before the justices relinquished their opposition to government efforts to restore the economy to health.[17]

With the end of the Court's resistance to economic regulation in the **Court Revolution of 1937,** the justices increasingly turned their attention to the civil rights arena. This new focus for Court activism was actually foreshadowed twelve years earlier. In *Gitlow v. New York* (1925), the Supreme Court, for the first time, extended the protections of the First Amendment to the states. However, that case did not lay down a strategy for incorporating additional provisions of the Bill of Rights into the Fourteenth Amendment.[18]

That step came in *Palko v. Connecticut* (1937), where Justice Benjamin Cardozo enunciated the principle that was to guide the interpretation of the Fourteenth Amendment for the next five decades. He held that the due process clause of the Four-

teenth Amendment applies to the states only those provisions of the Bill of Rights that are essential to a scheme of ordered liberty. This rule made an exception to Marshall's decision in the *Barron* case and at the same time furnished the necessary strategy for a selective incorporation of the Bill of Rights into the Fourteenth Amendment.

Despite the inherent limitations in Cardozo's rule, the Fourteenth Amendment became, as Table 11.4 shows, the vehicle by which the Supreme Court extended virtually all the protections of the Bill of Rights to the states. Congress cemented the national government's role in civil rights with the passage of the Civil Rights Act of 1964. This legislation, however, is based on the commerce power, not on the Fourteenth Amendment, leading some commentators to suggest that Congress is reluctant to use the Fourteenth Amendment as a legislative tool. Although the fervor of the civil rights movement has cooled considerably since the 1960s, the national government still has the major constitutional responsibility for guaranteeing all American citizens the full enjoyment of their civil rights and civil liberties.

The President and the Federal Courts

Enforcement of federal court decisions is only one part of the complex relationship between the president and the federal courts.[19] When viewed from a wider perspective, it is the president who decides how vigorously federal laws—antitrust, criminal, civil rights, drug, illegal immigration, tax, and so on—will be enforced. The president also establishes the policies the attorney general and the Justice Department will follow.

As the principal official responsible for the enforcement of federal laws, the attorney general directs the conduct of lawsuits involving the national government and supervises all United States attorneys and United States marshals. In consultation with the solicitor general, the attorney general decides whether cases where the United States is the losing party will be appealed to the Supreme Court. If such cases are appealed, the solicitor general appears as the attorney for the United States government.

Table 11.4
The Nationalization of the Bill of Rights by a
Process of Selective Incorporation into the
Fourteenth Amendment Due Process Clause

Freedoms	Binding on States	Cases
First Amendment		
Freedom of speech	Yes	*Gitlow v. New York* (1925)
Freedom of press	Yes	*Near v. Minnesota* (1931)
Free exercise of religion	Yes	*Hamilton v. Regents of California* (1934)
Establishment of religion; Separation of church and state	Yes	*Everson v. Bd. of Education* (1947)
Freedom of assembly	Yes	*De Jonge v. Oregon* (1937)
Second Amendment		
Right to bear arms	No	
Third Amendment		
Quartering of troops	No	
Fourth Amendment		
Right against unreasonable searches and seizures	Yes	*Wolf v. Colorado* (1949)
Exclusionary rule	Yes	*Mapp v. Ohio* (1961)
Fifth Amendment		
Grand jury indictment	No	*Hurtado v. California* (1884)
Right against self-incrimination	Yes	*Malloy v. Hogan* (1964)
Right to be informed of constitutional rights	Yes	*Miranda v. Arizona* (1966)
Right against double jeopardy	Yes	*Benton v. Maryland* (1969)
Sixth Amendment		
Fair trial	Yes	*Powell v. Alabama* (1932)
Public trial	Yes	*In re Oliver* (1948)
Speedy trial	Yes	*Klopfer v. North Carolina* (1967)
Impartial jury	Yes	*Parker v. Gladden* (1966)
Jury trial for all serious crimes	Yes	*Duncan v. Louisiana* (1968)
Confrontation of witnesses	Yes	*Pointer v. Texas* (1965)
Compulsory processes for obtaining witnesses	Yes	*Washington v. Texas* (1967)
Right to counsel		
In capital cases	Yes	*Betts v. Brady* (1942)
In felony cases	Yes	*Gideon v. Wainwright* (1963)
In cases involving a jail term	Yes	*Argersinger v. Hamlin* (1972)
Seventh Amendment		
Juries in civil cases	No	
Eighth Amendment		
Excessive bail or fines	No	
Cruel and unusual punishment	Yes	*Robinson v. California* (1962)
Ninth Amendment		
Right of privacy	Yes	*Griswold v. Connecticut* (1962)
Tenth Amendment		
Residual powers	Not applicable	

Other offices in the executive branch, such as the Treasury Department, also give the president ample opportunities to ensure that his policies on law enforcement are being carried out. Since the president can remove top bureaucrats, they have a stake in seeing that the presidential will is guiding their agency's activities.

Although the president cannot remove federal judges, his power to fill all vacant federal judicial posts (with the Senate's advice and consent) gives

REALIGNING THE SUPREME COURT

Some presidents, like Jimmy Carter, complete their term of office without making a single appointment to the Supreme Court. Others, such as Ronald Reagan, arrive at the presidency at a propitious time. As of early 1987, he has appointed two associate justices—Sandra Day O'Connor in 1981 and Antonin Scalia in 1986—and a new chief justice, William Rehnquist in 1986. Given the age and the poor health of several other justices on the High Court, it seems likely that Reagan will have an opportunity to make additional appointments to the Court.

Even if a president makes only one or two appointments, their influence can last through the administration of several presidents. William Brennan, for example, was appointed by Dwight Eisenhower in 1956 and Byron White by John Kennedy in 1962. They are still on the bench. By the end of his second term of office, Reagan will have appointed approximately half of all federal judges.

Despite these impressive numbers, even a single appointment to the Supreme Court, especially if it is the chief justice, can radically alter the Court. Rehnquist, if he matches the tenure of his two predecessors, will serve until after the turn of the next century. As a consequence, a president's appointees can establish (or terminate) a Court majority, whether liberal, conservative, or centrist, and can affect dramatically the substance and direction of the Court's policy making for a long period of time. President Reagan is close to ensuring that his appointments have this kind of impact.

cations, while also being sensitive to the representational aspects of their judicial appointments. During his 1980 presidential campaign, for example, Ronald Reagan felt compelled to promise to appoint a woman to the Supreme Court. He fulfilled this pledge in September 1981 with Sandra Day O'Connor's appointment to the High Court.

In other instances, the president must take into account the prominent political stature of an opponent or an ally. Dwight Eisenhower's appointment of Earl Warren as chief justice was in part due to Warren's political clout as governor of California and as a potential rival for the Republican nomination for president in 1952. Earlier, Franklin Roosevelt chose Hugo Black, then a senator from Alabama, to be his first appointment to the Supreme Court. Roosevelt's opponents in the Senate could hardly deny a seat on the Court to one of their own members, no matter how much they disliked the president. Two other chief justices, William Howard Taft and Charles Evans Hughes, were also prominent politicians whose reputations helped earn them the leadership of the nation's highest court.[20]

A president must also take such representational considerations as ethnicity, race, religion, and even geography into account when he considers someone for a judicial appointment. Although race is perhaps the most important, Antonin Scalia's Italian heritage was definitely a factor in Reagan's decision to appoint him to the Supreme Court. If Thurgood Marshall's seat should become vacant, the president would be under considerable pressure to appoint

him considerable leverage over the judiciary. Not surprisingly, the criteria for judicial appointments are highly political in nature. As a general rule, the president tries to ensure that his appointees share his ideological perspective, as Reagan did when he appointed William Rehnquist and Antonin Scalia to the Supreme Court. Somewhat more than 90 percent of all judicial appointees also come from the same political party as that of the president.

Certain political considerations, however, place limits on whom the president appoints to the federal bench. Presidents today must carefully assess a nominee's political stance and professional qualifi-

In addition to elevating William Rehnquist to Chief Justice, President Reagan has appointed Sandra Day O'Connor (the first woman) and Antonin Scalia (the first Italian-American) to serve on the Court.

WILLIAM H. REHNQUIST (b. 1924): CONTINUITY AND CHANGE IN THE SUPREME COURT

Every president wants his influence to extend beyond his tenure of office. One of the most lasting ways a president can achieve this goal is to remake the Supreme Court in his image. Ronald Reagan took an important step in that direction in June 1986 when he appointed William Rehnquist to be the sixteenth chief justice. Both ideologically and personally, Reagan and Rehnquist are cut from the same political cloth. In making his appointment, Reagan hoped that Rehnquist's intellect and affability would enable him to persuade the other justices to adopt the conservative vision of the Constitution.

No one doubts Rehnquist's intellectual abilities. Graduated first in his class from Stanford Law School in 1957, he practiced law in Phoenix before joining the Justice Department as an assistant attorney general during Richard

Nixon's administration. He quickly caught the eye of Nixon's inner staff, and was appointed to the Supreme Court in 1971 at the age of forty-seven. In his years on the Court, Rehnquist has honed his reputation as an able articulator of conservatism.

Rehnquist's jurisprudence

seems to be guided by three overarching principles. First, conflicts between individual rights and governmental authority should be resolved in favor of the government. Next, conflicts between the national government and the state governments should be resolved in favor of the states. And finally, questions whether to invoke the jurisdiction of the federal courts should, in most instances, be answered negatively. Although greatly oversimplified, this constitutes the heart of the conservative view of judicial power.

Whether Rehnquist's personality will enable him to become an effective leader is the crucial question. If he succeeds, it is quite clear that Rehnquist will move the Supreme Court in new, yet familiar, directions. At that point, the Rehnquist Court will be stamped by the personality of the chief justice.

another black to take his place. Sex is almost certainly going to be as important as race. Future presidents will be under considerable pressure to appoint additional women to the Supreme Court and to the lower federal courts. Justice O'Connor's successor will almost certainly be a woman.

Finally, we should note that presidential appointments, particularly to the Supreme Court, can have a dramatic effect on judicial policy making. Richard Nixon, for example, was determined to end the activism of the Warren Court. In just four years, 1969–1973, his appointments produced the shift from the bold policy making of the Warren Court to the more restrained approach of the Burger Court. Although Ronald Reagan has had to wait longer than Nixon, he has appointed two new jus-

tices and elevated Rehnquist to the position of Chief Justice as of early 1987, and seems on the verge of remaking the Court once more. Perhaps William Rehnquist will lead the Supreme Court into a fourth great era of policy making, while at the same time fulfilling Reagan's goal of changing the substance of Court policy making.

Given the number of the president's appointments to the federal bench, the Democrats fear that Reagan will be able to remake the federal judiciary in the same fashion that he remade the Civil Rights Commission. Despite stiff congressional opposition, Reagan was able to transform the Commission into a body far less liberal in its orientation. With a new chief justice on the Supreme Court, a new and more conservative majority may emerge rather quickly. If

The members of the Rehnquist Supreme Court

that happens, it is quite conceivable, but by no means certain, that the High Court's decisions could take an even sharper turn to the right and confirm the worst expectations of the Democrats.[21]

Owing to the role of the president in appointing justices to the federal bench, the courts cannot be isolated from the politics of the larger political system. Nor, in a representative form of government, should they be. Since the president is the only federal official elected by all the people, the chief executive is perhaps in the best position to ensure that the federal judiciary remains responsive, albeit indirectly, to the electorate.

Conclusion

During the course of American history, there have been periods when the federal courts have been relatively quiescent. Normally, however, the courts

have functioned as equal partners in the policy-making process. Judicial review, constitutional interpretation, and statutory interpretation ensure that the judiciary has the power to influence the development of public policy in any given area.

Moreover, the courts, especially the Supreme Court, must umpire the federal system, define the boundaries of the separation of powers, and determine the limits of governmental intrusion on the rights of the people. In carrying out these responsibilities, the Supreme Court has passed through three great eras of policy making, during which the justices have sought to resolve issues concerning the nature of the union, the government-business relationship, and the civil rights of individuals and disadvantaged groups.

Judges are aided in their policy-making efforts by the organization and structure of both the federal and the state courts. Yet policy making by the courts has not gone unchallenged. Congress, the president, the states, and certain powerful interests have all called for limits on judicial power. Advocates of judicial restraint have developed a series of arguments that envision a much more circumscribed role for the judiciary. But the Court Revolution of 1937 confirmed that the most effective restraints on Supreme Court activism are internal ones. At bottom, it is the Supreme Court that ultimately determines the scope and limits of its activism.

Although both Congress and the president can affect the policy-making activities of the courts, the president is often in a better position to do so. Enforcing federal court decisions, deciding which laws to enforce aggressively, selectively appealing certain cases, and appointing justices to the federal bench are the most obvious ways the president can exert pressure on the judiciary.

Despite efforts to counter court activism, the Supreme Court has shown that it can be a significant and independent policy maker, equal in importance to the president and Congress at critical times. *Brown v. Board of Education* (1954), which led to the desegregation of public schools, *Reynolds v. Sims* (1964) and *Wesberry v. Sanders* (1964), which resulted in the reapportioning of congressional districts and both houses of the state legislatures on an equal-population basis, *Heart of Atlanta Motel v. U.S.* (1964), which upheld Congress's use of the commerce power to enact civil rights legislation, and *U.S. v. Nixon* (1974), which restricted the reach of executive privilege and led to President Nixon's resignation, all attest to the important policy-making role of the Supreme Court over the last three decades. Indeed, one would be hard-pressed to cite a major policy area during that period in which the Court was not involved.

 ## Glossary

Civil liberties The political and personal freedoms usually found in a bill of rights or in other constitutional provisions that restrain the government from arbitrarily intruding on an individual's freedom.

Civil rights Positive acts of government that protect individuals and groups against arbitrary or discriminatory treatment by either government or private parties.

Constitutional interpretation The power of the courts to give meaning to the various clauses of the Constitution.

Court Revolution of 1937 A decisive reversal, led by Chief Justice Charles Evans Hughes and Associate Justice Owen J. Roberts, of the Supreme Court's opposition to the economic regulatory legislation of the New Deal.

Implied power A doctrine developed by John Marshall in *McCulloch v. Maryland* (1819), that used the necessary and proper clause to justify a broad interpretation of the Constitution.

Judicial review The power of the courts to determine the constitutionality of the acts of Congress, the president, or state officials.

National supremacy A second important doctrine developed by Marshall in the *McCulloch* case, which asserts that in instances of conflict between the national and state governments, the latter must give way.

Statutory interpretation The power of the courts to determine the meaning of the language of either federal or state laws and to decide whether those laws are in conformity with the Constitution.

Substantive due process A major doctrine forged by the Court during the 1890s that required both federal and state laws to meet the test of reasonableness, enabling the Court to thwart many of the efforts of the national and state governments to pass economic regulatory legislation.

Writ of habeas corpus A court order requiring executive authorities to appear before a judicial officer and provide evidence that the detention of a person is reasonable and legitimate.

Suggestions for Further Reading

Abraham, Henry J. *The Judicial Process.* 5th ed. New York: Oxford University Press, 1986. A superb comparative investigation of the courts in America, Britain, and France. The massive bibliography makes this work invaluable.

Abraham, Henry J., and Grace Doherty. *Civil Rights and Liberties in the United States.* 4th ed. New York: Oxford University Press, 1984. Meticulous and comprehensive review of the status of rights and liberties in this country.

Dworkin, Ronald. *Taking Rights Seriously.* Cambridge, Mass.: Harvard University Press, 1977. Although only a decade old, this work is widely regarded as a classic analysis of the principled underpinnings of law.

Jacob, Herbert. *Justice in America: Courts, Lawyers and the Judicial Process.* 4th ed. Boston: Little, Brown, 1984. One of the standard texts on the activities of the lower courts.

Johnson, Charles A., and Bradley C. Canon. *Judicial Policies: Implementation and Impact.* Washington: Congressional Quarterly Press, 1984. A scholarly but readable study on how judicial decisions are made, what forces influence them, and what impact they have.

McCloskey, Robert G. *The Modern Supreme Court.* Cambridge, Mass.: Harvard University Press, 1972. Despite being somewhat dated, this work contains a penetrating analysis of how the Supreme Court deals (or avoids dealing) with critical and divisive social issues.

Padover, Saul, and Jacob W. Landynski. *The Living U.S. Constitution.* 2d rev. ed. New York: Mentor, 1983. Includes a brief overview of the Constitutional Convention, sketches of the Founding Fathers, and digests of a number of leading Supreme Court decisions.

Pritchett, C. Herman. *Constitutional Law of the Federal System.* Englewood Cliffs, N.J.: Prentice-Hall, 1984. A distinguished political scientist's examination of the Court's shaping of the federal system.

Shapiro, Martin, and Rocco J. Tresolini. *American Constitutional Law.* 6th ed. New York: Macmillan, 1983. One of the best casebooks that examines how the Supreme Court has shaped the law of the land and how its activities have affected both the national and state governments.

Tribe, Laurence H. *American Constitutional Law.* Mineola, N.Y.: Foundation Press, 1978. A brilliant work that establishes various models to explain the Court's interpretation of the Constitution.

The legitimate object of government, is to do for a community of people, whatever they need to have done, but can not do, at all, or can not, so well do, for themselves—in their separate, and individual capacities.
Abraham Lincoln

The translation of values into public policy is what politics is all about.
Willard Gaylin

Chapter 12

Domestic Policy, Economic Management, and the Policy Process

Introduction

Policy is what politics is all about. Groups and individuals do not become involved in political activity primarily because it is fun (though it can be) or because they are driven by an insatiable hunger for power (though some are) or because they possess a noble sense of duty to their fellow citizens (though some do). Most engage in political activity because they are deeply concerned about some aspect of **public policy** and wish to influence the policy choices made by government. Such concern may arise because governmental activity is perceived as a threat to (or an opportunity for) personal profit or because government action is seen as the only effective way to treat a problem or condition that threatens the entire citizenry. Concern with public policy has always motivated political activity in the United States, providing the impetus for even the revolution that led to the nation's founding. Though seldom resulting in events as momentous for the course of human events as the American Revolution, clearly governmental policy deeply affects the lives of all citizens.

Today, what the government does about the supply of energy, the health and safety of the citizens, mass transit, pollution, the registration and control of handguns, abortion, the military draft, illegal aliens, **inflation,** unemployment, and a great many other policy concerns will make the lives of Americans better or worse and in many cases even longer or shorter. Of course, governmental policies do not have the same impact on all citizens. Indeed, much public policy is not intended to affect all citizens the same but to benefit some while burdening others. This unequal impact is what makes governmental policy the focus of political activity and what makes it so important to possess political influence in the policy process.

In earlier chapters, we looked at many of the principal players in the policy-making process. Here we consider how policy is made, and illustrate the types of policy government undertakes by discussing several areas of domestic policy, especially the policies involved in the politically crucial process of managing the economy.

The Policy Process

One useful way to examine how public policy is made and carried out is to break the process into its principal steps. Political scientists have identified five general, somewhat overlapping steps or stages in the policy-making process, beginning with agenda-setting and continuing through policy formulation, adoption, implementation, and ultimately to evaluation. By briefly examining each of these stages of the process, we should be able to clarify not only how public policy is made and carried out but also who is involved and what they are doing to affect policy outcomes.

Agenda-setting

Each of us as individuals have agendas for our personal lives—a list of things we are going to do or accomplish. Similarly, the **policy agenda** is the list of issues that the government will consider and on which it will make policy. We are seldom able to completely control our own personal agendas because others—friends, parents, professors, and so on—make demands on our time and help determine our agendas for us. In a like manner, the public policy agenda is affected by the demands of the public, organized interests, parties, and the outcomes of elections. Indeed, it is possible to think of politics generally as the effort to determine the agenda of the policy-making process. The government cannot act on all matters at once, so the most basic decision in politics is what to make policy about. Owing to the constraints of time and energy, most matters will receive no attention at all. Thus the first and most basic political objective to be gained is getting an issue on the agenda.

Political scientist E.E. Schattschneider stated the importance of the agenda-setting process most succinctly: "He who decides what politics is about runs the country." [1] Of course no one person, group, or institution determines what the entire policy agenda will be and thus "runs the country," but this statement emphasizes the often overlooked fact that setting the policy agenda ultimately determines the outcome of the policy process. It is important therefore to understand the forces that act to shape the policy agenda and thus set the parameters within which political debate and public policy making will occur.

Perhaps the most basic force that shapes the policy agenda is public opinion. What people consider legitimate for governmental action ultimately sets the boundaries of governmental policy making. Public opinion concerning the proper scope of government is most fundamentally determined by the set of shared political values on which the political community is based. Whether the people generally perceive any particular event or condition to be a public problem subject to governmental action for remedy depends on these values. In the United States, the value of economic individualism historically led people to perceive poverty as the result of individual failure rather than of social forces beyond the control of the individual, delaying the acceptance of government programs to combat poverty. The sanctity of private property and private enterprise among American political values continues to limit the policy agenda, preventing the consideration of comprehensive public solutions to many national problems. For example, the United States remains the only advanced industrial nation to lack a national health program, and the question of constructing a comprehensive system of public health care, often castigated as "socialized medicine," has never reached the policy agenda.

Our thinking is so shaped by our deeply held beliefs and values that it limits the range of events and conditions we perceive to be problems and also limits the range of policy alternatives we think of to those that fit our beliefs and values. The issues and alternatives that are not considered—political scientists often call them **nondecisions**—may be as numerous and important as those alternatives actually considered during policy making. Indeed, by definition they will be among the more far-reaching and system-altering alternatives; their absence from the policy agenda suggests that the impact of values is to generally bias the policy process toward the maintenance of the status quo.

Obviously, however, change in what is perceived to be the proper scope of governmental activity has occurred over the years. Such changes are usually due to changes in objective conditions in society or to the endeavors of political actors or to both.

New issues arise out of slow changes in the conditions of society and push their way onto the policy agenda. The demographic shift from a basically rural to a basically urban population, for example, presented a host of new policy questions and new needs for government regulation of more crowded and complex living conditions. Technological changes also have produced new policy issues. The development of air travel has been the basis for issues concerning access, safety, and noise, and new

HOMELESSNESS: A RISING ISSUE IN SEARCH OF THE POLICY AGENDA

It shows all the signs of a developing new condition that is slowly pushing its way into the nation's consciousness and as a result onto the policy agenda. First, new terms creep into common usage—"street people," "bag lady," "homeless." The new terms are necessary to describe the changes in the character of poverty in urban America. Of course, there have always been homeless, but rarely in such numbers, and perhaps never as visible. The nature of poverty is changing—it is increasingly an urban phenomenon—and the meaning of poverty is changing—it increasingly means homelessness, and that means being on the streets. Next, private interests become concerned and begin to organize to do something about the issue. Groups have established shelters and "warming centers" to provide relief. But homeless advocate groups know that without government help and funding, they cannot hope to deal with the rapidly expanding numbers. As a result, they begin to press their case through political participation. Third, the media sees a powerful human interest story in the homeless, and through news coverage and such programs as the dramatization of the life of a "bag lady" by Lucille Ball, the awareness of the nation is expanded with the mass emotional impact only TV can produce.

An issue has been born, but thus far the response by government has been minimal. Several state governments have begun to respond, however. In Massachusetts, the money allocated for shelters has gone from $500,000 in 1982 to $6,000,000 in 1985. Spending is also up in New York, in large part as a result of activist groups using litigation to press their cause. Overall, however, the response has been totally inadequate to deal with the worsening situation. Community groups report that homelessness is worse than at any time since the Great Depression, involving approximately two million people nationwide. Moreover, homelessness is affecting more families. As a result, the makeup of the homeless is changing, including more women and children among their ranks. According to one recent government study, 22 percent of the homeless are children. With such a large percentage being blameless children, perhaps the problem of homelessness will receive the attention it deserves.

Homeless in America—an increasingly common sight

developments in genetic engineering have already raised difficult new issues for government.

Sudden events or crises also cause changes in the policy agenda—natural catastrophes such as floods, severe storms, or outbreaks of disease or crises stemming from human activity such as a mine disaster or the near meltdown of a nuclear reactor. Really major crises, such as an economic depression or a foreign war, push virtually all other matters off the agenda and can deeply affect the value structure underlying the policy process. Understandably, then, many of the changes that shape American politics today stem from the 1930s and 1940s, decades in which the nation experienced both economic depression and a major foreign war. The Depression altered basic economic values enough to allow for a dramatic expansion of the scope of government. The Depression visited unemployment and economic need on so many that it was rationally impossible to assign responsibility for poverty to individual failure. Redefined as "misfortune," government action to aid the needy in society became acceptable, and social assistance programs have had a secure place on the policy agenda ever since.

Changes in conditions and crisis events provide the basis for putting issues on the policy agenda,

but they are not sufficient in themselves. Ultimately, people—political actors concerned about the underlying conditions or events—put issues on the agenda. Often a social condition can exist for many years without appearing on the policy agenda because no political actor has "made an issue of it." Public officials may adopt an issue in an effort to make their political reputation and link their public identity with a rising popular cause. Democrat Edward Kennedy has long championed and, for better or worse, has become associated with the cause of national health insurance, for example, whereas Republican Jack Kemp was out front in the cause of massive tax cuts to stimulate the economy. The president is in an unequaled position to affect the policy agenda. Since his every utterance receives nationwide attention, if he chooses to make an issue of something, he usually can. Nongovernmental actors such as interest groups are also important in bringing issues to the policy agenda.

The importance of political actors to the agenda-setting process suggests another subtle bias built into the policy process: Issues of concern to higher socioeconomic groups are more likely to reach the policy agenda. These people are more likely than people of lower socioeconomic status to be politically active, members of interest groups, understand the political system, and have the time and access to information necessary to manuever an issue onto the policy agenda. Moreover, policy makers are more inclined to consider issues raised by the higher-status citizens because they tend to have high-status backgrounds themselves and share the concerns and views of this sector of the population.

Policy Formulation

The formulation of policy simply means developing concrete policy proposals for dealing with problems on the policy agenda. Once the problem of energy shortages reaches the policy agenda, for example, it is necessary to address how energy availability will be improved. Should we increase production, reduce consumption, or both? Exactly how should we go about reducing consumption or increasing production? In answering such questions, policy is being formulated.

As we have seen, the president has become the chief legislator in the national government, and as such is the source or initiator of most national poli-

The presidency's command of media attention assures substantial power to set the political agenda.

cy. Central to the presidential role as a formulator of policy is the Office of Management and Budget (OMB). The OMB coordinates the budgetary requests of the agencies of the federal bureaucracy, issues guidelines for the development of such requests, and clears the federal budget before it is submitted to Congress. Since no president can be deeply involved in the many budgetary decisions, the OMB enjoys considerable autonomy, not only in formulating the budget, but also in formulating policy.

The Congress also contributes to the policy formulation process, much of which is conducted by the extensive staff of congressional committees. The Congress has greatly expanded its staff in recent years, giving it a source of information and policy alternatives beyond those flowing to it from the president through the OMB. A very important addition has been the Congressional Budget Office (CBO), the congressional equivalent of the OMB, and its parent committees, the House and Senate Budget Committees. The CBO, budget committees, and their staffs formulate a budget alternative to the president's.

Formulation is a very political process because decisions about how something is to be done will determine how the benefits and burdens of the policy are distributed. Therefore, the political actors involved in the agenda-setting process are also concerned in the formulation stage. It is at this stage in the policy process that much of the bargaining and compromise that plays such a central role in the American political scheme takes place. The iron triangles discussed in Chapter 8 greatly facilitate the process by bringing interest groups, congressional subcommittees, and executive agencies together into informal policy subsystems in which much policy formulation is accomplished.

BOOKS AND THE POLICY AGENDA

Normally, no single factor is wholly responsible for placing a new issue on the policy agenda. The time has to be ripe, and there must be a bold political entrepreneur willing to stake (or make) a political reputation on the issue. On several occasions in the twentieth century, books have played an extremely important role in making the time ripe and helping to dramatize an emerging issue. Four famous examples of such books are the following:

The Jungle, by Upton Sinclair, which, though focused largely on the plight of the immigrant in America, brought attention to the unsanitary conditions in meat-packing plants at the turn of the century. President Theodore Roosevelt among others was greatly impressed by the few pages devoted to a description of these conditions, which helped furnish the impetus for the Meat Inspection Act of 1906.

The Other America, by Michael Harrington, a best-selling book in the early 1960s, graphically described the grim circumstances of the American poor. Among those who read the book was President Kennedy, who decided to make the War on Poverty a central part of his administration and his planned run for reelection in 1964. A dog-eared copy of the book was one of Kennedy's posses-

sions found in the Oval Office after his assassination in 1963.

Unsafe at Any Speed, by consumer advocate Ralph Nader, strongly criticized the safety of certain American cars, especially GM's rear-engine Chevrolet Corvair, and helped to create the circumstances leading to the National Traffic and Motor Vehicle Safety Act of 1966. Nader's cause was greatly aided by a scandal that developed when it was revealed that GM had hired a private detective to try and collect gossip about Nader to discredit him and thus his book. Nader proved unimpeachable, however, and the book and GM's heavy-handed reaction to it made Nader's reputation. The Corvair was taken from the market, and Nader has become a major fixture in American politics.

Wealth and Poverty, by George Gilder, may be the most recent book of great significance. In it, Gilder lays out an explanation of poverty and its origins that is profoundly different from that on which the social legislation of the past two decades has been based. Described as the "supply-side Bible," the book has been an important influence on the thinking of many leading conservatives including members of the Reagan administration, helping to guide the current rightward movement in American public policy.

Policy formulation occurring within such subsystems can be criticized on a number of grounds. First, this highly decentralized process can result in uncoordinated and even inconsistent policy. Because the subgovernments have different political actors, policy formulation in different subsystems occurs in isolation. In effect, the government's right hand may not know what its left hand is doing. Iron triangles formulate policy that responds to separate and conflicting interests at the same time. This is to the political advantage of both officeholders and interest groups, but may produce inefficient and ineffective policy when taken as a whole.

Second, this sort of policy process may give too much power to well-organized and well-connected interest groups. When policy is formulated in rela-

tive isolation, with the main actors all having a vested interest in the policy, the public interest is likely to be overlooked or simply sacrificed to the interests of the members of the iron triangle and the bargaining and compromise process is largely or completely short circuited. For example, an iron triangle composed of (1) a subcommittee made up of Members of Congress from districts or states that serve as sites for military installations and/or defense industry plants, (2) interest groups made up of the armed forces and defense contractors, and (3) agencies of the Department of Defense, is unlikely to have deep disagreements over the need for increased defense spending. Similarly, another triangle involving (1) a subcommittee on the aged, (2) senior citizens' organizations like the Gray Panthers or the American Association of Retired Persons, and (3) the Social Security Administration is likely to formulate policies that tend to enhance Social Security benefits.

These examples illustrate a third problem. In such a highly decentralized policy process dominated by influential private interests, the government has neither the willingness nor the need to say no to anyone. It can, for example, say yes both to those wanting more for defense and to those wanting more for Social Security. The growth in the national government's budget deficit, according to this argument, is the result of the government's saying yes to demands for the reduction in taxes, and yes to the demands for retention of programs.

Policy Adoption

When an issue has reached the policy agenda and when specific policy responses have been formulated, policy must then be formally adopted or become law. This third stage of the policy process is what normally comes to mind when we speak of making policy—the image of government officials voting on legislative bills and the executive signing into law acts of the legislature. Many political actors seek to influence the outcome of these formal votes, but the actual decisions must be made by public officials.

The adoption process is the formal point of decision. Adoption or rejection of a policy alternative

WARNING: POLITICAL SCIENTISTS HAVE DETERMINED THAT TRYING TO MAKE SENSE OF NATIONAL PUBLIC POLICY MAY BE DANGEROUS TO YOUR MENTAL HEALTH

What is the national policy on the production, sale, and use of tobacco? The answer is that there is no one policy, but instead a set of inconsistent policies. Policy concerning tobacco is probably the clearest and most often cited example of inconsistent policy. One set of policies is produced by a network of policy subsystems made up of groups like the Tobacco Institute, the Retail Tobacco Distributors of America, and the tobacco growers; various agencies of the Department of Agriculture that administer tobacco programs; and the House and Senate Tobacco Subcommittees, whose members are drawn largely from tobacco-growing states. All these actors have a common interest in maximizing tobacco sales and the profits of the industry. As a result, the policy produced by this network of policy subsystems involves laws and appropriations dealing with tobacco subsidies—in effect, paying farmers to grow the commodity that is used almost solely for smoking.

A second, unrelated network of policy subsystems is made up of groups like the American Heart Association, the American Lung Association, and a variety of consumer protection groups; federal bureaucratic agencies like the Federal Trade Commission (FTC), Federal Communications Commission (FCC), and parts of the Department of Health and Human Services (HHS); and congres-

sional committees like the Senate Labor and Human Resources Committee. This network produces policies designed to discourage the use of tobacco, such as prohibiting the advertisement of cigarettes on radio and television, the production of public service messages warning of the dangers of its use, and requiring that an ominous warning be prominently displayed on cigarette packaging and printed advertisements.

Moreover, the warning has become more severe since first instituted in 1966, even while tobacco subsidies have been maintained and enlarged. Indeed, to the extent that the antitobacco policy is successful in discouraging consumption, more subsidies will be necessary to support the price of tobacco and maintain the profitability of the industry. Both policies can be justified as doing good for the political community, of course. One seeks to help protect the health of the population; the other seeks to secure the livelihood of whole regions of the nation dependent on the production of tobacco. They do not, however, constitute an internally consistent and rational body of public policy. Similar contradictions exist in many other policy areas. Our policy process appears to be designed to be responsive to contradictory demands, rather than to make sense as a consistent whole.

is certainly the result of political bargaining, compromise, and coalition building among a wide variety of governmental and nongovernmental political actors. But the adoption process brings an end to the political manuevering and forces officials to make a policy choice. Policy adoption specifies the output of the policy process and reveals the makeup of the political coalitions supporting and opposing policy alternatives. It is the point in the process where "push comes to shove." It is the point where debate turns to judgment.

However, government policy adoption does not only involve the decision to do something but also may involve government inaction or the decision to do nothing. Sometimes this means a formal vote to reject policy alternatives, but it can also mean simply never taking a vote at all on an issue on the policy agenda. This is a common fate of policy alternatives in the legislative process. The politics of the adoption stage of the policy process usually includes the efforts by political actors to either force a vote or avoid a vote on a policy proposal. If a vote can be delayed or avoided, a policy can effectively be killed.

Owing to the rules and procedures of the legislative process, at any of several steps it requires only a small minority of the whole to, in effect, veto policy initiatives. A simple majority of a congressional subcommittee, for example, perhaps as few as five or six, can block the progress of a bill toward the formal adoption vote of the whole house. The same is true at the full committee level; though requiring far more individual members for blockage, it is still a small minority of the whole. Of course, the president can also veto policy proposals as a minority of one in the adoption process. Just one-third plus one of the members of Congress are needed to sustain the president's veto. Thus, while unlikely to be able to get legislation of its own passed, a small minority can stop adoption of legislation it opposes if it concentrates its effort at critical stages of the process.

This characteristic of the policy process also tends to bias the process toward maintenance of the status quo, for it is comparatively easy for those supporting present policy, even if they are in the minority, to prevent change. A good example is the blockage by southern senators of civil rights legislation in the late 1940s through the early 1960s. A handful of southern conservative senators used the **filibuster** to block votes on civil rights legislation that was supported by majorities in the Senate as a whole and by the president. Because the rules of the Senate allow unlimited debate, these members simply talked and talked—filibustered—until the Senate agreed to move on to other business to get something done.

The American policy process is often criticized as designed more to prevent than to produce policy decisions. Political observers have expressed concern that with so many veto points, the system may become paralyzed, unable to adopt policies necessary to respond to the pressing problems of the day. The inability of the government to respond to the energy crisis in a consistent and coherent manner, despite the formulation of adequate policy programs, is an example. Again, the concern is with the power of minority interests to thwart the interests of the majority, or the public interest as a whole. On the other hand, it might be argued that the decentralized policy process is a vital aspect of the protection of minority interests and thus important for the maintenance of a responsive and democratic policy process.

Policy Implementation

Policy implementation means to put the policies adopted by governmental institutions into practice. Most policy that is adopted by government is not self-executing, but must be administered or enforced. Many policies actually consist of nothing more than general instructions to administrators. The details of implementation are often left to the experts in the implementation process, largely members of bureaucratic agencies, and thus implementation normally involves making policy about how general policy objectives will be accomplished. Since the actual impact of a policy—what it means in practice to the individual citizen—depends on how it is put into effect, this aspect of the policy process is very important. Of course, nothing so important is likely to be free of political struggle.

The first decision that must be made in implementating a policy is what organizational structure will be used to accomplish it. How a policy is implemented will depend on who does the implementing. A program might be placed in an old agency that is only marginally interested or even hostile to the new responsibilities the policy entails.

One way to fight a filibuster is to keep the Senate in session in order to wear down those filibustering. Here Senators prepare to sleep in the chambers in order to keep in session 24 hours a day. A strange spectacle for what some have termed the world's greatest deliberative body.

It can be placed in a new agency within an existing department, subject to the support or opposition of the larger entity of which it is a part. Or an entirely new and separate structure can be created for a new policy in an attempt to ensure its maximum effectiveness. Supporters and opponents of the policy will struggle over the apparatus of administration, knowing that even though formally adopted, the impact of the policy will be determined by the nature of its administration.

The administrative agency must then translate policy goals into concrete and specific rules, regulations, and behavioral guidelines. This process is subject to the political influence of a wide array of interested actors. As we have discussed earlier, agencies may tailor implementation rules and regulations to reflect the desires of powerful interest groups in exchange for support of the group with the legislature at budget approval time. Clearly, as one political scientist has written, policy implemen-

tation is really "a continuation of policy making by other means."[2]

Policy is made not only at the upper levels of bureaucracy in implementing rules and regulations but also at the "street level" where policy meets the public. The impact of policy on individual citizens depends ultimately on how street-level bureaucrats carry out these rules and regulations. A classic example is the police officer on the street. In an individual case, the law as applied means what the officer decides it means. For example, to Congress, the fifty-five mile-per-hour speed limit means people should be driving no more than fifty-five or be subject to the costs. The administrators of the policy, the state police in any individual state, may make the rule of implementation to arrest violators traveling at above sixty miles per hour. In effect the fifty-five mile-per-hour speed limit has been changed by administrative practice to a sixty-mile-per-hour speed limit.

State police are "street-level bureaucrats" implementing public policy.

Policy Evaluation

The distance between policy adoption and its implementation on the street is one reason that policies need evaluation. The purpose of evaluation is to determine whether the policy is being implemented as intended and, if so, if it is having the intended effect. Evaluation provides some feedback for the policy makers, so they can adjust the policy or its implementation to better produce intended effects or better avoid any undesirable unintended effects.

The principal policy-making institutions of government undertake a great deal of policy evaluation themselves, but they also get a lot of informal help from nongovernmental political actors. As we saw in our earlier discussion of Congress, the various congressional subcommittees are responsible for exercising oversight of the policy implementation process, monitoring the way their policies are implemented and the impact of the policies in society. Often legislation is passed with evaluation mechanisms written into the enabling act itself, requiring the collection of information that will allow Congress to evaluate results and effects of the policy. For example, the Equal Opportunity Act requires employment studies, so the impact of the act on the employment patterns of minorities and women can be assessed.

Policy would be evaluated by other interested participants in the political process even if Congress made no formal effort of its own, however. Policy and its impact on society is news, and the media play an important role in evaluation by monitoring and reporting the effects of government activity. Policy evaluation is thus as close as the morning newspaper on the doorstep and as common as the nightly television newscast. Interest groups are another source of policy evaluation. They are rarely a completely unbiased or objective source, but they can be relied on to point out problems caused by policy when they are affected in a disadvantageous manner. Attitude surveys of the public at large also serve as important sources of feedback on the impact and popularity of specific governmental policies. Policy makers interested in reelection are responsible for taking many of these polls, and they pay great attention to them.

More objective and systematic evaluation is undertaken by outside academic researchers and by policy analysts within the governmental bureaucracy itself. These are efforts to carefully measure the extent to which policy goals are realized and to determine the sources of policy failure. Evaluation may reveal that policy goals are not being realized owing to resistance by the agency or department charged with administering the policy. Or faults in the policy itself may be revealed—the policy may be too vague and subject to administrative misinterpretation, or perhaps the goals are actually undesirable and should be fundamentally altered. Policies nearly always result in unanticipated side effects, often in the form of human behavioral reactions that could not have been foreseen and which in some cases may be quite counterproductive. Policy can be adjusted to remove the incentive for this behavior.

Evaluation of the impact of policy in society can help to uncover new problems that may themselves

UNINTENDED CONSEQUENCES:
SOMETIMES FRIGHTFUL, SOMETIMES FREAKY

Public policy nearly always has consequences that are unforeseen at the time of adoption. Sometimes well-intentioned policies have unfortunate side effects that create serious new problems for society. In many other instances, human social behavior is altered in curious, but not damaging, ways. The rising problem of the homeless is an example of the occasionally frightful consequences of public policy, whereas the people of San Francisco provide us with a more "freaky" consequence of public policy.

Why is homelessness becoming such a serious problem? It seems odd that there are so many homeless now that the economy is performing fairly well. Although public policy is not entirely to blame, it has played an important role. First, the federal government has for a number of years supported the "deinstitutionalization" of patients from state mental hospitals. Institutionalization, it was argued, was cruel and impersonal. Many believed that it would be better for mental patients to be out in normal society. Besides, it was cheaper than providing adequate maintenance for such institutions. Unfortunately, normal society has often proven to be a cruel and impersonal place for these people too, and a place that fails to provide what even the poorest institutions did—shelter. About 20 percent of the homeless have once been in a state mental institution. Government policy bears at least partial responsibility for what has happened to them since.

A second policy-related cause is that federal money used over the years for urban renewal has resulted in the destruction of much of the low-cost, single-room-occupancy hotels the poor traditionally used for shelter. The rapid disappearance of this unlovely housing—approximately a million such units were destroyed between 1970 and 1980—and its replacement with more beautiful, higher-priced housing in downtown areas is another major cause of homelessness.

In a less serious vein, San Franciscans have responded to the rules of the road in a way that might never have happened in less "laid-back" New York or Washington, D.C. To encourage conservation and produce some traffic relief through car pooling, San Francisco permits cars with three or more passengers to take two fast lanes and bypass the $.75 toll on the Bay Bridge. In response, people line up at bus stops in suburban San Francisco and wait for cars to offer a ride downtown. By picking up two or more people, the driver saves time and money and the riders get where they are going. This special kind of commuting has been dubbed "the kindness of strangers," for each day riders are matched with new and unknown drivers. Some concerns have been voiced about personal safety with this system of casual carpooling, but the only serious consequence so far has been an estimated $1 million lost to the Bay Area transit system.

be placed on the policy agenda. Therefore, the policy process is to some extent cyclical, the final step or stage in the process—policy evaluation—functioning to supply information that helps to shape the first step in the process—setting the agenda. In this way, we can see the policy process as partially self-generating and thus perpetual.

Politics and the Types of Public Policy

Categorizing public policies into types is simply a means of organizing our thinking about policy—a way to get a handle on a complex and diverse sub-

ject. There are many ways of categorizing public policy, all of which provide important insights. Our discussion of types of policy and the politics that attend them is based on a typology that divides policies into categories according to the fundamental purpose of the policy. In this scheme, policies are either distributive, redistributive, or regulatory in character. We discuss each type in the following pages and look at a common example in American domestic politics.[3]

Distributive Policy

Distributive policies are government actions that distribute services or benefits to any number of individuals, groups, corporations, or communities. Some distributive policies give benefits to only one or a very few recipients, such as the loan guarantees for Chrysler in the late 1970s. But a distributive policy can also benefit a vast number of people, as the tax deductions for home mortgage payments and the provision of free public education. Other common examples of distributive policies include agricultural price support programs and the funding for construction projects of all types by the Army Corps of Engineers.

Although the benefits may be either relatively concentrated or dispersed, the costs of distributive policy are always widely shared. Because of this, the per capita payment for any one distributive policy is very small. The people who pay will be unaware of the costs of any particular distributive program or indifferent to them, because the personal impact is so slight. This greatly reduces the likelihood of organized resistance to a policy or program. Distributive policies appear to create only winners and no specific loser, though the costs of such programs result in higher general rates of taxation. For example, agricultural price supports most greatly benefit farmers, yet the cost is paid by all consumers in the form of higher taxes and higher food prices. Each individual consumer shoulders only a tiny fraction of the cost of these subsidies, however, and most are unaware of the effect on their food prices and taxes. Thus agricultural subsidies are not highly controversial and draw little organized effort to reduce or stop them. Farm groups that support such policies *are* highly organized, however, ensuring their continuation.

The best example of distributive policy, however, involves not economic interests, but communities. Almost every year, Congress passes a rivers and harbors bill that contains a large serving of what are commonly called pork barrel projects. These are construction projects, carried out by the Army Corps of Engineers, that may provide a city or local region with a new dam or a better harbor. Each locality, with the aid of its member of Congress, seeks authorization and funding for its own project without opposing the efforts of others to seek similar projects. Members of Congress from each affected area support the claims of others in return for support for the projects in their own district, a process known as **logrolling**. The result is that most such projects have many supporters and

COSTS AND CONSEQUENCES OF A DISTRIBUTIVE POLICY

Below are excerpts from an article by commentator Donald Lambro on the problems of our extensive system of farm subsidy programs. These programs are designed to ensure abundance by assuring the profitability of producing various food commodities. If priced entirely according to the free market's rules of supply and demand, these farm products would have to be in short supply to command a profitable price. The problem with farm subsidy programs is that they may produce abundance too effectively:

It is the cruelest paradox of our time: While starving human beings have become almost daily images on our television screens, U.S. warehouses and silos bulge with enough surplus food to feed most of the world's hungry people ... We produce too much food—so much, in fact, that the government buys up what can't be sold in national or world markets to prevent commodity prices from falling.

We sell or give a lot of it away through foreign-aid programs—but millions of tons of our farm productivity is simply stored away indefinitely in cavernous facilities ...

To give you an idea of how enormous this surplus is, consider these statistics:

■ In a nation of more than 240 million Americans, Uncle Sam has enough nonfat dry milk in storage to provide 23.7 quarts of milk for every man, woman and child in the United States.

■ We have enough butter in warehouses to provide every American with more than a pound of it.

■ We have enough cheese to give almost three pounds of it to everyone in our country.

Taxpayers pay for this dairy price-support program in multiple ways. First, they pay to purchase these and other surplus commodities ... By 1982, the program cost $2.6 billion ...

Second, taxpayers must pay to warehouse this stuff. Yearly storage costs: $32.8 million.

And, finally, consumers are forced to pay more for butter, milk and cheese products than they would under a free market, because of artificially inflated dairy prices propped up by the government's purchases. Needless to say, poor and low-income people are hurt most by such policies.

Army Corps of Engineer water projects are a classic example of distributive policy.

no opponents in Congress. Billions of tax dollars are distributed for hundreds of such projects across the country through the rivers and harbors legislation, yet, because the costs of pork barrel are widely dispersed and because the system materially benefits many communities and politically benefits the members of Congress representing these communities, it is seldom questioned or challenged.

Redistributive Policy

As the name suggests, **redistributive policies** are those through which government attempts to alter the relative allocation of wealth, income, or rights among broad classes or groups in society. Unlike distributive policy, redistributive policy necessarily involves clearcut winners and losers, and both potential winners and losers will be aware of the costs and benefits at stake. What is to be redistributed is normally money or power and status (often in the form of rights). Holders of wealth and power rarely share them willingly, and because money and power are useful in influencing the policy process, holders have the means to resist redistributive efforts. As a result, redistributive policy is politically controversial and furnishes incentives for those likely to benefit and those likely to bear the costs of redistribution to organize and participate. Redistributive policy has produced the sharpest political confrontations between ideological liberals (pro) and ideological conservatives (con) in American politics.

Owing to the formidable political forces arrayed against them, redistributive policies are difficult to

attain and perhaps even more difficult to retain. Important examples of redistributive policy include the Johnson administration's "War on Poverty," Medicare, the Voting Rights Act of 1965, and the graduated income tax. By 1986, the redistributive impact of the income tax had been greatly reduced by the attachment over time of a variety of credits, exemptions, exclusions, deductions, and other loopholes that tended to benefit high-income earners. As a result, the income tax had become only mildly redistributive if at all. Widespread dissatisfaction with the loophole-riddled system led to reform in 1986. The new structure will have just three graduated tax rates for individuals—15, 25 and 33 percent—when it is fully in effect in 1988. It should be somewhat more redistributive due to fewer loopholes for those in the upper income brackets. Johnson's War on Poverty programs, since 1968 lacking the presidential support and leadership that were so vital to their passage, have been gradually dismantled. More durable in the face of the resistance of wealth and power has been the Voting Rights Act of 1965, which redistributed rights rather than wealth. Specifically, it reduced the rights of the white political power structure to keep blacks from participating in politics and gave blacks the equal right to vote.

Despite resistance, a number of redistributive "welfare" policies are operating today. Some programs, though highly controversial when first instituted, have become well established and accepted. The first and best example of such a program is Social Security, which is so popular that as President Reagan discovered, a politician who talks loosely of tampering with it does so at great peril. Social Security has been successful because it benefits a broad proportion of the population, and everyone has a long-term stake in the system. Unemployment insurance has also become a well-established and accepted program. Under most circumstances, its costs are relatively low, and being unemployed is no longer widely regarded as the individual's personal failure.

Other redistributive policies are highly controversial, however. One such policy is Aid to Families with Dependent Children (AFDC). Though the program dates from the original Social Security Act in 1935, it has not become well accepted. The program is designed to give assistance to dependent children under eighteen who are living with only

This woman lives with her husband and 11 children in a two-room shack. They are among the many who suffer from poverty and hunger in the United States.

one parent or relative. When first adopted, the popular image of the average recipient was a white woman with children living in a small town, who had lost her husband in World War I or in an industrial or mining accident. Further, there were relatively few of them. Today, this image has changed to a black woman living in a large city, who is either an unwed mother or whose husband has left her. Moreover, the number of recipients has greatly increased in recent years. As a result, the public has increasingly perceived the program as having significant costs and a rather narrow and often undeserving clientele. The image does not necessarily conform to reality, but in politics, perceptions are often more important than reality.

Another highly controversial program is the food stamp program. Designed to assist the poorest in society to obtain food, the program helps almost 10 percent of all Americans. It is unpopular with conservatives because it is a "giveaway" program, and occasional scandals have resulted in criticism of its administration by both liberals and conservatives. The Reagan Administration has restricted eligibility, reducing the cost of the program to some extent.

Welfare programs like the AFDC or food stamp program are clearly perceived as redistributing significant sums from one group to another easily distinguishable group. The middle class is especially resentful of welfare programs, believing that it bears too much of the tax burden for the costs of such redistribution. Given the political weakness of recipient groups, it may seem surprising that such programs have survived at all. However, many redistributive policies also have a significant distributive component in the form of salaries to the middle-class administrative employees of the programs. Also, the distributive component of programs such as subsidized housing for the poor, generates income for the construction and banking industries. Such distributive benefits can be powerful sources of political promotion and defense of redistributive programs.

Regulatory Policy

Regulatory policies are designed to impose restrictions or limitations on the behavior of individuals and groups. They reduce the freedom to act of those they regulate, often defining specific forms of behavior as "criminal." The most extensive, though hardly the most controversial, variety of regulatory policies define criminal behavior against persons and property. More controversial are business regulatory policies such as those pertaining to pollution control or employee health and safety. Regulation may take the form of general rules of behavior or may extend to detailed control of the business, including entry into the business, standards of service, financial and accounting practices, and rates of charge.

Consumer protection legislation provides good examples of other forms of regulation. Such regulation often sets standards of quality or safety that must be met before products can reach the marketplace. New drugs and children's toys fall under this type of regulatory legislation. Another variety of consumer legislation requires businesses to give the consumer adequate information to make an informed decision, such as the regulations designed to

Environmental clean-up efforts are visible evidence of regulatory policies.

receives a grant of public authority for use in pursuing its private interest.

The independent regulatory commissions such as the Federal Communications Commission (FCC), the Securities and Exchange Commission (SEC), the Nuclear Regulatory Commission (NRC), and the like have especially been criticized for this kind of relationship. These regulatory commissions are often made up of experts drawn from the industries they are to regulate and intending to return to them. Indeed, a stint of government service is perceived to be a positive career move in some industries. The executive returns to private industry with valuable Washington contacts and wiser in the ways of the politics of regulation.

The existence of iron triangles also takes much of the sting out of government regulation. The influence of politically well-organized industries can be used to avoid much regulation that the industry might feel to be obnoxious and to soften the enforcement of that which is passed into law. Here too, members of congressional committee staffs and executive agencies commonly leave their jobs as regulators to accept positions in the industries they had been regulating.

Thus the regulatory atmosphere between government and the businesses regulated is often not as "adversarial" as one might assume. What the growth of government regulatory activity indicates, however, is the increasing involvement of the government in the economy and in the process of economic management. We turn now to the policies and problems of the national government in managing the economy.

protect the consumer from deceptive advertising practices or the Consumer Credit Protection Act, which requires creditors to provide borrowers with accurate information on the cost of financing credit purchases.

The formation of regulatory policy is usually accompanied by considerable political conflict among groups, one of which is normally seeking to impose governmental regulation on the other. The apparent outcome of the conflict is that someone wins and someone loses. But even where regulatory legislation is passed and enforcement apparatus is set up, the ultimate outcome of the regulatory process may leave it unclear who is really the winner and who is the loser. The regulated industry often comes to have such great influence with the regulating agency that the agency may be "captured," regulating in the interest of the regulated industry rather than in the interest of the public. In such a case, some argue, the regulated industry in effect

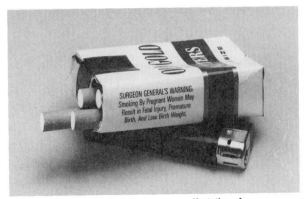

This prominent warning is one common manifestation of governmental regulatory policy.

Public Policy and the Management of the Economy

No policy area is of greater importance to the average American than the government's management of the economy. Yet few activities of government are more generally misunderstood. Government efforts to manage the economy are many and varied. In the following discussion we will try to shed some light on this complex and controversial policy area.

Of Politics and Economics

Americans often fail to appreciate the fundamental linkage between politics and economics, owing partly to the value we place on economic individualism and our attachment to the image of the free and self-regulating marketplace. That economics is what politics is mostly about, however, has long been a widely accepted notion among political thinkers of all types. Political theorists as different as James Madison, a principal author of the U.S. Constitution, and Karl Marx, the principal founding theorist of communism, base their arguments on the common view that economic conflict is the root cause of political conflict.

Evidence of the close connection between the economy and politics is everywhere in modern American government. As we discussed earlier, the federal executive bureaucracy is dominated by agencies and independent commissions implementing government economic regulatory policies. Their names indicate their economic function. A partial listing includes the Department of Labor, the Department of Commerce, the Treasury Department, the Department of Agriculture, the Department of Transportation, the Federal Trade Commission (FTC), the Securities and Exchange Commission (SEC), the Interstate Commerce Commission (ICC), the Commodity Futures Trading Commission (CFTC), Consumer Product Safety Commission (CPSC), and the National Labor Relations Board (NLRB).

The committee structure of the Congress that created many of these agencies reveals a similar attention to economic concerns. The standing committees in the House include Agriculture; Banking, Finance, and Urban Affairs; Education and Labor; Energy and Commerce; Merchant Marine and Fisheries; and Small Business. The committees in the Senate are also largely structured around economic concerns. The Budget Committee in each house, for example, helps formulate and move the federal budget toward adoption. This economic document is the single most important product of the policy system each year. The budget structures the policy debate throughout the term of Congress and is a key indicator of significant policy choices. Also, because budget-making involves decisions about total government spending, taxing, and borrowing, it is a key indicator and important element of government economic management.

Economic conditions also have important implications for the outcome of elections. Since the Great Depression first shook our unquestioned faith in the ability of the economy to regulate itself, we have both demanded more governmental regulation to stabilize the economy and increasingly held the government responsible for economic conditions. Though the government has become increasingly active in attempting to manage the economy, the general condition of the economy is not entirely or even mostly under the control of the federal government. It is often blamed (or given credit) for conditions that are largely beyond its control. Indeed, because the power to make economic policy is distributed among so many independent agencies, the national government has great difficulty planning and coordinating the economic policy power it does have. Nonetheless, when times are bad, we tend to punish the president and the candidates of the president's party.

Of course, the president and his party tend to claim the credit for the good times. Typically, they are rewarded with reelection and argue that this vote constitutes confirmation of (and a mandate for) their policies and the economic philosophies on which they are based. One indication of the increasing importance of economics in politics is the extent to which political debate deals with rival economic theories. Reference to these complex visions of how the economy works and to which public policy will maximize its health are common even in campaign rhetoric. Though not well understood by the public (or sometimes even by the politicians using them), these theories receive shorthand labels that the public can easily identify and that tend to become political rallying calls. The long debate between "monetarists" and "Keynesians" has recently been joined by calls for **"industrial policy"** and "supply-side economics," for example.

Monetarism is based on the belief that the nation's economic health is determined by the amount of money in circulation. Inflation occurs when too much money is in circulation, resulting in excess demand pulling up prices because of a relative lack of supply. Conversely, recession is primarily the result of too little money in circulation, which causes a relative lack of aggregate demand. Proper government economic management includes creating a steady and predictable growth in the money supply, at a rate approximately the same as the growth in productivity. According to the theory, this will promote growth in the economy and the creation of new jobs, without stimulating excessive demand and inflationary pressure on prices. Further, gently manipulating the aggregate supply of money is *all* the government should do. Subsequent decisions about the relative distribution of goods and services in the economy should be left entirely to the free market. Milton Friedman, one of the principal proponents of monetarism, argues that this maximization of the free market and minimization of the role of government is necessary to maintain political democracy.

Keynesianism, named for English economist John Maynard Keynes, advocates a much more active role for government in manipulating the level of aggregate demand in the economy. When demand is too little and the economy is stagnant or in recession, it is the task of government to stimulate demand. This should be done by pumping money into the economy through spending more than it takes in in taxes (deficit spending) and by creating public works programs and other public projects. Conversely, if aggregate demand is too great, Keynesianism calls for tax increases and reductions in government expenditures. What matters is the performance of the economy. Year-to-year budget balancing and the extent of the government's involvement in the economy are of secondary importance. A key distinction between monetarism and Keynesianism is the latter's advocacy of a positive role for government in the economy.

Currently prevalent supply-side economic theory shares with monetarism a faith in the ability of the free market to allocate resources and produce economic health. The theory argues, in essence, that people do not need to be encouraged to demand, but to produce, and thus focuses on the manipulation of supply rather than demand. In this way, it differs from both Keynesianism and monetarism. If people are encouraged to work, save, and invest in a free market, supply-siders argue, they will produce a greater supply relative to demand, lowering inflationary pressures and ensuring adequate demand (owing to relatively high income and low prices) to maintain healthy growth. The government policy needed to encourage harder work, more savings, and investment is sharply lower taxes. High taxes, especially progressive tax rates, discourage hard work because the more one makes, the more the government takes. Leaving the money in people's hands encourages increased productivity, removes the incentive to exploit tax loopholes and cheat on taxes, and increases the total wealth of the nation. Thus even though tax rates are lower, total national income will be higher, and so will be the total government revenues (Figure 12.1).[4]

This logic led Ronald Reagan to argue in his 1980 presidential campaign that he could cut taxes 30 percent, triple the defense budget, leave the social welfare "safety net" intact, and balance the

**Figure 12.1
The Laffer Curve**

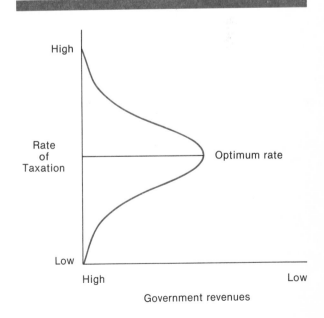

DAVID STOCKMAN (b. 1946):
A REVOLUTIONARY AS DIRECTOR OF
THE OFFICE OF MANAGEMENT AND BUDGET

In his book *The Triumph of Politics: Why the Reagan Revolution Failed,* David Stockman, Reagan's first director of the Office of Management and Budget (OMB), describes himself as a revolutionary who thought the times were ripe for ''drastic, wrenching changes'' in the established political process. Stockman actively sought the position as head of OMB, believing this agency was the key to altering the processes of government. He was quite correct in describing OMB as ''the needle's eye through which all policy must pass.'' From his position at OMB, he became the principle designer and advocate of an extensive plan to stem the flow of federal spending on social and welfare programs and reverse the direction of government policy established nearly fifty years earlier.

Stockman's revolutionary conservative agenda began to take shape at Harvard University where he was influenced by the thinking of political scientist J.Q. Wilson, sociologist Nathan Glazer, and especially Danial Patrick Moynihan, who was later elected senator from New York. In 1976, Stockman won election to the House of Representatives from Michigan. He quickly established himself as an opponent of big government and a supporter of business deregulation. Nearly al-

ways voting against funding for social programs, Stockman even opposed the federal ''bail-out'' for Chrysler Corporation, the only representative from auto-industry-dependent Michigan to take such a political risk. While a congressman, Stockman fell in with supply-side advocates such as economists Arthur Laffer and Jude Wanniski and Representative Jack Kemp of New York.

Having proven his conservative character and having been instructed in supply-side theory, he fit well into the Reagan camp in 1980. He also impressed Reagan himself when serving as a substitute for first John Anderson and later Jimmy Carter during Reagan's rehearsals for the televised debates. After the election and with the active backing of Kemp,

Stockman was selected to be director of OMB. He immediately began the task of reviewing every program in every agency in a search for ways to cut government spending. Suggested cuts included nutrition programs of the Agriculture Department, youth training programs of the Labor Department, the construction of VA hospitals, urban grant programs, and legal aid for the poor, to name but a few. Only Social Security and defense were to be spared the knife.

Stockman knew that the director of OMB would also be the political lightning rod for the administration, attracting the powerful bolts of opposition to such policies away from the president. Such a role is politically draining, and Stockman absorbed a lot of political electricity. However, he inflicted the greatest damage on himself. In an interview with *The Atlantic Monthly,* Stockman revealed his private doubts about his own budget calculations and the applicability of the supply-side notion of increased government revenues from lower rates of taxation. His credibility and influence suffered greatly from this indiscretion. Though he served at OMB for some time after, his ability to ''sell'' his revolution was severely impaired and his days in the administration clearly numbered.

budget all at the same time. A 25 percent "supply-side" tax cut was passed in 1981. Its failure to have the intended effect on the economy has been explained by supply-siders as due to continued excessive government spending and the need for still more drastic tax reductions.

By the mid-1980s, new economic conditions had begun to generate still another new economic viewpoint. Referred to as "industrial policy," it is a reaction to the declining health of many of the nation's basic industries in the face of stiff European and Japanese competition. In these countries, industries like steel and automobiles have benefited greatly from joint government-industry planning, investment, and trade strategies, and advocates of industrial policy argue that something similar is needed in the United States if we are to again compete successfully. Market forces alone will not enable American industry to recover. What is needed is government planning and coordination of investment and development, either to bring about the recovery of the old basic industries or to produce a smooth transition to new and better high-tech industries.

The public policy requirements and implications of each of these theories result in their being closely associated with differing political beliefs and philosophies. Conservatives are attracted to monetarism and supply-side economics because both call for a small role for government in economic management and a correspondingly large role for the free market. Liberals tend to be attracted to Keynesianism and the notion of industrial policy because they require government to play a positive role in ensuring economic equity, fairness, health, and stability, as well as softening the cruelest consequences of the operation of the free market.

The Legal Foundations of Government Economic Management

The Employment Act of 1946 placed the principal responsibility for the development of economic policy on the president. In taking such a step, Congress and the American people recognized that a laissez-faire, hands-off attitude toward the economy on the part of the federal government was no longer possible or desirable. In the minds of many people, the Great Depression had destroyed the myth of the efficiency of unregulated capitalism. Yet, as we have seen, the debate still rages over the proper role of the national government in the economic arena.

Recent *Economic Reports,* which are prepared by the Council of Economic Advisers as required by the Employment Act, have carried on this ideological debate. For example, the *Economic Report* for 1982 argues that "political freedom and economic freedom are closely related. ... No nation in which the government has the dominant economic role has maintained broad political freedom; economic conditions in such countries are generally inferior to those in comparable nations with a predominantly market economy."[5] This supply-side vision of how the economy works is disputed by Keynesians who point to the economic successes of the Scandinavian countries and Japan where government intervention in the economy is more pervasive than in the United States.

The *Economic Report,* which is sent to the Joint Economic Committee of Congress, outlines the president's proposals for the realization of the three goals of the Employment Act. First, the president is responsible for formulating economic policies that will ensure maximum employment. Traditionally, this has meant that the president should develop countercyclical economic policies if the unemployment rate rises above 4 to 6 percent. In the last decade, the precise point at which such policies should be adopted has crept upward as the unemployment rate has continued to rise. Jimmy Carter, a Democratic president, was pressured to advance policies that called for the government to be the employer of last resort; that is, if jobs are not being created in the private sector fast enough to keep the unemployment rate below a given percentage rate, then the government should create public employment jobs and hire the unemployed to fill them. Ronald Reagan, a Republican president, has been urged to promote policies that will foster job creation in the private sector. Such jobs, Republicans argue, have a future, whereas government employment is largely make-work and a dead end.

Second, the president is responsible for proposing economic policies that will ensure maximum production. Ideally, government policy should encourage a growth rate of approximately 4 percent after inflation. Such a rate of growth will result in an increase in output and enhance the overall strength of the economy. Once again, Democrats and Republicans differ as to the nature of the policies most likely to contribute to healthy economic growth. Democratic administrations tend to adopt policies that will benefit workers and consumers. Republican administrations tend to develop policies that make it easier for business interests to expand their plants and facilities.

Finally, the Employment Act makes the president responsible for proposing economic policies that ensure economic stability. The administration's policies should strive to foster price stability, that is, an inflation rate that does not exceed the overall growth rate of the economy. Of the three goals, price stability has been historically the most difficult to achieve. A number of factors, such as government deficits, cost of living increases for Social Security retirees, and wage increases that exceed productivity gains, contribute to what many economists see as an inflationary bias in the American economy. Other economists, among them Robert Heilbroner, have gone so far as to say that inflation is the contemporary way that capitalism manifests its inherent instability.[6] Before the Great Depression, this instability was manifested by periodic economic crises—panics, depressions, and recessions. According to this group of economists, the policies designed to end those periodic crises have created an inflationary bias to economic activity.

In addressing the problem of how to cope with inflation, Democrats and Republicans differ. Democrats accuse Republicans of proposing policies that place a higher priority on fighting inflation than reducing unemployment. In the trade-off between inflation and unemployment, Republicans contend that curbing inflation will in the long run lead to a lowering of the unemployment rate. As a part of his plan to attack the inflationary spiral of the 1970s, President Reagan's economic policies were designed to slow the growth of federal spending. His decision in June 1983 to reappoint Paul Volcker as chairman of the **Federal Reserve System** signaled his endorsement of a policy of monetary restraint, that is, a policy that limits the growth of the money supply by affecting both the amount of currency in circulation and interest rates. The huge governmental deficits that are a result of the president's tax cuts and increased defense spending augment inflationary pressures, however, and in time may offset the gains achieved by a restrictive **monetary policy**.

As chairman of the Federal Reserve Board, Paul Volcker has immense power in economic policy. Many credit Volcker with both the deep recession and high unemployment of 1982 and the subsequent recovery and lowered inflation rate of more recent years.

The widespread disagreement among economists, political scientists, and politicians about the most effective way to reach the goals of the Employment Act suggests several conclusions. First, the American economy is so complex and the level of understanding so limited that competing policies are inevitable. Second, the ideological debate over economic policies reveals that the ends of such policies are not entirely economic, but are advocated as means to reach certain desired political and social goals. Finally, economic policies are as much the result of political pressure as they are of economic theory. For example, virtually all analysts are agreed that an intense lobbying effort by the banking community was directly responsible for the repeal, before it even went into effect, of the 10 percent withholding provision on savings and interest in July 1983.

Thus the normal pattern of economic policy making—limited knowledge, value conflict, and pressure politics—influences both the formulation of the budget and the substance of economic policies. This pattern sets boundaries to the economic policies, the likelihood of significant reallocations, and the extent of change that is possible in any given year or administration.

Fiscal Policy as an Instrument of Economic Management

Since the Great Depression and World War II, governmental policy makers have recognized that **fiscal policy** (taxing and spending policy) can be used to manage the economy, albeit in a crude way. John Maynard Keynes had reasoned that the gross national product (GNP), that is, the sum total of all goods and services produced in any given year, was a compound of consumer spending (C) plus investment expenditures (I) plus government expenditures (G) (the equation is GNP = C + I + G). He went on to argue that a government could, by manipulating its tax and spending policies, significantly affect all parts of the equation. For example, a reduction in the individual income tax rate would put more money in the hands of consumers, leading to increased spending by consumers. Or an increase in capital investment taxes would lead to less investment spending by businesses. Government spending at an increased level would have an expansionary effect, whereas reduced government spending would have a deflationary impact on the economy.

Today, both Keynesians and supply-side economists acknowledge that fiscal policy can exert a powerful inflationary or recessionary effect. Nor is this awareness limited to economists. Every wage earner is conscious of tax-withholding provisions that reduce take-home pay markedly. Huge governmental deficits have prompted calls for a balanced-budget amendment. More than ever before, the federal budgetary process is being exposed to intense scrutiny by both politicians and the public.

An analysis of the federal budget can give us at least a partial answer to several questions about the relationship between the political and economic systems. First, from what perspective can the budget be viewed as the government's response to inputs from the environment? The allocation of public resources should reflect in some fashion the results of competition among groups and interests with varying amounts of power and influence. Next, in what ways can the federal budget be employed as an instrument of economic management? Since more than 20 percent of the nation's GNP is accounted for by government spending, manipulation of taxing and spending policies can have a powerful expansive or contractive impact on the economy.

Third, is the pattern of federal spending an accurate indicator of the nation's priorities? From a commonsense point of view, whatever the government spends the most money on may be regarded as one of the top priorities. Finally, how have spending patterns changed over time? By looking at a long-enough period, we should be able to determine whether Democratic administrations have, in fact, had a different set of expenditure priorities than Republican administrations. This type of analysis should furnish some insight into the influence of party philosophy on budgetary matters. An examination over time should also reveal changes in the pattern of interest group influence. If expenditures go up, the influence of a group may be increasing, and vice versa. Most significant, an analysis over time gives us firm data on how well the government has been able to meet the mandates of the Employment Act of 1946.

Thus the federal budget represents one set of fundamental political decisions. Priorities are established, spending levels are determined, the tax burden allocated, and a deficit or surplus predicted. The expenditure side of the budget sets the nation's priorities and spending levels, in other words, "who gets what."

Over the last decade, expenditures for national defense and Social Security, including Medicare, have been the nation's top two priorities and have accounted for nearly 60 percent of all federal spending.[7] For most of that decade, spending for interest on the national debt, health, and veterans' benefits and services rounded out the top five expenditures. These last three budget functions accounted for nearly 30 percent of federal expenditures. The top five functions accounted for better than 85 percent of federal expenditures. Table 12.1 shows how budget outlays have been distributed during three recent fiscal years.

Viewed over time, budgetary and resource allocations can indicate important shifts in political

Table 12.1
Budget Outlays by Function (in billions)

	1987*	1986*	1985
National Defense	$282.2	$265.8	$252.7
Social Security	212.2	200.1	188.6
Net Interest	148.0	142.7	129.4
Income Security	118.4	118.1	128.2
Medicare	70.2	68.7	65.8
Health	35.0	35.7	33.5
Education, Training, Employment and Social Services	27.4	30.7	29.3
Veterans' Benefits and Services	26.4	26.6	26.4
Transportation	25.5	27.1	25.8
Agriculture	19.5	25.9	25.6
International Affairs	18.6	17.1	16.2
Natural Resources and Environment	12.0	12.9	13.4
General Science, Space and Technology	9.2	8.9	8.6
Administration of Justice	6.9	6.8	6.3
Community and Regional Development	6.5	7.9	7.7
General Government	6.1	6.3	5.2
Energy	4.0	4.4	5.7
General Purpose Fiscal Assistance	1.7	6.2	6.4
Commerce and Housing Credit	1.4	3.8	4.2
Allowances	.8	0	0
Undistributed Offsetting Receipts	−38.1	−35.8	−32.8
Total Budget Outlays	994.0	979.9	946.3

* Figures for 1986 and 1987 are estimates

Source: *U.S. Budget in Brief, Fiscal Year 1981*, Table 3.

power or demographic trends. Expenditures for income security (various welfare programs) have risen dramatically in the last ten years, whereas federal expenditures for commerce and housing credit are the only instances of an absolute decline. The rise of health expenditures reveals both the demographic trend of an aging population and the increased political power of older Americans.

Certain values such as anticommunism have supported a high level of spending for national defense throughout the same period. Other values like economic individualism and limited government have acted as constraints on government spending in the areas of public assistance, pollution control, and the development of solar energy. Expenditures for social programs for the disadvantaged, critics of the president insist, have been the principal focus of budget cuts by the Reagan administration.

The tax side of the federal budget reveals how the tax burden has been allocated, that is, who pays the costs of government. The sharpest rise in the tax burden has come from increases in social insurance taxes. In 1964, social insurance taxes accounted for 18 percent of the tax dollar. Twenty-three years later, social insurance taxes had risen to 30

Figure 12.2
The Federal Government Dollar (1987 Estimate)

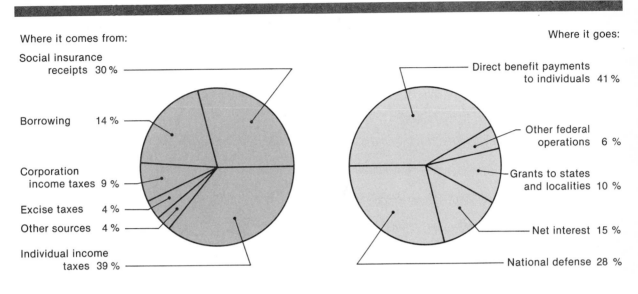

Where it comes from:

Social insurance receipts 30 %

Borrowing 14 %

Corporation income taxes 9 %

Excise taxes 4 %

Other sources 4 %

Individual income taxes 39 %

Where it goes:

Direct benefit payments to individuals 41 %

Other federal operations 6 %

Grants to states and localities 10 %

Net interest 15 %

National defense 28 %

Source: *U.S. Budget in Brief, Fiscal Year 1986*

percent of the tax dollar. Given the problems with the Social Security system, future tax increases to finance that system are highly likely.

During the last two decades, corporate taxes as a percentage of the tax dollar declined from 20 percent in 1964 to 9 percent in 1987. Far less dramatic has been the decline in personal income taxes. In 1964, personal income taxes accounted for 41 percent of the tax dollar. By 1987, personal income taxes had declined by only 2 percent to 39 percent of the tax dollar. As these two sources of the tax dollar have declined, borrowing as a share of the budget dollar has increased from 5 percent in 1964 to 14 percent in 1987 (Figure 12.2).

The allocation of the tax dollar does not disclose that over the last twenty years, capital gains taxes have been revised downward, which has directly benefited the more affluent classes. Income from municipal bonds, another tax haven for upper-income groups, remained untaxed, whereas interest on savings accounts was fully taxed. In these and other ways, wealthy individuals have had the benefit of tax provisions not normally within the reach of even the middle class. Moreover, nearly one out of six of the nation's largest profitable corporations—including one with earnings of more than $1

billion—paid no corporate taxes on 1981 profits, according to an independent tax study,[8] highlighting the fact that major corporations could also use pre-1987 tax laws in ways that smaller businesses could not. It was concern over inequities like this that led to a groundswell of support for tax reform in 1986.

Several other dimensions of the federal budget can also illustrate the impact of fiscal policy on the economy. As noted earlier, federal government expenditures have accounted for approximately one-fifth of total GNP for more than four decades. If all levels of government spending are included, the total government share of GNP rises to approximately one-third. Although government expenditures as a fraction of GNP have remained relatively stable, government spending has still had an inflationary impact, because in the last forty years a budget surplus has been recorded in only eight years. Budget deficits have also contributed to the upward trend in interest rates, especially over the last decade. Despite the almost constant deficit spending, the national debt as a fraction of total GNP has actually gone down. In 1964, the national debt stood at $316.8 billion and was 51.2 percent of GNP. By 1986, the national debt had grown to more

DEFICIT, DEFICIT, WHO'S RESPONSIBLE
FOR THE DEFICIT?

Before coming to power in 1981, the Republican party had for many years complained about the Democrats' constantly raising federal spending and their tendency to spend more money than they raised in tax revenues. All this spending and debt were damaging the economy, they argued, stifling private initiative and investment, driving up interest rates, and leaving future generations with a huge national debt to pay. They, in contrast, were the party of fiscal responsibility and balanced budgets. So when they came to power behind an extremely conservative president in 1981, everyone expected a change. And things did change. In Reagan's first term, federal spending increased by nearly one-third, and the size of the total federal debt increased by almost 75 percent! People were so unconcerned with the size of the deficit that they returned Mr. Reagan to office for four more years. By the end of his fifth year in office, the amount of debt added during his tenure exceeded that accumulated in all the administrations of the preceding thirty-nine presidents. The deficit had grown so large that just the interest paid on the debt in 1984 was more than the entire budget submitted by President Kennedy in his last year in office!

During the 1984 presidential election the Democrats decided to run against the Republicans using much the same arguments the Republicans had lost elections with for decades. They complained about the Republicans' spendthrift approach to national defense and pointed to the huge deficit that would ruin the economy and punish future generations with high interest payments. Of course, the Democrats had to overlook the fact that all the money the Republicans spent had been approved by the Democratic controlled House of Representatives, as were the budgets that resulted in the huge deficits.

Such reversals in position are not all that unusual in American politics, but they are confusing. They tend to lead to some cynicism about the integrity of both parties as well, and they certainly do not help us assign blame for the deficit problem. Perhaps we, the voters, are really to blame. We have never responded electorally to the party that tried to run on the issue of high deficits, whether it was the Republicans or more lately the Democrats. We have also wanted to enjoy the benefits of tax cuts without suffering the loss of our favorite programs and personal governmental benefits. The result, as we should have known, is higher deficits. The responsibility may thus lie with "the people." Unfortunately, it may not be the same people who ultimately will have to pay the bill.

than $2 trillion, yet as a fraction of GNP the debt had declined to 47 percent.

In recent years, the national government has made budgetary funds available for loan guarantees to ailing corporations. It is highly doubtful, for example, whether Chrysler Corporation could have avoided bankruptcy without federal loan guarantees. Defense contractors like Boeing have also been assisted by federal loan guarantees. Even urban areas in the northeastern regions of the country have sought relief from their financial difficulties by attempting to secure such loans. If these are not sufficient, then direct subsidies or government contracts to provide a service are sometimes available. Amtrak, the nation's rail passenger service, is a case in point.

In addition to these areas of economic impact, the increase in federal government spending has been of direct benefit to the state governments. As of fiscal 1987, federal grants to state and local governments accounted for approximately 10 percent of the budget dollar. Just a decade earlier, such grants were so insignificant that they were not even included in the budget summaries. In some instances, these grants now account for as much as 20 percent of some state budgets. Without them, state and the local governments would be forced to raise taxes or cut services, politically difficult choices. Federal grants to the states have been immune from President Reagan's budget cutting. Rather than eliminate them, the president has proposed that such grants be converted into block grants, that is,

SLAYING THE DEFICIT DRAGON: WILL GRAMM–RUDMAN WORK?

In late 1985, Congress passed a tough (some would say frightening) deficit reduction bill popularly referred to as Gramm-Rudman (after its principal sponsors). As originally passed, this act bound Congress to a series of budget targets moving from a $144 billion deficit in 1987 to a balanced budget in 1991. Each year on August 20, the Office of Management and Budget and the Congressional Budget Office would jointly forecast whether the budget meets the targets set by Gramm-Rudman. If so, all can relax until the following year. If not, the Gramm-Rudman procedure would swing into action. First, the General Accounting Office (GAO) was to compile a list of across-the-board cuts, split equally between domestic and military programs, that would bring the budget into compliance with the Gramm-Rudman targets. The GAO-determined budget then would become the document the president would enforce—unless the Congress could come up with its own plan by September 30 and the president signed it into law.

Neither the bill's supporters nor its critics liked Gramm-Rudman's automatic, across-the-board

Senators Phil Gramm (left) R—Texas and Warren Rudman R—New Hampshire

cuts, which removed from Congress the responsibility for making hard choices among programs. Instead, it was hoped that the prospect of indiscriminate cuts in domestic (except Social Security) and military programs would force the Congress and the president into accepting their responsibility for making spending cuts and taxing increases in order to reduce the deficit. Many felt that this transfer of executive authority to a legislative agency like the GAO was unconstitutional, however. Acting on such concern Representative Mike Synar (D–OK) moved to have the Supreme Court rule on this provision of the law. The Court did find this provision to be an unconstitutional violation of the separation of powers, thus weakening the automatic across-the-board threat of the legislation and tossing responsibility back into the Congress's contentious lap.

Without the discipline inherent in its original procedures, it seems unlikely that Gramm-Rudman's yearly budget targets will be met by Congress. What does seem certain is that if Congress and the president are ever going to come to grips with the deficit it will involve hard choices requiring compromises, and suffering, all around.

federal funds available to the states for spending with fewer federal restrictions.

Other Tools of Economic Management

Closely related to the fiscal policies described in the last section are a number of other policies that reach beyond the budget to shape the economy in subtle but significant ways. Monetary policies, tariff policies, trade agreements, attitudes toward organized labor, economic regulations, safety and environmental regulations, energy policies, and government-owned services are among the most obvious governmental actions that powerfully affect the economic climate. These policies can be grouped under four general categories: monetary policy, economic development policy, economic regulatory policy, and government ownership.

Monetary policy: The Federal Reserve System, often referred to as "the Fed," has the primary responsibility for formulating and administering monetary policy. Monetary policy is concerned with regulating the amount of money in circulation and the availability of credit. To discharge its responsibilities, the Federal Reserve System has three principal tools that can be employed to affect the growth in the money supply and interest rates. First, and most important, the Fed can use open market operations—the buying and selling of government securities—to determine the money supply. When the Fed purchases government bonds, the effect is to increase the money supply. When the Fed sells government bonds, the effect is to decrease the money supply. In this way, the Fed can readily affect the amount of money available for economic growth.

Second, the Fed can affect the money supply by manipulating the discount rate, that is, by raising or lowering the rate that member banks have to pay for borrowing funds from Federal Reserve banks. If the discount rate is raised, the effect is to increase interest rates to private borrowers as well. This, of course, has a dampening effect on the economy. If the discount rate is lowered, the effect is to cause interest rates to decline, making it easier for private borrowers to carry out their plans for expansion. Such plans have a stimulating effect on the overall economy.

The third and least used way the Fed affects the money supply is through the manipulation of reserve requirements, that is, by raising or lowering the amount that member banks must keep on deposit to pay back their depositors. If the reserve requirement is raised, member banks have less money available to lend; consequently, the money supply grows at a much slower rate. If the reserve requirement is lowered, member banks have more money to lend, and the money supply can grow more rapidly.

Since most of the decisions of the Fed are made in secret, it is only after the fact that the decisions of that body are known to the public. If the Fed is acting to expand the money supply, there will be a downward trend in the prime rate (the interest rate that banks charge their biggest and best customers). Other borrowers may pay up to 1.5 percent more than the prime rate to borrow money. When the Fed acts to contract the money supply, there is upward pressure on the prime rate. As the prime rate climbs, business activity slows and the economy grows more slowly. The main objective of the Fed is to act in such a way that the economy grows at a healthy rate. Too rapid a rate of growth feeds inflationary pressures. Too severe a contraction of the money supply can send the economy into recession. Thus the Fed is constantly trying to determine what balance between expansion and contraction of the money supply will have the intended effect on the growth rate of the economy.

Economic development policy: Federal government policies can foster certain enterprises. For example, in the early years of the airline industry, the government subsidized that industry by granting generous mail contracts to the air carriers. Even earlier, the government had subsidized the building of the first transcontinental railroad through land grants to the Union Pacific and the Central Pacific. Today, most urban mass transportation systems operate with a government **subsidy.** Indeed, without such a subsidy, fares would be so high that large numbers of people could not afford mass transport.

Tax preferences are another tool the government can use to promote business activity. By adopting the appropriate tariff structure, the government can protect and promote domestic firms. By accelerating the depreciation schedule, businesses are encouraged to modernize their plants. By lowering the

Urban rapid transit systems are part of economic infra-structure provided by government.

rate at which capital gains are taxed, investment activity is encouraged. By taxing the "windfall" profits of the oil companies at a lower rate, the government can foster the development of new oil reserves. By adopting the appropriate tax provisions, the government can promote a land use policy that discourages farmland conversion to residential, commercial, or industrial use. The use of such tax expenditures (so called because they cost the government revenue) to subsidize and promote business activity has been extensive. Indeed, the impact on the economy in general and business activity in particular of the elimination of many such tax expenditures is one source of concern with the recent tax reform legislation.

Government also promotes business activity through providing government services. The airline industry benefits from government provision of weather information, air traffic controllers, and security personnel. The business community in general benefits from such services as the preparation of economic forecasting data. Among the most important sources for such data are *The Statistical Abstract of the United States,* various census reports, Federal Reserve bulletins, the *Economic Report of the President,* and Department of Commerce and Department of Labor publications.

Calculating the cost of government promotion efforts is extremely difficult. Many such efforts are not called government promotion, but bear names like grants-in-aid, loan guarantees, price supports, stabilization programs, tax incentives, and so on. In each instance, however, federal funds are being employed to promote or protect economic activity. These activities have become so ingrained in the economic system that any attempt to end them would result in serious economic dislocation. Moreover, the beneficiaries of government promotion efforts insist that such programs serve the public interest as well as their private interests. However, such policies are both distributive and redistributive in nature, and in this case the redistribution does not favor the poorest and most needy classes.

Economic regulatory policy: Since the Great Depression, the federal government, much to the chagrin of certain elements of the business community, has adopted a host of regulatory measures. Some regulation of the economy had occurred as early as the 1880s with the creation of the Interstate Commerce Commission. But it was the economic collapse of the 1930s that inaugurated widespread federal intervention in the economy. The real flood of economic regulation is a phenomenon of the last half-century. Yet economist Lester Thurow maintains that the American economy is one of the least regulated industrial economies in the world.[9]

Government regulatory activity takes many forms, but most regulations are administered by the independent regulatory commissions, which were established by Congress. Among the most important are the Environmental Protection Agency (EPA), the Federal Communications Commission (FCC), the Federal Power Commission (FPC), the previously mentioned Interstate Commerce Commission (ICC), the National Labor Relations Board (NLRB), the Nuclear Regulatory Commission (NRC), and the Securities and Exchange Commission (SEC).

All these agencies have significant powers to regulate economic activity within their jurisdiction. Safety standards found in Occupational Safety and Health Administration rules set guidelines employ-

ers must follow. Rate regulations, route certificates, and licensing requirements are pervasive in the transportation industries. Affirmative action guidelines, minimum wage laws, and child labor restrictions are examples of government regulations affecting businesses in their employment practices. Clean air standards, rules for the disposal of nuclear wastes, and strip-mining regulations determine the conditions under which energy is produced by public utilities. In each of these instances, government regulation is an attempt to achieve one or more of the following goals: to control monopoly and oligopoly, to regulate labor-management relations, to shield the economically powerless, to protect the environment, and to offset the deficiencies of market forces.

Hardly any significant arena of economic activity is free from government regulation. President Reagan is responding to pleas that many government regulations are unnecessary, burdensome, and counterproductive, and has been able to draw support from both liberals and conservatives in some of his deregulation efforts. Both groups applauded

Charlie Daniel in the Knoxville Journal

government deregulation of the transportation industry, for example, Liberals favoring the increased competition that deregulation would bring, whereas conservatives approved of the reduction in government intervention.

Government Ownership: Public ownership of enterprises that compete directly or indirectly with private enterprises is not a widely known tool of economic management. Yet the federal government operates more than 20,000 businesses with assets of more than $11 billion. These businesses include the Government Printing Office, the world's largest publishing company; Social Security, the world's largest insurance system; the Veteran's Administration, the nation's largest health care system; the National Forest Service, the nation's largest timber company; the Postal Service, the nation's largest mail delivery company; and the Tennessee Valley Authority, one of the nation's largest public utilities. Contrary to the general impression, some government businesses actually make a profit. So many Americans now travel abroad, for example, that the Passport Agency over the years has increased its fiscal surplus.

Virtually all the services provided by these government entities could be supplied by privately held companies doing business under government contract, and proposals to do so have been made at various times. But little political pressure for such transfer of services to private enterprise has been generated. Moreover, some government businesses, such as the postal service, have used existing laws to prevent privately owned companies from competing with them.

Government ownership has also been used as a prop for troubled businesses like the Amtrak rail passenger system. There is no evidence to indicate that Amtrak will ever be able to operate at a profit without government subsidies. Urban transportation systems, whether bus or rail, are often run by a government entity. Those that are privately owned, without exception, require government subsidies to continue in existence.

Government ownership is employed by policy makers as simply one more tool for the purpose of managing the overall performance of the economy. The government-owned unemployment insurance system is a good example. The system protects the purchasing power of individuals who, for a variety

The Kentucky Dam, one part of the extensive holdings of the Tennessee Valley Authority (TVA)

of reasons, become unemployed. If that buying power were lost completely, the economy could, if the numbers were large enough, be thrown into recession. A government-owned insurance system not only assists the unemployed in gaining the necessities of life but it also has a stabilizing effect on the overall economy. Many other government businesses have the same dual effect of protecting the economically weak and stabilizing the larger economy.

Conclusion

Public policy and the policy-making process in the United States are complex. Public policies can be classified into at least three functional types—distributive, redistributive, and regulatory—each of which has its own peculiar characteristics of process and impact. Generally, the policy process can be divided into five interacting and overlapping steps or stages. The final stage (policy evaluation) tends to generate information that restimulates the first step (agenda setting) creating a self-sustaining policy cycle. The process is extremely fragmented, which contributes both to its responsiveness to narrowly organized interests and to problems of policy inconsistency.

For political scientists, an analysis of the interaction of the political and economic systems is essential to understanding how the American political system processes economic inputs, how economic management policies are formulated, and how the nation establishes its spending priorities. Overall, the best source for the analysis of these various factors is the federal budget. It is also important to examine the entire range of tools that the government uses to manage the economy.

All the federal economic management tools—fiscal policy, monetary policy, economic development, regulation, and government ownership—are the ZWsubject of sharp debate between liberals and conservatives, Keynesians and supply siders. An important element of this ideological debate is the way each group makes use of, or tries to overcome, the strongly held values of economic individualism and limited government. Each firmly believes that if its policies are adopted, the economy will function more efficiently.

Policies that merely ensure efficient functioning of the economy, however, leave unanswered the larger questions of the proper relationship between political authority and corporate power. If the issue of efficiency is the only one analyzed by public policy makers, a powerful bias in favor of the existing system is being built into public policies, and it is unlikely that the larger issues of what goals the government should choose in formulating economic policy will be fully addressed.

 ## Glossary

Distributive policy Government actions that distribute economic benefits to large numbers of people in specific categories, such as business and agriculture.

Federal Reserve System Banking regulatory agency that is principally responsible for monetary policy and for controlling the amount of credit available and the amount of currency in circulation.

Filibuster Tactic of a Senator or small group of Senators to exploit the Senate's unlimited debate rules to "talk a bill to death"—holding the floor to prevent a bill from coming to a vote until the Senate moves on to other business. A three-fifths vote is required for "cloture"—cutting off debate to end a filibuster.

Fiscal policy The spending, taxing, and debt policies of the national government, controlled basically by the Congress and president and reflected in the federal budget.

Industrial policy A form of economic planning that calls for government-directed investments designed to aid in or initiate the process of shifting resources from outmoded to modern, or "high-tech," industries.

Inflation A general rise in prices that results in a corresponding decline in the purchasing power or value of money.

Keynesianism The theory that government spending can be used to regulate the economy, especially as a tool to counter economic slumps.

Logrolling The practice of legislators trading their voting support on a measure in return for support on another measure. A legislator may agree to support a government project for a colleague's district in return for support for another project for his or her home district, for example.

Monetary policy Government policy, set by the Federal Reserve Board, that regulates the amount of money in circulation to stimulate or decrease aggregate demand.

Monetarism An economic theory proposed by Milton Friedman holding that the supply of money is the major determinant of national economic health and that an excess supply is the principal cause of inflation.

Nondecision The failure of an issue to receive a hearing or to be consciously considered by decision makers. This failure is due largely to the limits imposed on the policy agenda by deeply held consensual values in society.

Policy agenda The list of issues and problems to be addressed and acted upon by the formal policy adoption institutions.

Public policy A course of action followed by government in dealing with an issue or problem.

Redistributive policy Actions of government that use the resources collected from one broad class of people to improve the condition of another broad class.

Regulatory policy Government decisions designed to control the activities of individuals or groups, such as regulation of fair trade practices in business.

Subsidy A government grant of money to a specific group, for example, government price supports for agricultural commodities.

 ## Suggestions for Further Reading

Alt, James E., and K. Alec Chrystal. *Political Economics.* London: Wheatsheaf, 1983. A sophisticated treatment of the relationship between politics and economics.

Bauer, Raymond A., and Kenneth J. Gergen, eds. *The Study of Policy Formation.* New York: Free Press, 1968. A collection of original essays dealing with theoretical and methodolgical problems in the study of public policy.

Boskin, Michael J., and Aaron Wildavsky, eds. *The Federal Budget: Economics and Politics.* San Franscisco: Institute for Contemporary Studies, 1982. Excellent essays on how the budget is made, various means for controlling it, and current trends in federal fiscal policy.

Cobb, Roger W., and Charles D. Elder. *Participation in American Politics: The Dynamics of Agenda Building.* Boston: Allyn and Bacon, 1972. Useful and very influential discussion of how problems get on the policy agenda in the American policy process.

Dye, Thomas R. *Understanding Public Policy.* Englewood Cliffs, N.J.: Prentice-Hall, 1981. Examines a number of the most influential models of policy analysis and compares their utility with that of case studies.

Gilder, George. *Wealth and Poverty.* New York: Basic Books, 1981. The controversial view of poverty and its origins that is the foundation for supply-side policy advocates.

Haveman, Robert, ed. *A Decade of Federal Anti-Poverty Programs.* New York: Academic Press, 1977. A series of excellent articles dealing with the origins and accomplishments of the War on Poverty.

Peters, Guy B. *American Public Policy: Process and Performance.* New York: Franklin Watts, 1982. A good general introduction to the policy process, some substantive areas of public policy, and policy analysis.

Nadel, Mark V. *The Politics of Consumer Protection.* 2d ed. Indianapolis: Bobbs-Merrill, 1975. Addresses the sources and uses of political influence in the adoption of consumer protection legislation.

Reich, Robert. *The Next American Frontier.* New York: Times Books, 1983. An excellent and politically influential analysis of the contemporary American political economy and a persuasive argument for an industrial policy.

Stone, Alan. *Regulation and its Alternatives.* Washington: Congressional Quarterly Press, 1982. A wide-ranging and insightful study of the nature, justification, and politics of economic regulatory policy.

Thurow, Lester C. *The Zero-Sum Society: Distribution and the Possibility for Economic Change.* New York: Basic Books, 1980. A thought-provoking treatment of the limitations of the disaggregated American policy process in addressing and solving America's fundamental economic problems.

Wilson, James Q., ed. *The Politics of Regulation.* New York: Basic Books, 1980. Examines regulatory policy in nine agencies within the context of an explanatory theory.

Let us join in creating a new endeavor—not a new balance of power, but a new world of law—where the strong are just, the weak secure, and the peace preserved.
John F. Kennedy

Chapter 13

Foreign Policy and International Affairs

Introduction

In certain critical respects, American foreign policy is rooted in perceptions of the nation's basic interests and values. These interests and values determine America's foreign policy goals, among which freedom of the seas, free trade, and a commitment to free institutions rank near the top. Despite the primacy of these goals and widespread public opinion in their favor, the United States does not and cannot have a single, unified foreign policy.

Political, economic, ideological, and sometimes religious circumstances dictate a collection of policies—toward the Soviet Union, China, the Middle East, the **North-South division**, Northern Ireland, Iran, arms control, grain exports, and so on. Very often, these circumstances are beyond the control of the American government. The United States is only one of 160 sovereign states, each of which has its own foreign policy, which may be contrary to our own.

Foreign policies are also limited by the uncertainties and complexities inherent in international affairs. Although these uncertainties are often aggravated by the use of overheated political rhetoric, a government will carefully assess the risks, costs, and resources needed to act on the rhetoric. Normally, governments are not disposed to take unnecessary risks that may damage trade, bring about a break in diplomatic relations, or result in hostilities. Rather they seek a stable environment, preferably one that reduces uncertainties and therefore the probability of hostilities.

Three Basic Principles of International Affairs and Defense

Despite changing circumstances and unavoidable uncertainties, American foreign policy is guided by three basic principles. First, the national government has exclusive power in the fields of international affairs and defense. The Constitution bans the states from entering into treaties, alliances, and confederations; even interstate compacts must be approved by Congress. Nor can states engage in war or armed conflict unless actually invaded. For states, war is strictly a defensive affair. Indeed, states are forbidden to maintain a standing armed force or warships during peacetime.

Although the national government's power is divided between Congress and the president, as Table 13.1 indicates, the president is dominant. In the international arena, the president is the sole official, legitimate voice of the American government. The Supreme Court has confirmed on a number of occasions the president's authoritative role in international affairs. By contrast, the justices have done very little to enhance the role of Congress in this area.

Civilian supremacy is a second basic principle that guides American foreign policy, as we can see from the organizational structure of the American government. The president, who is commander in chief, and all the top Defense Department officials are required by the Constitution to be civilians. Congress, a civilian body, declares war, appropriates money for the armed services, and establishes military law. Finally, the Court of Military Appeals, the highest military court, has civilian judges appointed by the president and confirmed by the Senate.

The third basic principle concerns the scope of constitutional authority over international affairs. Unlike the legislative power of Congress, which rests on Article I, Section 8, foreign policy and national defense policy is conducted under the authority of United States as a sovereign state. Article I, Section 8, contains a list of enumerated powers that restrict the scope of legislation. When the United States acts as a sovereign state, it can do virtually anything that any other sovereign state can do. Even though the federal government cannot do what the Constitution forbids, the range of powers in these areas is much broader and has been interpreted more loosely than that for legislation.

Influences on Foreign Policy

Although the president dominates the formulation and implementation of American foreign policy, such policy is neither developed nor adopted in a vacuum. Besides the executive agencies that affect foreign policy making, Congress, interest groups, the media, and public opinion all have a role to play. Although the latter three have no constitutional foundation, no president can ignore their influence. For example, Presidents Lyndon Johnson and Richard Nixon found their options during the Vietnam

Table 13.1
Powers and Roles of the President in Foreign Affairs

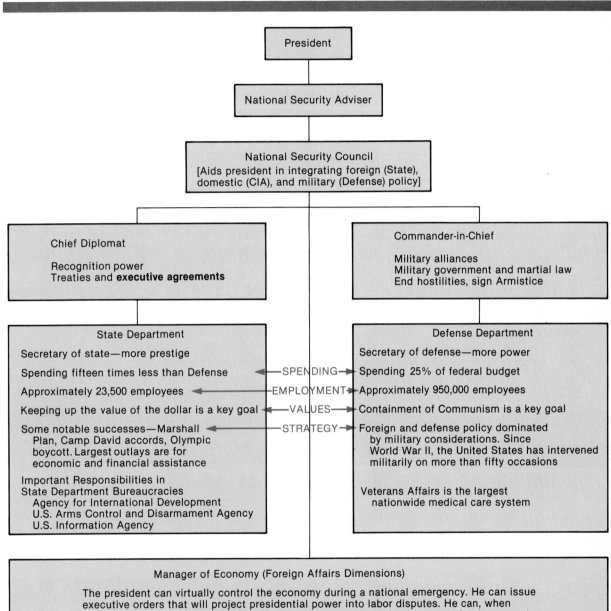

"THE BAD NEWS IS WE SHOT DOWN THE WRONG SATELLITE... THE GOOD NEWS IS THAT WE GOT THE ONE THAT TRANSMITS 'MTV'......!"

war limited by antiwar groups and an increasingly hostile public opinion.

The following sections examine the constraints placed on presidential ability to act in foreign policy by Congress, interest groups, the media, public opinion, and international organizations.

Congress

As we noted earlier, the Constitution divides the responsibility for foreign affairs between the Congress and the president. Since the Constitution's framers obviously wanted power to be shared, the question may well be asked, Why does the executive so overshadow the legislative branch? Congress is at a disadvantage for four principal reasons.

First, Congress is not organized to formulate carefully prepared policy alternatives to meet problems that arise. As Table 13.1 indicates, the president enjoys the benefit of a well-organized foreign policy establishment that contrasts vividly with the fragmented authority found in Congress. The professional staff of congressional committees simply cannot compete with the National Security Council, the State Department, and the Defense Department. Congressional staffers lack both the expertise and the sources of information these executive agencies have long enjoyed.

Second, Congress, unlike the presidency, is a deliberative body that requires consent by a number of its committees and a majority of its members. As a consequence, Congress is rarely able to act quickly and decisively. Although the president will consult widely on any given action, he does not need the consent of his subordinates before he acts.

Third, Congress is made up of 435 representatives and 100 senators. As legislators, they usually address local concerns rather than national issues. By contrast, the American people view the president as the spokesman for national interests. He is the only official who can speak authoritatively for the national government in foreign affairs and the only one who can meet with other heads of state as a coequal.

Finally, unlike the chief executive, Congress has no intelligence-gathering apparatus and often lacks unbiased and disinterested sources of information. By contrast, the Central Intelligence Agency (CIA), an executive agency, performs this function and reports directly to the president.

Despite these disadvantages, Congress can influence foreign policy, as the following examples illustrate. Congress: can refuse to ratify treaties (Wilson's League of Nations); passed the War Powers Act, which limits the president's power to commit troops; imposed sanctions against South Africa despite President Reagan's opposition; cut defense appropriations (including Star Wars); limited aid to the Contras in Nicaragua.

Interest Groups

Agriculture, business, and labor all attempt to influence certain aspects of foreign policy. Despite American differences with the Soviet Union, for example, American farmers have lobbied hard for continued grain sales to that nation. The Department of Agriculture has, for the most part, supported the farmers' position. Veteran's groups, religious groups, ethnic groups, and women's groups have all, on occasion, attempted to influence the development or implementation of foreign policy. Even college students can get into the act. On many campuses, students have demanded that the Reagan administration take a harder line against apartheid in South Africa. They have also pressured university trustees to end their investments in companies doing business in that country.

Media

Newspapers, magazines, radio, and above all, television can have an impact on foreign policy. As a purveyor of information to the public, the media may create a climate of public opinion that in turn brings pressure to bear on both Congress and the president. This pressure can act as a restraint on the

MAJOR EXECUTIVE AGENCIES THAT IMPINGE ON FOREIGN AFFAIRS

Foreign policy is neither formulated nor implemented in a vacuum. The president and the secretary of state must often consider the advice of other executive agencies. In some instances, these agencies may actually determine what policy is adopted.

Agency	Activities
Special Agency for Trade Negotiation	Aids the president in developing trade policy and trade agreements. Deals with problem areas (such as the trade imbalance with Japan) to ensure a healthy balance of trade.
Department of the Treasury	The value of the dollar in international markets, the balance of payments, and monetary negotiations are Treasury concerns. It also registers and licenses ships engaged in foreign commerce as well as collects customs duties and import tariffs.
Department of Commerce	Assists with international trade matters, sales of American goods, and loans to international applicants. Sends delegations to trade missions abroad to promote American exports.
Department of Agriculture	Offers agricultural advice to developing countries, limits (competing) agricultural imports, and tries to expand the international market for American agricultural products.
Department of Justice	Attempts to control drug traffic (much of which comes from outside the United States), to impede the flow of illegal aliens into this country, and to deport undesirables. The naturalization of legal immigrants is also a Justice Department responsibility.

THE MEDIA AND POLITICAL REALITY

Within moments after the Reagan-Gorbachev summits in Geneva and Reykjavik were announced, the American press reacted (or overreacted) with saturated coverage weeks and months before the agendas were finalized. Did the press raise or depress hopes and expectations for such important meetings? Overall, the press tended to raise expectations, especially in the pivotal area of arms control. Officials at the White House felt compelled to play down the importance of these meetings, arguing that for the public to hope that some sort of arms reduction agreement could be arranged in a few hours was unrealistic. Allowing the media to evaluate the summit meetings' accomplishments in terms of the expectations they had created would make the president's efforts appear to be a failure. The president's image makers understood the need to lower public expectations to ensure the appearance of success regardless of what happened. Clearly, the press's power to shape political reality can influence the behavior of even the leader of a world superpower.

percent of the American public think it very important that the value of the dollar be kept up, whereas only 29 percent think it very important for the United States to bring a democratic form of government to other countries.[1]

International Organizations

Up to this point, we have focused on those factors in foreign policy making that are largely internal to the United States. But U.S. foreign policy is also affected by other actors on the international scene, among them international organizations.

The United States belongs to more than two hundred international organizations, yet only a handful of them have a significant impact on foreign policy. These include the United Nations, the World Bank, the North Atlantic Treaty Organization (NATO), and the Organization of American States (OAS). The members of these organizations represent, respectively, virtually all the sovereign states in the world, an economic entity enmeshed in North-South economic problems, an alliance committed to the containment of Soviet communism, and a regional body with members from every country in this hemisphere except Cuba.

formulation and implementation of policy, as our earlier Vietnam example indicates. An astute president, however, can also use the media to get his message across. President Reagan's weekly radio broadcasts enabled him to build support for his action against Libyan terrorism and for his policy of **constructive engagement** with South Africa.

Public Opinion

An aroused or apathetic public can limit the foreign policy options of the president. Despite a concerted effort on the part of the Reagan administration to mobilize support for military aid to the Contras in Nicaragua, little public support has been forthcoming. As a consequence, Congress has been reluctant to accede to the administration's requests for funds for military aid.

Although most Americans profess a commitment to free institutions and to democracy, they also have a strong interest in the economic content of this nation's foreign policy goals. For example, 90

AMERIKA

In February, 1987, the American Broadcasting Company broadcast a twelve-hour mini-series, *Amerika*. The focus of the series was upon a Soviet take-over of the United States in the 1990s. Understandably, the scenario of Soviet rule is completely unpleasant. However, *Amerika* is also a commercially televised effort to portray how totally evil the Soviet menace is often perceived to be. It is uncertain to what extent public images, especially if cast in black and white, influence the formulation of foreign policy or vice-versa. There may be substantial danger, though, in oversimplification. Depicting only the worst elements of the Soviet Union (and its East European allies) may result in a somewhat distorted picture of the superpower that competes with us. It also complicates the determination of what our policies toward that country should realistically entail.

The U.S. role in the founding and maintenance of the United Nations is the strongest evidence of the dominance of internationalism since World War II.

From this brief list, we can also identify the major thrusts of American foreign policy in terms of both ideology and economic development. Ideologically, NATO gives institutional form to the **East-West conflict.** The United States as a superpower dominates this organization, just as the Soviet Union, the world's other superpower, dominates its principal military alliance, the Warsaw Pact. Although overshadowed by the ideological conflict, the issues surrounding economic development are now recognized as vital to the United States's national interest. The World Bank gives the United States an opportunity to project its influence into North-South problems.

Many third-world countries, including Mexico, Argentina, and Brazil in this hemisphere, are staggering under a huge national debt owed to foreign banks.[2] Creative leadership by the United States is necessary to relieve some of this burden. As the *Report of the National Bipartisan Commission on Central America* (known also as the Kissinger Commission)

emphasizes, if the United States does not take such steps for humanitarian reasons, it should do so out of self-interest. The turmoil in Central America, the report insists, is due as much to poverty as it is to communist subversion.[3] The Kissinger Commission's point is quite simple; nations with healthy, growing economies are less susceptible to foreign intrigues.

Phases of American Foreign Policy

American foreign policy has passed through several overlapping phases. As the nation grew and the industrial revolution spread, domestic and international circumstances shaped the nation's responses to world affairs. Today's foreign policies are partly the result of preceding developments. Let us turn now to a discussion of the historical circumstances in which these policies have their origin.

Isolationism: Foreign Policies to the 1890s

During this initial phase, the nation's foreign policy was shaped both by public policies and situational factors. The public policies included the ideas enunciated in George Washington's Farewell Address and the Monroe Doctrine. Washington's Farewell Address in 1797 warned the new nation against entanglement in military alliances with European powers. This sentiment was so much in keeping with American perceptions that the United States did not enter into a long-term, peacetime, military alliance with Europe until 1949, the year the NATO **Treaty** went into effect. Two years earlier, the United States had signed the RIO Pact, a military alliance with nations from this hemisphere.

The Monroe Doctrine, actually the brainchild of Secretary of State John Quincy Adams, was announced in 1823 by President James Monroe in his annual message to Congress. Monroe affirmed this nation's opposition to European intervention in the affairs of North or South America, declaring that the Americas were no longer open to colonization by European powers. Any attempt by such powers to extend their regimes in this direction would be regarded as an unfriendly act.

Both Monroe and Adams were determined to stop the so-called Holy Alliance from aiding Spain in a reconquest of the Latin American countries that had recently gained their independence from that nation. Monroe tempered this bluntness by saying that the United States would not interfere with existing colonies in the New World, nor would the United States interfere in European affairs.[4]

Although the Monroe Doctrine had little influence at the time it was issued, its continuing importance can be traced to the fact that it elucidates certain basic principles of American foreign policy: resistance to foreign intervention, a commitment to national self-determination, and a desire to protect and extend republican institutions. These principles have guided American foreign policy ever since and most foreign policy statements refer either directly or indirectly to them. American intervention in World War I and II can be explained by reference to these principles, as can American opposition to the Soviet Union's international ambitions.

Certain situational factors contributed to isolationist sentiments and also to the success of the Monroe Doctrine. Two great oceans separated the

This painting depicts President Monroe enunciating the "Monroe Doctrine".

United States from Europe and Asia. This geographic isolation enabled Americans to remain free from involvement in the wars of Europe and to make it costly for Europeans to wage war in this hemisphere. Not until the twentieth century did technological innovations make distance less of a factor in calculating United States foreign policy interests.

American energies were also directed toward the domestication of the continent throughout the nineteenth century rather than toward engagement in the events of Europe. The presence of the frontier stimulated the pioneer spirit, and Horace Greeley's famous injunction, "Go West, young man, go West!" was heeded by many.[5] Settling the land, building towns and cities, and organizing new states were endeavors that were a part of the nation's "manifest destiny." Americans had little time for what was happening beyond the nation's boundaries. There was simply too much work to do at home.

World Outlook/Imperialism: From the 1890s to the End of World War I

The American frontier had disappeared by the 1890s, and energy that had been expended internally was now directed abroad. Other countries were acquiring spheres of influence, and the United

THE "BRITISH" MONROE DOCTRINE

John Quincy Adams, secretary of state under President Monroe (1817–1824), is correctly credited with formulating the Monroe Doctrine. But this foreign policy statement was even more ingenious than most contemporaries of Adams thought. Originally, the British government had made overtures to the United States to coauthor a joint doctrine. Such an agreement would have enabled the British to interfere in the Western Hemisphere, perhaps even against American national interests.

From the British perspective, a bilateral agreement with the United States would protect Britain's political and economic interests in the New World. Politically, such an agreement would forestall the reconquest of Latin America by Spain and the Holy Alliance. Economically, it would ensure that Latin American markets would remain open to British trade. The British also felt that the United States would be unable to resist having the world's most powerful navy on its side in any conflict with Old World nations.

Adams, recognizing that Britain had these interests to protect, decided the United States could safely issue a unilateral declaration. He knew the United States was incapable of defending the Western Hemisphere against European adventurism, but he also knew the British would have no choice other than to defend the hemisphere for the United States. The strategy worked. Gradually, as the nineteenth century progressed, the United States assumed from the British protection of its own hemisphere. In the meantime, Adams had placed the British in the position of having to defend American interests from European incursions.

Theodore Roosevelt's "Big Stick" is viewed as a manifestation of U.S. imperialism.

States as an emerging power followed suit. Africa and Southeast Asia became the object of the **imperial** ambitions of England, Germany, Italy, France, Belgium, the Netherlands, and Portugal. By contrast, the United States looked to the Pacific, where it acquired the Philippines in the Spanish-American War in 1898 and annexed Hawaii and Samoa. In the Orient, the United States sought to open new markets and to secure favorable trade relations with Japan and China.

During this same period, the United States protected American businesses in foreign countries. Critics condemned American involvement in Latin America as "dollar diplomacy." Latin Americans, of course, deeply resented the American government's efforts on behalf of corporate interests. In time, the United States established **protectorates** in Cuba, Haiti, Nicaragua, and Santo Domingo. Given this history, the motives behind the recent American involvement in Central America are viewed with suspicion by many people in that region.

American intervention in Latin America was the direct consequence of presidential policy making. President Theodore Roosevelt announced the Roosevelt Corollary to the Monroe Doctrine in 1904. Essentially, the corollary called for the United States to act as the policeman of the Western Hemisphere. In the 1930s, President Franklin Roosevelt renounced his cousin's corollary and introduced the Good Neighbor Policy. Despite the Good Neighbor policy and other policies of mixed intentions and effect like President John Kennedy's Alliance for Progress, the United States has continued to intervene in Latin American affairs up to the present day.

Neo-Isolationism: From the Rejection of the League of Nations Treaty to the Signing of the RIO Pact in 1947

American disillusionment following World War I led to a revival of isolationist sentiment. The dangers of entanglement in European wars that George Washington had warned against had been bitterly confirmed by the war and by the **treaty** negotiations that followed. Although the European nations had paid lip service to Woodrow Wilson's Fourteen Points as a basis for peace negotiations, the victors were determined to exact immense reparations from Germany. President Wilson did convince the warring powers to set up a League of Nations, but the United States Senate resisted further entanglement in European affairs. When the League of Nations Treaty was brought before the Senate by President Wilson, it was soundly defeated.

These Nicaraguan "contras" equipped with U.S. M–60 machine guns reflect a continuation of an interventionist attitude toward Latin America on the part of the United States.

With Hitler's rise to power, United States disillusionment with Europe grew even deeper. The United States attempted to remain aloof from the growing conflict by passing neutrality legislation in the 1930s, but as Hitler's armies overran Europe, Americans reluctantly began to see Nazi Germany as a direct threat to the nation's interest. Even then, the United States resisted entering the war for more than two years after the outbreak of hostilities in 1939. During this period, the United States aided Great Britain and the Allied cause in a number of ways. Ultimately, such aid proved insufficient, and following the bombing of Pearl Harbor by the Japanese and a German declaration of war in December of 1941, the United States entered the war as a combatant.

Internationalism: From World War II to the Present

The foreign policy of the immediate postwar period was dominated by the Truman Doctrine. (Table 13.2 summarizes foreign policy changes since World War II.) The centerpiece of that doctrine was the European Recovery Program, popularly known as the Marshall Plan. Named for Truman's secretary of state, the Marshall Plan was designed to rebuild the war-torn economies of Europe and Japan, and by so doing to stop the growing influence of communism in these countries. Many scholars regard the Marshall Plan as the most successful of all United States foreign policies.

The Marshall Plan was a landmark because for the first time, economic assistance was employed as a major instrument of foreign policy. But when the cold war between the United States and the Soviet Union heated up, economic assistance became subordinated to military assistance. By the 1980s, military expenditures were fifteen times greater than economic assistance.

Foremost among the goals of the Truman Doctrine was the containment of communism. To check the spread of Soviet power into the free world, the Truman Doctrine called for measures of **collective security.** As a consequence, the United States entered into a number of long-term, multilateral military alliances, the most important of which is the North Atlantic Treaty Organization (NATO). Containment of Soviet communism, however, was not restricted to Europe. American involvement in both

Table 13.2
U.S. Foreign Policy Changes Since World War II

1. The United States has abandoned isolation in favor of a world leadership role.

2. Nonalignment (neutrality) has been displaced by an emphasis on collective security. The most important multilateral military alliances are the RIO Pact (1947), NATO (1949), ANZUS (1951), SEATO (1954). Bilateral alliances with West Germany and Japan are also in effect.

3. The United States has chosen to intervene in the affairs of other countries rather than working through international organizations to settle conflicts. American policy in Central America and the occupation of the Caribbean island of Grenada are cases in point. The United States has not used the United Nations, the World Court, the Organization of American States, or the Contadora group in seeking a resolution of the turmoil in these regions.

4. The United States has replaced economic assistance with military assistance and military preparedness as the primary thrust of American efforts in world affairs. Despite the success of the Marshall Plan compared with the military outcomes in Korea and Vietnam, economic development policies have been relegated to a secondary position.

5. Use of America's economic strength to achieve diplomatic goals has been relatively ineffective. Nor has America been willing to make the necessary long-range commitment to economic development in the Third World. To blunt communist insurgencies in those countries could possibly require a commitment of approximately fifty years of economic aid.

Korea and Vietnam can be traced directly to containment policy. The Reagan administration has also used the language of containment to justify an American presence in Central America and in the Caribbean basin.

American foreign policy in the post-Vietnam era seems to be in a transitional period, for a number of reasons. First, Marxism (communism) is no longer perceived as a monolithic force. The breakdown of solidarity in the communist world has occurred in several areas. Border conflicts between the Soviet Union and China and between China and Vietnam have heightened tensions among the largest communist countries. China, Romania, and Yugoslavia were among the communist countries who refused to support the Soviet boycott of the 1984 Summer Olympics. (Table 13.3 summarizes defense policy changes since World War II.)

Second, attempts at detente with Russia and China on the part of the United States and its Western European allies suggest a drift away from containment. When the United States urged its NATO allies not to sell the Soviet Union the equip-

Table 13.3

Defense Policy Changes Since World War II
[Based on The National Security Act of 1947]

1. Poor coordination between the State and War departments led to the establishment of the National Security Council. Its principal responsibility is to integrate foreign, domestic, and military policy to secure the national interest.

2. The problems of coordinating three separate armed services persuaded Congress to create the Defense Department, which encompasses all three branches. Although interservice rivalry has been reduced, the branches still view one another as competitors for defense dollars.

3. As a result of problems encountered with intelligence gathering during the war years, the Central Intelligence Agency (CIA) was established. Despite this reorganization effort and congressional attempts at oversight of the CIA, the agency's role in domestic surveillance, the failure to anticipate the assault on the American embassy in Iran, and the covert operations in Nicaragua have led many people to believe that serious problems persist.

4. A lack of comprehensive economic planning brought about the establishment of a series of executive agencies with three chief functions: to develop plans for converting the economy from a peacetime basis to a war setting, to develop and implement a program of civil defense and to develop and implement national disaster relief programs.

ment necessary to build a natural gas pipeline to Western Europe, the allies could not be persuaded. Moreover, where containment resulted in armed intervention, the results were frustrating. For many Americans, Korea and Vietnam were disillusioning experiences and reinforced their distrust of and weariness with foreign involvements. One of the bitterest lessons of these wars was the revelation of the limits of American military power.

Third, the Middle East has become a focus of American concern. **OPEC,** Israel, Lebanon, Libya, and Iran now command some of the attention that formerly was expended on the East-West ideological struggle. It is hard to view the conflicts in this region in purely ideological terms. Religious fundamentalism and religious cleavages are much more powerful explanatory factors. The war between Iran and Iraq, for example, simply cannot be explained in terms of the East-West split. OPEC oil politics, traditional ethnic rivalries stretching back several thousand years, and the Islamic revival present new challenges to American policy makers.

Fourth, economic challenges to American supremacy have proliferated. West Germany, Japan, and the OPEC countries have each in its own

way damaged the American economy. These economic conflicts have also called into question the United States's commitment to free trade. A flood of imports, particularly autos and steel from Japan, has led domestic manufacturers to call for protection from what they view as unfair competition. The race with Japan to build the next generation of supercomputers may well determine whether the United States will remain the dominant economic power in the West.

Finally, the third-world countries have posed challenging questions about the U.S. role in economic modernization. Critics of American military involvement in El Salvador and Nicaragua, Kissinger Commission members, and the Contadora group all call for economic assistance for Central America along the lines of a Marshall Plan. The North-South division of the world according to level of economic development is perceived to be more crucial than the ideological split between East and West. The large bloc of neutral nations siding with neither the Soviet Union nor the United States views the tensions between the two superpowers as the greatest threat to world peace. These nations see the arms race as a dangerous waste of the world's

CONTAINMENT POLICY

Originally enunciated in the July 1947 issue of *Foreign Affairs* by diplomat George Kennan (who discreetly authored the article as "Mr. X"), the essence of containment was to limit Soviet influence outside its borders. Kennan, the American ambassador to the Soviet Union, argued that communism would continue to expand unless containment became an integral part of American foreign policy. It did. In 1947, for example, President Truman announced the Truman Doctrine. Basically, the doctrine called for American assistance to those countries threatened by, or actually undergoing, communist-inspired insurrections. The doctrine was first applied to Greece and Turkey. Two years later, NATO (North Atlantic Treaty Organization) was formed and became a main defense system of North America and Western Europe against further Soviet expansion. Both Greece and Turkey became NATO members.

GEORGE C. MARSHALL (1880–1959) AND THE EUROPEAN RECOVERY PLAN

For nearly a half-century (1902–1951), George C. Marshall served his country with great distinction. He was commissioned as an officer in the regular army in 1902 and fought in World War I. During World War II, Marshall, now a general, was chairman of a combined chiefs of staff and won great praise as the principal Allied strategist. Immediately after the war, he went to China as a special ambassador.

President Harry Truman appointed Marshall secretary of state in January 1947. In this post, Marshall formulated the European Recovery Plan, popularly known as the Marshall Plan. Under the plan, the United States spent in excess of $13 billion to rebuild the war-torn economies of Europe and Japan. In only three years, 1948–1951, American aid did much to repair the damage done in both the Allied and Axis countries.

The Marshall plan is widely regarded as the most successful of all American foreign policies. The plan was not only an economic success, as the health of the West German and Japanese economies attest, but it also averted the political upheavals that might have led to communist insurgencies in Western Europe. In 1953, Mar-

shall was awarded the Nobel Peace Prize for his role in European reconstruction.

Poor health forced Marshall to resign as secretary of state in 1949. One year later, in the midst of the Korean war, President Truman asked Marshall to serve as secretary of defense. Congress held Marshall in such high regard that it set aside the rule that the secretary of defense must be a civilian. In 1951, Marshall now seventy-one years old, resigned as secretary of defense and retired from public life.

It is somewhat ironic that a man who fought in two world wars and spent most of his adult life in the military should be best remembered for his civilian contributions. Yet the father of the Marshall Plan was both soldier and statesman. Few others in the twentieth century have contributed so much to American democracy.

---

precious resources that could otherwise be allocated to reducing the poverty of the third world.

New Challenges in Foreign Policy

After World War II ended in 1945, the United States emerged as the only major industrialized society whose economy was still intact and the only military power armed with nuclear weapons. At that time, there were only about 60 other sovereign governments on the planet, and few of these were located in Africa or Asia. Forty years later, the international situation had changed dramatically. By 1985, a total of about 160 governments belonged to

the United Nations, the United States had become a debtor nation,[6] and five other countries had accumulated nuclear arsenals.[7] For the United States, the world had become decidedly more competitive and more dangerous. These changes also brought new foreign policy challenges.

The North and the South

The newly independent and developing countries of the Southern Hemisphere (Latin America, Africa, the Middle East, and East and South Asia) represented a new force in world politics. These formerly colonial societies began to demand (in many cases not without justification) a share of the unprece-

THE PROBLEMS OF COMBATING INSURGENCY IN EL SALVADOR

El Salvador is an embattled small country in Central America that is torn between extreme leftist and rightist forces. The left is far from united and is fighting a protracted guerilla war with the government. The right also employs violence to achieve its goal of retaining power. Both extremes often engage in terrorist acts.

José Napoleon Duarte, El Salvador's politically moderate president, once remarked that if the average Salvadoran could be confident that tomorrow would be just a little better than today, the radical leftists in the hills would have no popular support. For most people, revolution is a last resort, a signal that political and economic problems have overwhelmed the society. In the case of El Salvador, military assistance may be necessary to defeat the leftist rebels, but economic assistance is crucial to blunt their appeal. Economically prosperous societies, history suggests, do not provide a fertile ground for revolution.

nomic assistance, whereas others are actually in economic competition with the United States. The answers are also embarrassing because the United States has never really resolved the contradictions between humanitarian aid and political prudence. Even at the height of the Ethiopian famine, for example, some American leaders were reluctant to ship food to millions of starving Ethiopians because Ethiopia has a Marxist regime.[9]

The less-developed countries occasionally single out the United States as a savior, but more frequently as an exploiter. Third-world critics complain that the United States betrays its ideals by supporting repressive and authoritarian regimes, for example, Shah Reza Pahlavi in Iran from 1941 until 1979 and Ferdinand Marcos in the Philippines from 1965 until the scandal surrounding the presidential election in 1986 drove him from power.

United States foreign policy, however, must balance an array of contradictory factors. Although it is true that foreign policy is in part geared to supporting regimes friendly to American interests, that does not tell the whole story. A great problem fac-

dented prosperity that the West had enjoyed throughout most of the postwar period.

In the West, these nations were politely referred to as less-developed countries (LDCs). As the gap between the rich North and the poor South grows greater, the LDCs find it increasingly difficult to comprehend or support American foreign policy. Why, for example, does the United States spend a billion dollars a day on defense and delivers only a few billion a year in economic aid to developing societies?[8] Both domestic and foreign commentators on American policy also ask how Americans justify consuming nearly 30 percent of the earth's available resources, even though they account for only approximately 5 percent of the planet's population?

Answers to such questions are both complicated and embarrassing. They are complicated because the LDCs themselves are experiencing uneven economic development. Some LDCs, such as Bahrain, Costa Rica, and Taiwan, are much better off than others, such as Haiti, South Yemen, and Djibouti. Dozens of LDCs desperately need American eco-

THE EARLY DEMISE OF PAX AMERICANA

Until 1945, the United States was the only superpower. America's military presence in Western Europe and throughout the Pacific basin, its monopoly of nuclear weapons, and the fact that its economic capacity and productivity was intact and unsurpassed should have meant a period of relative peace and prosperity. It didn't. The United States only enjoyed the latter (briefly), while vainly pursuing the former (indefinitely). By the early 1950s, the United States was involved in an Asian land war, and the Soviet Union was quickly developing a nuclear arsenal. The "American peace" was short-lived, primarily because of the fast-changing world that emerged after 1945. With the proliferation of new sovereign states, the economic revival of and eventual competition with West Germany and Japan, and the emergence of developing nations with natural resources much needed in the West, the United States became inescapably aware that even the influence of a superpower has perceptible limits.

FOUR WORLDS

Political scientists after 1945 characteristically divided the planet into three worlds: (1) the Western democracies of North America and Western Europe, (2) the communist countries of Eastern Europe, and (3) the rest of the world, composed for the most part of developing countries. This rather arbitrary division was later extended to include a fourth category: those countries in the developing areas that had achieved impressive and rather sudden national wealth as the result of a quadrupuling of oil prices in the middle 1970s. This newest group of countries caused, at least temporarily, severe economic dislocations in the rest of the developing world, which lacked much-needed natural resources. The increase in oil prices hurt the oil-poor developing countries even more than the industrialized ones, since they had fewer financial resources with which to purchase a necessary ingredient of their progress. From this experience we now realize that lumping a group of countries into one category on the basis of similar needs and aspirations may mask their different economic situations or rates of modernization.

ing policy makers is that it is often difficult to discern at what point the costs of supporting a friendly regime become greater than the benefits. Recent events in the Philippines supply vivid evidence of such a dilemma. By the mid-1980s, the Marcos regime had been in power for nearly two decades and had during this period alienated a good part of the Filipino citizenry. Worse yet, corruption had all but destroyed one of the most promising economies in East Asia. Nor was the country free of political turmoil. The number of communist insurgents had risen from approximately sixteen thousand in the early 1980s to around thirty thousand by the end of 1985, certainly a sign of political desperation.

When Marcos forces attempted to steal the 1986 presidential election through widespread fraud at the ballot box, it was clear that no hope remained for the regime. In the year or so before the election, the United States had wisely begun to distance itself from Marcos by supporting the moderate and democratic elements led by Corazón Aquino. Fortunately, the disaffection of the Filipino armed forces

and the withdrawal of American support led to Marcos's peaceful exit.

Now that the corruption of the Marcos regime is well known, American policy makers must ask why they did not know earlier. Why did Marcos's anticommunist rhetoric blind policy makers to the degradation of democratic ideals that was occurring in the Philipines? Are there any lessons to be learned from this experience that should guide American policy in Central America?

Terrorism

Although the support of friendly regimes is fraught with uncertainties, the problem of international terrorism presents even greater difficulties for American policy makers. Because terrorism falls completely outside the normal channels of international relations, governments are often at a loss as to how to combat it. Under normal circumstances, the United States, like other sovereign states, can choose to have diplomatic relations with other governments. States can also forge trade agreements, establish military alliances, provide for cultural exchanges, formulate arms control agreements, and develop economic assistance programs.

Sovereign states can also, as the United States with Cuba, Iran, and North Korea, have no formal diplomatic relations. Countries antagonistic toward one another may very well go even farther and undertake boycotts and sanctions.[10] The ultimate recourse, of course, is war. All these measures are perceived to be of some benefit to at least one of the parties involved. Many of these measures lend some stability and predictability to international relations.

What makes international terrorism so terrible is its outlaw nature. Terrorists operate on their own and respect neither international law nor diplomatic courtesy. They are typically motivated by ethnic, ideological, or religious hostilities that are destructive of democratic ideals. All too often, they hold the United States responsible for their problems because they see the American government as supporting regimes that have produced the conditions they oppose. As a result, United States citizens are popular targets, because at any given time there are millions of Americans abroad, most of whom are civilians, who can be counted on to be easy victims.

The aftermath of a terrorist bombing of the LaBelle discotheque in
Berlin in April 1986

Such attacks allow terrorists to carry out one of
the principal goals of their organizations: to demonstrate the helplessness of government to protect in-
nocent people. This also explains why democratic
societies are the most attractive targets for terrorists.[11] In open societies, terrorists can come and
go and conspire as they please. Moreover, should a
democratic government take measures to police its
society more harshly, the terrorist becomes the
victor because the government has been forced to
undermine its own democratic ideals.

Combating terrorism is further complicated by
governments that either sponsor terrorism, as Libya
does on a regular basis, or engage in terrorist acts, as
Iran did when it seized the American Embassy in
Tehran along with its occupants. What does a
country whose citizens are imperiled do then? Increasingly, American foreign policy makers and
their counterparts in other democracies are treating

terrorists as pirates were dealt with hundreds of
years ago—as the enemies of the entire human race.

Under the right circumstances, the activities of
terrorists can be thwarted.[12] Several rings have been
broken and numerous terrorists have been caught
and brought to trial. In mid-1986, for example, the
hijackers of the Italian cruise ship, the *Achille Lauro,*
were tried and convicted in an Italian court. Since
terrorism is an international problem and terrorist
groups have been known to cooperate with one
another even though they may be separated by
thousands of miles, international approaches must
be developed to counter terrorism.

This is easier than it sounds. An important first
step would be to secure international agreement on
what constitutes terrorism and what constitutes acceptable interference in another nation's affairs.
The United States has been the target of much criticism in this respect. Terrorist acts committed by the

secret police of American allies have rarely been denounced. As one observer has asked, "Did we ever attempt to curb Savak, the Shah of Iran's murderous secret police, whom we helped supply and train?" [13]

Many foreign political leaders, including some of this nation's allies, viewed the mining of Nicaragua's harbors as an unacceptable interference by the United States in the affairs of a sovereign state. When the United States refused to accept the jurisdiction of the World Court in its dispute with Nicaragua, it appeared to many people throughout the world that America was flaunting international law.

Direct military action by the United States against a country either harboring terrorists or sponsoring terrorism has produced mixed results. When U.S. Navy fighter aircraft forced the Eygptian airliner carrying the hijackers of the Italian ship *Achille Lauro* to land in Sicily, the United States was accused of combating terrorism with terrorism and with violating international law. Nor did the Italian government prove helpful. One of the suspected planners of the hijacking was allowed to leave Italy despite American protests.

When the United States attacked Libya in April 1986, several of its allies refused to cooperate.

Others condemned the American action as another act of American terrorism. Shortly after the attack, several people, including a British citizen, lost their lives to terrorist reprisals. How likely is it that military action will actually lead to a reduction in terrorism? Can we break the law to preserve the law? Under what conditions do the ends justify the means?

There are, of course, no easy answers to such questions. Terrorism is difficult to predict or to prevent. Most governments can only react to terrorism. Very often, the options policy makers have at their disposal seem woefully inadequate. Still, the Soviet Union has cooperated with the United States in trying to prevent certain forms of terrorism. In a rare act of international cooperation between the two superpowers, the United States and Russia signed an agreement in June 1985 to monitor (and possibly stop) the acquisition of nuclear weapons by terrorist organizations. Preventing the ultimate nightmare is obviously in both countries' national interest.

Yet as long as there is ambiguity about what constitutes terrorism, about the right of one nation to interfere in the internal affairs of another nation, and about the reach of international law, violence

TRADING ARMS FOR HOSTAGES: DO THE ENDS JUSTIFY THE MEANS?

The foreign policy arena frequently forces policy makers to face the possibility of achieving highly desirable ends, but only through the use of highly questionable means. The determination of when the ends justify the means in such situations is a true test of the policy makers' foreign policy savvy, political and, in some cases, even moral judgement. The ends justifying the means was a question in the controversy that arose late in 1986 when it was revealed that President Reagan's National Security Council had been, for a period of about eighteen months, shipping arms to Iran in return for help in securing the release of American hostages being held by terrorists in Lebanon. President Reagan attempted to justify the arms deal by arguing that the ends (supporting moderate elements in Iran, improving relations with this important Middle Eastern power, and helping with the release of the hostages) justified the means (supplying arms and spare parts to a terrorist state still led by the despised Ayatollah Khomeini). The opinion polls indicated that the vast majority of the people did not agree, however. The polls also indicated that by engaging secretly in such deals while publicly promising never to bargain for hostages, Reagan had badly damaged his credibility. Moreover, because the trade involved an officially designated terrorist state, the entire operation was of questionable legality. No one questioned the motives of the administration or the desirability of the ends sought, but the means employed called the judgement and credibility of the president and his closest advisors into question.

in the international arena cannot be unequivocally and universally condemned nor effectively and legitimately combated.

Domestic Considerations in Foreign Policy

As we have noted on several occasions in this chapter, foreign policy is neither formulated nor imple-

mented in a vacuum. In the last two sections we explored what might be termed the international environment of American foreign policy making. We must now turn to an examination of those factors arising from domestic politics that influence how the United States will act in the international arena.

Although most Americans decide for whom to vote on the basis of issues close to home, elections in the United States do have important foreign policy implications. The party or ideological persuasion that wins a majority in Congress and the candidate who wins the presidency brings to public office values that, for example, will shape decisions on whether to grant or withhold economic and military aid, will influence their commitment to arms control negotiations, and will affect the types of trade agreements that will be pursued. In these and many other ways, the values American policy makers hold influence the conduct and outlook of dozens of governments who either rely on or are antagonistic to us.[14]

Even values as seemingly remote from international affairs as religious convictions can have an impact on foreign policy. The past two decades have witnessed a resurgence of religious sentiments. A record number of Americans now watch or listen to Christian television or radio programs and send their children to increasingly available Christian schools. Not surprisingly, some of this sentiment has spilled over into politics.

We can cite two examples of this trend. Pat Robertson, a foremost evangelical personality, announced he was seriously considering running for the Republican presidential nomination in 1988. With the four to six million people that he reaches daily through his Christian Broadcasting Network, it appears that Robertson has the nucleus for a national political campaign. Reverend Jerry Falwell's 1985 visit to South Africa was widely perceived as reinforcing the Reagan administration's policy of constructive engagement with the South African government. At a nationally broadcast news conference, Falwell insisted that more radical measures, such as economic sanctions, were unnecessary. Naturally, the administration was pleased with such news coverage.

The Christian evangelical movement, combined with the Reagan administration's conservative dis-

In response to Libyan involvement in the LaBelle Disco bombing President Reagan sent U.S. bombers to attack Tripoli. This photo of the destruction of the Libyan Naval academy shows the results of one response to terrorism.

position, has also contributed to a very strong posture of support for anticommunist regimes. Critics argue that a racist regime in South Africa is as evil as a communist regime in the Soviet Union. Neither serves the ultimate policy goals of the American government. But supporters of anticommunist governments maintain that although apartheid is repugnant to American ideals, the South Africans do not threaten vital American interests in the same way that the Soviets do.

Most of the world's governments consider their main policy goals to be political and economic survival, but American policy makers operate in a different environment. They must take into account the views of groups who are espousing philosophical and moral causes that are often at odds with one another, while seeking to implement policies that are supportive of the world's democracies. But is it always safe or even wise for the United States to

fashion foreign policies that are consistently supportive of other democracies? A case in point is the nearly unequivocal backing the United States has given Israel since its inception in 1948. Of course, since Israel is the predominant military power in the Middle East, the support is as strategic as it is idealistic. At the same time, the Middle East includes many countries whose own policies may favor the United States but are hostile to Israel. Such countries, particularly Saudi Arabia, are strategic allies because of their vast resources of oil and natural gas and their opposition to a Soviet presence in the Middle East.

The situation becomes further complicated when other American allies are considered. Most Western European countries and Japan, for example, are far more dependent on Middle Eastern oil than is the United States,[15] and, out of self-interest, are less favorably disposed toward Israel. Thus even

One sign of unrest among South Africa's Black majority is this burned out train in Soweto. The South African government's reluctance to abandon its racist "aparthied" policies presents the U.S. with a thorny foreign policy issue.

America's allies may be unable to develop foreign policies free of conflict and contradiction. Governments, whether democratic or authoritarian, pursue their own interests and, given human limitations, the people must hope that their leaders understand what those interests really are.[16]

In both domestic and foreign policy making, the American government is usually mindful of public opinion. Unfortunately for policy makers, there are many publics. When President Truman recognized the state of Israel in 1948, he did so in opposition to the secretary of state and the State Department, who did not want to risk antagonizing friendly Arab governments. But 1948 was also a presidential election year in which Truman was running for a full term of his own.[17] He had to consider the possible impact of his decision on both Jewish and non-Jewish voters who were very favorably disposed toward the recognition of Israel.

Pressures for Change in American Foreign Policy

Owing to the constantly changing conditions in the international arena, most of which are beyond American control, it is extremely difficult to evaluate the consistency, coherence, and effectiveness of foreign policy in nonpartisan, objective terms. The world in which American policy makers must operate is inconsistent, sometimes irrational, and always exceedingly complex. Nevertheless, certain pressures for change in United States foreign policy are apparent.

The limited success, some would say the failure, of military intervention since World War II has led policy makers to exercise greater caution in the exertion of force. The huge costs, the uncertainty of the outcome, and the danger of conflict growing beyond control have all led to a more skeptical attitude about the effectiveness of military solutions to the world's political and economic problems. Congress, after Vietnam, has adopted a much more critical attitude toward American military involvement. The War Powers Act, which is designed to limit the president's ability to commit troops abroad, is the most important indicator of Congress's new stance.

Public opposition to the Vietnam war, to the commitment of military advisers to El Salvador, and to military aid to the Contras in Nicaragua have made Congress and the president more aware of how hostile public opinion can limit the discretion of public officials. Although not nearly so intense in the 1980s, the opposition to a registration for a possible draft is also a good barometer of the attitudes of young people toward compulsory military service. Despite the charges by some public officials that the all-volunteer armed service has left the nation dangerously weak, any attempt to resurrect the draft would bring down on Congress a storm of opposition.

Fear of nuclear war, the strength of the international peace movement, and the reluctance of the United States's European allies to accept automati-

AN(OTHER) AMERICAN FOREIGN POLICY DILEMMA

The United States recognized Israel in 1948, minutes after the Israelis declared their statehood. From that time, American foreign policy in the Middle East has been fraught with difficulty. The United States has diplomatic relations with most of the Arab states hostile to Israel. Such a stance has required a careful balancing act between a pro-Israel position and a (not always successful) attempt to have cordial relations with Arab governments. The United States position was made somewhat easier in 1979 when Egypt and Israel signed a peace treaty and exchanged ambassadors. But because of American refusal to recognize the Palestine Liberation Organization, its acquiescence in the Israeli occupation of land Arab states claim as their own, and its support for Israel's strong military posture, many Arab governments believe the United States is not sufficiently sensitive to their interests.

cally more advanced nuclear weapons have all produced pressures for change. Many United States allies have also questioned our commitment to arms reduction. Shrewd moves by Mikhail Gorbachev, the Soviet leader, have seemingly put the American president on the defensive. Despite his efforts to counter Gorbachev and to get the arms negotiations with the Soviets moving again, Reagan is still perceived as the reluctant party. Nor did the meetings between Reagan and Gorbachev in Geneva (1985) and in Reykjavik (1986) produce any breakthroughs in the arms talks. While both leaders have good reasons for wanting an agreement, neither will get everything he wants in any possible outcome.

Both Republicans and Democrats have joined in attacking what is widely perceived as an oversized defense budget. The federal budget now allocates approximately 25 percent of all federal dollars to national defense. In the light of deficits exceeding $230 billion dollars a year and of the imperatives of Gramm-Rudman, cutting the size of the deficit also means slowing the growth of defense expenditures. Public opinion polls reveal that a majority of Americans think deficits should be reduced in part by reducing the Pentagon's budget. The media coverage of defense contractors charging excessive amounts for spare parts has reinforced this perception.

The increasing recognition of economic development as the most effective method of thwarting communism has led many to question the United States role in the underdeveloped world. The economic split between North and South is beginning to overshadow the ideological conflict between East and West. Although weakened by the oil glut, OPEC's emergence as an economic cartel is a classic example of how economics, more than ideology, can affect American foreign policy (and the debt of third world countries). The same is true for the upheavals in Latin America, Africa, and Asia, which are better understood from a North-South perspective than from an East-West perspective.

The limited success of military measures has also led to a renewed interest in economic development programs modeled after the Marshall Plan. Widely regarded as one of the United States's greatest successes in world affairs, the Marshall Plan could be adapted to overcome contemporary obstacles to development in the third world. Such a course of action would, as the Kissinger Commis-

"STAR WARS" A WEAPONS SYSTEM OR A FOREIGN POLICY TOOL?

Both nuclear superpowers understand that a nuclear exchange would destroy not only their respective countries but most of the world as well. This concept is appropriately referred to as MAD (mutual assured destruction). Until recently, few envisioned any feasible defense against incoming missiles with nuclear warheads. The strategic defense initiative (nicknamed Star Wars) is intended to change all that by intercepting and destroying the missiles after they are launched and before they reach their targets. Whether SDI will work (experts are to be found on both sides of the issue) does not detract from SDI's utility as a negotiating advantage of the United States in arms limitation talks with the Soviet Union. The Soviet Union is understandably impressed with both American technology and the fact that it can ill afford to match it. Its efforts to have the United States reduce the scope of SDI, if not abandon it completely, appear to have resulted in a new Soviet flexibility in arms control negotiations.

sion argues, be a more effective barrier to the spread of communism than mere reliance on military force.

Conclusion

As we approach the end of the twentieth century, the planet seems smaller, more vulnerable to acts of terrorism, and, frighteningly, more in danger of destruction by nuclear warfare. In this complex and uncertain environment, American foreign policy makers must assess risks, calculate costs, search for peaceful solutions, and attempt to reduce the likelihood of all-out war with the Soviets.

The uncertainty, the ideological antipathy, and forty years of hostility and distrust between the two superpowers ensure that the two countries will continue to allocate huge sums of money for national defense. From the perspective of the developing countries, these expenditures are a shameful waste of money in a world where millions live in poverty, suffer from malnutrition and hunger, and die unnecessary deaths from diseases that have been virtually unknown in the industrial world for decades.

The economic challenges the world faces present the United States with an unmatched opportunity to provide humanitarian leadership. By adapting the ideas behind the Marshall Plan to the contemporary period and to the needs of the developing world, the United States could within the next half-century raise the standard of living of countless millions. Such action will require courage, vision, perseverance, patience, and luck.

We can expect no quick fix, however. There will be discouraging setbacks, progress will be excruciatingly slow, and many countries receiving aid will show little gratitude. But if these steps are not taken, the poverty of the third world will prove a fertile ground for the seeds of Marxist ideology. If past history is any guide, once a nation is lost to communism, it is lost to democracy as well.

 Glossary

Collective security   A defense arrangement by which several countries, as in the North Atlantic Treaty Organization (NATO), agree to come to one another's assistance in the event of a foreign attack. An attack upon one member nation is therefore considered as an attack on all member nations.

Constructive engagement   A term used to describe the Reagan administration's approach to reforming the apartheid policy of the South African government. The administration considers this policy less extreme and more productive than other, more radical measures.

East-West conflict   A description of the ideological competition and the confrontational approach of the United States and the Soviet Union and their allies in NATO and the Warsaw Pact, respectively.

Executive agreement   An agreement between the president of the United States and the head of one or more sovereign states, typically about trade. Unlike treaties, such agreements do not require senatorial consent. In recent years, executive agreements have outnumbered treaties by a ratio of at least four to one.

North-South division A phrase used to describe the division of the world into the rich, industrialized, largely white, countries of the Northern Hemisphere and the poor, developing, largely nonwhite, countries of the Southern Hemisphere. Emphasizes economics rather than ideology as a basis for world conflicts.

Imperialism The political domination of one country by another. Usually, the mother country is independent, whereas the dominated country is treated legally as a colony. Socialists use the term to include economic domination of one country by another regardless of the existing political relationship.

OPEC The acronym for Organization of Petroleum Exporting Countries. Most of OPECs' members are countries of the Middle East. OPEC meets semiannually in an attempt to set oil production quotas and prices. In recent years, these efforts have been largely unsuccessful.

Protectorate A political term used to describe the domination of a weaker country by a stronger one. Major world powers, including the democracies, have established protectorates in countries that have a vital natural resource to prevent an adversary from doing the same.

Treaty A formal agreement reached by two or more countries that has been ratified by their respective governments. Treaties are a major source of international law. In the United States, the president initiates the treaty-making process, but all treaties must be ratified by a two-thirds vote of the Senate.

 ## Suggestions for Further Reading

Almond, Gabriel A. *The American People and Foreign Policy.* 2d ed. Boulder, Colo.: Greenwood Press, 1977. An early but still very relevant study of the influence of public opinion on foreign policy decisions and their implementation.

Falk, Richard. *Human Rights and State Sovereignty.* New York: Holmes and Meier, 1981. The question of how far the United States should go and is willing to go to protect human rights in the rest of the world is treated in this readable book.

Feinberg, Richard E. *The Intemperate Zone: The Third World Challenge to U.S. Foreign Policy.* New York: Norton, 1983. This work offers a penetrating and provocative analysis while displaying a comprehensive knowledge of the strategic and moral issues involved.

Feld, Werner J. *American Foreign Policy: Aspirations and Reality.* New York: Wiley, 1984. Carefully examines how the complexities and uncertainties of world affairs place limits on the United States's efforts to control its destiny and affect the international arena.

Halberstam, David. *The Best and the Brightest.* New York: Random House, 1972. A terrifying analysis of how the best-informed minds in government can make tragic mistakes and miscalculations in foreign policy decision making.

Kennedy, Robert F. *Thirteen Days.* New York: Norton, 1971. A well-written novel could not provide greater suspense than this narrative of the Cuban missile crisis in 1962 by the brother of the president and one of the most important decision makers then in government.

Kissinger, Henry. *White House Years.* Boston: Little, Brown, 1979. An inside, if self-serving, account of the formulation and implementation of policy in foreign affairs during the Nixon and Ford administrations.

Kubalkova, V., and A.A. Cruickshank. *International Inequality.* New York: St. Martin's, 1981. A comparison of how communist, developing, and Western countries view international politics.

LaFeber, Walter. *Inevitable Revolutions: The United States in Central America.* New York: Norton, 1983. Hailed as the best book on Central America in more than one hundred years. The author's dissection of the U.S. role in Central America makes for sometimes painful reading.

Ray, James Lee. *Global Politics.* 2d ed. Boston: Houghton Mifflin, 1982. Examines the role of the United States in world affairs. Also includes a good overview of the history of American foreign policy.

Spanier, John, and Eric M. Uslaner. *Foreign Policy and the Democratic Dilemma.* 3d ed. New York: Holt, Rinehart and Winston, 1982. How the sometimes hardball and cruel diplomatic game in the world is played out by those who must also consider their commitment to democratic ideals.

Tuchman, Barbara. *The March of Folly: From Troy to Viet Nam* New York: Knopf, 1984. Recounts in a brilliant fashion how political leaders and nations have stumbled from one military debacle to another.

She from old fountains doth new judgment draw,
Till, word by word, the ancient order swerves
To the true course more nigh; in every age
A little she creates, but more preserves.
George E. Woodberry
"My Country"

Chapter 14

Continuity and Renewal

Chapter Outline

Introduction
Values and the Policy Process
Change and the Future of American Politics
Appropriate Strategies for Political Change
Conclusion

Introduction

Before examining the various dimensions of political change, let us recall what we view as the central emphases of this text. Throughout this work, we have focused on values—the values held by those who get involved in politics, who go to the polls to vote, who join interest groups, and who actually make the public policies that affect our lives. This focus on values underpinned our analysis of political parties and interest groups, the institutions of the national government and the public policies produced by that government. No understanding of American politics, we are convinced, can be complete without a careful exploration of the ways that values impinge on the political process in general and the policy process in particular.

Foremost among the values that pervade American politics are those found in the Declaration of Independence and the Constitution. Also of critical importance are underlying or **inherited values.** They influence both group and party activity and the cost and resource allocations found in the federal budget. Together, these values have a significant impact on the inputs and the outcomes of the policy process.

Values and the Policy Process

Three basic conclusions about the policy process follow from our analysis of American politics. First, analysis at the level of values indicates that public policies are, for the most part, consistent with the values of the people most likely to vote. In a **majoritarian** electoral system, this is not particularly surprising. It does indicate, however, that the protection of minority interests depends largely on to what degree those interests are perceived as consonant with majority preferences. When such consonance is lacking, the American form of government will be far less responsive to minorities.

Second, the values held by those who are politically active and the claims of special interests have played important roles in the policy-making process. Critics of existing policy such as the Reverend Jesse Jackson, Kalman Silvert, and Howard Zinn insist that only by increasing political participation, especially by politically inactive groups, including the disadvantaged, can this nation enhance the pro-

cess of determining the common good.[1] Increased political participation by such groups, they argue, is also necessary before the nation can be assured of a fairer and more equitable cost and resource allocation. Under the present pattern of policy making, dairy farmers, for example, are the beneficiaries of public policies that raise substantially the cost of dairy products to the American consumer. For these critics, the crucial question is whether the benefits to dairy farmers outweigh the costs to consumers.

Third, budget analysis reveals that present policies support a high level of defense spending and that the tax structure, until the Tax Reform Act of 1986, provided wealthy individuals and large corporations some tax advantages. Defense expenditures account for more than 25 percent of the federal budget and corporate income taxes account for less than 10 percent. This pattern of budgetary allocations reflects the nation's strongly held values of anticommunism and economic individualism. At the same time, large numbers of Americans are disturbed, as the Gramm-Rudman deficit reduction act reveals, by the imbalance between revenues and expenditures. Yet fundamental revisions in budgetary allocations are, we believe, unlikely until there is a change in the value structure of the most politically active individuals and groups.

For many critics of American government, the inequities and persisting problems in the policy process can be traced directly to the traditional pattern of policy making, that is, to the impact of inherited values, pressure politics (or "client" politics as James Q. Wilson terms it), and incremental change on the entire policy-making process. Inherited values such as economic individualism and limited government constrain policy making on such environmental problems as acid rain and toxic wastes. Pressure politics, as the dairy farmer example reveals, works to the advantage of special interests. When policies are enacted to address particular problems, incremental change ensures gradual policy shifts and a piecemeal approach rather than comprehensive changes.

Many believe the United States has the resources to manage its problems much more effectively. For a variety of reasons, we simply lack the political will and the appropriate values to attack the nation's problems head on. The problems of the economy (such as the balance of payments in foreign trade and the trade-off between inflation and

Nearly 30% of the national budget flows through this building, the Pentagon, seat of the Department of Defense.

unemployment), of the environment (acid rain, toxic wastes), of the society (abortion, drug abuse, crime, and poverty) and of foreign affairs (the East-West conflict and North-South relations) are all exacerbated by the current configuration of values.

In any event, the American nation could almost certainly come to grips more effectively with the short-run problems of the use and abuse of national power and the short-run vagaries of the economy.[2] Many opponents and even some of the supporters of the Reagan administration see the American presence in Central America as an ineffective use of national power. American intervention can succeed, these groups claim, only if military force is coupled with a long-range plan for economic development.

At present, the emphasis is almost solely on military force with little thought given to the economic problems of that troubled region. Economic perplexities at home could also be more satisfactorily resolved if the federal budget deficit were reduced and a trade policy adopted that alleviated the balance of payments problem.

Until these short-run difficulties are addressed more effectively, the United States will find the mid-run problem of the challenge of socialism to be quite formidable. Both democracy and capitalism are under attack throughout the world, but particularly in the developing countries of the Southern Hemisphere. As a nation, we must respond not only to the ideological conflict with the Soviet Union

POLITICS, ECONOMICS, AND IDEOLOGY

Political inquiry remains a fascinating quest because there are few universally agreed-on answers to the fundamental questions of politics. Much the same is true for economic inquiry as well. Unlike engineering problems or problems that can be solved by advances in technology, political and economic issues often get bogged down in ideological debates. Under what conditions should the government intervene in the economy? Is the free market the most efficient allocator of resources in a modern, industrialized state? What are the most effective governmental instruments for ensuring economic growth? Does government have a responsibility to alleviate social ills? What criteria should be used to determine the proper balance between economic growth and environmental protection? The answers to these queries depend to a large extent on who is asked. Liberals, conservatives, libertarians, capitalists, socialists, ecologists, and humanists will argue forcibly for their point of view. Disturbing or reassuring, the health of the American democracy rests on the wise choices of the American people among competing policy alternatives.

(the East-West split) but also to the pleas of third-world countries for economic assistance (the North-South division).

There appear to be two great historical "ifs" that condition our response to this challenge. If the Vietnam experience is an accurate guide, American military intervention will not forestall, except briefly, the demands for revolutionary change that are sweeping through the poor nations of the world. If the post-World War II experience of Europe and Japan is an accurate guide, this nation's most effective response to the economic problems of the developing countries will consist of a plan of economic development similar to the Marshall Plan.

Unless we confront the mid-run problems successfully, we cannot address the long-run problem of the transformation or reconstruction of the material basis of American civilization. Internationally, the nation's basic industries are not competing effectively with either Japan or West Germany. The decline of the so-called smokestack industries has

resulted in closed plants and lost jobs in many parts of the industrial Northeast. In certain respects, we are losing the shirt off our back (a shirt, incidentally, that was probably made in some Asian country).

Domestically, the nation's infrastructure is crumbling. Bridges, highways, railroads, dams, and soil erosion control are all in need of a massive infusion of governmental funds. Those who live in the snowbelt are all too familiar with the potholes in the streets and on the highways that plague drivers every spring. Cleaning up existing hazardous waste sites continues to strain budgetary resources.

Despite disagreement about specifics, resolving the nation's persisting problems appears to call for both continuity and renewal. The values embedded in the Declaration of Independence and the Constitution provide the bedrock for continuity. On the other hand, renewal seems possible only if compre-

The collapse of a 100 foot section of the Connecticut Turnpike (I-95) dramatically emphasized rising concern over the condition of the nation's transportation infrastructure. The prevention of similar incidents in the future is a matter of governmental policy.

hensive changes are undertaken. These changes involve increasing the levels of political participation, an enhanced understanding of the proper role of the national government in the nation's economy, and a more widely based commitment to ensuring that all Americans have a chance to share in the American dream.

Change and the Future of American Politics

Significant change in the American form of government, we believe, can come about only if ways can be found to increase dramatically the level and quality of political participation. Leftist critics of the economic system such as Michael Harrington insist that many of the barriers to increased participation are economic.[3] Political scientists have long been aware that the socioeconomic status of an individual or a group determines to a large extent the level of political participation. Yet if we are to come closer to Abraham Lincoln's definition of democracy as government of the people, by the people, and for the people, we must find answers to the difficult problem of mobilizing the individuals and groups who traditionally have not been politically active.[4]

Other critics suggest that ordinary citizens must become aware of and guard against the undue influence of concentrated economic power.[5] Large corporations and multinational firms can exert an unhealthy influence on a democratic political system. If the citizenry is not alert to this danger, the fact of economic privilege may in time erode the content of individual political rights.

The danger of overregulation or the stifling of the entreprenurial spirit must be avoided as well. Job creation, economic growth, and technological innovation all depend to a large extent on economic incentives. To remain a world economic power, the nation must insist on the public accountability of business without incurring the economic stagnation due to unnecessarily restrictive governmental policy.

We must, however, never lose sight of the goal of a more just society. Economic, racial, and sexual inequality are barriers to the complete realization of democracy. If an individual cannot get a good education and then compete with others on an equal

THE DISTRIBUTION OF WEALTH AND INCOME IN THE UNITED STATES

Despite a progressive income tax that has been in place for nearly three-quarters of a century and numerous social programs that are more than a half-century old, the redistribution of wealth and income from the haves to the have-nots has been minimal at best. The wealthiest 2 percent of American families own 30 percent of all privately held financial assets, whereas the poorest 20 percent have a negative net worth. The top 20 percent of American families earn 49 percent of all income, and the bottom 20 percent earn only 4 percent. Approximately 15 percent of all American families fall below the government-defined poverty line.

These statistics pose some troubling questions for the American people. How much disparity in wealth and income is permissible in a democratic society? Does the government have a responsibility to ensure a minimal standard of living for the disadvantaged? Should there be an economic bill of rights comparable to the Bill of Rights found in the Constitution? Have government efforts to aid the disadvantaged simply been ineffective or is the distribution of wealth and income an accurate reflection of the distribution of human talents? What accounts for the persistence of poverty in one of the world's richest nations? In seeking answers to these questions and in the quest for a more just society, Americans will be engaged in a searching inquiry into the American character and into the reach of American democracy.

basis for jobs and housing because of racial or sexual prejudice, the substance of American democracy for that person remains an empty promise.

Yet, as Samuel Huntington tells us, we must not despair. "Critics say that America is a lie because its reality falls so far short of its ideals. They are wrong. America is not a lie; it is a disappointment. But it can be a disappointment only because it is also a hope."[6] While we strive for a just society, we must not let the quest for equality lead to a numbing sameness that destroys individual initiative. Although it is difficult to achieve, Americans must find an appropriate balance between the ideals of equality and individualism. Too much stress on either impedes both justice and creativity, limiting our innate potential.

By relating political change to the influence of competing interest groups, the institutions of government, and to policy outcomes, we can gain a clearer understanding of what is necessary to achieve change and what impact change will have on the American political process. Table 14.1 highlights various dimensions and consequences of change.

Revolutionary change is one type of change. No stable political system, regardless of ideological outlook, encourages or facilitates revolutionary change. Despite their claims to be revolutionary regimes, communist countries quickly take steps to ensure that another revolution does not topple them from power. The Soviet Union has also intervened directly or indirectly in the internal affairs of such neighboring communist countries as Czechoslavakia, Hungary, and Poland, when the Communist party's rule was threatened. When China under Mao urged the Red Guards to engage in perpetual revolution, the results produced chaos and set back economic development by more than a decade.

In the United States, the American Revolution can be viewed as a successful attempt at revolutionary change. Yet our Constitution does not provide for any future revolutions. Indeed, any attempt to overthrow the government today would be viewed not only as subversive but also illegal.

Comprehensive changes are another type. Comprehensive changes in stable political systems are uncommon. Over the course of American history, the most important comprehensive changes occurred during times of national crisis—the Civil War and the Great Depression. The Civil War en-

ded the threat posed by the states rights advocates to national sovereignty, whereas the Great Depression changed significantly the role of the national government in regulating the economy, assuring citizens of minimal economic well-being, and protecting their civil rights and civil liberties.[7] In addition, the origins of many contemporary social programs can be traced directly to Franklin Roosevelt whose New Deal was an effort to overcome the depression.

Changes that are perceived as far-reaching are also likely to provoke opposition. The civil rights movement is a case in point. When blacks undertook a series of actions to secure their rights, they were opposed on nearly every front by whites who were determined to protect the status quo. Until the Supreme Court struck down the legal segregation of the nation's public schools, whites even had the law on their side. After the *Brown* decision, whites had to find new grounds for their resistance. Blacks have had to wage a long and bitter conflict to secure their rights. Even today that struggle is not over.

In less momentous times and with less controversial issues, the typical environment and pattern of policy making is stability, incremental change, and moderate conflict. To have any hope of success, those who seek change must take this pattern of policy making into account, adapting their tactics to the type of change they are seeking and recognizing the likelihood of conflict arising out of their efforts.

As Table 14.2 suggests, a conflict will be severe or moderate depending on existing conditions. In 1787, the Founding Fathers disagreed on some issues but agreed on many others. As a result, the Constitutional Convention fostered only moderate conflict. In contrast, by the 1860s, northern and

Table 14.1
Dimensions of Change

TYPE OF CHANGE	RELATIVE INFLUENCE OF COMPETING INTERESTS	INSTITUTIONS	POLICY OUTCOMES
Incremental	Pattern of interests remains stable; decisions based on bargains and compromises	Basically unaltered	Gradual policy redirection
Comprehensive	Substantial changes in the pattern of interest competition	Basically unaltered	Far-reaching innovations or historic reversals of policies
Revolutionary	Pattern of interests transformed; new interests appear, others disappear	Substantial alteration	Policy dramatically reoriented

Table 14.2
Paradigm of Conflict

	MODERATE	SEVERE
ATTITUDES		
Leaders and activists	Convergent	Divergent
Nonelites	Convergent	Divergent
LINES OF CLEAVAGE	Overlapping (cross-cutting)	Nonoverlapping (cumulative)
THREATS TO WAY OF LIFE	Absent	Present
Elites	Secure	Threatened
Aspiring groups	Successful	Frustrated
POLITICAL INSTITUTIONS PROVIDE:		
Negotiations but not decisions	No	Yes
Decisions without consent	No	Yes
Agreed processes for negotiating consent and arriving at decisions	Yes	No

southern leaders differed on virtually all issues affecting the two regions. The result was the Civil War, the most severe conflict ever to engulf the nation.

Appropriate Strategies for Political Change

Given the upheavals and the uncertainties that accompany revolutionary change, a prudent strategy, from a tactical point of view, is to seek change through group activity. Like-minded individuals who band together under able leadership can bring pressure to bear on a government to change its policies. Such a strategy is essentially the democratic method of reorienting a political system.

Only when all avenues of peaceful change have been blocked by those in power should a group seek its goals by other means. Thomas Jefferson, in the Declaration of Independence, justified the American Revolution on the grounds of a long series of usurpations and tyrannies. It was only after more than a decade of such abuses that a majority of the American colonists were willing to resist British rule.

Yet the pursuit of change through group activity carries a certain amount of risk. A group is less than

a majority. No major category of the American population defined by a single criterion, whether it be occupation, income, religion, ethnic group, gender, or region, constitutes a majority. As a first step then, groups seeking change must attempt to unite with other groups. Coalition building, however, is an extremely difficult task, as Jesse Jackson found in the 1984 Democratic presidential primaries when he sought to build a "rainbow coalition" of blacks, Hispanics and whites, men and women, and the unemployed and poverty stricken.

In general, for change to be successful, reform groups must identify the appropriate strategy and assess realistically their ability to implement that strategy in the pursuit of their goals. Table 14.3 outlines the options available to groups seeking change. The first two strategies, forming an independent or a new coalition party, often contain a large element of ideology. As a consequence, they have rarely been successful in American politics at the national level. Despite numerous attempts, not since the Civil War has the effort to create a new coalition party succeeded in electoral politics.[8] Theodore Roosevelt failed with the Progressive party in 1912, Robert LaFollette with the Progressive party in 1924, George Wallace with the American Independent party in 1968, and John Anderson with his Independent party in 1980. Nor have third-party movements, as distinguished from minor parties, lasted beyond two or three presidential elections.

League of Women Voters holds a pre-election debate on Capitol Hill.

Table 14.3
Alternative Strategies and Political Change

GOALS	MEMBERS/ INTERESTS	APPROPRIATE STRATEGY
Comprehensive Acceptable to neither party	Few—homogene-ous	Form an indepen-dent party
Comprehensive Acceptable to neither party	Numerous—hetero-geneous	Form a new coali-tion party
Narrow (influence in a limited area) Acceptable to both parties	Few—heterogene-ous	Form a pressure group
Comprehensive Acceptable to one party	Numerous—hetero-geneous	Join in a coalition with an existing party

Indeed, none of the parties just mentioned has survived. The political lesson seems plain: Advocates of change should avoid these two strategies.

The latter two strategies, forming a pressure group or joining in a coalition with an existing party, are more pragmatic and thus more in keeping with the traditional pattern of American policy making. The third, pressure group, strategy describes the existing method of interest-based politics and is often applauded by apologists for the American system as one of the strengths of a **pluralist society.**[9] Unfortunately, this strategy forecloses efforts at comprehensive changes that would result in a sweeping redirection of present policies. It should be considered only by groups that are basically satisfied with the system and are seeking only incremental changes in public policies.

By contrast, the fourth strategy, joining in a coalition with an existing party, assumes the desirability or necessity of comprehensive change. This strategy attempts to increase the level of political participation so power and decision making may be shared across a broad range of issues. Jesse Jackson's effort to register black voters and to insert planks protective of the economic interests of his "rainbow" coalition in the 1984 Democratic platform is a recent example of an attempt to seek comprehensive change. Although his success in the primaries and at the Democratic Convention was limited, there can be little doubt that Jackson awak-

ened many leaders in the Democratic party to constituencies they could not safely ignore if they hoped to win future presidential elections.

Conclusion

Successful political change must be in harmony with the value structures of politically active individuals and groups. Without a doubt, the most important sources of American values are the Declaration of Independence and the Constitution. The Declaration not only justified the American Revolution but also set forth brilliantly the fundamental principles of American political philosophy. That philosophy called for the protection of the natural rights of equality, life, liberty, and the pursuit of happiness. The Constitution insisted on popular sovereignty and, while granting impressive powers to the national government, placed limits on the exercise of those powers. As a consequence, we are largely free to pursue whatever goals we wish. Popular sovereignty and limited government have largely been realized. Only the natural right of equality has yet to be fully accepted.

It is not surprising then that the rising demand for equality by blacks and other minorities and by women has proven so potent in the twentieth century. The Fourteenth Amendment equal protection jurisprudence forged by the Warren Court and the

Pursuit of change through group activity seems a certainty in a nation of such diversity.

NANCY LANDON KASSEBAUM (b. 1932): CONTINUITY AND RENEWAL IN KANSAS

Senator Nancy Landon Kassebaum of Kansas represents both continuity and renewal in American politics. First elected in 1978, she is the first woman to win a Senate seat who was not the widow of a member of Congress. Her victory was thus symbolic of the rising importance of women as a political force. Senator Kassebaum's election also reflected continuity, however, in that she is a member of an old political family and heir to the influence and advantages such membership brings. She is the daughter of Alf Landon, a former governor of Kansas and Republican candidate for president in 1936.

Alf Landon was soundly beaten by FDR in his presidential bid, but the Landon name is still potent in Kansas politics. Though he initially opposed his daughter's candidacy because he thought Kansas was not ready for a woman senator, she skillfully used her Landon name and turned her relative inexperience in politics to her advantage. Her campaign slogan, "A fresh face, a trusted Kansas name," succinctly captured both aspects of her campaign. She presented herself as a homemaker rather than just another politician, and outpolled eight other candidates in the Republican primary including another, more politically experienced woman. Her name and disarming tactics worked again in the general election against a popular Democrat.

Despite her relative inexperience, Kassebaum has had an impact in the Senate and has gained the respect of both her fellow senators and her constituents. She tends to reflect her conservative Kansas Republican roots on domestic economic matters, but has displayed a rather independent and liberal stance in her role as a member of the Foreign Relations Committee. She has made the most news as a member of the Western Hemisphere Affairs Subcommittee, favoring the Panama Canal Treaty initiated by President Carter and voicing strong criticism of Reagan administration policy toward Central America.

In 1980, Kassebaum registered another first for women when she served in the symbolically important post of temporary chair of the Republican National Convention. Her service was impressive enough to earn her mention as a possible vice presidential candidate in that same year. Though she has blazed trails for women in politics, she is a moderate on most "women's issues." She favored the Equal Rights Amendment, for example, but did not feel that its defeat was a mistake of awesome proportions. She has endorsed federal funding for abortion, but only in the limited circumstances of rape, incest, or endangerment of the mother's life.

Kassebaum is widely praised as a hard worker in the Senate and, given her growing popularity in heavily Republican Kansas, will most likely remain in the Senate as long as she wishes. Now in her second term, her seniority will soon assure her influential positions on the important Budget and Commerce committees. Given this record, Senator Kassebaum may well go on to establish other important firsts for women in American politics in the years ahead.

proposed Equal Rights Amendment are different manifestations of the way the ideal of equality can be used in seeking change.

Since the Jacksonian era of the 1830s, political equality has been a notable part of the democratic creed and a growing part of American practice. Yet if political, racial, and sexual inequality are increasingly viewed as unacceptable in a just society, it is difficult to conceive what logic can be found that would deny the extension of this argument to the elimination of the worst forms of economic inequality.

If the extension of equality is the logic of democracy, ultimately all barriers to equality will fall. Nor would the destruction of those barriers necessarily mean the denial of the individualism that the founders of this nation strove to protect in the Constitution. Equality and individualism can be realized together, but it will require astuteness on the part of the American people. Ideally, the removal of inequities that limit liberty and the pursuit of happiness should encourage the full realization of every individual's potential. Such a goal expresses both the continuity of traditional ideals and the renewal of those ideals that give life and vitality to the American republic.

 ## Glossary

Inherited values   Values that Americans have acquired as a result of the nation's history. The ideals of popular sovereignty, limited government, and political equality, embedded in the Declaration of Independence and the Constitution, and the values of anticommunism and economic individualism are critical to an understanding of American politics.

Lines of cleavage   A political concept that seeks to classify how and why individuals and groups differ on critical issues. If most people agree on some issues and disagree on others, the lines of cleavage are said to be overlapping. If, however, society becomes polarized, the lines of cleavage are viewed as cumulative and the resulting political conflicts are likely to be severe.

Majoritarian politics   An approach to policy making that emphasizes the benefits that accrue to large numbers of people. Critics contend that majoritarian politics ignores the needs of the disadvantaged and the underrepresented who must bear the tax burden without receiving the benefits of governmental programs.

Pattern of interests   A phrase used to describe the relative strength and influence of competing groups. In the United States, business, farm, and labor groups are considered more powerful than civil rights, environmental, and urban groups.

Pluralist society   A society made up of heterogeneous groups that compete for political influence. Public policies are largely the result of that competition.

 ## Suggestions for Further Reading

Domhoff, G. William. *Who Rules America Now? A View for the Eighties.* Englewood Cliffs, N.J.: Prentice-Hall, 1983. Argues that a self-conscious elite occupies the dominant positions in both our economic and political systems.

Friedman, Milton, and Rose Friedman. *Free to Choose: A Personal Statement.* New York: Avon, 1980. A Nobel laureate economist and his wife champion the virtues of a free market economy and decry the fact that the United States has strayed from this libertarian vision.

Gilder, George. *Wealth and Poverty.* New York: Basic Books, 1981. An ambitious attempt to update Adam Smith's *Wealth of Nations* that has captured the imagination of conservatives, libertarians, and neoconservatives.

Heilbroner, Robert L. *Business Civilization in Decline.* New York: Norton, 1976. One of the most widely read economists outlines his views of the coming transition to the postindustrial era.

Lasch, Christopher. *The Culture of Narcissism: American Life in an Age of Diminishing Expectations.* New York: Norton, 1979. A brilliant and provocative indictment of contemporary American culture by a leftist social critic.

Pole, Jack R. *The Pursuit of Equality in American History.* Berkeley: University of California Press, 1978. Examines from an historical perspective the value that Alexis de Tocqueville saw as the distinguishing characteristic of American democracy.

Thurow, Lester. *The Zero-Sum Society: Distribution and the Possibilities for Economic Change.* New York: Basic Books, 1980. Argues forcibly that most of the economic problems faced by the United States will be exceedingly difficult to resolve because the solutions necessitate winners and losers and political leaders are extremely reluctant to make those kinds of decisions.

Notes

Chapter One

1. The classic study of Jeffersonian economics is Joseph Dorfman, "The Economic Philosophy of Thomas Jefferson," *Political Science Quarterly* 55:98–121 (March 1940).

2. Kenneth M. Dolbeare and Patricia Dolbeare, *American Ideologies: The Competing Political Beliefs of the 1970s*, 3rd ed. (Chicago: Rand-McNally, 1976), explore the political thought of various groups who would seek far-reaching changes in the structure of American politics.

3. Milton Friedman has won many adherents to his point of view that an inextricable link exists between a capitalist economy and a democratic form of government. See Milton Friedman, *Capitalism and Freedom* (Chicago: University of Chicago Press, 1962), and Milton Friedman and Rose Friedman, *Free to Choose* (New York: Harcourt Brace Jovanovich, 1980).

4. Office of Management and Budget, *The United States Budget in Brief, Fiscal Year 1987* (Washington, D.C.: Government Printing Office, 1986), Tables 3 and 4. This document is the source for all the budgetary figures used in this chapter.

5. Charles Redenius, *The American Ideal of Equality: From Jefferson's Declaration to the Burger Court* (Port Washington, N.Y.: Kennikat, 1981), pp. 18–21, 36–37, and 113–114.

6. An excellent survey of the economic transformation can be found in William G. Shepard, *Market Power and Economic Welfare* (New York: Random House, 1979).

7. For a provocative argument on what reforms are necessary, see Philip Green, *Retrieving Democracy* (Totowa, N.J.: Rowman and Allanheld, 1985).

8. Paul Blumberg, *Inequality in an Age of Decline* (New York: Oxford University Press, 1980), pp. 9–64.

9. For the renewal of concern with civil rights for blacks, see Carl M. Brauer, *John F. Kennedy and the Second Reconstruction* (New York: Columbia University Press, 1977).

10. Alexis de Tocqueville, *Democracy in America* (New York: Random House, 1945), 1:452.

11. George Kenan (writing as "X"), "The Sources of Soviet Conduct," *Foreign Affairs* 24:566–582 (1947), is widely regarded as the most able analysis of the origins of containment as a foreign policy.

12. Robert Heilbroner, *An Inquiry into the Human Prospect: Revised and Updated for the 1980s* (New York: Norton, 1980), pp. 47, 54, 68.

13. Joan Edelman Spero, *The Politics of International Economic Relations*, 2nd ed. (New York: St. Martin's, 1981), explores both East-West and North-South tensions. See also, Richard E. Neustadt and Ernest R. May, *Thinking in Time: The Uses of History for Decision-Makers* (New York: Free Press, 1986), for a provocative analysis of how history can serve policy makers faced with difficult choices.

Chapter Two

1. The nature of democracy is explored in Robert Dahl, *A Preface to Democratic Theory* (Chicago: University of Chicago Press, 1956); Charles Frankel, *The Democratic Prospect* (New York: Harper, 1962); Joseph Schumpeter, *Capitalism, Socialism, and Democracy*, 3d ed. (New York: Harper, 1950); and Giovanni Sartori, *Democratic Theory* (Westport, Conn.: Greenwood, 1973).

2. For contrasting perspectives on American history, see Daniel Boorstin, *The Americans: The Democratic Experience* (New York: Random House, 1973), and Howard Zinn, *A People's History of the United States* (New York: Harper, 1980).

3. See Michael Harrington, *The Next America: The Decline and Rise of the United States* (New York: Holt, 1981), for a work that advocates a radical expansion of rights.

4. Robert McCloskey, *The American Supreme Court* (Chicago: University of Chicago Press, 1960), and G. Edward White, *The American Judicial Tradition* (New York: Oxford University Press, 1976), support this contention.

5. J. R. Pole, *The Pursuit of Equality in American History* (Berkeley: University of California Press, 1978), pp. 333–341.

6. Thomas Jefferson, *The Portable Thomas Jefferson,* edited by Merrill Peterson (New York: Viking, 1975), p. 291.

7. David Wood, *Power and Policy in Western European Democracies,* 2d ed. (New York: Wiley, 1982), pp. 101–124.

8. An excellent overview of this subject is Robert Heilbroner, *The Making of Economic Society,* 6th ed. (Englewood Cliffs, N.J.: Prentice-Hall, 1980).

9. One scholar who would so argue is Friedrich von Hayek. See his *The Road to Serfdom* (Chicago, University of Chicago Press, 1944).

10. Many European nations have been plagued by slow economic growth over the last decade. In an attempt to cure their economic woes, some nations have turned to the right, others to the left. Britain and France are examples of this phenomenon. See Charles Redenius, "The Supply-Side Alternative: Reagan and Thatcher's Economic Policies," *Journal of Social, Political and Economic Studies* 8(2):189–209 (1983), for an exploration of the British experience.

11. For an analysis of the ties between government and business in Japan, see J. Halliday, *A Political History of Japanese Capitalism* (New York: Pantheon, 1975).

Chapter Three

1. Seymour Martin Lipset, *The First New Nation* (New York: Heinemann, 1964).
2. For contrasting views of the Declaration, see Carl Becker, *The Declaration of Independence* (New York: Random House, 1970), and Garry Wills, *Inventing America: Jefferson's Declaration of Independence* (Garden City, N.Y.: Doubleday, 1978).
3. Jack R. Pole, *The Pursuit of Equality in American History* (Berkeley, Calif.: University of California Press, 1978), p. 56, and Charles M. Redenius, *The American Ideal of Equality: From Jefferson's Declaration to the Burger Court* (Port Washington, N.Y.: Kennikat, 1981), pp. 11–14.
4. Alexis de Tocqueville, *Democracy in America,* Vol. 1 (New York: Random House, 1945), pp. 3, 55.
5. Herbert Aptheker, *A History of the American People,* Part 2, *The American Revolution* (New York: International Publishers, 1960), pp. 100–110, offers some trenchant criticisms.
6. Baptists, Quakers, and Methodists, among others, offered a critique of church-state unity. All these groups drew on a tradition of religious dissent that dated back to the Civil War in England of the 1640s. See Christopher Hill, *The World Turned Upside Down* (New York: Penguin Books, 1976), for a careful analysis of the contribution of the religious dissenters.
7. The Magna Carta was signed in 1215 by King John. He was persuaded to do so by nobles disgusted with his arbitrary rule. The document is often cited as the beginning of British constitutionalism.
8. Mercantilism's days, however, were numbered. In 1776, the same year as the Declaration of Independence, Adam Smith published his *Wealth of Nations,* which remains the classic statement of capitalism. The influence of Smith's book spread rapidly and quickly became the veritable bible of American capitalism.
9. John Locke, *Two Treatises on Government,* in William Ebenstein, ed., *Great Political Thinkers: Plato to the Present,* 4th ed. (New York: Holt, 1969), p. 418.
10. Many English parliamentarians, such as Edmund Burke, strongly supported compromise with the colonies. Unfortunately, Burke was in a minority.
11. In his *Two Treaties on Government* published in 1689–1690.
12. Crane Brinton, *The Anatomy of Revolution* (New York: Random House, 1965), offers a comparative analysis of revolution employing the two-phase approach.
13. Bernard Bailyn, *The Ideological Origins of the American Revolution* (Cambridge, Mass.: Harvard University Press, 1967), and Gordon Wood, *The Creation of the American Republic, 1776–1789* (Chapel Hill: University of North Carolina Press, 1969), are indispensable to an understanding of this period.
14. Page Smith, *The Shaping of America* (New York: McGraw-Hill, 1980), reports on the later careers of the revolutionary generation in Chapter 48, "Whatever Happened to the Founding Fathers," pp. 785–801.
15. Paine got into trouble by living up to his name in the French Revolution, where he was even too radical for France's extremists. At one point, he was thrown into prison and avoided the guillotine only through the intervention of American diplomats.
16. The English Bill of Rights was promulgated in 1691, the American equivalent in 1791.
17. We examine the bargains and compromises at the Constitutional Convention in the next chapter.

Chapter Four

1. This period in American history is carefully explored in Forrest Mc Donald, *E Pluribus Unum: The Formation of the American Republic, 1776–1790* (Boston: Houghton Mifflin, 1965).
2. Alexander Hamilton, John Jay, and James Madison, *The Federalist Papers,* edited by Clinton Rossiter (New York: New American Library, 1961), p. 322.
3. Bernard Schwartz, *The Great Rights of Mankind: A History of the Bill of Rights* (New York: Oxford University Press, 1977), pp. 156–160.
4. The impact of this change in leadership on the development of American ideals is explored in Charles M. Redenius, *The American Ideal of Equality: From Jefferson's Declaration to the Burger Court* (Port Washington, N.Y.: Kennikat, 1981), pp. 14–21.
5. For a penetrating analysis of what the Founding Fathers meant by federalism, see Martin Diamond, "The *Federalist's* View of Federalism," in George C. S. Benson, ed., *Essays in Federalism* (Clarement, Calif.: Institute for Studies in Federalism of Claremont Men's College, 1961), pp. 21–64.
6. Not everyone has gladly accepted the virtues of congressional dominance. In his classic study, *Congressional Government* (Boston: Houghton Mifflin, 1885), Woodrow Wilson, the only political scientist to be elected president, pilloried the idea of legislative leadership.
7. For the development of executive power, see Thomas E. Cronin, *The State of the Presidency,* 2d ed. (Boston: Little Brown, 1980).
8. Louis W. Koenig, *The Chief Executive,* 4th ed. (New York: Harcourt Brace Jovanovich, 1981), explores this phenomena.
9. Marshall's constitutional contributions are analyzed in Leonard Baker, *John Marshall: A Life in Law* (New York: Macmillan, 1981).
10. A good overview of federal expenditures for each fiscal year can be found in *The United States Budget in Brief,* issued annually in late January by the Government Printing Office.
11. The Supreme Court has also fashioned a variety of doctrines to deal with the problems of obscenity and pornography, church-state relations, the permissible scope of the rights of assembly and petition, and constitutionally acceptable limits on the derived rights of association and dissent.
12. The process of, and the controversy surrounding, the incorporation of the Bill of Rights into the Fourteenth Amendment is detailed in C. Herman Pritchett, *The American Constitution,* 3d ed. (New York: McGraw-Hill, 1977), pp. 416–482.

Chapter Five

1. U.S. Bureau of the Census, *1977 Census of Governments* 8(2):1.
2. The originator of this imagery is Morton Grodzins. It is more fully discussed in "Centralization and Decentralization in the American Federal System," in Robert A. Goldwin, ed., *A Nation of States* (Chicago: Rand McNally, 1963).
3. David Caputo and Richard L. Cole, *Urban Politics and Decentralization: The Politics of General Revenue Sharing* (Lexington, Mass.: D.C. Heath, 1974). Still among the more enlightening studies of general revenue sharing.

4. John J. Harrigan, *Politics and Policy in States and Communities,* 2d ed. (Boston: Little, Brown, 1984), p. 42.

5. The Lone Jack example and statistics are taken from Harrigan (1984), p. 42, cited above.

Chapter Six

1. The complex nature of political socialization has led political scientists to develop a variety of theories—accumulation, biopolitics, cognitive development, identification, and interpersonal transfer, among others—to explain how and why socialization occurs as it does. Richard E. Dawson, Kenneth Prewitt, and Karen S. Dawson, *Political Socialization,* 2d ed. (Boston: Little, Brown, 1977) provides some interesting insights into this process.

2. Bruce M. Borthwick captures this milieu in his *Comparative Politics of the Middle East* (Englewood Cliffs, N.J.: Prentice-Hall, 1980), pp. 199–200.

3. David M. Billeaux and Terry Warburton, "The Politics of Music Videos: Is the Median the Message?", unpublished paper presented to the national meeting of the Popular Culture Association, 1985.

4. Roger D. Cobb and Charles Elder, *Participation in American Politics: The Dynamics of Agenda-Building* (Boston: Allyn and Bacon, 1972) examines the agenda-setting process generally and the matter of nonissues specifically.

5. Oscar Lewis, *The Children of Sanchez* (New York: Random House, 1961). This volume is must reading for those who seek to understand the perspective of the economically disadvantaged.

6. Robert S. Erikson, Norman R. Luttbeg, and Kent L. Tedin, *American Public Opinion: Its Origins, Content and Impact,* 2d ed. (New York: Wiley, 1979), p. 83.

7. Ibid, p. 178.

8. Ibid.

9. The improvements in polling techniques are examined in Bernard Hennessy, *Public Opinion,* 3d ed. (Belmont, Calif.: Brooks/Cole, 1981).

10. Robert Weissberg, *Public Opinion and Popular Government,* (Englewood Cliffs, N.J.: Prentice-Hall, 1976). An excellent source for the role and problems of public opinion in democratic government.

11. Michael Corbett, *Political Tolerance in America: Freedom and Equality in Public Attitudes* (New York: Longman, 1982). Provides a full discussion of this aspect of public opinion.

12. See Charles W. Roll, Jr. and Albert H. Cantril, *Polls, Their Use and Misuse in Politics* (New York: Basic Books, 1972) for discussion and examples of how poll results can be manipulated to reflect what the pollster desires.

13. Weissberg, *Public Opinion and Popular Government.* See especially Chapters 6 and 7 for a discussion of these and other issues on which opinion has diverged from policy.

14. See Benjamin I. Page and Robert Y. Shapiro, "Effects of Public Opinion on Policy," *American Political Science Review* 77 (1983): 170–190, and Alan D. Monroe, "Consistency Between Public Preferences and National Policy Decisions," *American Politics Quarterly* 7 (1979): 3–19.

15. See Raymond Wolfinger and Steven J. Rosenstone, *Who Votes* (New Haven: Yale University Press, 1980), for a full discussion of voting patterns.

16. Lester W. Milbrath and M.L. Goel, *Political Participation: How and Why People Get Involved in Politics,* 2nd ed. (Chicago: Rand McNally, 1977), pp. 45–59, discusses research concerning these matters.

17. See Samuel C. Patterson and Gregory A. Caldeira, "Getting Out the Vote: Participation in Gubernatorial Elections," *American Political Science Review* 77: 675–689 (1983), for a discussion of the importance of electoral closeness and competition in races for governor.

18. Angus Campbell et al., *The American Voter* (New York: Wiley, 1960) is the landmark study of voting behavior.

19. Ibid. The role of parties as perceptual filters is more fully discussed in Campbell, Chapter 6.

20. Gerald Pomper et al., *The Election of 1984* (Chatham, N.J.: Chatham House Publishers, 1985), p. 67.

21. David B. Hill and Norman Luttbeg, *Trends in American Electoral Behavior,* 2d ed. (Itaska, Ill.: Peacock, 1983) discusses five important electoral trends.

22. For a full discussion, see Paul R. Abramson, John H. Aldrich, and David W. Rohde, *Change and Continuity in the 1980 Election,* rev. ed. (Washington, D.C.: Congressional Quarterly Press, 1983).

23. Hill and Luttbeg, *Trends in American Electoral Behavior,* p. 50.

Chapter Seven

1. Vermont case cited in Lewis Lipsitz, *American Democracy* (New York: St. Martin's, 1986), p. 97.

2. For a full discussion of the Oklahoma redistricting story, see *Congressional Quarterly Weekly Reports,* July 10, 1982, pp. 1670–1673.

3. In Maine, the electors are selected by congressional districts; thus any candidate carrying a district will receive an electoral vote even if failing to win statewide.

4. For a discussion of the possibilities of realignment owing to changes in the loyalties of the young, see Gerald Pomper, "The Presidential Election," and Wilson Carey McWilliams, "The Meaning of the Election," both in Gerald Pomper et al., *The Election of 1984* (Chatham: N.J. Chatham House, 1985).

5. Seymour Martin Lipset, "The Elections, the Economy and Public Opinion: 1984," *Political Science* (Winter 1985).

6. Herbert Alexander, *Financing Politics,* 3d ed. (Washington D.C.: Congressional Quarterly Press, 1984).

7. David E. Price, *Bringing Back the Parties* (Washington, D.C.: Congressional Quarterly Press, 1984), Chap. 8.

8. *Statistical Abstract 1985* (Washington, D.C.: Department of Commerce, 1984).

9. Congressional Quarterly, *Dollar Politics* (Washington, D.C.: Congressional Quarterly Press, 1974), pp. 66–69.

10. Figures on PAC contributions are derived from FEC statistics for 1984.

11. Laurily K. Epstein and Gerald Strom, "Election Night Projections and West Coast Turnout," *American Politics Quarterly:* 479–491 (1981), find no evidence of an impact on turnout of early projections. John E. Jackson, "Election Night Reporting and Voter Turnout," *American Journal of Political Science*: 615–635 (1983), found that supporters of the projected winner (Reagan) were somewhat more likely to stay home from the polls than those of the projected loser due to early projections.

12. Quoted in Richard Reeves, "On Political Books," *Washington Monthly,* December 1977, p. 58.

13. Thomas E. Patterson, *Mass Media Elections: How Americans Choose Their Presidents* (New York: Praeger, 1980), pp. 153–159.

14. Thomas E. Patterson and Robert D. McClure, *The Unseeing Eye: The Myth of Television Power in National Politics* (New York: Putnam, 1976), p. 111.

15. David O. Sears and Richard E. Whitney, "Political Persuasion," in Ithiel de Sola Pool et al., *Handbook of Communication* (Chicago: Rand McNally, 1973), pp. 253–289.

Chapter Eight

1. Kay Lehman Schlozman and John T. Tierney, "More of the Same: Washington Pressure Group Activity in a Decade of Change," *Journal of Politics*, 45:356 (1983).

2. Kay Lehman Schlozman and John T. Tierney, *Organized Interests and American Democracy* (New York: Harper and Row, 1985).

3. Lester W. Milbrath, *Washington Lobbyists* (Westport, Conn.: Greenwood, 1976), is a classic study.

4. For an analysis of the impact of these organizations, see Herbert Alexander, *PACs: What They Are, How They Are Changing Political Campaign Financing Patterns* (Grass Roots Guide, 1979).

5. Richard Kluger, *Simple Justice: The History of Brown v. Board of Education and Black America's Struggle for Equality* (New York: Knopf, 1976), is the definitive study. See also Stephen L. Wasby, "Interest Groups in Court: Race Relations Litigation," in Alan J. Cigler and Burdett A. Loomis, eds., *Interest Group Politics* (Washington, D.C.: Congressional Quarterly Press, 1983).

6. Ronald Hrebenar and Ruth K. Scott, *Interest Group Politics in America* (Englewood Cliffs, N.J.: Prentice-Hall, 1982), includes some intriguing arguments in this regard.

7. Roberto Michel, *Political Parties, A Sociological Study of The Oligarchical Tendencies of Modern Democracies*. Trans. by Eden-Cedar Paul. New York: Dover Publisher, 1959.

8. Thomas R. Dye, *Who's Running America? The Carter Years* (Englewood Cliffs, N.J.: Prentice-Hall, 1979), is a contemporary statement of elitist politics. Similar arguments are made in G. William Domhoff, *Who Rules America Now? A View for the Eighties* (Englewood Cliffs, N.J.: Prentice-Hall, 1983).

9. Theodore Lowi, *The End of Liberalism*, 2d ed. (New York: Norton, 1979), argues this position very persuasively.

10. *Gallup Opinion Index*, February 1966, p. 14, American National Election Survey, CFS, 1984.

11. Norman Nie, Sidney Verba, and John Petrocek, *The Changing American Voter* (Cambridge, Mass.: Harvard University Press, 1976), traces the key behavioral changes.

12. Bryon E. Shafer, "Anti-Party Politics," in *Public Interest* 63:95–111 (Spring 1981), skillfully identifies the contributing factors.

13. The classic statement of this thesis is by Maurice Duverger, *Political Parties: Their Organization and Activity in the Modern State*, trans. Barbara and Robert North (New York: Wiley, 1954).

14. For the impact of third parties, see Howard R. Penniman, "Presidential Third Parties and the Modern American Two-Party System," in William Crotty, ed., *The Party Symbol* (San Francisco: Freeman, 1980), pp. 101–117. See also Daniel A. Mazmanian, "Third Parties in Presidential Elections," in Jeff Fishel, ed., *Parties and Elections in an Anti-Party Age* (Indianapolis: Indiana University Press, 1978).

15. Ruth K. Scott and Ronald Hrebenar, *Parties in Crisis: Party Politics in America* (New York: Wiley, 1979); Bruce A. Campbell and Richard J. Trilling, *Realignment in American Politics: Toward a Theory* (Austin: University of Texas Press, 1980); Seymour Martin Lipset, ed., *Party Coalitions in the 1980s* (San Francisco: Institute for Contemporary Studies, 1981), present various sides of this debate.

16. Walter Dean Burnham, "American Politics in the 1970s," in William N. Chambers and Walter Dean Burnham, eds., *The American Party System*, 2d ed. (New York: Oxford University Press, 1975), is a useful commentary on Ladd's thesis.

Chapter Nine

1. David J. Vogler, *The Politics of Congress*, 3d ed. (Boston: Allyn and Bacon, 1980), pp. 160–188, argues that there are three categories of committees—power (Appropriations, Rules, Ways and Means, for example), policy (Banking, Housing and Urban Affairs, Energy and Natural Resources, and Foreign Relations), and constituency (Interior and Insular Affairs, Merchant Marine and Fisheries, and Public Works and Transportation) committees.

2. For a severe critique of Congress, see Mark J. Green, James M. Fallows, and David R. Zwick, *Who Runs Congress? The President, Big Business or You?* (New York: Bantam, 1972).

3. Edward S. Greenberg, *The American Political System* (Boston: Little, Brown, 1983), p. 317.

4. Cited in Theodore L. Becker, *American Government* (Boston: Allyn and Bacon, 1976), pp. 218–219.

5. Morris Fiorina, *Congress: Keystone of the Washington Establishment* (New Haven, Conn.: Yale University Press, 1977), p. 5; Congressional Quarterly, *Electing Congress* (Washington, D.C.: Congressional Quarterly Press, 1978), p. 9.

6. Patricia Hurley and Kim Q. Hill found that only about 17 percent of the population can accurately report how their representative had voted on any issue. See "The Prospects for Issue Voting in Contemporary Congressional Elections," *American Politics Quarterly* 8:446 (October 1980). That economic conditions have less impact on congressional elections than commonly thought is discussed in John R. Owens and Edward C. Olsen, "Economic Fluctuations and Congressional Elections," *American Journal of Political Science* 24:469–493 (August 1980).

7. Thomas E. Mann and Raymond E. Wolfinger, "Candidates and Parties in Congressional Elections," *American Political Science Review* 74:627 (September 1980).

8. 377 U.S. 533 (1964), at 565.

9. The various factors that impinge on the decisions of members of Congress are explored in Aage R. Clausen, *How Congressmen Decide* (New York: St. Martin's, 1973).

10. A careful scrutiny of the legislative process can be found in Walter J. Oleszek, *Congressional Procedures and the Policy Process* (Washington, D.C.: Congressional Quarterly Press, 1978).

11. Morris S. Ogul, *Congress Oversees the Bureaucracy* (Pittsburgh: University of Pittsburgh Press, 1976), analyzes the various facets of the oversight function.

12. George C. Edwards III, *Presidential Influence in Congress* (San Francisco: Freeman, 1980), examines the power relationship between the two branches.

13. William S. Livingston, Lawrence C. Dodd, and Richard L. Schott, eds., *The Presidency and the Congress: A Shifting Balance of Power* (Austin, TX: University of Texas Press, 1979), includes readings representing a range of perspectives.

14. Lance T. LeLoup, *The Fiscal Congress: Legislative Control of the Budget* (Westport, Conn.: Greenwood, 1980), assesses this Congressional effort.

15. The legislative history of this landmark statute is the subject of Stephen K. Bailey, *Congress Makes A Law* (New York: Columbia University Press, 1950).

Chapter Ten

1. The darker side of presidential power is explored in Jim Heath, *Decade of Disillusionment: The Kennedy-Johnson Years* (Bloomington: Indiana University Press, 1975).

2. For a well-reasoned analysis of leadership in a democracy, see James McGregor Burns, *Leadership* (New York: Harper, 1978).

3. Charles Redenius, *The American Ideal of Equality: From Jefferson's Declaration to the Burger Court* (Port Washington, N.Y.: Kennikat, 1981), pp. 40–41.

4. Various facets of the president's role as party leader are examined in David Broder, *The Party's Over* (New York: Harper, 1971).

5. Richard Neustadt, *Presidential Power: The Politics of Leadership from FDR to Carter* (New York: Wiley, 1979), argues that presidential power rests basically on the president's ability to persuade.

6. Other instruments of executive authority are analyzed in Louis Koenig, *The Chief Executive*, 4th ed., (New York: Harcourt Brace Jovanovich, 1981).

7. A cross-national comparison of economic policies can be found in Charles Redenius, "Thatcherism and Reaganomics: Economic Policy Making in Great Britain and the United States," *Journal of Political Science* 10(2):96–113 (Spring 1983).

8. Alexander George, *Presidential Decision Making in Foreign Policy* (Boulder, Colo.: Westview, 1980), treats some of the difficulties presidents face in this arena.

9. Richard Pious, *The American Presidency* (New York: Basic Books, 1979), is both comprehensive and insightful.

10. For a good discussion of the politics of bureaucratic decision making and the role of agency clientele, see Francis E. Rourke, *Bureaucracy, Politics, and Public Policy*, 4th ed. (Boston: Little, Brown, 1986).

11. Cited in Hugh Heclo, *A Government of Strangers: Executive Politics in Washington* (Washington, D.C.: Brookings Institution, 1977), p. 103.

12. In Britain, elections must be held at least once every five years, but that is the only limitation a prime minister faces. It doesn't always work, of course, but the prime minister can call an election whenever the party leadership believes the party has the best chance of retaining or increasing its parliamentary majority.

13. Ironically, the Twenty-second Amendment has yet to apply to a Democratic president. None has survived or been elected to a second term. By contrast, two Republican presidents, Eisenhower and Reagan, were denied the opportunity to seek a third term.

14. The French choose their president by majority popular vote. A national referendum in 1962 abolished their electoral college. As a result, their system may be more democratic as well, for reasons we discussed in Chapter 7.

15. From 1836 to 1860 and from 1876 to 1896, for example, no president was able to succeed himself in office, because his party refused to renominate him or because he lost the election.

16. Garner, who was Franklin Roosevelt's vice president from 1933 to 1941, left Washington after his second term vowing never to return. He never did.

17. Article I, Section 3.

18. Article II, Section 1.

19. Interestingly, incumbent vice presidents have not been very successful presidential candidates. Martin Van Buren in 1836 was the last sitting vice president to win a presidential election. Incumbent vice presidents Richard Nixon in 1960 and Hubert Humphrey in 1968 both lost.

20. This is probably why neither Ronald Reagan nor Gerald Ford expressed much enthusiasm for the idea of having Ford be the vice presidential candidate in 1980. A former president as vice president would be constitutionally permissible, but politically difficult.

Chapter Eleven

1. Alexis de Tocqueville, *Democracy in America*, Phillips Bradley, ed. (New York: Knopf, 1944), p. 280.

2. Robert G. McCloskey, *The American Supreme Court* (Chicago: University of Chicago Press, 1960), pp. 16–18.

3. Arthur J. Goldberg, *Equal Justice: The Warren Era of the Supreme Court* (Evanston, Ill.: Northwestern University Press, 1971), examines the policy making of this great activist Court.

4. For a somewhat critical analysis of Rehnquist's judicial philosophy, see David L. Shapiro, "Mr. Justice Rehnquist," *Harvard Law Review* 90:293–357 (1976).

5. Robert Jackson, *The Struggle for Judicial Supremacy* (New York: Octagon, 1941), is the classic work on the Court Revolution of 1937.

6. A balanced treatment of the transition from the Warren Court to the Burger Court can be found in Stephen L. Wasby, *Continuity and Change: From the Warren Court to the Burger Court* (Pacific Palisades, Calif.: Goodyear, 1976).

7. The jurisprudence of the Warren Court is brilliantly analyzed in G. Edward White, *The American Judicial Tradition* (New York: Oxford University Press, 1976), pp. 317–368.

8. On this point, see the controversial analysis by Bob Woodward and Scott Armstrong, *The Brethren: Inside the Supreme Court* (New York: Simon and Shuster, 1979).

9. C. Herman Pritchett, *Congress Versus the Supreme Court, 1957–1960* (Minneapolis: University of Minnesota Press, 1960), analyzes one of Congress's most concerted efforts to alter the appellate jurisdiction of the Supreme Court.

10. An excellent set of readings that probe various facets of the judicial process can be found in Walter Murphy and C. Herman Pritchett, eds. *Courts, Judges and Politics*, 3d ed. (New York: Random House, 1979).

11. S. Sidney Ulmer, *Supreme Court Policy Making and Constitutional Law* (New York: McGraw-Hill, 1986), explores the High Court's decisional processes.

12. It should be noted that the Declaration of Independence is a statement of American political philosophy rather than law. See Charles Redenius, *The American Ideal of Equality: From Jefferson's Declaration to the Burger Court* (Port Washington, N.Y.: Kennikat Press, 1981), for an interpretation of the role of the ideal of equality in American history.

13. Jackson's efforts also had the unintended effect of inducing millions of adult whites, most of whom opposed Jackson, to register to vote.

14. In *Mapp*, the Supreme Court was extending the same exclusionary rule to the state courts that had been binding on the federal courts since *United States v. Weeks* (1914).

15. During the Civil War, President Lincoln took the unprecedented step of ignoring the writ of habeas corpus. Many people, including Chief Justice Taney, felt that despite the precarious times Lincoln's actions were unjustified. Others felt that the president had committed an impeachable offense.

16. For a lively account of how the right to counsel was incorporated into the Fourteenth Amendment, see Anthony Lewis, *Gideon's Trumpet* (New York: Random House, 1964).

17. Following Franklin Roosevelt's landslide victory in 1936, he offered a plan that would increase the size of the Supreme Court from 9 to 15 members. Roosevelt's aim was to pack the Court with his appointees and end resistance to his legislative goals. Although the plan was defeated in Congress, Roosevelt achieved his objective without any new appointments when Hughes and Roberts joined the liberals to form a new majority. Their change in voting behavior is often referred to as "the switch in time that saved nine."

18. C. Herman Pritchett, *The American Constitution*, 3d. ed. (New York: McGraw-Hill, 1977), pp. 416–482, includes a careful analysis of the incorporation of the Bill of Rights into the Fourteenth Amendment.

19. The relationship between the president and the federal courts is examined in Henry J. Abraham, *Justices and Presidents: A Political History of the Appointments to the Supreme Court* (Baltimore: Penguin, 1975).

20. Taft has been the only man to be elected president and also appointed to the Supreme Court. Hughes had come close to being elected president in 1916 as the Republican nominee.

21. However, several Supreme Court justices have disappointed their presidential mentors by being too liberal or too conservative once on the bench. Earl Warren, for example, turned out to be both more liberal and more activist than Eisenhower would have liked.

Chapter Twelve

1. E. E. Schattschneider, *The Semisovereign People* (New York: Holt, Rinehart and Winston, 1960), p. 68.

2. Robert L. Lineberry, *American Public Policy* (New York: Harper and Row, 1977), p. 71.

3. Theodore J. Lowi, "American Business, Public Policy, Case Studies, and Political Theory," *World Politics* (July 1964), pp. 667–715.

4. Charles Redenius, "The Supply-Side Alternative: Reagan and Thatcher's Economic Policies," *Journal of Social, Political and Economic Studies* (2): 189–209 (Summer 1983).

5. Council of Economic Advisers, *The Economic Report of the President, 1982* (Washington, D.C.: Government Printing Office, 1982), p. 85.

6. Robert Heilbroner, *An Inquiry into the Human Prospect: Updated and Reconsidered for the 1980's,* (New York: Norton, 1980), p. 113.

7. The statistics in this and the following paragraphs are drawn from *The United States Budget in Brief* (Washington, D.C.: Government Printing Office, 1986), and earlier years.

8. *Effective Corporate Tax Rates in 1981* (Arlington, Va: Tax Analysts, 1982), provides the relevant statistics.

9. Lester Thurow, *The Zero-Sum Society* (New York: Basic Books, 1980), pp. 7–9.

Chapter Thirteen

1. Survey by the American Institute of Public Opinion (known more popularly as the Gallup Poll) for the Chicago Council on Foreign Relations, November 17–26, 1978.

2. Not that we are setting a good example. By 1985, the United States had become a debtor nation for the first time since 1914 and had accumulated a national debt approaching $3 trillion.

3. *Report of the National Bipartisan Commission on Central America* (Washington, D.C.: United States Government Printing Office, 1984), pp. 4–5, 126–127.

4. Since in 1823 the United States was too weak to interfere anywhere in Europe, this was an easy commitment to keep.

5. Even today people continue to heed Greeley's advice. By the 1980 census, California had become the most populous state, owing to migration from other states (and illegal immigration from Mexico).

6. This occurred during the last six months of 1985.

7. The Soviet Union, Britain, France, China, and India, in that order, have tested nuclear devices.

8. See, for example, Ruth Sivard, ed., *World Military and Social Expenditures, 1982* (Leesburg, Va.: World Priorities, 1982). In 1982, the United States spent about $60,000 per soldier under arms, the Soviet Union about $32,000.

9. The Ethiopians suffered more from their government than most other nations. During the worst part of the famine in 1984, the government spent $250 million to commemorate the tenth anniversary of the coup that brought the Marxists to power while entire provinces of the country were literally starving to death.

10. Nor does mutual antagonism have to interfere in otherwise normal relationships. The United States, for example, still imports millions of dollars worth of pistachio nuts from Iran each year.

11. Which is why totalitarian systems are infrequent targets. They are not immune, however, as the kidnapping of four Soviet diplomats in Beirut in 1985 makes clear. Three were returned, but one was murdered.

12. See, for example, Antony J. Blinken, "The New Terrorism," *New Republic,* 192(13):12–13 (April 1, 1985).

13. Nicolaus Mills, "The Ethics of Terrorism: The Trap of Toughing It Out," *Commonweal,* July 12, 1985, p. 389.

14. When it seemed that Jimmy Carter might win the 1976 presidential election Soviet diplomatic personnel tried to meet with him to ascertain his views. Then a private citizen, Carter wisely refused. Apparently, the Soviets, like many Americans, did not know (nor had they heard of) the former governor of Georgia.

15. By the early 1980s, the United States imported only 3 percent of its oil from the Persian Gulf. For more than a decade, the United States had gradually decreased its dependency on Middle Eastern oil through conservation, use of other sources, and the helpful arrival of an oil glut by 1984.

16. Unhappily, that is not always the case. Heads of government may pursue goals that are both irrational and injurious to their countries' interests. Iran since 1979 may be cited as an example. It is important to remember, though, that the "rational" approach of the West may not be comprehended or appreciated elsewhere.

17. Truman became an "accidental" president in April 1945, when Franklin Roosevelt died shortly after beginning his fourth term in office.

Chapter Fourteen

1. See Kalman H. Silvert, *The Reason for Democracy* (New York: Viking, 1977), for a representative portrait of this point of view.

2. Robert L. Heilbroner, *An Inquiry into the Human Prospect: Updated and Reconsidered for the 1980s* (New York: Norton, 1980), pp. 151–153, sees the United States as facing short run, mid-run, and long-run problems. Our discussion is based on Heilbroner's approach.

3. For his most recent foray against the inequities of our economic system, see Michael Harrington, *The New American Poverty* (New York: Holt, Rinehart and Winston, 1984).

4. E.E. Schattschneider, *The Semi-Sovereign People: A Realist's View of Democracy* (Hinsdale, Ill.: Dryden, 1975), provides a classic critique of pluralism's inability to overcome the evils of low levels of participation.

5. Arthur I. Blaustein, ed., *The American Promise: Equal Justice and Economic Opportunity* (New Brunswick, N.J.: Transaction Books, 1982), is a good collection of essays that espouses this position.

6. Samuel P. Huntington, "American Ideals versus American Institutions," *Political Science Quarterly* 97(1):37 (Spring 1982).

7. The constitutional implications of these far-reaching changes are ably explored in Alfred E. Kelley and Winfred A. Harbison, *The American Constitution: Its Origins and Development,* 6th ed. (New York: Norton, 1982).

8. Frank J. Sorauf, *Party Politics in America,* 5th ed. (Boston: Little, Brown, 1984), includes a careful review of the failures of third-party movements.

9. Both the strengths and weaknesses of pluralism are carefully analyzed in Robert A. Dahl, *Dilemmas of Pluralist Democracy* (New Haven, Conn.: Yale University Press, 1982).

Appendix A

THE DECLARATION OF INDEPENDENCE

In Congress, July 4, 1776.

A Declaration by the Representatives of the United States of America, in General Congress assembled. When in the Course of human Events, it becomes necessary for one People to dissolve the Political Bonds which have connected them with another, and to assume among the Powers of the Earth, the separate and equal Station to which the Laws of Nature and of Nature's God entitle them, a decent Respect to the Opinions of Mankind requires that they should declare the causes which impel them to the Separation.

We hold these Truths to be self-evident, that all Men are created equal, that they are endowed by their Creator with certain unalienable Rights, that among these are Life, Liberty, and the Pursuit of Happiness—That to secure these Rights, Governments are instituted among Men, deriving their just Powers from the Consent of the Governed, that whenever any Form of Government becomes destructive of these Ends, it is the Right of the People to alter or abolish it, and to institute new Government, laying its Foundation on such Principles, and organizing its Powers in such Forms, as to them shall seem most likely to effect their Safety and Happiness. Prudence, indeed, will dictate that Governments long established should not be changed for light and transient Causes; and accordingly all Experience hath shewn, that Mankind are more disposed to suffer, while Evils are sufferable, than to right themselves by abolishing the Forms to which they are accustomed. But when a long Train of Abuses and Usurpations, pursuing invariably the same Object, evinces a Design to reduce them under absolute Despotism, it is their Right, it is their Duty, to throw off such Government, and to provide new Guards for their future Security. Such has been the patient Sufferance of these Colonies; and such is now the Necessity which constrains them to alter their former Systems of Government. The History of the present King of Great-Britain is a History of repeated injuries and Usurpations, all having in direct Object the Establishment of an absolute Tyranny over these States. To prove this, let Facts be submitted to a candid World.

He has refused his Assent to Laws, the most wholesome and necessary for the public Good.

He has forbidden his Governors to pass Laws of immediate and pressing Importance, unless suspended in their Operation till his Assent should be obtained; and when so suspended, he has utterly neglected to attend to them.

He has refused to pass other Laws for the Accommodation of large Districts of People, unless those People would relinquish the Right of Representation in the Legislature, a Right inestimable to them, and formidable to Tyrants only.

He has called together Legislative Bodies at Places unusual, uncomfortable, and distant from the Depository of their Public Records, for the sole Purpose of fatiguing them into Compliance with his Measures.

He has dissolved Representative Houses repeatedly, for opposing with manly Firmness his Invasions on the Rights of the People.

He has refused for a long Time, after such Dissolutions, to cause others to be elected; whereby the Legislative Powers, incapable of Annihilation, have returned to the People at large for their exercise; the State remaining in the mean time exposed to all the Dangers of Invasion from without, and Convulsions within.

He has endeavoured to prevent the Population of these States; for that Purpose obstructing the Laws for Naturalization of Foreigners; refusing to pass others to encourage their Migrations hither, and raising the Conditions of New Appropriations of Lands.

He has obstructed the Administration of Justice, by refusing his Assent to Laws for establishing Judiciary Powers.

He has made Judges dependent on his Will alone, for the Tenure of their offices, and the Amount and payment of their Salaries.

He has erected a Multiple of new Offices, and sent higher Swarms of Officers to harrass our People, and eat out their Substance.

He has kept among us, in Times of Peace, Standing Armies, without the consent of our Legislatures.

He has affected to render the Military independent of, and superior to the Civil Power.

He has combined with others to subject us to a Jurisdiction foreign to our Constitution, and unacknowledged by our Laws; giving his Assent to their Acts of pretended Legislation:

For quartering large Bodies of Armed Troops among us:

For protecting them, by a mock Trial, from Punishment for any Murders which they should commit on the Inhabitants of these States:

For cutting off our Trade with all Parts of the World:

For imposing Taxes on us without our Consent:

For depriving us, in many cases, of the Benefits of Trial by Jury:

For transporting us beyond Seas to be tried for pretended Offences:

For abolishing the free System of English Laws in a neighboring Province, establishing therein an arbitrary Government, and enlarging its Boundaries, so as to render it at once an Example and fit Instrument for introducing the same absolute Rule into these Colonies:

For taking away our Charters, abolishing our most valuable Laws, and altering fundamentally the Forms of our Governments:

For suspending our own Legislatures, and declaring themselves invested with Power to legislate for us in all Cases whatsoever.

He has abdicated Government here, by declaring us out of his Protection and waging War against us.

He has plundered our Seas, ravaged our Coasts, burnt our towns, and destroyed the Lives of our People.

He is, at this Time, transporting large Armies of foreign Mercenaries to compleat the works of Death, Desolation, and Tyranny, already begun with circumstances of Cruelty and Perfidy, scarcely paralleled in the most barbarous Ages, and totally unworthy the Head of a civilized Nation.

He has constrained our fellow Citizens taken Captive on the high Seas to bear Arms against their Country, to become the Executioners of their Friends and Brethren, or to fall themselves by their Hands.

He has excited domestic Insurrections amongst us, and has endeavoured to bring on the Inhabitants of our Frontiers, the merciless Indian Savages, whose known Rule of Warfare, is an undistinguished Destruction, of all Ages, Sexes and Conditions.

In every stage of these Oppressions we have Petitioned for Redress in the most humble Terms: Our repeated Petitions have been answered only by repeated Injury. A Prince, whose Character is thus marked by every act which may define a Tyrant, is unfit to be the Ruler of a free People.

Nor have we been wanting in Attentions to our British Brethren. We have warned them from Time to Time of Attempts by their Legislature to extend an unwarrantable Jurisdiction over us. We have reminded them of the Circumstances of our Emigration and Settlement here. We have appealed to their native Justice and Magnanimity, and we have conjured them by the Ties of our common Kindred to disavow these Usurpations, which, would inevitably interrupt our Connections and Correspondence. They too have been deaf to the Voice of Justice and of Consanguinity. We must, therefore, acquiesce in the Necessity, which denounces our Separation, and hold them, as we hold the rest of Mankind, Enemies in War, in Peace, Friends.

We, therefore, the Representatives of the UNITED STATES OF AMERICA, in General Congress Assembled, appealing to the Supreme Judge of the World for the Rectitude of our Intentions, do, in the Name, and by Authority of the good People of these Colonies, solemnly Publish and Declare, That these United Colonies are, and of Right ought to be,

Free and Independent States; that they are absolved from all Allegiance to the British Crown, and that all political Connection between them and the State of Great-Britian, is and ought to be totally dissolved; and that as Free and Independent States, they have full Power to levy War, conclude Peace, contract Alliances, establish Commerce, and to do all other Acts and Things which Independent States may of right do. And for the support of this declaration, with a firm Reliance on the Protection of divine Providence, we mutually pledge to each other our lives, our Fortunes, and our sacred Honor.

Appendix B

THE CONSTITUTION OF THE UNITED STATES OF AMERICA *

We the people of the United States, in Order to form a more perfect Union, establish Justice, insure domestic Tranquility, provide for the common defence, promote the general Welfare, and secure the Blessings of Liberty to ourselves and our posterity, do ordain and establish this Constitution for the United States of America.

Article I

SECTION 1.   All legislative Powers herein granted shall be vested in a Congress of the United States, which shall consist of a Senate and House of Representatives.

SECTION 2.   The House of Representatives shall be composed of Members chosen every second Year by the People of the several States, and the Electors in each State shall have the Qualifications requisite for Electors of the most numerous Branch of the State Legislature.

No person shall be a Representative who shall not have attained to the Age of twenty five Years, and been seven Years a Citizen of the United States, and who shall not, when elected, be an Inhabitant of that State in which he shall be chosen.

Representatives and direct [Taxes] [1] shall be apportioned among the several States which may be included within this Union, according to their respective Numbers [which shall be determined by adding to the whole Number of free Persons, including those bound to Service for a Term of Years, and excluding Indians not taxed, three fifths of all

other Persons].[2] The actual Enumeration shall be made within three Years after the first Meeting of the Congress of the United States, and within every subsequent Term of ten Years, in such Manner as they shall by Law direct. The Number of Representatives shall not exceed one for every thirty Thousand, but each State shall have at Least one Representative; and until such enumeration shall be made, the State of New Hampshire shall be entitled to chuse three, Massachusetts eight, Rhode Island and Providence Plantations one, Connecticut five, New-York six, New Jersey four, Pennsylvania eight, Delaware one, Maryland six, Virginia ten, North Carolina five, South Carolina five, and Georgia three.

When vacancies happen in the Representation from any State, the Executive Authority thereof shall issue Writs of Election to fill such Vacancies.

The House of Representatives shall chuse their Speaker and other Officers; and shall have the sole Power of Impeachment.

SECTION 3.   The Senate of the United States shall be composed of two Senators from each State [chosen by the Legislature thereof],[3] for six Years; and each Senator shall have one Vote.

Immediately after they shall be assembled in Consequence of the first Election, they shall be divided as equally as may be into three Classes. The Seats of the Senators of the first Class shall be vacated at the Expiration of the second Year, of the second Class at the Expiration of the fourth Year, and of the third Class at the Expiration of the sixth Year, so that one third may be chosen every second

---

* The spelling, capitalization, and punctuation of the original have been retained here. Brackets indicate passages that have been altered by amendments to the Constitution.

[1] Modified by the Sixteenth Amendment.

[2] Modified by the Fourteenth Amendment.

[3] Repealed by the Seventeenth Amendment.

Year [and if Vacancies happen by Resignation, or otherwise, during the Recess of the Legislature of any State, the Executive thereof may make temporary Appointments until the next Meeting of the Legislature, which shall then fill such Vacancies.] [4]

No Person shall be a Senator who shall not have attained to the Age of thirty Years, and been nine Years a Citizen of the United States, and who shall not, when elected, be an Inhabitant of that State for which he shall be chosen.

The Vice President of the United States shall be President of the Senate, but shall have no Vote, unless they be equally divided.

The Senate shall chuse their other Officers, and also a President pro tempore, in the Absence of the Vice President, or when he shall exercise the Office of President of the United States.

The Senate shall have the sole Power to try all Impeachments. When sitting for that Purpose, they shall be on Oath or Affirmation. When the President of the United States is tried, the Chief Justice shall preside: And no Person shall be convicted without the Concurrence of two thirds of the members present.

Judgment in Cases of Impeachment shall not extend further than to removal from Office, and disqualification to hold and enjoy any Office of honor, Trust or Profit under the United States; but the Party convicted shall nevertheless be liable and subject to Indictment, Trial, Judgment, and Punishment, according to Law.

SECTION 4.   The Times, Places and Manner of holding Elections for Senators and Representatives, shall be prescribed in each State by the Legislature thereof; but the Congress may at any time by Law make or alter such Regulations, except as to the Places of chusing Senators.

[The Congress shall assemble at least once in every Year, and such Meeting shall be on the first Monday in December, unless they shall by Law appoint a different Day.] [5]

SECTION 5.   Each House shall be the Judge of the Elections, Returns and Qualifications of its own Members, and a Majority of each shall constitute a

[4] Modified by the Seventeenth Amendment.

[5] Changed by the Twentieth Amendment.

Quorum to do Business; but a smaller Number may adjourn from day to day, and may be authorized to compel the Attendance of absent Members, in such Manner, and under such Penalties as each House may provide.

Each House may determine the Rules of its Proceedings, punish its Members for disorderly Behaviour, and, with the Concurrence of two thirds, expel a Member.

Each House shall keep a Journal of its Proceedings, and from time to time publish the same, excepting such Parts as may in their Judgment require Secrecy; and the Yeas and Nays of the Members of either House on any question shall, at the Desire of one fifth of those present, be entered on the Journal.

Neither House, during the Session of Congress, shall, without the Consent of the other, adjourn for more than three days, nor to any other Place than that in which the two Houses shall be sitting.

SECTION 6.   The Senators and Representatives shall receive a Compensation for their Services, to be ascertained by Law, and paid out of the Treasury of the United States. They shall in all Cases, except Treason, Felony and Breach of the Peace, be privileged from Arrest during their Attendance at the Session of their respective Houses, and in going to and returning from the same; and for any Speech or Debate in either House, they shall not be questioned in any other Place.

No Senator or Representative shall, during the Time for which he was elected, be appointed to any civil Office under the Authority of the United States, which shall have been created, or the Emoluments whereof shall have been encreased during such time; and no Person holding any Office under the United States, shall be a Member of either House during his Continuance in Office.

SECTION 7.   All Bills for raising Revenue shall originate in the House of Representatives; but the Senate may propose or concur with Amendments as on other Bills.

Every Bill which shall have passed the House of Representatives and the Senate, shall, before it become a Law, be presented to the President of the United States; If he approves he shall sign it, but if not he shall return it, with his Objections to that

House in which it shall have originated, who shall enter the Objections at large on their Journal, and proceed to reconsider it. If after such Reconsideration two thirds of that House shall agree to pass the Bill, it shall be sent, together with the Objections, to the other House, by which it shall likewise be reconsidered, and if approved by two thirds of that House, it shall become a Law. But in all such Cases the Votes of both Houses shall be determined by yeas and Nays, and the Names of the Persons voting for and against the Bill shall be entered on the Journal of each House respectively. If any Bill shall not be returned by the President within ten Days (Sundays excepted) after it shall have been presented to him, the Same shall be a Law, in like Manner as if he had signed it, unless the Congress by their Adjournment prevent its Return, in which Case it shall not be a Law.

Every Order, Resolution, or Vote to which the Concurrence of the Senate and House of Representatives may be necessary (except on a question of Adjournment) shall be presented to the President of the United States; and before the Same shall take Effect, shall be approved by him, or being disapproved by him, shall be repassed by two thirds of the Senate and House of Representatives, according to the Rules and Limitations prescribed in the Case of a Bill.

SECTION 8.   The Congress shall have Power To lay and collect Taxes, Duties, Imposts and Excises, to pay the Debts and provide for the common Defence and general Welfare of the United States; but all Duties, Imposts and Excises shall be uniform throughout the United States;

To borrow Money on the credit of the United States;

To regulate Commerce with foreign Nations, and among the several States, and with the Indian Tribes;

To establish a uniform Rule of Naturalization, and uniform Laws on the subject of Bankruptcies throughout the United States;

To coin Money, regulate the Value thereof, and of foreign Coin, and fix the Standard of Weights and Measures.

To provide for the Punishment of counterfeiting the Securities and current Coin of the United States;

To establish Post Offices and post Roads;

To promote the Progress of Science and useful Arts, by securing for limited Times to Authors and Inventors the exclusive Right to their respective Writings and Discoveries;

To constitute Tribunals inferior to the supreme Court;

To define and punish Piracies and Felonies committed on the high Seas, and Offences against the Law of Nations;

To declare War, grant Letters of Marque and Reprisal, and make Rules concerning Captures on Land and Water;

To raise and support Armies, but no Appropriation of Money to that Use shall be for a longer Term than two Years;

To provide and maintain a Navy;

To make Rules for the Government and Regulation of the land and naval Forces;

To provide for calling forth the Militia to execute the Laws of the Union, suppress Insurrections and repel Invasions;

To provide for organizing, arming, and disciplining the Militia, and for governing such Part of them as may be employed in the Service of the United States, reserving to the States respectively, the Appointment of the Officers, and the Authority of training the Militia according to the discipline prescribed by Congress;

To exercise exclusive Legislation in all Cases whatsoever, over such District (not exceeding ten Miles square) as may, by Cession of particular States, and the Acceptance of Congress, become the Seat of the Government of the United States, and to exercise like Authority over all Places purchased by the Consent of the Legislature of the State in which the Same shall be, for the Erection of Forts, Magazines, Arsenals, dock-Yards, and other needful Buildings;—And

To make all Laws which shall be necessary and proper for carrying into Execution the foregoing Powers, and all other Powers vested by this Constitution in the Government of the United States, or in any Department or Officer thereof.

SECTION 9.   The Migration or Importation of such Persons as any of the States now existing shall think proper to admit, shall not be prohibited by the Congress prior to the Year one thousand eight hundred and eight, but a Tax or duty may be imposed on such Importation, not exceeding ten dollars for each Person.

The Privilege of the Writ of Habeas Corpus shall not be suspended, unless when in Cases of Rebellion or Invasion the public Safety may require it.

No Bill of Attainder or ex post facto Law shall be passed.

[No Capitation, or other direct, Tax shall be laid, unless in Proportion to the Census or Enumeration herein before directed to be taken.] [6]

No Tax or Duty shall be laid on Articles exported from any State.

No Preference shall be given by any Regulation of Commerce or Revenue to the Ports of one State over those of another; nor shall Vessels bound to, or from, one State, be obliged to enter, clear, or pay Duties in another.

No Money shall be drawn from the Treasury, but in Consequence of Appropriations made by Law; and a regular Statement and Account of the Receipts and Expenditures of all public Money shall be published from time to time.

No Title of Nobility shall be granted by the United States; And no Person holding any Office of Profit or Trust under them, shall, without the Consent of the Congress, accept of any present, Emolument, Office, or Title, of any kind whatever, from any King, Prince, or foreign State.

SECTION 10.   No State shall enter into any Treaty, Alliance, or Confederation; grant Letters of Marque and Reprisal; coin Money; emit Bills of Credit; make any Thing but gold and silver Coin a Tender in Payment of Debts; pass any Bill of Attainder, ex post facto Law, or Law impairing the Obligation of Contracts, or grant any Title of Nobility.

No State shall, without the Consent of the Congress, lay any Imposts or Duties on Imports or Exports, except what may be absolutely necessary for executing its inspection Laws; and the net Produce of all Duties and Imposts, laid by any State on Imports or Exports, shall be for the Use of the Treasury of the United States; and all such Laws shall be subject to the Revision and Control of the Congress.

No State shall, without the Consent of Congress, lay any Duty of Tonnage, keep Troops, or

[6] Modified by the Sixteenth Amendment.

Ships of War in time of Peace, enter into any Agreement or Compact with another State, or with a foreign Power or engage in War, unless actually invaded, or in such imminent Danger as will not admit of delay.

Article II

SECTION 1.   The executive Power shall be vested in a President of the United States of America. He shall hold his Office during the Term of four Years, and, together with the Vice President, chosen for the Same Term, be elected, as follows.

Each State shall appoint, in such Manner as the Legislature thereof may direct, a Number of Electors, equal to the whole Number of Senators and Representatives to which the State may be entitled in the Congress; but no Senator or Representative, or Person holding an Office of Trust or Profit under the United States, shall be appointed an Elector.

[The Electors shall meet in their respective States, and vote by Ballot for two Persons of whom one at least shall not be an Inhabitant of the same State with themselves. And they shall make a List of all the Persons voted for, and of the Number of Votes for each; which List they shall sign and certify, and transmit sealed to the Seat of the Government of the United States, directed to the President of the Senate. The President of the Senate shall, in the Presence of the Senate and House of Representatives, open all the Certificates, and the Votes shall then be counted. The Person having the greatest Number of Votes shall be the President, if such Number be a Majority of the whole Number of Electors appointed; and if there be more than one who have such Majority, and have an equal Number of Votes, then the House of Representatives shall immediately chuse by Ballot one of them for President; and if no Person have a Majority, then from the five highest on the List the said House shall in like Manner chuse the President. But in chusing the President, the Votes shall be taken by States, the Representation from each State having one Vote; A quorum for this Purpose shall consist of a Member or Members from two thirds of the States, and a Majority of all the States shall be necessary to a Choice. In every Case, after the Choice of the President, the Person having the greatest Number of Votes of the Electors shall be the Vice President. But if there should remain two or more who have equal Votes, the Senate shall chuse from them by Ballot the Vice President.] [7]

The Congress may determine the Time of chusing the Electors, and the Day on which they shall give their Votes; which Day shall be the same throughout the United States.

No Person except a natural born Citizen, or a Citizen of the United States, at the time of the Adoption of this Constitution, shall be eligible to the Office of President; neither shall any Person be eligible to that Office who shall not have attained to the Age of thirty five Years, and been fourteen Years a Resident within the United States.

[In Case of the Removal of the President from Office, or of his Death, Resignation, or Inability to discharge the Powers and Duties of the said Office, the same shall devolve on the Vice President, and the Congress may by Law provide for the Case of Removal, Death, Resignation or Inability, both of the President and Vice President, declaring what Officer shall then act as President, and such Officer shall act accordingly, until the Disability be removed, or a President shall be elected.] [8]

The President shall, at stated Times, receive for his Services, a Compensation, which shall neither be encreased nor diminished during the Period for which he shall have been elected, and he shall not receive within that Period any other Emolument from the United States, or any of them.

Before he enter on the Execution of his Office, he shall take the following Oath or Affirmation:—"I do solemnly swear (or affirm) that I will faithfully execute the Office of President of the United States, and will to the best of my Ability, preserve, protect and defend the Constitution of the United States."

SECTION 2. The President shall be Commander in Chief of the Army and Navy of the United States, and of the Militia of the several States, when called into the actual Service of the United States; he may require the Opinion, in writing, of the Principal Officer in each of the executive Departments, upon any Subject relating to the Duties of their respective Offices, and he shall have Power to grant Re-

[7] Changed by the Twelfth Amendment.

[8] Modified by the Twenty-fifth Amendment.

prieves and Pardons for Offences against the United States, except in Cases of Impeachment.

He shall have Power, by and with the Advice and Consent of the Senate, to make Treaties, provided two thirds of the Senators present concur; and he shall nominate, and by and with the Advice and Consent of the Senate, shall appoint Ambassadors, other public Ministers and Consuls, Judges of the supreme Court, and all other Officers of the United States, whose Appointments are not herein otherwise provided for, and which shall be established by Law; but the Congress may by Law vest the Appointment of such inferior Officers, as they think proper, in the President alone, in the Courts of Law, or in the Heads of Departments.

The President shall have Power to fill up all Vacancies that may happen during the Recess of the Senate, by granting Commissions which shall expire at the end of their next Session.

SECTION 3. He shall from time to time give to the Congress Information of the State of the Union, and recommend to their Consideration such Measures as he shall judge necessary and expedient; he may, on extraordinary Occasions, convene both Houses, or either of them, and in Case of Disagreement between them, with Respect to the Time of Adjournment, he may adjourn them to such Times as he shall think proper; he shall receive Ambassadors and other public Ministers; he shall take Care that the Laws be faithfully executed, and shall Commission all the Officers of the United States.

SECTION 4. The President, Vice President and all civil Officers of the United States, shall be removed from Office on Impeachment for, and Conviction of, Treason, Bribery, or other high Crimes and Misdemeanors.

Article III

SECTION 1. The judicial Power of the United States, shall be vested in one supreme Court, and in such inferior Courts as the Congress may from time to time ordain and establish. The Judges, both of the supreme and inferior Courts, shall hold their Offices during good Behavior, and shall, at stated Times, receive for their Services, a Compensation, which shall not be diminished during their Continuance in Office.

SECTION 2.   The judicial Power shall extend to all Cases, in Law and Equity, arising under this Constitution, the Laws of the United States, and Treaties made, or which shall be made, under their Authority;—to all Cases affecting Ambassadors, other public Ministers and Consuls;—to all Cases of admiralty and maritime Jurisdiction;—to Controversies to which the United States shall be a Party;—to Controversies between two or more States; [—between a State and Citizens of another State;—] [9] between Citizens of different States,—between Citizens of the same State claiming Lands under Grants of different States, [and between a state, or the Citizens thereof, and foreign States, Citizens or Subjects.] [10]

In all Cases affecting Ambassadors, other public Ministers and Consuls, and those in which a State shall be Party, the supreme Court shall have original Jurisdiction. In all the other Cases before mentioned, the supreme Court shall have appellate Jurisdiction, both as to Law and Fact, with such Exceptions, and under such Regulations as the Congress shall make.

The Trial of all Crimes, except in Cases of Impeachment, shall be by Jury; and such Trial shall be held in the State where the said Crimes shall have been committed; but when not committed within any State, the Trial shall be at such Place or Places as the Congress may by Law have directed.

SECTION 3.   Treason against the United States, shall consist only in levying War against them, or in adhering to their Enemies, giving them Aid and Comfort. No Person shall be convicted of Treason unless on the Testimony of two Witnesses to the same overt Act, or on Confession in open Court.

The Congress shall have Power to declare the Punishment of Treason, but no Attainder of Treason shall work Corruption of Blood, or Forfeiture except during the Life of the Person attainted.

Article IV

SECTION 1.   Full Faith and Credit shall be given in each State to the public Acts, Records, and judicial Proceedings of every other State. And the Congress may by general Laws prescribe the Manner in which such Acts, Records and Proceedings shall be proved, and the Effect thereof.

SECTION 2.   The Citizens of each State shall be entitled to all Privileges and Immunities of Citizens in the several States.

A Person charged in any State with Treason, Felony, or other Crime, who shall flee from Justice, and be found in another State, shall on Demand of the executive Authority of the State from which he fled, be delivered up, to be removed to the State having Jurisdiction of the Crime.

[No Person held to Service or Labour in one State under the Laws thereof, escaping into another, shall, in Consequence of any Law or Regulation therein, be discharged from such Service or Labour, but shall be delivered up on Claim of the Party to whom such Service or Labour may be due.] [11]

SECTION 3.   New States may be admitted by the Congress into this Union; but no new State shall be formed or erected within the Jurisdiction of any other State; nor any State be formed by the Junction of two or more States, or Parts of States, without the Consent of the Legislatures of the States concerned as well as of the Congress.

The Congress shall have Power to dispose of and make all needful Rules and Regulations respecting the Territory or other Property belonging to the United States; and nothing in this Constitution shall be so construed as to Prejudice any Claims of the United States, or of any particular State.

SECTION 4.   The United States shall guarantee to every State in this Union a Republican Form of Government, and shall protect each of them against Invasion, and on Application of the Legislature, or of the Executive (when the Legislature cannot be convened) against domestic Violence.

Article V

The Congress, whenever two thirds of both Houses shall deem it necessary, shall propose Amendments to this Constitution, or on the Application of the Legislatures of two thirds of the several States, shall call a Convention for proposing Amendments,

---

[9] Modified by the Eleventh Amendment.

[10] Modified by the Eleventh Amendment.

[11] Repealed by the Thirteenth Amendment.

which, in either Case, shall be valid to all Intents and Purposes, as Part of this Constitution, when ratified by the Legislatures of three fourths of the several States, or by Conventions in three fourths thereof, as the one or the other Mode of Ratification may be proposed by the Congress; Provided that no Amendment which may be made prior to the Year One thousand eight hundred and eight shall in any Manner affect the first and fourth Clauses in the Ninth Section of the first Article; and that no State, without its Consent, shall be deprived of its equal Suffrage in the Senate.

Article VI

All Debts contracted and Engagements entered into, before the Adoption of this Constitution, shall be as valid against the United States under this Constitution, as under the Confederation.

This Constitution, and the laws of the United States which shall be made in Pursuance thereof; and all Treaties made, or which shall be made, under the Authority of the United States, shall be the supreme Law of the Land; and the Judges in every State shall be bound thereby, any Thing in the Constitution or Laws of any State to the Contrary notwithstanding.

The Senators and Representatives before mentioned, and the Members of the several State Legislatures, and all executive and judicial Officers, both of the United States and of the several States, shall be bound by Oath or Affirmation, to support this Constitution: but no religious Test shall ever be required as a Qualification to any Office or public Trust under the United States.

Article VII

The Ratification of the Conventions of nine States, shall be sufficient for the Establishment of this Constitution between the States so ratifying the Same.

Done in Convention by the Unanimous Consent of the States present the Seventeenth Day of September in the Year of our Lord one thousand seven hundred and Eighty seven and of the Independence of the United States of America the Twelfth. IN WITNESS whereof we have hereunto subscribed our Names,

Attest

WILLIAM JACKSON
Secretary

GO. WASHINGTON
Presid'. and deputy from Virginia

DELAWARE
Geo. Read
Gunning Bedford jun
John Dickinson
Richard Basset
Jaco. Broom

MASSACHUSETTS
Nathaniel Gorham
Rufus King

CONNECTICUT
Wm. Saml. Johnson
Roger Sherman

NEW YORK
Alexander Hamilton

NEW JERSEY
Wh. Livingston
David Brearley.

Wm. Paterson.
John. Dayton

PENNSYLVANIA
B. Franklin
Thomas Mifflin
Robt. Morris
Geo. Clymer
Thos. FitzSimons
Jared Ingersoll
James Wilson.
Gouv. Morris

NEW HAMPSHIRE
John Langdon
Nicholas Gilman

MARYLAND
James McHenry
Dan of St. Thos. Jenifer
Danl. Carroll.

VIRGINIA
John Blair
James Madison Jr.

NORTH CAROLINA
Wm. Blount
Richd. Dobbs Spaight.
Hu. Williamson

SOUTH CAROLINA
J. Rutledge
Charles Cotesworth Pinckney
Charles Pinckney
Pierce Butler.

GEORGIA
William Few
Abr. Baldwin

Articles in addition to, and amendment of the Constitution of the United States of America, proposed by Congress and ratified by the Legislatures of the several states, pursuant to the Fifth Article of the original Constitution.

Amendment I [12]

Congress shall make no law respecting an establishment of religion, or prohibiting the free exercise thereof; or abridging the freedom of speech, or of the press; or the right of the people peaceably to assemble, and to petition the Government for a redress of grievances.

Amendment II

A well regulated militia, being necessary to the security of a free State, the right of the people to keep and bear arms, shall not be infringed.

Amendment III

No Soldier shall, in time of peace be quartered in any house, without the consent of the owner, nor in time of war, but in a manner to be prescribed by law.

Amendment IV

The right of the people to be secure in their persons, houses, papers, and effects, against unreasonable searches and seizures, shall not be violated, and no warrants shall issue, but upon probable cause, supported by oath or affirmation, and particularly describing the place to be searched, and the persons or things to be seized.

Amendment V

No person shall be held to answer for a capital, or otherwise infamous crime, unless on a presentment or indictment or a Grand Jury, except in cases arising in the land or naval forces, or in the militia, when in actual service in time of war or public danger; nor shall any person be subject for the same offence to be twice put in jeopardy of life or limb; nor shall be compelled in any criminal case to be a witness against himself, nor be deprived of life, liberty, or property, without due process of law; nor shall private property be taken for public use, without just compensation.

[12] The first ten amendments were passed by Congress on September 25, 1789, and were ratified on December 15, 1791.

Amendment VI

In all criminal prosecutions, the accused shall enjoy the right to a speedy and public trial, by an impartial jury of the State and district wherein the crime shall have been committed, which district shall have been previously ascertained by law, and to be informed of the nature and cause of the accusation; to be confronted with the witnesses against him; to have compulsory process for obtaining witnesses in his favor, and to have the assistance of counsel for his defence.

Amendment VII

In Suits at common law, where the value in controversy shall exceed twenty dollars, the right of trial by jury shall be preserved, and no fact tried by a jury, shall be otherwise reexamined in any Court of the United States, than according to the rules of the common law.

Amendment VIII

Excessive bail shall not be required, nor excessive fines imposed, nor cruel and unusual punishments inflicted.

Amendment IX

The enumeration in the Constitution, of certain rights, shall not be construed to deny or disparage others retained by the people.

Amendment X

The powers not delegated to the United States by the Constitution, nor prohibited by it to the States, are reserved to the States respectively, or to the people.

Amendment XI—(Ratified February 7, 1795)

The Judicial power of the United States shall not be construed to extend to any suit in law or equity, commenced or prosecuted against one of the United States by Citizens of another State, or by Citizens or Subjects of any Foreign State.

Amendment XII—(Ratified June 15, 1804)

The Electors shall meet in their respective states, and vote by ballot for President and Vice-President, one of whom, at least, shall not be an inhabitant of the same state with themselves; they shall name in their ballots the person voted for as President, and in distinct ballots the person voted for as Vice-

President, and they shall make distinct lists of all persons voted for as President, and of all persons voted for as Vice-President, and of the number of votes for each, which lists they shall sign and certify, and transmit sealed to the seat of the government of the United States, directed to the President of the Senate;—The President of the Senate shall, in the presence of the Senate and House of Representatives, open all the certificates and the votes shall then be counted;—The person having the greatest number of votes for President, shall be the President, if such number be a majority of the whole number of Electors appointed; and if no person have such majority, then from the persons having the highest numbers not exceeding three on the list of those voted for as President, the House of Representatives shall choose immediately, by ballot, the President. But in choosing the President, the votes shall be taken by states, the representation from each state having one vote; a quorum for this purpose shall consist of a member or members from two-thirds of the states, and a majority of all the states shall be necessary to a choice. [And if the House of Representatives shall not choose a President whenever the right of choice shall devolve upon them, before the fourth day of March next following, then the Vice-President shall act as President, as in the case of the death or other constitutional disability of the President.] [13]—The person having the greatest number of votes as Vice-President, shall be the Vice-President, if such number be a majority of the whole number of Electors appointed, and if no person have a majority, then from the two highest numbers on the list, the Senate shall choose the Vice-President; a quorum for the purpose shall consist of two-thirds of the whole number of Senators, and a majority of the whole number shall be necessary to a choice. But no person constitutionally ineligible to the office of President shall be eligible to that of Vice-President of the United States.

Amendment XIII—(Ratified on December 6, 1865)

SECTION 1.   Neither slavery nor involuntary servitude, except as a punishment for crime whereof the party shall have been duly convicted, shall exist

within the United States, or any place subject to their jurisdiction.

SECTION 2.   Congress shall have power to enforce this article by appropriate legislation.

Amendment XIV—(Ratified on July 9, 1868)

SECTION 1.   All persons born or naturalized in the United States, and subject to the jurisdiction thereof, are citizens of the United States and of the State wherein they reside. No State shall make or enforce any law which shall abridge the privileges or immunities of citizens of the United States; nor shall any State deprive any person of life, liberty, or property, without due process of law; nor deny to any person within its jurisdiction the equal protection of the laws.

SECTION 2.   Representatives shall be apportioned among the several States according to their respective numbers, counting the whole number of persons in each State, excluding Indians not taxed. But when the right to vote at any election for the choice of electors for President and Vice President of the United States, Representatives in Congress, the Executive and Judicial officers of a State, or the members of the Legislature thereof, is denied to any of the male inhabitants of such State, being [twenty-one] [14] years of age, and citizens of the United States, or in any way abridged, except for participation in rebellion, or other crime, the basis of representation therein shall be reduced in the proportion which the number of such male citizens shall bear to the whole number of male citizens twenty-one years of age in such State.

SECTION 3.   No person shall be a Senator or Representative in Congress, or elector of President and Vice President, or hold any office, civil or military, under the United States, or under any State, who having previously taken an oath, as a member of Congress, or as an officer of the United States, or as a member of any State legislature, or as an executive or judicial officer of any State, to support the Constitution of the United States, shall have engaged in insurrection or rebellion against the same, or given aid or comfort to the enemies thereof. But

---

[13] Changed by the Twentieth Amendment.

[14] Changed by the Twenty-sixth Amendment.

Congress may by a vote of two-thirds of each House, remove such disability.

SECTION 4. The validity of the public debt of the United States, authorized by law, including debts incurred for payment of pensions and bounties for services in suppressing insurrection or rebellion, shall not be questioned. But neither the United States nor any State shall assume or pay any debt or obligation incurred in aid of insurrection or rebellion against the United States, or any claim for the loss or emancipation of any slave, but all such debts, obligations and claims shall be held illegal and void.

SECTION 5. The Congress shall have power to enforce, by appropriate legislation, the provisions of this article.

Amendment XV—(Ratified on February 3, 1870)
SECTION 1. The right of citizens of the United States to vote shall not be denied or abridged by the United States or by any State on account of race, color, or previous condition of servitude.

SECTION 2. The Congress shall have power to enforce this article by appropriate legislation.

Amendment XVI—(Ratified on February 3, 1913)
The Congress shall have power to lay and collect taxes on incomes, from whatever source derived, without apportionment among the several States, and without regard to any census or enumeration.

Amendment XVII—(Ratified on April 8, 1913)
The Senate of the United States shall be composed of two Senators from each State, elected by the people thereof, for six years; and each Senator shall have one vote. The electors in each State shall have the qualifications requisite for electors of the most numerous branch of the State legislatures.

When vacancies happen in the representation of any State in the Senate, the executive authority of such State shall issue writs of election to fill such vacancies: *Provided,* That the legislature of any State may empower the executive thereof to make temporary appointments until the people fill the vacancies by election as the legislature may direct.

This amendment shall not be so construed as to affect the election or term of any Senator chosen before it becomes valid as part of the Constitution.

Amendment XVIII—(Ratified on January 16, 1919)
SECTION 1. After one year from the ratification of this article the manufacture, sale, or transportation of intoxicating liquors within, the importation thereof into, or the exportation thereof from the United States and all territory subject to the jurisdiction thereof for beverage purposes is hereby prohibited.

SECTION 2. The Congress and the several States shall have concurrent power to enforce this article by appropriate legislation.

SECTION 3. This article shall be inoperative unless it shall have been ratified as an amendment to the Constitution by the legislatures of the several States, as provided in the Constitution, within seven years from the date of the submission hereof to the States by the Congress.[15]

Amendment XIX—(Ratified on August 18, 1920)
The right of citizens of the United States to vote shall not be denied or abridged by the United States or by any State on account of sex.

Congress shall have power to enforce this article by appropriate legislation.

Amendment XX—(Ratified on January 23, 1933)
SECTION 1. The terms of the President and Vice President shall end at noon on the 20th day of January, and the terms of Senators and Representatives at noon on the 3d day of January, of the years in which such terms would have ended if this article had not been ratified, and the terms of their successors shall then begin.

SECTION 2. The Congress shall assemble at least once in every year, and such meeting shall begin at noon on the 3d day of January, unless they shall by law appoint a different day.

SECTION 3. If, at the time fixed for the beginning of the term of the President, the President elect shall have died, the Vice President elect shall become President. If a President shall not have been chosen before the time fixed for the beginning of his term, or if the President elect shall have failed to qualify, then the Vice President elect shall act as President

---

[15] The Eighteenth Amendment was repealed by the Twenty-first Amendment.

until a President shall have qualified; and the Congress may by law provide for the case wherein neither a President elect nor a Vice President elect shall have qualified, declaring who shall then act as President, or the manner in which one who is to act shall be selected, and such person shall act accordingly until a President or Vice President shall have qualified.

SECTION 4. The Congress may by law provide for the case of the death of any of the persons from whom the House of Representatives may choose a President whenever the rights of choice shall have devolved upon them, and for the case of the death of any of the persons from whom the Senate may choose a Vice President whenever the right of choice shall have devolved upon them.

SECTION 5. Sections 1 and 2 shall take effect on the 15th day of October following the ratification of this article.

SECTION 6. This article shall be inoperative unless it shall have been ratified as an amendment to the Constitution by the legislatures of three-fourths of the several States within seven years from the date of its submission.

Amendment XXI—(Ratified on December 5, 1933)
SECTION 1. The eighteenth article of amendment to the Constitution of the United States is hereby repealed.

SECTION 2. The transportation or importation into any State, Territory, or possession of the United States for delivery or use therein of intoxicating liquors, in violation of the laws thereof, is hereby prohibited.

SECTION 3. This article shall be inoperative unless it shall have been ratified as an amendment to the Constitution by conventions in the several States, as provided in the Constitution, within seven years from the date of the submission hereof to the States by the Congress.

Amendment XXII—(Ratified on February 27, 1951)
No person shall be elected to the office of the President more than twice, and no person who has held the office of President, or acted as President, for more than two years of a term to which some other person was elected President shall be elected to the

office of President more than once. But this Article shall not apply to any person holding the office of President when this Article was proposed by the Congress, and shall not prevent any person who may be holding the office of President, or acting as President, during the term within which this Article becomes operative from holding the office of President or acting as President during the remainder of such term.

Amendment XXIII—(Ratified on March 29, 1961)
SECTION 1. The District constituting the seat of Government of the United States shall appoint in such manner as the Congress may direct:

A number of electors of President and Vice President equal to the whole number of Senators and Representatives in Congress to which the District would be entitled if it were a State, but in no event more than the least populous State; they shall be in addition to those appointed by the States, but they shall be considered, for the purposes of the election of President and Vice President, to be electors appointed by a State; and they shall meet in the District and perform such duties as provided by the twelfth article of amendment.

SECTION 2. The Congress shall have power to enforce this article by appropriate legislation.

Amendment XXIV—(Ratified on January 23, 1964)
SECTION 1. The right of citizens of the United States to vote in any primary or other election for President or Vice President, for electors for President or Vice President, or for Senator or Representative in Congress, shall not be denied or abridged by the United States or any State by reason of failure to pay any poll tax or other tax.

SECTION 2. The Congress shall have power to enforce this article by appropriate legislation.

Amendment XXV—(Ratified on February 10, 1967)
SECTION 1. In case of the removal of the President from office or of his death or resignation, the Vice President shall become President.

SECTION 2. Whenever there is a vacancy in the office of the Vice President, the President shall nominate a Vice President who shall take office upon confirmation by a majority vote of both Houses of Congress.

SECTION 3. Whenever the President transmits to the President pro tempore of the Senate and the Speaker of the House of Representatives his written declaration that he is unable to discharge the powers and duties of his office, and until he transmits to them a written declaration to the contrary, such powers and duties shall be discharged by the Vice President as Acting President.

SECTION 4. Whenever the Vice President and a majority of either the principal officers of the executive departments or of such other body as Congress may by law provide, transmit to the President pro tempore of the Senate and the Speaker of the House of Representatives their written declaration that the President is unable to discharge the powers and duties of his office, the Vice President shall immediately assume the powers and duties of the office as Acting President.

Thereafter, when the President transmits to the President pro tempore of the Senate and the Speaker of the House of Representatives his written declaration that no inability exists, he shall resume the powers and duties of his office unless the Vice President and a majority of either the principal officers of the executive department or of such other body as Congress may by law provide, transmit within four days to the President pro tempore of the Senate and the Speaker of the House of Representatives their written declaration that the President is unable to discharge the powers and duties of his office. Thereupon Congress shall decide the issue, assembling within forty-eight hours for that purpose if not in session. If the Congress, within twenty-one days after receipt of the latter written declaration, or, if Congress is not in session, within twenty-one days after Congress is required to assemble, determines by two-thirds vote of both Houses that the President is unable to discharge the powers and duties of his office, the Vice President shall continue to discharge the same as Acting President; otherwise, the President shall resume the powers and duties of his office.

Amendment XXVI—(Ratified on July 1, 1971)

SECTION 1. The right of citizens of the United States, who are eighteen years of age or older, to vote shall not be denied or abridged by the United States or by any State on account of age.

SECTION 2. The Congress shall have power to enforce this article by appropriate legislation.

Appendix C

PRESIDENTIAL ELECTIONS, 1789–1986

Year	Candidates	Party	Popular Vote	Electoral Vote
1789	**George Washington**			69
	John Adams			34
	Others			35
1792	**George Washington**			132
	John Adams			77
	George Clinton			50
	Others			5
1796	**John Adams**	Federalist		71
	Thomas Jefferson	Democratic-Republican		68
	Thomas Pinckney	Federalist		59
	Aaron Burr	Democratic-Republican		30
	Others			48
1800	**Thomas Jefferson** ‡	Democratic-Republican		73
	Aaron Burr	Democratic-Republican		73
	John Adams	Federalist		65
	Charles C. Pinckney	Federalist		64
1804	**Thomas Jefferson**	Democratic-Republican		162
	Charles C. Pinckney	Federalist		14
1808	**James Madison**	Democratic-Republican		122
	Charles C. Pinckney	Federalist		47
	George Clinton	Independent-Republican		6
1812	**James Madison**	Democratic-Republican		128
	DeWitt Clinton	Federalist		89
1816	**James Monroe**	Democratic-Republican		183
	Rufus King	Federalist		34
1820	**James Monroe**	Democratic-Republican		231
	John Quincy Adams	Independent-Republican		1
1824	**John Quincy Adams** ‡	Democratic-Republican	108,740 (30.5%)	84
	Andrew Jackson	Democratic-Republican	153,544 (43.1%)	99
	Henry Clay	Democratic-Republican	47,136 (13.2%)	37
	William H. Crawford	Democratic-Republican	46,618 (13.1%)	41
1828	**Andrew Jackson**	Democratic	647,231 (56.0%)	178
	John Quincy Adams	National Republican	509,097 (44.0%)	83
1832	**Andrew Jackson**	Democratic	687,502 (55.0%)	219
	Henry Clay	National Republican	530,189 (42.4%)	49
	William Wirt	Anti-Masonic		7
	John Floyd	National Republican	33,108 (2.6%)	11
1836	**Martin Van Buren**	Democratic	761,549 (50.9%)	170
	William H. Harrison	Whig	549,567 (36.7%)	73
	Hugh L. White	Whig	145,396 (9.7%)	26
	Daniel Webster	Whig	41,287 (2.7%)	14

Year	Candidates	Party	Popular Vote	Electoral Vote
1840	William H. Harrison * (John Tyler, 1841)	Whig	1,275,017 (53.1%)	234
	Martin Van Buren	Democratic	1,128,702 (46.9%)	60
1844	James K. Polk	Democratic	1,337,243 (49.6%)	170
	Henry Clay	Whig	1,299,068 (48.1%)	105
	James G. Birney	Liberty	62,300 (2.3%)	
1848	Zachary Taylor * (Millard Fillmore, 1850)	Whig	1,360,101 (47.4%)	163
	Lewis Cass	Democratic	1,220,544 (42.5%)	127
	Martin Van Buren	Free Soil	291,263 (10.1%)	
1852	Franklin Pierce	Democratic	1,601,474 (50.9%)	254
	Winfield Scott	Whig	1,386,578 (44.1%)	42
1856	James Buchanan	Democratic	1,838,169 (45.4%)	174
	John C. Fremont	Republican	1,335,264 (33.0%)	114
	Millard Fillmore	American	874,534 (21.6%)	8
1860	Abraham Lincoln	Republican	1,865,593 (39.8%)	180
	Stephen A. Douglas	Democratic	1,382,713 (29.5%)	12
	John C. Breckinridge	Democratic	848,356 (18.1%)	72
	John Bell	Constitutional Union	592,906 (12.6%)	39
1864	Abraham Lincoln * (Andrew Johnson, 1865)	Republican	2,206,938 (55.0%)	212
	George B. McClellan	Democratic	1,803,787 (45.0%)	21
1868	Ulysses S. Grant	Republican	3,013,421 (52.7%)	214
	Horatio Seymour	Democratic	2,706,829 (47.3%)	80
1872	Ulysses S. Grant	Republican	3,596,745 (55.6%)	286
	Horace Greeley	Democratic	2,843,446 (43.9%)	66
1876	Rutherford B. Hayes	Republican	4,036,572 (48.0%)	185
	Samuel J. Tilden	Democratic	4,284,020 (51.0%)	184
1880	James A. Garfield * (Chester A. Arthur, 1881)	Republican	4,449,053 (48.3%)	214
	Winfield S. Hancock	Democratic	4,442,035 (48.2%)	155
	James B. Weaver	Greenback-Labor	308,578 (3.4%)	
1884	Grover Cleveland	Democratic	4,874,986 (48.5%)	219
	James G. Blaine	Republican	4,851,981 (48.2%)	182
	Benjamin F. Butler	Greenback-Labor	175,370 (1.8%)	
1888	Benjamin Harrison	Republican	5,444,337 (47.8%)	233
	Grover Cleveland	Democratic	5,540,050 (48.6%)	168
1892	Grover Cleveland	Democratic	5,554,414 (46.0%)	277
	Benjamin Harrison	Republican	5,190,802 (43.0%)	145
	James B. Weaver	People's	1,027,329 (8.5%)	22
1896	William McKinley	Republican	7,035,638 (50.8%)	271
	William J. Bryan	Democratic; Populist	6,467,946 (46.7%)	176
1900	William McKinley * (Theodore Roosevelt, 1901)	Republican	7,219,530 (51.7%)	292
	William J. Bryan	Democratic; Populist	6,356,734 (45.5%)	155
1904	Theodore Roosevelt	Republican	7,628,834 (56.4%)	336
	Alton B. Parker	Democratic	5,084,401 (37.6%)	140
	Eugene V. Debs	Socialist	402,460 (3.0%)	
1908	William H. Taft	Republican	7,679,006 (51.6%)	321
	William J. Bryan	Democratic	6,409,106 (43.1%)	162
	Eugene V. Debs	Socialist	420,820 (2.8%)	

Year	Candidates	Party	Popular Vote	Electoral Vote
1912	Woodrow Wilson	Democratic	6,286,820 (41.8%)	435
	Theodore Roosevelt	Progressive	4,126,020 (27.4%)	88
	William H. Taft	Republican	3,483,922 (23.2%)	8
	Eugene V. Debs	Socialist	897,011 (6.0%)	
1916	Woodrow Wilson	Democratic	9,129,606 (49.3%)	277
	Charles E. Hughes	Republican	8,538,221 (46.1%)	254
1920	Warren G. Harding *	Republican	16,152,200 (61.0%)	404
	(Calvin Coolidge, 1923)			
	James M. Cox	Democratic	9,147,353 (34.6%)	127
	Eugene V. Debs	Socialist	919,799 (3.5%)	
1924	Calvin Coolidge	Republican	15,725,016 (54.1%)	382
	John W. Davis	Democratic	8,385,586 (28.8%)	136
	Robert M. La Follette	Progressive	4,822,856 (16.6%)	13
1928	Herbert C. Hoover	Republican	21,392,190 (58.2%)	444
	Alfred E. Smith	Democratic	15,016,443 (40.8%)	87
1932	Franklin D. Roosevelt	Democratic	22,809,638 (57.3%)	472
	Herbert C. Hoover	Republican	15,758,901 (39.6%)	59
	Norman Thomas	Socialist	881,951 (2.2%)	
1936	Franklin D. Roosevelt	Democratic	27,751,612 (60.7%)	523
	Alfred M. Landon	Republican	16,681,913 (36.4%)	8
	William Lemke	Union	891,858 (1.9%)	
1940	Franklin D. Roosevelt	Democratic	27,243,466 (54.7%)	449
	Wendell L. Wilkie	Republican	22,304,755 (44.8%)	82
1944	Franklin D. Roosevelt *	Democratic	25,602,505 (52.8%)	432
	(Harry S Truman, 1945)			
	Thomas E. Dewey	Republican	22,006,278 (44.5%)	99
1948	Harry S Truman	Democratic	24,105,587 (49.5%)	303
	Thomas E. Dewey	Republican	21,970,017 (45.1%)	189
	J. Strom Thurmond	States' Rights	1,169,063 (2.4%)	39
	Henry A. Wallace	Progressive	1,157,172 (2.4%)	
1952	Dwight D. Eisenhower	Republican	33,936,234 (55.2%)	442
	Adlai E. Stevenson	Democratic	27,314,992 (44.5%)	89
1956	Dwight D. Eisenhower	Republican	35,590,472 (57.4%)	457
	Adlai E. Stevenson	Democratic	26,022,752 (42.0%)	73
1960	John F. Kennedy *	Democratic	34,227,096 (49.9%)	303
	(Lyndon B. Johnson, 1963)			
	Richard M. Nixon	Republican	34,108,546 (49.6%)	219
1964	Lyndon B. Johnson	Democratic	43,126,233 (61.1%)	486
	Barry M. Goldwater	Republican	27,174,989 (38.5%)	52
1968	Richard M. Nixon	Republican	31,785,148 (43.4%)	301
	Hubert H. Humphrey	Democratic	31,274,503 (42.7%)	191
	George C. Wallace	Amer. Independent	9,899,557 (13.5%)	46
1972	Richard M. Nixon †	Republican	45,767,218 (60.6%)	520
	(Gerald R. Ford, 1974)			
	George S. McGovern	Democratic	28,357,668 (37.5%)	17
1976	Jimmy Carter	Democratic	40,274,975 (50.6%)	297
	Gerald R. Ford	Republican	38,530,614 (48.4%)	240
1980	Ronald Reagan	Republican	43,899,248 (51.0%)	489
	Jimmy Carter	Democratic	36,481,435 (42.3%)	49
	John Anderson	Independent	5,719,437 (6.6%)	0

Year	Candidates	Party	Popular Vote	Electoral Vote
1984	Ronald Reagan	Republican	54,455,075 (59%)	525
	Walter F. Mondale	Democrat	37,577,185 (41%)	13

* Died in office.

† Resigned.

‡ Chosen by the House of Representatives.

Note: Because only the leading candidates are listed, popular vote percentages do not always total 100%.

Index